MOTHER AND DAUGHTER

MOTHER

and

DAUGHTER

THE LETTERS OF
ELEANOR AND ANNA
ROOSEVELT

EDITED BY BERNARD ASBELL

FROMM INTERNATIONAL PUBLISHING CORPORATION

New York

Published in 1988 by Fromm International Publishing
Corporation, 560 Lexington Avenue, New York, NY

Acknowledgment and thanks are expressed to the following persons for permitting
quotation of letters used in this book: Franklin D. Roosevelt, Jr., literary executor of
the Estate of Anna Eleanor Roosevelt, for the letters of Eleanor Roosevelt; James A.
Halstead, M.D., for the letters and other papers of Anna Roosevelt Halstead, and for
his own letters and other papers; Elliott Roosevelt, for two of his own letters; John
Boettiger, for making available numerous documents including the letters of his
father, John Boettiger.

Library of Congress Cataloging-in-Publication Data

Roosevelt, Eleanor, 1884-1962.
   Mother & daughter: the letters of Eleanor and Anna Roosevelt/
edited by Bernard Asbell.
      p.   cm.
   Reprint. Originally published: New York: Coward, McCann &
Geoghegan, c1982.
   Includes index.
   ISBN 0-88064-108-8: $9.95
   1. Roosevelt, Eleanor, 1884-1962—Correspondence.   2. Roosevelt,
Anna, 1906-1975—Correspondence.   3. Presidents—United States—
Wives—Correspondence.   4. Presidents—United States—Children—
Correspondence.   I. Roosevelt, Anna, 1906-1975.   II. Asbell,
Bernard.   III. Title.   IV. Title: Mother and daughter.
E807.1.R48A4   1988
973.917'092'2—dc19
[B]   88-16572
                                                            CIP

To the memory of my mother

THE WHITE HOUSE
WASHINGTON

Wednesday night
Sept 10th

Anna darling, I've thought of you often & wished for you & yet been glad you did not come for these hectic days. Father wants you both to come when you can spend a long week end at least & I think he will pay for the trips as he wants it. He lets you choose some inheritances to & speak.

The funeral was nice & simple,

Letter from Eleanor Roosevelt to Anna Roosevelt Halsted, September 10, [1941].
From The Halsted Collection, Franklin D. Roosevelt Library, Hyde Park, New York.
Copyright © Franklin D. Roosevelt, Jr.

INTRODUCTION

When the two-year labor of this book was mere days away from completion I learned something about its origins that I had not known. Anna Roosevelt's widower, Dr. James A. Halsted, who in recent years has taken a serious interest in biography, was commuting weekly from his home in Hillsdale, New York, to attend a writing course of mine in Connecticut. One night after class he handed me a sheet of paper, suggesting I use it (or not use it) in my book in any way I liked. It was his personal memorandum of Anna's intentions regarding a memoir that she did not live to produce. Parts of Jim's memo I knew; other parts surprised me:

> I said over and over again to Anna during the years of our life together: "You *must* write your memoirs. You have so much to say which no one else knows. . . . You owe it to history."
>
> Such manouevring fell on deaf ears. Anna's life in the public eye had ended with her mother's death. Or so she thought. At least she did not want to dredge up anything she had buried. . . .
>
> After her mother died Anna became, perhaps unwillingly, more prominent . . . partly because she was the only female among four brothers. She rather liked the new role. . . .
>
> One day, Professor Frank Freidel, a biographer of FDR, stopped in to see us on his way from Cambridge to Hyde Park, basically to have another try at persuading Anna to write. After a long talk, Anna tentatively gave in. Later, more definitely, she said to me: "I'll ask Bernie Asbell to interview me as many times as he needs to, and he can write my book."
>
> Anna died within eighteen months. I later pushed the idea further with Asbell after discussing it with Professor Freidel, who heartily agreed on the man to do it. . . .

What Anna had told me of her intention was quite different. We had become friends, she and Jim and I joining for a meal or a visit fairly regularly, after I had completed my second book about her father, *The F.D.R. Memoirs*, published in 1973, to which she had furnished an introduction. On one of these visits in 1974 and in succeeding conversations she indicated a book was on her mind by telling me all the reasons she didn't want to write one: Her brother Elliott had done one she deplored and she didn't want to appear that she was answering it. She'd never kept a diary and feared she wouldn't remember tellings that were most worth telling. Maybe she didn't know anything—and had never known anything—worth telling. And anyway, who *cared* what she thought.

Her reluctance was quite convincing. One day a publisher asked if I could arrange a luncheon meeting of the three of us so that he could assess whether "there might be a book in her." To my surprise, she agreed to join us. Yet I didn't question the face value of her stated resistance to doing a memoir.

In ensuing weeks, Anna, while reiterating that she had no story she burned to write, did say—several times—that there were certain matters (I gathered they concerned relationships between her mother and father, between her parents and their five children, and, I believe, Anna's assessment of the relationship between FDR and Lucy Mercer Rutherfurd) that she wished to "set straight" for the future. We devised a plan to spend a day together every month or so with a tape recorder. I'd prod and plumb, she'd dredge; knowing we enjoyed each other's talk, we were confident we'd dig out what there was to dig. The end product—at least this was all she stated to me of her intention—would be a tape that she could deposit in the Roosevelt archive at Hyde Park, to remain unavailable to researchers until some time or circumstance which she need not at that moment yet define. We'd take our time and first see what our conversations produced. The prospect delighted me. It meant serving a friend through an activity of pure pleasure, with no professional commitment, which at that moment I did not feel available to make.

We agreed to begin the following April—of 1975—upon her return with Jim from a vacation trip to Mexico and California. While in California, Anna learned she had cancer. She declined rapidly. On December 1, Anna died.

In 1976, just as he says, Jim repeatedly opened the question of my pursuing the book that Anna so ambivalently had in mind. I felt—though hesitated to state it bluntly to her widower—that if a potential book had truly resided in her unique experiences and recollections, the possibility of capturing it had now passed. The book had to come *from* Anna, not be *about* her.

Jim invited me to inspect two transfer cases of Anna's papers, most of them more private than those included among her letters willed to the Franklin D. Roosevelt Library at Hyde Park. Some fascinating items, but they lacked the critical mass that might justify a major project. Dr. William R. Emerson, director of the FDR Library, estimated for me, when I inquired, that his archivists would finish their work of sorting Anna's collection of letters in mid-1976. Yes, he confirmed, I would probably find it contained some extraordinarily worthwhile material.

A year slipped by—to Memorial Day, 1977, and a ceremony at the library to dedicate a portrait of Anna that Jim had commissioned. It was a watercolor by Elizabeth Shoumatoff, who was painting Anna's father in the same medium and style on April 12, 1945, at Warm Springs, Georgia, when he slumped into unconsciousness and died. On that Memorial Day I looked at a few samples of Anna's letters to her mother—and of Eleanor Roosevelt's letters to Anna.

A clear, compelling story presented itself from those samples of letters. Not because they mentioned famous people Anna—or, for that matter, Mrs. Roosevelt—had known, nor great events witnessed. Not because new anecdotes might enrich, even alter, our perception of the most famous man in their private lives, a towering public man of his century. These newsy, busy, chattering letters between a mother and daughter that spanned half a century tell—vividly, immediately, intimately—what cannot be gleamed from answers in a tape-recorded interview, no matter how penetrating and clever the questions. As no posed self-portraiture can do, these scribbled exchanges within the family come as close as the written word can to answering the question:

What was it like—every day—to *be* a Roosevelt?

"Letters show the direction of a person's life," writes Dorothy Lobrano Guth, in introducing her compilation of the *Letters of E. B. White*. "They capture, in an informal, but immediate way . . . sometimes in a way that is embarrassing to the letter writer . . . his character, his relationships with others, his hopes and disappointments." "Like all letters," write Justin G. Turner and Linda Levitt Turner in their preface to *Mary Todd Lincoln—Her Life and Letters*, "these have far greater value as evidence than the most candid diary or autobiography. Each one was written on a particular day under a specific impulse, with no thought that it would be judged in a larger context, or, for that matter, read by anyone other than the person to whom it was addressed."

Personal letters reveal truth not always by being truthful. We can learn about a person by what she chooses to conceal—from herself as well as from others. For example, Mrs. Roosevelt conveys the strains of managing four rambunctious sons not so much by what she explicitly writes, but by what she uncomfortably pokes at, then hastens to cover over: ". . . I loved seeing Elliott but . . . we think so little alike on many things that tho' I love him, I have to be careful when with him & that means that short visits are better than long ones!" We see a lifetime of tense, itchy acceptance by Eleanor of Sara Delano Roosevelt's controlling ways, covered over by forbearing smiles, until Eleanor writes a startling outpouring to Anna on the day of her mother-in-law's burial: ". . . I kept being appalled at myself because I couldn't feel any real grief or sense of loss & that seemed terrible after 36 years. . . ."

Anna's letters, too, are as expressive in their evasions as in their forthrightness. Anna cultivates here, year by year, a lifelong technique of communicating one side of what she feels about her mother: As an adolescent on her first tour of Europe, Anna is lavish in reminding her mother in every letter how she is missed. Decades later, there is a manner almost approaching flattery when Anna repeatedly refers with admiration to her mother's position in the world. Yet the reader is hard put to find the slightest overt hint of the uncertainty and uneasiness that Anna feels throughout her life about her place in her mother's heart.

"Anna always used to tell me," says Jim Halsted, "that her mother was very unpredictable and inconsistent in bringing up her children. Inconsistent in her feelings—sweet and lovely one hour, and the next hour very critical, very demanding, very difficult to be with. You could never quite tell what she really meant. This is very troubling to a child, not to be able to rely on the feelings of a parent. Nevertheless, Anna was always very, very admiring of her mother, of course, and also loving of her, so there was great uncertainty, insecurity. I don't think she ever discussed any of that with her mother. She talked to me about it quite a lot.

"I think she felt she could count on her father, count on his consistency of affection, in a way she couldn't with her mother. Of course, the most memorable case of her mother's withdrawal of warmth—this was when Anna was a mature adult—was when Mrs. Roosevelt* returned to the White House right after the President's death, when Mrs. Roosevelt had just found out that Lucy Mercer had been to the White House for dinner, and that Anna had been hostess. Mrs. Roosevelt could show this bitter, cold anger and *did*, and made Anna feel very badly. Anna tried to explain that her father was lonely and had this great responsibility, and Anna had to make a quick decision as to whether she would give in to the idea of Lucy coming to dinner and spending the evening. And Anna decided in favor of it because it was going to help her father, which was what her job was during that year and a half toward the end of the war."

Once seeing these letters, I had no hesitation in concluding that the right way to tell Anna's story—for Anna to tell her own story—was through this intimate correspondence with her mother, augmented by background notes.

That decision, instead of simplifying the project, as one might first expect, made it vastly more difficult, laborious and prolonged. All one has to do to understand why is to read the sample of one of Eleanor Roosevelt's hastily scrawled letters shown on page 6. The pattern of when she runs words together and when she breaks them in the middle is beyond human analysis. In 1950, when her secretary became ill, Mrs. Roosevelt took up typing for her business correspondence, seeking some extra practice in her letters to Anna. On August 21, she typed about her handwriting problem, and an inherited tremble that complicated it:

"My trembling is only bad in writing, it does not bother me in typing at all. Might not be so harmfull as far as legibility goes if I had not written so carelessly for years so that I run all my words together. It is emotional in part at least for I notice if I am upset about something that is the way it shows up. Nevertheless I type so slowly that it is going to be hard to make it a habit as nothing seems important enough to put on paper this way, and I leave words out constantly because my thoughts outrun my fingers. . . ."

The task of deciphering and typing the letters in Anna's collection—Mrs. Roosevelt's alone number almost a thousand—took almost a year. I hereby nominate my research assistant, Laura Hagfeldt, as the world's most skilled reader of Eleanor Roosevelt's handwriting. I doubt that any of the archivists at Hyde Park would dispute that nomination, nor care to compete for it. This book would not have been completed—indeed, would not have gone forward beyond the terrors of reading the first few letters—without Laura's dedication, patience and meticulousness.

Many typographical oddities in the pages that follow will appear to be typographical errors. Unless we—annotator, research assistant, proofreaders and editors—have slipped up, they are not errors, but are reproductions of

---

*For the first several years of Anna's and Jim's marriage, Jim Halsted continued to address his mother-in-law as "Mrs. Roosevelt."

errors and idiosyncrasies appearing in the letters themselves (for example, Mrs. Roosevelt's capricious spellings of her grandchildren's names: Buzzy, Buzzie, Buz; Sisty, Sistie; Johnny, Johnnie). In the main, we corrected the letters only for what appeared to be typing errors.

I wish to express special gratitude to Franklin D. Roosevelt, Jr., literary executor of his mother's estate, for his permission to quote from the letters of Eleanor Roosevelt.

Bernard Asbell

CHAPTER I

March 29, 1916–Autumn, 1918

On March 4, 1913, thirty-one-year-old Franklin D. Roosevelt and his wife Eleanor, standing beneath the glistening dome of the Capitol in Washington, excitedly witnessed the inauguration of President Woodrow Wilson. The couple had attended this awesome ceremony once before. In 1905, thirteen days before their marriage, they witnessed the oath taking of Theodore Roosevelt, Eleanor's uncle and Franklin's distant cousin, their excitement intensified by the coming New York wedding and the new President's consent to attend it.

Young Roosevelt, an early supporter of Wilson for the Democratic nomination, was important not for his political power or experience (being merely a state senator in New York) but for his name, which cousin Ted had made famous as a Republican name. So Franklin's invitation to the Wilson festivity was a payoff. Minutes after the swearing-in, Wilson's newly announced secretary of the navy, Josephus Daniels, whom Roosevelt had met at the Democratic convention, asked Franklin if he'd like to be assistant secretary. The young man surprised the older one, so Daniels later wrote, by accepting without a moment's hesitation.

Franklin and Eleanor excitedly departed for their New York town house on East Sixty-fifth Street and for their Hudson Valley estate at Hyde Park to pack their belongings and scoop up their three children: Anna, about to turn seven; James, five, and Elliott, two and a half.

Exactly a week later, Anna, no doubt prodded by her mother, composed the first letter of her life—at least, the earliest known. In effect, it is a thank-you note to her baby-sitter, FDR's imperious mother, Sara Delano Roosevelt, who, having tended the children at Sixty-fifth Street, had returned to Hyde Park. There is a certain ironic appropriateness in thus opening a collection of letters recording a mother-daughter relationship, since Anna and Eleanor often agreed in later life (say other family members) that until Anna was a teenager Granny directed Anna's upbringing far more than Eleanor did.

By autumn the Roosevelts rented a gaslit home at 1733 N Street, N.W., belonging to Eleanor's Auntie Bye, Anna Roosevelt Cowles. The house, as described years later by Elliott, was "one of a red-brick row, indistinguishable from its neighbors, with an unfenced, handkerchief-sized lawn in front and a miniature garden in the rear."

Anna and James were visiting their Hudson Valley relatives when Eleanor wrote her first known letter to her daughter. It seems a detached and emotionless letter. But emotionless the young mother was not.

Since the day Anna was born, Eleanor felt helpless as a mother. She even projected upon her pediatrician, a Dr. Holt, whom she described as "the great baby doctor of that period," a feeling of "great contempt for the ignorance and foolhardiness of any young woman who would have a baby without knowing even the rudiments of how to care for it." Eleanor's self-description was merciless: "I had never had any interest in dolls or in little children, and I knew absolutely nothing about handling or feeding a baby. . . . For years I was afraid of my nurses, who . . . were usually trained English nurses who ordered me around quite as much as they ordered the children."

Eleanor tells of an evening during Anna's infancy when the Roosevelts expected dinner guests on their nurse's night out. Instead of slipping into slumber following her evening bottle, baby Anna began to squawl fiercely— just as the door knocker announced the first arrivals. Grateful that she had one of Washington's first telephones, Eleanor, not yet dressed, frantically rang up their family doctor. His surprisingly calm suggestion was that the baby "might have a little wind, and was I sure I had gotten up all the bubbles after her last bottle?" Years later Eleanor confessed, "I did not dare tell him I had completely forgotten to put her over my shoulder, and had no idea whether the bubbles had come up or not." As soon as baby Anna burped and "went to sleep like a lamb," Eleanor "registered a vow that never again would I have a dinner on the nurse's day out."

Other family anecdotes are vital to understanding Eleanor's difficulty in cultivating a comfortable sense of the role of woman and mother, a difficulty that is to seep through all the letters, all the years, to follow. "Once when Jimmy had a bad case of poison ivy," Anna has told, "Mother arrived from New York and I took her immediately to Jimmy's bedside, explaining how much he was suffering. I'll never forget my surprise when Mother calmly said, 'You silly boy, you ought to know better than to get near poison ivy!'" The ethic of her family, Anna concluded, was that when illness or injury struck, "the emphasis was on courage and keeping quiet about whatever pain we felt."

James has revealed that the "warmest moments" he can recall with his mother were when she would occasionally lie beside him to read aloud—not for the sake of personal warmth in itself but to get him to stay put: "As a boy I had to have my 'quiet times.' . . . It is sad she seldom had other occasions to unbend."

That recollection triggers another, a more painful one, in James's mind: When Elliott was about five, a sickliness and weakness in his legs induced doctors to strap him into leg braces (which many doctors today might argue was more likely to further weaken Elliott's legs than to help strengthen them). One day at Campobello Island, where Eleanor and the children customarily summered, the young mother went shopping with a friend on the New Brunswick mainland. While she was away, Elliott, hampered by his braces, stumbled into a fire and badly burned himself. Next day, Eleanor began a long, chatty letter to FDR in Washington with the word of "the splendid cruise" to St. Andrew's, stringing out other chitchat, finally mentioning that the children burned some litter behind the house and that the beach now looked quite nice, adding, as though incidentally, "When I got home I found that poor baby Elliott had fallen into the ashes. . . . The ashes got under the strops of his braces and burned . . . but he only cried a little. . . . Nurse says that they are only skin burns."

It is during that illness of Elliott's—before the burning incident—that Eleanor had occasion to write her first letter to her daughter. With Elliott's illness, the arrival less than a month earlier of baby John, and Franklin, Jr., demanding attention as a one-and-a-half-year-old, Eleanor had taken Anna and James out of school and shipped them up to Hyde Park for what turns out to be a repeatedly extended visit to Granny and other relatives in other mansions on both banks of the Hudson.

Perhaps no sentence in a long life of correspondence by Eleanor is as self-descriptive of her place in the family—rather, her clear sense of nonplace, nonmotherhood, nonpersonhood—as one in the letter to Anna of April 4: "Wee babs [John, born March 13] is getting so cunning & now has a bath in his rubber tub & Miss Spring [their nurse] says she knows you'll love to see him."

"*. . . The house seems very quiet without you. . . .*"

1733 N Street
Washington, D.C.
[ca. March 29, 1916]

Dearest Anna,

The house seems very quiet without you & James but Elliott [age five and a half] is better & now & then I hear his voice. He was very pleased to have your little doll & bathtub & played with them yesterday. When he heard you were gone he said he'd go when he was better & he thought anyway you'd bring him a present!

Wee babs is very well & so is Franklin who is just now breakfasting with Father downstairs. Father will be with you Sunday & Monday & then I hope you will be home on Tuesday.

Tell James I will write tomorrow & give him my love, also G'ma. Much love to you dear.

Devotedly,
Mother

Wednesday

". . . [Elliott] has had a horrid time. . . ."

1733 N Street
Washington, D.C.
[April 4, 1916]

Dearest Anna,

I was glad to get your letter & it was nice to hear from Father how you both were & what a lovely day you all had at Hyde Park.

Tell James, Elliott was so pleased with his letter & do write him too for he has had a horrid time & being in bed again is pretty hard but I hope he'll soon be well enough to be up & then you can both come back.

Wee babs is getting so cunning & now has a bath in his rubber tub & Miss Spring says she knows you'll love to see him. Franklin is well & was so glad to see Father today.

I've sent your books & music on to Grandmama & you & James must try to keep up.

Much love to you & James.

Your devoted,
Mother

April 4th

". . . Miss Spring sends her love. . . . Your devoted Mother."

1733 N Street
Washington, D.C.
April 12th [1916]

Dearest Anna,

Your letter was a real pleasure & I would have answered sooner but I've had a good many visitors. Elliott is much better & will be dressed tomorrow. He wants me to thank you so much for his toys, they are a great pleasure for he is tired of being in.

Do write us how you get on with your swimming. I am so glad you are both learning & it is for you to go to Helen's class though you ought to be a good deal ahead of such little girls.

I am glad you like your maid, she will be my maid too when you come back as Martha is leaving in a few days.

Franklin is getting so big & says many new words & wee baby is so sweet. Miss Spring sends her love & so does Elliott.

Your devoted Mother.

By May, Elliott is well enough to be sent to Hyde Park too so that Eleanor can concentrate on the care of her babies. Apparently a tutor has now been engaged to help Anna and James catch up with their studies.

". . . Consider him your special charge. . . ."

1733 N Street
May 21st [ca. 1916]

Dearest Annakins

Father & I have agreed to take a little french boy for a year in the name of you three chicks. We pay the extra amount to eke out what the French government gives for his support but we want you three to consider him your special charge. You have a little money to give away & you have a good many things of your own. You can write to him in french, tell him about yourselves, send him kodaks & ask him to write you about himself & in that way you can find out what he needs. His name is Henri Bouland, & he was born on Aug. 14th, 1908, his address is Villicroze, Var. I think Var. is a province between Marseilles & Nice but you can look it up on the map. He has an older brother & a younger sister & his Father has been killed at the front. I don't know whether his mother is living or not.

Monique has had the measles, do write & tell her you are sorry.

This letter is for the boys as well as for you as I haven't time to write to each one of you. I'm sure you are all very happy & I think of you beginning work today & hope you will both do your best to make up all you have missed. Kisses to my two boys & kind messages to Connochie & love to my big girl from her devoted

Mother

Transporting the family on the long journeys to Campobello Island was an annual ordeal for Eleanor, but it had its rewards. "Mother always liked it," recalls James, "because she had her own home here, which she ran." Sara lived in a separate house nearby—when she did not choose to spend her summer in Europe. "Father loved life on the island more than any of us, but got to spend the least time there. . . . It was rugged, my father's kind of place more than my mother's, but we children never minded its inconveniences."

The safari from New York to "Campo" would commence with a six-hour train trip to Boston. Traveling was rarely light, even though forty to fifty trunks, valises, boxes and barrels went ahead by express to Eastport, Maine, to be ferried to Welchpool, and by horse-drawn dray up the inclines of the island until local laborers completed the haul with wheelbarrows. Meanwhile, in Boston, the family spent a night at a certain dowdy hotel, the same every year, a stop that Sara insisted on because *her* father had always stayed there. Late the next night the family bunked down in a Pullman train to Ayer's Junction where they switched to an older, shabbier train heated by a coal stove for the journey to Eastport. On the train, Indians hawked basketsful of handcrafts. At Eastport, Eleanor and Nurse herded their brood into a carriage for a trip to the dock. There they waited for the tide to be right so a motorboat could cross to the island. From the island dock, they rowed to their own pier, and the children, refreshed by the arrival, scampered up a hill to the enormous barn-red heap of rooms that they modestly called "the cottage."

With Father remaining in Washington, letter writing to and from "Campo" became active, although letters might be delayed for days.

". . . A few people were drowned but it is a nice day to-day. . . ."

[Campobello Island]
July 10, 1915

Dear Mother and father
I hope you will come on the 15 of July. Aunt Margaret [wife of Eleanor's brother Hall] and her baby arrived here safly, the baby is very pritty. We have had awful storm yesterday and a few people were drowned but it is a nice day to-day. Kiss Gradma for me

Love from Anna

p.s. Mr. Byron son was drowned at Nova Scotia and his body was brought to the village and they had a very lage funeral.

"Dear Father . . . You may hear some shreiks . . ."

Campobello Island
[Summer, ca. 1916]

Dear Father
I hope it is not too hot in Washington and that you do not have to take a bath at two o'clock in the morning. Will you please bring two life preserves so that we can swim. We have allready been in swimming with Mary and James. We all send our love.

Love from
Anna

[ca. 1916]

Dear Father,
Will you please come and say good-night to James and if it is not to late, I am going up now to put something in James' bed and you may hear some shreiks when you come in.

Anna

"It's no wonder," Anna has written, "that I wanted to be a boy instead of a girl, and that Father was my childhood hero—not politically or as a world leader—just as a man and *my* father. . . . When I was twelve years old, we had moved to a house at 2131 R Street in Washington, and I had joyfully acquired a puppy police dog at a Red Cross raffle in Dutchess County, N.Y., where I took two 25-cent chances with my own money. The dog became my closest companion. . . . Every morning, Father and I and Chief, the police dog, would walk the mile and a half or so from the house to my school. After leaving me, Father would walk on down to his Navy Department office, taking Chief with him. Those walks I remember because he talked about all sorts of things I liked to hear about—books I was reading, a cruise we might be going to take down the Potomac River the following week end, the historic old Virginia houses Father planned to show us."

Mother's companionship, in contrast, was not what an experience-eager girl thought of as fun. "She felt a tremendous sense of duty to us," Anna was to allow many years later. "It was part of that duty to read to us, and to hear our prayers before we went to bed, but she did not understand or satisfy the need of a child for primary closeness to a parent. . . . Mother was a terribly conscientious person. She tried, you always felt she was doing her darndest to do the right thing by her children, or to get across to them the things that she felt were right and the things that she felt were wrong. She didn't have too much sense of humor about it during those years of developing."

An unfair judgment? Eleanor herself poignantly confirms it: "It did not come naturally to me to understand little children or to enjoy them. Playing with children was difficult for me because play had not been an important part of my own childhood."

Communication within the family—between husband and wife, between parents and children, was taut, distant, unrevealing. "I cannot recall any of us," James has written, "being counseled by our parents or given any particular piece of advice. I cannot imagine going to my parents with a problem. When we had problems, we handled them ourselves or went to our grandmother. But you did not discuss *personal* problems with Granny. I never remember being in her bedroom. Nor, for that matter, in my mother's very often. Certainly not when she was in bed. I remember romping with Father in his bed, but we never romped with Mother or Granny. . . . Mother was always stiff, never relaxed enough to romp. . . . She found it easier to give than to get, to do for than to have done for her. Mother loved all mankind, but she did not know how to let her children love her. . . . Mother once undertook to read to Anna and me about the birds and the bees—literally, the birds and the bees. All I remember is the pollination of flowers. She never was tempted to try that again. As we grew up, we certainly never spoke of sex to our mother or grandmother. Nor did Father do his duty. I learned from other children, I suppose. Or by experimentation. Later we were able to joke about sex with Father, but only lightly."

Relatively late in her life (long after her mother offered her daughter the premarital admonition that "sex was an ordeal to be borne"), Anna began writing notes about and to herself, perhaps for a possible memoir. After her death, I found these notes in her attic, kept separate from the papers she had willed to the Hyde Park Library. One of these memos recalled: ". . . Another traumatic experience for me . . . indicative of the taboos and inhibitions of that time within the social structure in which I was brought up . . . haunted me through various types of persecution dreams for many years. Finally, in my latish teens I asked my mother why, at the age of three or four I had my hands tied, above my head, to the top bars of my crib whenever I went to bed. Her answer was simply that I masturbated and this was the prescribed cure. Later (I have no idea how much later but it can't have been long because I was still sleeping in the 'big' nursery at Hyde Park), I remember graduating to 'bells': aluminum-type contraptions which covered my hands and had air holes in them. Cloth pieces were attached which were made firm around my wrists. These were 'heaven' to me because I made up marvelous stories: the holes were windows in castles; people lived behind those windows and had wonderful adventures. The answer from Mother was given in a tone which precluded any further questions—if I had any. The indication was clearly that I had had a bad habit which had to be cured and about which one didn't talk!"

The noncommunicative relationship—or communicated nonrelationship—between preadolescent Anna and her terrified mother was infinitely complicated by the place in both of their lives of servants—by Mother's terror of them and the child's increasing skill at manipulating them. This, too, is the subject of a self-searching and revealing essay I found in Anna's attic box:

"What happens to a child's security and development when his first learning pattern is that he is required to pay allegiance [to] two separate hierarchies? The first hierarchy is that of the nanny or nurse, and a governess is in the picture too if there are older siblings. This hierarchy bathes, teaches the unwelcome task of washing behind the ears, brushing the teeth night and morning, toilet training, dressing and undressing, and the rule of handwashing before meals and before presenting oneself to the second hierarchy. The second hierarchy is that of the parents and, in my case, the only grandparent alive when I came into the world and the most solidly [at first Anna had written "puzzlingly," but crossed it out, substituting "solidly"] important individual in this category in my earliest childhood.

"At about the age of four I had learned that the nurse group did not have to command my respect because they came and went, always replaced by someone else with the usual human differences in training emphasis, severity and kind of punishment, empathy or the opposite toward the 'charges.' At an early age I learned to judge, sometimes fairly, sometimes not, and to try wiles and my own brand of cunning in making life as easy as I thought possible for myself.

"The same age brought the realization that the second group did remain constant, and quite obviously had power over the first group, as well as ultimate power over me. Also, this second group were surrounded by surrogate 'nurses' who catered to their individual needs: a personal maid for my grandmother, and male and female people who cleaned the house, cooked and served the meals, and washed and ironed. At Hyde Park, the only place I really thought of as home, there was an additional surrogate group who took care of another aspect of the lives of the permanent hierarchy: the farmer and his helpers, the coachman and his helpers (in my earliest years) and later the chauffeur, and the gardeners.

"Obviously, the permanent group provided an important segment of childhood security. To varying degrees, depending on the personal characteristics of the parents and grandparent, affection and love could be counted on.

"But [childhood dependence on] a consistent, warm and spontaneous love was muted to accommodate to circumstance: emotional display was abhorrent in company; a goodbye or hello kiss was an off-hand, perfunctory affair; a squeeze from Granny in public meant she was talking about you in adult fashion to another adult and I felt only [her] condescension and [my] embarrassment because I couldn't understand and suspected 'double-talk'; a pat on the head from an 'outsider' adult had the same effect on me. On the other hand, when I was sent down to say Good Morning to Granny as she finished her breakfast in bed, her kiss and hug were indeed warm—almost suffocating as my own daughter complained when she was very young and going thru much the same childhood routine as I had, and to whom I explained that Granny's bosom was a bit too ample and therefore somewhat like a pillow held against your face against your will. I don't remember much about Mother's and Father's greetings in the early mornings except for perfunctory kisses from each of them on our cheeks as we or they arrived at the breakfast table. But Mother made quite a ritual out of evening prayers and 'tucking the chicks into bed.' I think Father joined in once in a while. Mother came to the nursery for this ritual. We knelt at her knee for prayers, and at our bedsides if we were alone with the nurse. If nurse complained of our behavior, Mother's disapproval was quite evident, usually expressed by dampening down the warmth of her goodnight hug and kiss."

The following paragraph, on a separate scrap of paper, appears to follow the preceding, and unfortunately trails off incomplete:

"What specificly caused my childhood puzzlements? In early years only stories from books gave me a hint that not everyone in the world lived as we did. Later on, but still early in my childhood I read for myself and developed powers of observation which engendered all sorts of varying emotions in me. Having never experienced hunger, poverty, war, death, the everyday injustices of humans one to the other . . .."

Anna gives no hint as to whether her child's mind held her parents responsible for the misdemeanors of the "first hierarchy." Having endured at least four nurses in the first five years of her life, each of a different style of cruelty, Anna cannot be said to have been nurtured in a surround that stimulated easy trust.

Clearly, the star of the four was an English nanny the children secretly called "Old Battle-ax." Determined to divest Anna of her childish taste for nonsense and to teach her once and for all to act like a lady, Old Battle-ax one day, as Brother James recalls, "pushed Sis to the floor, knelt on her chest and cuffed her about." She punished a prank of Elliott's by shoving him in a closet, turning its key so furiously it broke off. Untroubled, she just left him there for several hours until Father came home. Franklin, Jr., claims he suffers from claustrophobia to this day from experiencing the same punishment. To rebuke James for staring in fascination while she smeared hot English mustard heavily on her lunch, she forced him to eat the entire contents of the jar. Today, more than sixty years later, he cannot bear to taste even the mildest mustard. Disbelieving one day Jimmy's claim that he had brushed his teeth, Old Battle-ax dressed him in Anna's clothing, bedecked his back with a sign, I Am a Liar, and put him out to parade on East Sixty-fifth Street before his friends. The relevance of this incident to our story is not Jimmy's unforgettable humiliation, but Eleanor's response to the incident. She openly wept over his humiliation, an expression Eleanor did not easily give herself to. But fire the nurse? An unthinkable affront, not only to Old Battle-ax, whom Eleanor feared, but to Granny, who had picked her. After all, a child's pain, while heart-plucking, is soon forgotten, isn't it?

Firing Old Battle-ax soon became not only thinkable, but inescapable, when she was caught at true sin. One day Eleanor discovered in the bottom drawer of Old Battle-ax's bureau a cache of empty gin and whiskey bottles.

America's entry into the war in the spring of 1917 almost obliterated family time with Father, except for Anna's precious morning walks to school. In other ways, too, the war invaded Eleanor's life. She stepped up her reliance on hired nurses, and committed herself to a demanding schedule at the Red Cross canteen.

". . . Doctor Hardin came and sewed it up. . . ."

[2131 R St., N.W.
Washington, D.C.]
March 17th, 1918

Dear Grandmama

Thank you ever so much for your dear letter. Mother cut her finger badly yesterday in a bread machine down at the canteen, and Doctor Hardin came and sewed it up. Violet Spencer came for lunch yesterday, and we played with the cat after lunch . . . and then I went to a consort which my school gives every year. . . .

Last Friday I did not go to school because there was a case Hun pox. That same afternoon I went to hear Abbé Cabanel who had been in the trenches. . . . James is going to have his tonsils taken out next Tuesday, and he is looking forward to it.

With lots of love
Anna

". . . Granny betted one dollar that he would not. . . ."

Hyde Park
Monday [1918]

Dear Mother,
　Last week we went to the races with Aunt Betty and Uncle Rosy [Mr. and Mrs. James Roosevelt Roosevelt; he was F.D.R.'s older half-brother]. There were some trotting and pacing races. It was very exciting. Uncle Rosy bet Granny a dollar the horse he liked best would win and Granny betted one dollar that he would not. Granny won the dollar and gave it to me and I was given another dollar by Aunt Betty which she had won off Uncle Rosy at golf. With those two dollars and my savings I was able to get a War Saving Stamp. So I have bought two War Savings since you left. My arith. book has not come and I am very anxious to start.
　Did you know that Polly Raymond, Mrs Low's granddaughter, was run down by an autombile the other day. She was on her bicycle and thought she could get accross the road in time. The car did not see her and ran into her and knocked her off her bicycle. She was badly bruised but is getting all well again.

[no signature]

". . . I wish I could go to the [war] mouvie. . . ."

Hyde Park
[July 2, 1918]

Dear Mother
　. . . I have got a little cold so I am staying in bed to day. George cut Dicky's nails the other day and by a mistake he snipped a little bit of the flesh so poor Dicky has been standing on one leg for two or three days. Yesterday morning Dr. Smith came to see me and said the same thing about me as Dr. Vehslage in New York. James went to the war mouvies yesterday as he said Father had said that he could go to the next thing like that. I wish I could go to the mouvie as I have never been and James says it is such fun, but it does not matter because I will enjoy it all the more when I do go.
　Is not it too bad about Quentin Roosevelt [Theodore Roosevelt's son, killed in World War I]. I am glad Father reached the first stage of his journey in safty.
　I have finished "Little Women" and I liked it very very much, I am now reading "Little Men" which is a continuation of "Little Women."

With lots of love
Anna

Excuse writing.
July 2, 1918

In Franklin's position of social as well as governmental importance, Eleanor played her part dutifully, undertaking "a kind of social life I had never known before, dining out night after night and having people dine with us about once a week." Observing Washington custom, newly arrived Eleanor in the winter of 1913–14 spent tedious afternoon upon afternoon, loaded down by a carful of children, leaving calling cards at the homes of other official families: "I tried at first to do without a secretary, but found that it took me such endless hours to arrange my calling list, and answer and send invitations, that I finally engaged one for three mornings a week."

The part-time secretary was Lucy Page Mercer, twenty-two when she was hired late in 1913, and securely established in Washington and New York society. As Eleanor needed Lucy's assistance, Lucy needed Eleanor's pay. The Mercer family had fallen on hard times.

Lucy's mother, Minnie Leigh Tunis, was once described by *The Clubfellow and Washington Mirror* as "easily the most beautiful woman in Washington society for a number of years, and to be invited to one of her dinners was in itself a social distinction that qualified one for admission to any home." She married Carroll Mercer, a retired army major and descendant of the Carrolls of Carrollton. He was a founder of the Chevy Chase Club (where Franklin golfed) and prominent in the Metropolitan Club (Franklin's favorite dining and partying place). The marriage was socially perfect, an adornment to Minnie's standing, but a personal failure almost from the beginning. The couple lived separately through most of the years of Lucy's life. Mercer, a drunkard unable to support his wife and two daughters, was to die a pauper. Minnie went to work in New York as an "inside decorator," a field of self-support in which she was also to train Lucy.

At the Roosevelt residence, Lucy's duties were more than secretarial. In the spring of 1914, when Eleanor and the children were visiting Hyde Park, Franklin wrote his wife upon returning to work in Washington—the first mention of the young lady in the family correspondence:

Dearest Babs—

> Arrived safely and came to the house and Albert [the chauffeur] telephoned Miss Mercer who later came and cleaned up. Then a long day at the office and dinner alone at 7:30. . . .

About Lucy Mercer it has been said that "every man who ever knew her" fell in love with her (although, despite her constant round of social events with proper companions, Lucy's young life is not known to have included a romantic attachment with any eligible young man). While tall—five feet nine inches—she was surpassingly graceful, with sympathetic yet mysterious blue eyes, a voice described as having "the quality of dark velvet," and light hair usually said to be blond although she described it as brown. Her exquisite manners and aura of modest reserve made her a most agreeable listener, which contributed to a man's feeling of importance. She is what Sara Roosevelt always believed a woman should be, one who strives to please a man, never to challenge him. And she was commandingly competent at the tasks that inundated Eleanor. A friend of Lucy's, Aileen Tone, who had held a similar job for Henry Adams, told how Lucy, whom she called a "charmer," would plant herself on the living-room floor and spread bills, letters, and invitations about, making order of them in a twinkle. When Eleanor lacked a woman for a dinner party, she readily invited Lucy.

What do we know of Franklin and Lucy's wartime romance? Concerning the period between 1913, when Eleanor hired Lucy, and the spring of 1917, when the United States declared war, absolutely nothing except the one time that Lucy "came and cleaned up." In the summer of 1917 Franklin arranged a weekend cruise on the *Sylph,* the smaller of two presidential yachts, customarily available to the assistant secretary of the navy. "It worked out *wonderfully!*" Franklin wrote Eleanor, listing his passengers: "The Charlie Munns, the Cary Graysons, Lucy Mercer and Nigel Law, and they all got on splendidly." (Charles A. Munn was a Harvard acquaintance of FDR; his wife, the former Mary Astor Paul, a co-volunteer with Eleanor at the Red Cross. Dr. Cary T. Grayson was President Wilson's physician and medical director of the Navy. Nigel Law was Third Secretary of the British Embassy.) Eleanor was not among the passengers because a week earlier she herded her brood to their summer at Campobello, where Franklin insisted she stay. Clearly she became nervous about what may have been going on in Washington. And he was nervous too. He writes:

> . . . I really can't stand that house all alone without you, and you were a goosy girl to think or even pretend to think that I don't want you here *all* the summer, because you know I do! But honestly *you* ought to have six weeks straight at Campo, just as *I* ought to, only you can and I can't! I *know* what a whole summer here does to people's nerves and at the end of *this* summer I will be like a bear with a sore head until I get a change or some cold weather—in fact as you know I am unreasonable and touchy now—but I shall try to improve.

In 1918 Anna was twelve, a time of early stirrings to reach—tentatively, fearfully, crankily—for independence from her parents, particularly from her mother. In any case, it can scarcely be expected to have been a smooth year between Anna and Eleanor. As it turned out—and Anna was not to know why for some years to come—the year was disastrous, Eleanor's attention seized by a devastating discovery. Franklin returned from a battlefront tour of Europe with double pneumonia, so ill he had to be carried off his naval ship on a stretcher. In their New York home, Eleanor's first instinct was to find some practical way to help him. She leafed through correspondence she found in his luggage, presumably to see if she could help him catch up with replies. She was stunned to find a packet of letters from Lucy. "The bottom dropped out of my own particular world," she wrote a friend about it a quarter century later, still not rid of the aftertaste, "and I faced myself, my surroundings, my world, honestly for the first time. I really grew up that year."

(Not surprisingly, these letters have been destroyed, leaving us with no clue to how ardent they were as love letters; all we know is Eleanor's reaction to them. This led me to speculate in an earlier book [1973] on the remote possibility "that Eleanor, whose emotions are fragile, may have overreacted to what the letters said." Since then, however, James Roosevelt has published "a rather well-kept secret" that "there came to light during this time a register from a motel in Virginia Beach [where Lucy's maternal family was rooted] showing that Father and Lucy had checked in as man and wife and spent the night." If this "well-kept secret" is true, and if it indeed "came to light during this time," it may have been one of Eleanor's exhibits in the confrontation she demanded with Franklin—and which apparently included the presence of Franklin's mother.)

Eleanor offered Franklin "his freedom" to marry Lucy if he felt he could accept the consequences for the children. Apparently the children were not the only consideration. For one thing, there was Lucy's Catholicism, which would prevent her from marrying a divorced father of five. Also, Sara, moving in to take charge in her accustomed way, decided that the family could cover up and live with the scar of her son's indiscretion, but not with the disgrace of a family divorce. Using the lever that fit her hand best, she threatened to cut off Franklin's income if he did not give up Lucy. Perhaps the pivotal argument was the one to be made by Louis Howe, Roosevelt's elfin assistant and political adviser, who was determined to steer Franklin Roosevelt one day into the presidency. Howe asserted that a divorce would demolish Roosevelt's ambition for a political future. The young father and young mother, according to their son James, "agreed to go on for the sake of appearances, the children and the future, but as business partners, not as husband and wife, provided he end his affair with Lucy at once, which he did. After that, Father and Mother had an armed truce that endured to the day he died."

One can only speculate as to how Anna received, interpreted and was affected by the fearful currents that radiated through the stricken home during the autumn and winter of 1918. All we have is a letter that Anna scrawled to her father when he was confined to his room, swept by a fever:

". . . *Mother will kiss you for me.* . . ."

[Autumn, 1918?]

Dear Father
I am sending you these little pictures of indians and boy scouts, you can make a very nice little picture if you put them together. Ask Mother to put them together for you, and stand them up against something. I hope you feel better, and will be all right again very soon. Goodby Father I wish I could kiss you. Mother will kiss you for me

Love from
Anna

CHAPTER II

February 21, 1923–ca. 1931

Between 1918 and early 1923 (for Anna, ages twelve to almost seventeen), correspondence between mother and daughter came to a virtual halt. They were rarely apart for long. If they had occasion to write, apparently the letters were lost.

From 1923 until about 1928 the preserved letters are almost all from Anna to her mother. Presumably, Eleanor's to Anna have disappeared because Anna had not yet acquired the Roosevelt habit of squirreling every scrap of paper that contained a scribble. Perhaps that's just as well. This short-term predominance of Anna's letters (after which, for the remainder of this volume, Eleanor's letters far outnumber her daughter's) gives high visibility to the blooming of Anna's mind and interests, her enthusiasms and curiosities. The new Anna has a great deal to say.

If this is a time of growth for the two Roosevelt women, it is also a time of great events and great trial.

The first event, which could hardly be called unexpected, was the death on August 14, 1919, of Eleanor's Grandmother Hall—actually her surrogate mother. Before Eleanor turned ten she lost her adoring, adored, hard-drinking and emotionally helpless father—less than two years after the death of her unadoring, unadored mother. Perhaps the significance here of Grandmother Hall's death is a self-descriptive reflection (in writing) it soon draws from Eleanor Roosevelt:

"Her interest had always been centered in her family and even my children, her greatgrandchildren. . . . Her love clouded her judgment. . . . I wondered then and I wonder now, if her life had been a little less centered in her family group, if that family group might not have been a great deal better off. If she had had some kind of life of her own, what would have been the result? I think I remember that when she was young she painted rather well. Could she have developed that talent? . . . Her willingness to be subservient to her children isolated her, whether they realized it or not; and it might have been far better, for her boys at least, had she insisted on bringing more discipline into their lives simply by having a life of her own.

"My grandmother's life had a considerable effect on me, for even when I was young I determined that I would never be dependent on my children by allowing all my interests to center in them. The conviction has grown through the years. In watching the lives of those around her, I have felt that it might have been well in their youth if they had not been able to count on her devotion and her presence whenever they needed her.

"Up to a certain point it is good for us to know that there are people in the world who will give us love and unquestioned loyalty to the limit of their ability. I doubt, however, if it is good for us to feel assured of this without the accompanying obligation of having to justify this devotion by our behavior.

"My grandmother could judge others, but never her own children. She seemed to be able to wipe their faults out of her consciousness and to let them begin after each failure with a clean slate. Her gratitude for their affection was something almost pathetic and showed how little else she had in life. It is hard sometimes to realize what factors in our experience have influenced our development, but I am sure that my grandmother's life has been a great factor in determining some of my reactions to life. . . ."

The next important event occurred in July 1920, when Eleanor received a telegram from San Francisco, where her husband was attending the Democratic National Convention. The wire was signed by Roosevelt's boss at the Navy Department:

> MRS FRANKLIN D ROOSEVELT
> CAMPOBELLO NB
> IT WOULD HAVE DONE YOUR HEART GOOD TO HAVE SEEN THE
> SPONTANEOUS AND ENTHUSIASTIC TRIBUTE PAID WHEN FRANK-
> LIN WAS NOMINATED UNANIMOUSLY FOR VICE PRESIDENT TO-
> DAY STOP ACCEPT MY CONGRATULATIONS AND GREETINGS
> STOP WILL YOU BE GOOD ENOUGH TO SEND MY CONGRATULA-
> TIONS AND GREETINGS ALSO TO HIS MOTHER AS I DO NOT KNOW
> HER ADDRESS
>
> JOSEPHUS DANIELS

"I am sure that I was glad for my husband," Eleanor wrote many years later, after becoming First Lady, "but it never occurred to me to be much excited. . . . I felt detached and objective, as though I were looking at someone else's life. This seems to have remained with me down to the present day. I cannot quite describe it, but it is as though you lived two lives, one of your own and the other which belonged to the circumstances that surround you."

The Roosevelts decided to take fourteen-year-old Anna on their campaign visit to the Ohio home of James M. Cox, the presidential nominee. Eleanor is effusive about Anna's debut on the political stage: "She was pretty, her light golden hair, which at that time was long, attracted a good deal of attention, and everyone was as kind to her as could be. For her the day was over far too quickly." That is not what Anna is to recall thirty-eight years after the event: "I haven't the slightest memory of being much made over. What I do remember is that I was made to wear a navy blue alpaca dress, which the family thought was simply beautiful but which I hated because it scratched, and that I had a private bathroom at the Cox's place, which I thought was really something."

The Cox-Roosevelt ticket was overwhelmingly defeated, chiefly a national rejection of Woodrow Wilson's zeal for a League of Nations that would include the United States.

Next summer, in a burst of postelection vengeance, a Republican Senate subcommittee chairman accused the previous administration's navy leadership of negligence in office, which threw Roosevelt's name across ugly headlines. Burning with indignation, Roosevelt demanded and obtained an appearance before the committee, where he effectively refuted the accusations. Leaving steamy Washington, he headed for Campobello Island to rejoin his family. During that week his body was incubating the virus of poliomyelitis.

Arriving at Campobello, Roosevelt immediately sought the peace of mind he always found in sailing and fishing. Preparing his tackle aboard the tiny sailboat *Vireo,* which he bought to teach his sons to sail, he slipped and fell overboard. By Roosevelt's own account:

"I'd never felt anything so cold as the water. . . . It seemed paralyzing. . . . The next day we landed on the island. There was a blue haze over it, pungent with burning spruce. All that day we fought a forest fire. Late in the afternoon we brought it under control. Our eyes were bleary with smoke; we were begrimed, smarting with sparkburns, exhausted. We plunged into a freshwater pool on the island to revive ourselves. We ran in our bathing suits along the hot, dusty roads to the house.

"I didn't feel the usual reaction, the glow I'd expected. Walking and running couldn't overcome the chill. When I reached the house the mail was in, with several newspapers I hadn't seen. I sat reading for a while, too tired even to dress. I'd never felt quite that way before.

"The next morning when I swung out of my bed my leg lagged, but I managed to move about and to shave. I tried to persuade myself that the trouble with my leg was muscular, that it would disappear as I used it. But presently it refused to work, and then the other. . . ."

Next day an elderly local physician, disregarding the patient's complaints of weakness in the legs, a dull ache in his back, and recurrent teeth-chattering chills, diagnosed the condition as a cold. The aching spread, his temperature rose to 102 degrees, and three days later, his body immobile from the chest down, Roosevelt learned he had the disease he always dreaded his children might contract, infantile paralysis.

Much has been written about the reactions to this devastating event of

Franklin's mother and wife, and what has been called "a battle to the finish between these two remarkable women for Franklin's soul." That battle was one day to be dramatized in a play and movie, *Sunrise at Campobello*.

But an unvoiced drama was to lurk, darkly, fearfully. Jimmy, thirteen, standing on the porch at Campobello, watching Father carried out on a stretcher, felt "as young and scared as little Johnny"—who was only five. Jimmy continues: "Just the month before he came to Campobello, I thought, this big, wonderful father of mine had taken me to see the Dempsey-Carpentier world's heavyweight championship fight in Jersey City, and on the way out I got pulled away from him in the crowd and was scared to death until he found me. Would he ever, I wondered, take me anywhere again?"

Anna, fifteen, at least as frightened, desperately hungry for clues to her father's fate—the family's fate, *her* fate—hid in her closet to listen when the doctors used her bedroom to discuss their diagnosis. That is when and where she heard for the first time, the foreshortened and foreboding medical word "polio":

"Mother became more and more busy. . . . I gradually grew accustomed to a new relationship with Father—a relationship where I had to go to his room and sit on a chair or at the foot of his bed when I wanted to talk to him. For some months my knowledge that he was suffering made me shy with him. But gradually his gaiety, his ability to poke fun at himself as he learned to move himself around through the use of his arms, broke down the tension we had been feeling. . . .

"Every time I saw him walking, with great effort, on his crutches, for as long a distance as he possibly could, I couldn't help but feel a wrench in my heart. I would see him walk out our Hyde Park driveway, oh so slowly, and see the beads of perspiration on his forehead after he'd gone a short distance.

"But then his own spirit was transmitted to all of us. He apparently knew it would be a shock for us to realize that the useless muscles in his legs would cause atrophy. . . . So Father removed the sadness by showing us his legs. He gave us the names of each of the muscles in them, then told us which ones he was working hardest on at that moment. He would shout with glee over a little movement of a muscle that had been dormant. So, gradually, I almost forgot that he had once had well-developed muscles. The battle Father was making became a spirited game."

That fall, back in their New York house on East Sixty-fifth Street, Anna was enrolled in Miss Chapin's School where she felt brushed aside by cliquey girls she didn't know, lonely, ignored, all reflections of new moods that bewildered her at home. She selected as a target for her resentment not Father, not Mother, not Grandmother, but, of all people, Louis Howe, the brooding-eyed, hunched-over, ash-laden ex-reporter who had decided a decade ago to become a man of significance and power by making Franklin D. Roosevelt President, and who responded to Roosevelt's affliction by renewing his devotion full time—in fact, by moving in with the Roosevelts. He was the only person in the Roosevelt constellation who was equally close to Eleanor and Franklin. Sara detested Howe through all those previous years—not only as the unattractive person she found him to be, but for the despicable world of politics she perceived him as tempting her Franklin into—and she detested him still. Not without political skills herself, Sara cultivated an effective approach to the problem.

"Granny, with a good insight into my adolescent nature," Anna recalled, "started telling me that it was inexcusable that I, the only daughter of the family, should have a tiny bedroom in the back of the house, while Louis enjoyed a large, sunny front bedroom with his own private bath. Granny's needling finally took root. At her instigation, I went to Mother one evening and demanded a switch in rooms."

"Because of constant outside influences," Eleanor was later to write discreetly, her mother-in-law still being vigorously alive, "the situation grew in her [Anna's] mind to a point where she felt that I did not care for her and was not giving her any consideration. It never occurred to her that I had far less than she had. . . . I realize now that my attitude toward her had been wrong. She was an adolescent girl and I still treated her like a child and thought of her as a child. It never occurred to me to take her into my confidence and consult with her about our difficulties or tell her just what her father was going through. . . . It never occurred to me that the time comes, particularly with a girl, when it is important to make her your confidante. If I had realized this I might have saved Anna and myself several years of real unhappiness. . . .

"As it was, I am responsible for having given her a most unhappy time, and we can both of us be extremely grateful for the fact that finally the entire situation got on my nerves and one afternoon in the spring, when I was trying to read to the two youngest boys, I suddenly found myself sobbing as I read. I could not think why I was sobbing, nor could I stop. . . . I found an empty room . . . locked the door and poured cold water on a towel and mopped my face. I eventually pulled myself together, for it requires an audience, as a rule, to keep on these emotional jags. That is the one and only time I ever remember in my entire life having gone to pieces in this particular manner. . . .

"The effect, however, was rather good on Anna, because she began to straighten out, and at least she poured some of her troubles out and told me she knew she had been wrong and that I did love her, and from that day to this our mutual understanding has constantly improved.

"Today no one could ask for a better friend than I have in Anna, or she has in me. Perhaps because it grew slowly, the bond between us is all the stronger. No one can tell either of us anything about the other; and though we might not always think alike or act alike, we always respect each other's motives, and there is a type of sympathetic understanding between us which would make a real misunderstanding quite impossible."

The relish of Anna's new grown-upness spills from her first letters after the long hiatus, when, in the early winter of 1923, her parents are visiting Florida, and Anna teases her mother with hints of the sin that she knows her mother most dreads—yielding to the curse of alcohol—although quickly assuring her that it was "disgusting."

". . . A Welsh rabbit with some sort of booze in it. . . ."

49 East 65th Street
New York, N.Y.
[February 21, 1923]

Dear Mother and Father,

. . . The boys are now bemoaning their fate because they don't have a holiday tomorrow and I do!

. . . This evening Elliott and I spent half an hour cleaning out his three aquariums. It was some dirty job. I think I prefer cleaning up after dogs than after fish!

I had a very nice time out at Dorothys in Flushing last Saturday. The only thing that nearly killed me was that we had (after returning from the movies at 11.30 at night (Friday) a Welsh rabbit with some sort of booze in it. Every body thought it was delicious but I thought it was a disgusting mess, and it didn't like me at all as we went to bed right after it. We also had a glass of beer. In spite of the Welsh rabbit I had a very good time and liked the whole family very much.

Last Saturday night I went with Mr. Black [Van Lear Black, a business associate of FDR] and Jessie to a show given by darkies, called "Liza," which was mostly bum, though quite peppy!

Nobody went to church last Sunday, because Elliott had an appointment with another boy and I was very sleepy and also had a cold coming on which miraculously disappeared Monday morning!!

Everybody seems happy in the house. The only thing that gets my goat every Friday is your linen closet, and that's because it takes so long because I'm not used to it.

I hope you are having a good time.

Lots of Love Anna.

P.S. Elliott & I wrote to Jimmie the other day.

In the summer of 1924 Anna was sent for a riding and desert-camping vacation at the Arizona home of Eleanor's lifelong friend, Isabella Greenway, who had a daughter about Anna's age. The adventure was marred only by the anticipation of another trip to follow immediately: to Newport, Rhode Island, and Anna's "coming out" during Tennis Week.

The family tension and the battle that swirled around that event were still to stir Anna forty-three years later when I first met her in her Washington home. My transcript of her comments forms the best backdrop of the "Newport letters":

"These are most complicated and fascinating creatures, both these parents of mine. Because in many ways they never gave up form. . . . Things were done in a certain way.

"When I got to the age of seventeen [Anna is in error; the correct age is eighteen], I was *informed* that I had to come out in society, and I *died*. And I *wasn't* going to come out. And Granny said, 'You are.' And I went to

Mother, and she said, 'Yes, you must.' And my mother . . . *made* me come home and go to Newport for what they call 'Tennis Week' . . . to stay with her cousin Susie Parish, who was *really* Old Guard. . . . She made me go there, and I completely abhorred this stuff to such an extent that Cousin Susie had to procure two young men to go to the dances with me. But Mother made me do this. It was Granny who took me to get the clothes for this business."

You were angry, I asked Anna, because your mother didn't oppose the blind obedience to form?

"She didn't oppose it. She didn't help me a bit. That's why I've always said I grew up in a most inconsistent—and I felt this for a long time—a very difficult atmosphere to think through. Because on the one hand, here were my parents with their [liberal] political and social views, and the people and the conversations I was listening to at meals; and, on the other hand, here I was being *forced*. I couldn't go out with a young man without a chaperone. So Mother was the same [as all those other society people she often criticized].

"Now, Father, you couldn't draw into this. He'd just say, 'That's up to Granny and Mother. You settle all this with them.' I couldn't go to Father on this. He wouldn't give me the time of day."

". . . I wish Newport would blow up & bust. . . ."

[Warren, Arizona]
Tuesday July 29, 1924

Dearest Ma—

Here's a letter at last—better late that never!

. . . A week ago today we went underground in the mine here at Bisbee. They dropped us in a cage 2200 ft. in less than a minute & a half. It was a little scary, but good fun! Then we walked for miles underground, with our little miners lamps. In that dim light you could see the copper gleaming in the rocks. It was so hot that the perspiration just ran down us in rivers, & when we reached the top we nearly froze to death.

On Wednesday Uncle John ["Uncle" John Greenway was not actually Anna's uncle] took the 3 of us over to Ajo where Uncle John's mine is. Its all surface mining & is the biggest copper mine in the U.S. One night we lay out on the prairies, which is something I'd always wanted to do, & it was lovely. The rocks all around us were the most gorgeous colors. We had one or two good rides but it was so hot we didn't do much during the day.

Yesterday we went to Fort Huachuca for the day. The country is even prettier around there than here because there's more timber on the mountains & there's been more rain so everything is greener. . . .

I love it out here, the people are so friendly & hospitable, & everything is so "big." The thought of Newport is even more unattractive than ever. I'll look sweet in an evening dress. Two patches on my shoulders are burnt brown, my neck & a large V on my neck are brown, my face is brown & my arms as far as the elbows. Gee! I wish Newport would blow up & bust.

I'm leaving here on August 1st & I'll wire you particulars.
. . . Loads of love to everyone, & piles for yourself,

Anna

"*. . . A good education for a girl for one week . . .*"

Newport, R.I.
Tuesday [August 12, 1924]

Dearest Ma—
This *is* a strange place! Even more formal than I imagined. . . . The dances start tonight (one every night from now on!) so maybe I won't feel so belligerent tomorrow morning. How those dances scare me! . . .
Newport seems to me a good education for a girl for one week when she comes out, but for a boy its the worst in the world, even for a day. They think they're young princes because all the females do is to spend their times running after said males. . . .
The two boys staying here (Albert Wall & Cortland Parker) are very nice. Ones a regular parlor snake & the other is more of a student. I haven't quite made him out yet. . . .
Please Bring me 2 more shirts for the knickers . . . one or two more under shirts & some more sateen bloomers if they come up from the wash (& 1 middy blouse). . . .

Loads of love to you [and] Pa,
Anna

P.S. Only lunches & teas so far so I'm still alive.
P.P.S. The English in this letter is fierce in spots, please excuse it.

Having "come out" in society, there remained yet another obligatory rite for the proper formation of a young lady and prospective wife, at least as Granny saw it: an ocean trip to Europe. Again, Anna's own words best introduce her letters from Rome—her "own words" coming from notes I found in her attic box after Anna's death:
"Rome with Granny when I was 18—winter: We shared a cabin for the Atlantic crossing which was so many decks down that the rough seas made the riled up ocean water outside the porthole resemble submarine underwater travel; First night out I was sea sick—corkscrew motion of ship, both rolling & pitching. Granny didn't feel we should have a private bath (too expensive) so we both traveled down rolling corridors to the bath tub. We did have our own toilet and basin. *And* Granny had her own personal maid who traveled with us, and shared a cabin with someone else. I liked the maid—a French Canadian girl. The gal caught the eye of one of the young officers. She was

also assigned by Granny to chaperone me when I wanted to walk around the deck. The officer would join us, and the 3 of us would go and sit behind some abuttment—which I'm sure was away from the 1st Class section & where therefore we were not being observed by anyone who would tell Granny. I think the trip took a good 2 weeks—& we landed in Naples. Drove with Granny in a rented, horsedrawn Victoria over the Amalfi Drive. I had discovered that the Italians liked my blue eyes and very blond hair so I used my wiles on the driver, pointing to the seat beside him where I wanted to be—rather than far down & behind, where Granny sat. She didn't like my idea but finally agreed—because the driver was quite ancient. To this day I don't know if the driver was kidding me or not—but I got him to allow me to drive the horse—after he demonstrated to me that in Italy a carriage horse is trained to go ahead if you put pressure on the reins and to stop if you let the reins go slack. Anyway the horse seemed to go along well for me.

"Granny's intellectual adventurousness: Why should she have planned (before we left the U.S.) for us to have an audience with the Pope at the Vatican? She had grown up a Unitarian and became a *low* church Episcopalian only when she married my grandfather. Also, why did she pull strings in the U.S. to make it possible for her to have a private audience with Il Duce? (Our visit came at the height of Mussolini's popularity and success with raising the standard of living of some Italians. Our Amalfi driver showed us many villas, tucked into the hills, built by 'Italians who made their money in the U.S., brought it home and spent it on these villas and on living well.' Our driver attributed this to Mussolini, and also gave credit to him for curing unemployment and putting people to work. Granny was much impressed. This driver was one of many who talked similarly then."

". . . *you're just a little coo-coo if you're a Democrat!* . . ."

January 16th, 1925

Dearest Ma—

The ocean trip has been piles of fun. I've never slept so much in all my life and I only fed the fishes [a family euphemism for seasickness] once, the first day. . . .

Our first day at Gib[raltar] we motored to Algeciras and I loved it. The little white stucco houses reminded me of Mexico, and it was also like Mexico in that everyone looks so poor. The only prosperous place we passed was a large bullfarm. The owner was riding through one of the fields, and he certainly was picturesque in his Spanish dress, and on the peachiest looking horse I've seen in ages. We also saw some peasant women kneeling beside a stream and scrubbing clothes. In spite of looking so poor all the people seem so happy. There seem to be at least a dozen children to each family and they all live together in a little 2 by 4 room, but still they look husky and healthy.

So far, we've done most of our sight-seeing with Mr. and Mrs. Cook. I like Mrs better than Mr. because Mr. and I disagree about almost everything, but most especially politics. He thinks you belong in the Insane Asylum if you believe Lafolette [Senator Robert M. La Follette, Sr., Wisconsin Progressive] right about anything and you're just a little coo-coo if you're a Democrat!

Loads and loads of love to you and Pop and the boys,

Anna

". . . These blow-outs [with Granny] are usually started by me . . . but . . ."

Hotel Windsor
Via Veneto
Rome
January 27th,
1925

Dearest Mum—

I feel as if I hadn't written to you for ages, but I told Granny she stole all my thunder by writing you all the news nearly every day, so now she swears she isn't going to write till I've written you a good long epistle! So far Granny and I haven't hit it off so badly. Every now and then we have grand blowouts that would be quite amusing for an outsider! But, I'll have to own that somehow or other these blow-outs are usually started by me and my fault, but thats not invariably the case! Anyway, the blow-outs are not too frequent and Miss Bates [brought as a chaperone] (who arrived here last Monday) is a great help and a perfect dear. . . .

Last Saturday we went to Saint Peters. It seemed to me it was so big and full of Popes statues and large cherubs and paintings that it was more like a museum than a church. It seemed very impressive, especially looking up from the back of the church straight up to the nave—the proportions were so wonderful. Somebody told us the only time St. Peters was really appropriate was for large Papal ceremonies, when the whole place was filled with the scarlet tunics and purples. . . .

We have had two Italian lessons. I can say one or two words but so far I haven't dared air my small knowledge in broad day-light! . . .

Tomorrow is Pa's birthday so tonight Granny is sending a cable. [Granny was allowing for delay. FDR's birthday was January 30.] Tell Pa I wish I could be there to give him his 84 (he is that old isn't he, by now!) spankings and one to grow on. Tell him I'd only give him 43 kisses, though!

I do wish you were here Ma. I keep thinking when I pass funny little shops & see an old dirty winding street, what fun we could have exploring together. . . .

What is Pa's address in Fla.? . . .

Much, much love to you and Pop,

Anna

P.S. The check is for the breeches & stockings on Abercrombie bill.

". . . they all seem to take for granted that they are the one & only . . ."

Hotel Windsor
Via Veneto
Rome
Feb 11th, 1925

Dearest Mums—

. . . Tonight Granny is having quite a dinner party here. Granny is having an old Baron something or other and Mr. and Mrs. Randal MacIver, and I'm having nearly every young person I know in Rome! Namely: Mr. Holman (2nd Sec. of Brit. Em.) & his sister & Cousin Miss Andrews & Copley and Lord Castlereagh. We were all going to see the Coliseum [Colosseum] by moonlight but the moon will not oblige tonight so I guess we will either go to one of the big hotels and dance or stay here and talk. Mr. Holman and his sister are the nicest of the bunch because they've both got splendid senses of humor and are loads of fun. Lord C. is nice but a little heavy. I can't make out whether it is because he is shy or just naturally dumb!

Tom Amory is also staying at this hotel now and I've had some good times with him, going to the movies & hotels to dance.

Ma, you can't imagine how many letters I've been getting from Robert, it is something fierce! As soon as I landed in Naples I wrote him the letter I told you I was going to write him, telling him a few things which I'm afraid he won't appreciate much. Of course, I haven't had a letter in answer to it yet & I haven't written since, but I'm very curious to see what his answering letter will be! I've also had loads of letters from Sidney and several from Curt [Anna's first mention of Curtis Dall, her senior by ten years, whom she was soon to marry] and they all seem to take for granted that they are the one & only in my thoughts! I don't suppose I can help that but honestly Ma, I'm perfectly certain that when I get home I won't be any more anxious to be engaged than I was when I left. That doesn't mean I don't like any of these people as much as ever but it just means that I have so much fun with other people that I'm not in the least ready to say I'm sure I like one person more than any others on earth. I know you know all this allready, but I just felt like saying it so I did.

Miss Bates & I are doing a great deal of sight-seeing and I'm getting to love certain things. I do so wish you were here. I miss you like everything too & I think when I see you I'll have so much to say I'll talk for a full week straight. Tell the kids I loved their letters and please to write again.

As always loads & loads of love, Anna.

". . . a well-fed, flabby, unintelligent . . . and totally unnecessary human being, sqweeked in, . . ."

Hotel Windsor
Via Veneto
Rome
February 25, 1925

Dearest Mums—

Yesterday Miss Bates and some 60 odd other people and I had an audience with the Pope. I was much disappointed, because I had at least expected to have the audience in a lovely room, and I expected it would be rather impressive. Instead, we were all put, in a circle, in a large, very plain room to wait for the Pope. After about half an hour a man came in and told us to kneel, then the Pope, looking like a well-fed, flabby, unintelligent, (though I've heard he is very intellectual) and totally unnecessary human being, sqweeked in, in carpet slippers, attended by a sleepy, fat military something or other. He gave everyone his hand so that they could kiss his ring, then he muttered a few words of blessing, & it was over. When his ring came under my nose I tried to get a look at it, instead of kissing it, but that was enough to show him I was an awful heretic so he moved on before I got a good look! Miss Bates and I wanted to get a look at the Palace but every direction we turned in we ran into a Swiss Guards bayonet, or spear! . . .

Tom Amory and I have been out sight-seeing all morning on foot. First, we went to the rag market, which is interesting, because sometimes you see some lovely bits of old tapestries and silks there, and also because it is fun to hear the people bargaining. . . . Then to the Theatrum Marcelli. You can't get in there but between the old, low arches, regular caves are scooped out where whole families live. We walked all the time so we wandered through a great many filthy, smelly, typical little Roman streets, and several times we went in their little dark holes to see what they were like. Our excuse each time was to ask where something was, but the stench was something fierce so, beleive me, we didn't stay long inside!

I have been to see Signora Agresti (the lady Mr. Morganthau [Morgenthau] gave me a letter to) and she gave me a lot of dope on farming [Anna had been considering the study of agriculture at Cornell] and is going to give me some reading matter; but she says it is impossible to spend a night on a farm some where. She says in the first place, she doesn't think they'd take Miss Bates and me in for the night and in the second place that they are suspicious of strangers and I couldn't learn a thing about their lives in one night. On the way to Florence, in the car, I am going to try to get pictures of some of the farms and families, but that seems to be the best I can do. The whole thing is really no easy job, as you'd realize if you were over here alone with Granny. If I had you to sort of help me every now and then it would be different. And if we could take our lunch & drive out into the country and have a real look at the farms it would again be different. But it is all much more easily planned on that side of the ocean than it is done on this side!

I am hoping to get a letter from you before I leave here. I really want one badly! . . .

Love to Pop & the boys & loads to yourself,

Anna

Upon Anna and Granny's return in the late spring of 1925, family talk turned to Anna's near future, now that she had finished at Miss Chapin's. "In my home environment," Anna later recalled, "it was taken for granted that the boys in the family went to college (. . . if at all possible, where their fathers had . . .). My mother mentioned several times that she and Father thought it would be wise for me to learn 'to do something' by which I could earn my living if necessary. College for me was never even discussed that I remember. My grandmother . . . was most outspoken: Girls who went to college were very apt to be 'old maids' and become 'bookworms'—the latter a dire threat to any girl's chance of attracting a husband!"

Evidently, college for Anna *was* discussed, whether Anna chose to remember it or not. She didn't like the idea one bit. Father wanted her to apply for the four-year course at Cornell (not necessarily with the plan of completing it). At least he'd like Anna to give the first year of it an honest try. Anna made a counteroffer: one semester of a course in "practical" agriculture at Cornell. Henry Morgenthau, a family friend, advised Eleanor that Anna ought first to attend a summer course at the Geneva (New York) State Experimental Station. Anna was so opposed, she refused to speak to her mother all the way to Geneva.

Years later, in writing and speaking of her faint brush with higher education, Anna was to convince herself (or try to appear to) that she welcomed these experiences. In a magazine article after her father's death: "When I was eighteen or nineteen, Father and I had serious talks about my studying agriculture, the idea being that I would be able to help him with his many agricultural projects on the acres around our house at Hyde Park. These included a farm where there were chickens, cows and pigs, acres of woods, some fruit orchards and some grain fields." In her lengthy initial interview with me: "I was the only girl—you better remember this. A girl to Father was—well, she didn't have to earn her own living. He belonged to *that* generation. . . . When I was a little girl I would be one, for instance, who wanted to ride horseback with him. And I started riding on the saddle in front of him. And he wanted me to be—he liked to talk to me about his trees. In fact, he got me very interested in his experimentation with trees and the types of soil we had around Hyde Park. You see, at that time we had around two thousand acres, and orchards which seemed to do fairly well around there. These were things that were very personal to him—questions like, 'How did you *use* trees?' This is why he got into developing shelter belts of trees when he first became President. . . . So I went to Cornell for a short course in agriculture when I was nineteen—just before I got married."

"Just now," Eleanor wrote Franklin at Warm Springs, "I am more worried about Anna than anyone. I do hope at Cornell at least her name will mean little and she'll get some of the foolishness out of her."

Apparently she didn't, which brought some measure of glee to her younger brother Elliott, who was chafing under his own hostilities toward study at Groton School, near Boston. Elliott chortles in a letter home: "I don't know what the Alpha Phi [a Cornell sorority] is yet, but I understand Anna got into [it] just so she could go to a certain dance. Pretty soft I think!! Several Yale boys have been up here and have mentioned her. They think she will probably get flunked out or something like that because she never seems to be at the college at all."

The battle over school was not the only source of tension. Anna's rage at her mother over the eminent position of Louis Howe continued. Howe was resented not only for taking Anna's room, brother James wrote, but also for "moving mother into the spotlight of public life. Anna accused him of stealing mother's attentions from her. He did. And he did not care. He felt mother was needed more in public than in her private life, that she had a higher destiny than merely being a mother. Anna was sacrificed to the cause, as we all were in a way. Anna argued bitterly with mother about this sacrifice, and when she got to college she refused to answer mother's letters."

While angry with her mother in 1925, there's much evidence that she was feeling warmly toward her father. But the evidence largely misleads. The previous year during the Tennis Week festivities at Newport, she was told by "this gossipy old cousin, Susie Parish," of her father's escapade with Lucy Mercer, of the near wreckage of her parents' marriage, finally helping Anna make sense of a coldness, a deadness, in her parents' dealings with one another, so different from the cheery warmth she recalled between them when she was a child. It helped explain, among other things, why Mother was now building—for *herself*—a cottage, more than a mile away from the Big House at Hyde Park, in the woods on the other side of Route 9, along a stream called Val-Kill.

Cousin Susie, recalled Anna in a conversation with me one day, described the episode "as 'this horrible thing.' I couldn't talk to my mother about it. I didn't know *who* to talk to. This 'horrible thing' had happened—this woman named Lucy Mercer almost running off with Father. In those days you used the term 'an *affair*.' And this had been, so Susie said, 'very much gossiped about at the time,' but that 'thank goodness, nothing had happened.' Nothing except that it had hurt Mother very deeply. But there was no divorce, you see, so 'nothing had happened.'

"Well, a year later"—presumably, this is shortly before Anna's pouting departure for school—"out of the blue, my *mother* told me about it. I was a year older, of course. And I remember my first reaction was that I was *mad— mad* at Father for having at one time hurt Mother."

"So," I said, "even though angry with your mother for 'forcing' you to school, you now felt defensive of her?"

"Yes, isn't that funny? Because I was a *woman*, you see. You can sympathize as a woman. This could easily happen to *me*. At least, that's the rationale I realized later on to explain my immediate reaction, but I didn't realize it then."

As though all that were not enough: "The most visible family tension, in Anna's eyes," her son John Boettiger later wrote, "was that between Eleanor and Sara; and her awareness of that tension must have served as a convenient mask for her less conscious—and probably more frightening—experience of serious tension between her parents. . . . She was to say, many years later and after she had divorced [Curtis Dall, her first husband], that she married to get away from the constraints of her family, and particularly the tension and feeling of oppressiveness she still associated with her mother and grandmother. An underlying motive, coexisting uneasily with her desire for freedom, may have been a wish to be properly cared for by an older man (Curtis was ten years her senior): as the young Sara was cared for by the older James; as Eleanor [had] dreamed of an idyllic life with her father [Elliott]; and perhaps as Anna may have wished, inside herself, to be her father's helpmate."

Whatever the sources and explanations, soon—and seemingly out of nowhere—came the opening sentence of the letter that follows, that "The day is drawing nigh" for a dinner party to announce the engagement of nineteen-year-old Anna Roosevelt to twenty-nine-year-old Curtis Dall, a securities salesman for Lehman Brothers, tall, lean, with a receding hairline, whose chief interests seem bounded on the south by Wall Street and its style of male camaraderie built upon the sport of money; on the west by class reunions at Princeton football games, and on the north by horsemanship and hunting in Westchester County and the Adirondacks. "I got married when I did," she was one day to assert bluntly, "because I wanted to get out."

Anna and Curtis married in early June 1926, when Anna had just turned twenty. On the eve of the wedding, Anna has recalled, "my mother asked me if there was anything about 'the intimacies of marriage' I would like to ask her. My answer was a firm 'NO': I had learned a little, so very little as I later discovered, but I had definitely learned at that particular time what one did and did not talk about with one's parents."

The wedding was followed by a honeymoon voyage aboard the S.S. *Empress of France* to Great Britain.

". . . gosh-darn the dinner—I'm getting cold feet! . . ."

[Geneva, N.Y.]
1/18/26

Dearest Ma—

"The day is drawing nigh" and I'm beginning to wish that the dinner could be held without me! I'd love to watch it over the banisters in my pajamas! Can't I?

In all my letters to the great Aunts etc. I haven't mentioned the dinner but I have said it was going to be announced on the 23rd. Should I have done that? I have a feeling maybe I shouldn't! But, believe me I'm *not* going to write those darn letters over again! . . .

I'm glad these two weeks are up—but—gosh-darn the dinner—I'm getting cold feet!

Last night I wrote a paper until two o'clock, but tonight, I'm going skating after supper & to bed as soon as I get in, so as to be rested on Friday & Sat. & Sun.!

I waited on table the other night & earned 35 cents for myself! I also broke 2 dishes & spilled a plate of soup down my back carrying the large tray on my shoulder!

Curt said he would meet me at the station Friday a.m.—Oodles of love

Anna

". . . my inglorious way of terminating my college career. . . ."

Monday Feb. 8th [1926]
Infirmary

Dearest Mums—

Here is a letter at last! Last Tuesday night I started my reasons for being sent here, by loosing everything I'd eaten for the past two weeks. The next day I had my usual, fever, chills, aches & pains. That afternoon I was sent down here and told I had a touch of grip or "Flu." Thursday my temperature went way down & I thought I was alright, but Friday it went to my intestines, and took the form of bad dyheria (spelling?), which lasted until yesterday, in spite of all the medicine they stuffed in me! Of course, my piles also started in and behaved badly. So up until this morning I've had nothing but boiled milk & dry toast. I couldn't even drink plain water with the result that at present I'm pretty weak. However I had an egg for breakfast this morning and I'm having a little meat for lunch.

Curt went to Pittsburgh last Thursday on a business trip, and came here yesterday by way of Buffalo. The Doctor thinks I ought to be able to leave by tomorrow, so Curt is staying over, & we'll go home tomorrow by the 12.30 if I don't feel to wobbly. . . .

I am rather ashamed, Ma, of my inglorious way of terminating my college career, but I don't exactly see how I could have helped it!

Best love to Pop and to you. Tell Father to remember his figure! . . .

Much love,
Anna

P.S. Curt just came in and says to give you his love.

A.

". . . hard to tell whether Father is walking better or not. . . ."

[Warm Springs, Georgia]
[Monday, April 12, 1926]

Dearest Mums—

It was great to get your letter this morning. The enclosed was from Emily Smith saying that she was so sorry our wedding days clashed, but could not change her plans!

Curt arrived here Saturday morning & is staying till Wednesday morning, and we're having a blissful time.

Will it fit in with your plans if I leave here next Tues. the 20th, getting to New York Wed. noon. There are so many things you & I have got to plan, that I'd like to get home at least a day before you start South.

Ma, its awfully hard to tell whether Father is walking better or not. He doesn't walk very much, & doesn't exercise over much. However he does handle himself better & can go up 2 steps. He is entirely "off" Dr. MacDonald now—Says he was ruining his legs—might get him to walk but would deform his legs. Dr. Abbott was here & started him off on this tack, as far as I can gather. Dr. A. told him he must wear 2 braces. He now wants to . . . spend the summer between Warm Spr., Hyde Park & N.Y.! I don't know whether you know all this, but anyhow, it sounds interesting!

The one & only topic of conversation is *Warm Springs*!

I'm getting a wonderful tan & having a fine time.

Love to the kids & Jimmie. Lots of love to you from Curt & me,

Anna

". . . I think my [ring] size is either 3½—4—or 4½! . . ."

Warm Springs
Friday [April 16, 1926]

Dearest Mum—

I've just telegraphed you that I am leaving here Monday instead of Tuesday.

When I first arrived I wrote Dot and Gaillard asking them if they would be bridesmaids, but have not heard from them. Could you telephone Dot do you suppose & tell her I want to give her a ring anyhow, so please to come in & get fitted? Gaillard, Helen & Martha I'll have to guess at from my own size. I'm enclosing a piece of cardboard the size of my little finger & a piece of elastic which *unstretched* is just my size. I think my size is either 3½—4—or 4½! Gaillard's size is ½ smaller than mine. Helen & Martha are my size. The numbers I am taking from the ones written on the ring thing in the front hall. The enclosed cardboard is rather a loose fit for me. If Kay & Nicky haven't been in, call up Kay & tell her to tell Nicky. If my roundabout method is no good, well—I guess the good old lady who is making these rings will have [to] add on a little more steam!

I miss Curt terribly since he left on Wed. morning. We had such a great time. Curt got quite a tan & looked fine—and as for me I'm getting quite niggerish. . . .

Much, much love,

Anna

". . . Our cabin is peachy . . ."

S.S. Empress of France
Wed P.M. [ca. June 1926]

Dearest Mums and Dad,

We got your wire as soon as we got on board—We loved it!

Both of you can well imagine what kind of a time we are having. Absolutely perfect, are the only possible words that describe it.

Gosh! we owe a lot to you two. And don't forget that we think a great deal of you.

Our cabin is peachy and we've chosen nice space on the starboard deck, about amid-ships for our deck-chairs. Now we are going to reserve a "table for two" in the dining-room. (excuse me—I meant "mess-hall!")

With a great deal of love to all the family, and loads & loads to both of you,

Anna & Curt.

P.S. Dont forget to write us soon c/o F.L. & Tr. Co. London—Lots of love!
C.

". . . Curt wants to know what he is to call you! . . ."

Burlington Hotel. W.1.
[London]
Saturday June 19th [1926]

Dearest Mums—

We have been here now since Wednesday afternoon. . . . Our room here is peachy. We lead a very leisurely life—breakfast in bed(!) and our other meals just wherever we darn please!

Here is some real news for you. We have hauled off and bought one of those tiny English cars, a "Peugeot". It is a runabout, and is painted a French blue. Curt joined the Royal Automobile Club, and they will help us with road maps, etc. This is not as extravagant as it sounds as we bought the car for £165 and the garage guarantees to take it back in three weeks, and pay us £125, so all our transportation thru England and Scotland will cost us £40. The club dues are £2—1 for one year.

So far we haven't called on anyone! We're going to pay a few calls tomorrow afternoon, however. . . .

We start off in our car on Wednesday morning early. . . .

The ocean trip was great, too. The weather was rather bad, but it wasn't very rough. It will amuse you to know that we only met 2 people the whole way over—and they were a young couple who introduced themselves and played games with us twice!

We are not getting our return passage until we get back here in about 3 weeks, so you see we are not worrying about the exact date on which we sail! . . .

Curt is terrible the way he mimics the English accent in talking to elevator boys etc.—He says I spoil it by bursting out laughing! You would too, if you could hear the strange noises forthcoming from his throat! . . .

Oodles & oodles of love from us both to you,

Anna

P.S. Curt wants to know what he is to call you!

". . . hated to say good-bye to our little 'Sassy' . . ."

Burlington Hotel. W.1.
Thursday July 15, '26

Dearest Mums—

I feel rather guilty, as this is only my second letter to you since we left! . . . We have had *such* a glorious trip! . . .

We arrived [at York] at 12.30 at night, having run out of gas at 11.30, three miles outside—pushed the car for a mile and a half, & finally met a kind soul who sold us half a gallon! . . . And finally (ran out of ink)[letter continues in pencil] back here yesterday afternoon, in time to return the car and book a passage on the Celtic the day after tomorrow. . . .

The Celtic stops at Boston, probably on Sunday afternoon the 27th or Monday morning. We stop there for about 2 hours, and we wondered if you couldn't all (or as many as possible) come down & say hello to us. [FDR, Eleanor and their boys had been summering at Marion, Mass.] It would be wonderful to see you, if only for a few seconds, or minutes.

We hated to say good-bye to our little "Sassy" (the car) this morning for the last time. We couldn't have had a more wonderful time.

Love to all, and loads & loads to you from us both,

Anna

After Anna's marriage, Eleanor reshaped her life to accentuate independence—from her husband, from her mother-in-law.

She took up residence in Val-Kill Cottage. To keep up appearances, Eleanor occupied her room at the Big House when Franklin had important visitors there. Val-Kill also became the full-time residence of two close friends, Nancy Cook and Marion Dickerman, whom Eleanor met in the women's division of the Democratic State Committee. Miss Cook was a lawyer and headed the women's division; Miss Dickerman, an educator and social activist. They were an enterprising pair and seemed to stir an entrepreneurial spirit in Eleanor, the trio converting part of the cottage to a furniture factory to create jobs for underemployed farm lads of Dutchess County. In addition, they bought a girls' finishing school in Manhattan, the Todhunter School, where Eleanor taught American history, English and current events to older girls ("because I considered that it took less training . . . than to teach the younger").

Between the previous letter and the next, two great family events occurred. First, on March 25, 1927, Anna became the mother of a girl, third in a line to be named Anna Eleanor. Like her mother, she was often called "Sis" or "Sister," but her nickname eventually settled to a distinctive "Sistie" (often spelled "Sisty"). The second event was that in November 1928 Franklin D. Roosevelt was elected governor of New York. While her social duties as the state's first lady often tied Eleanor to the creaky, Victorian executive mansion in Albany, in a way the new prominence freed her for new forms of independence. When she was at Val-Kill or at Todhunter—more than half the time—she was quite on her own, unencumbered by family. Franklin's secretary, Marguerite (Missy) LeHand, who was invited into residence at the mansion, occupying a room next to the governor's, became, in actuality, his hostess most of the time.

". . . [They said Elliott] had an excellent mind . . . original & exceptional."

Parents House, Groton
March 2d, 1929

Anna darling,
   The baby came up comfortably on Tuesday last to Albany & seems quite at home & everyone is crazy about her. She sleeps & eats well. I had Dr. Shaw come to see her on Thursday morning & she greeted him smilingly & was sweet until she spied his bag then she put her hands to her ears & howled! Nothing would console her & she did not stop till he left! . . .
   Yesterday [I] had quite a good part of the afternoon here & a most satisfactory time with Elliott. Father & I had evolved a plan but I feared it would not please Elliott instead of which he seems delighted. He is going to graduate here & we are going to find the best possible tutoring school & let him spend next year there taking the necessities for college but also taking some side things he's never had a chance to take here which will mean that he will enter college well ahead of his necessary work & perhaps knowing a little more what subjects are of the greatest interest to him. . . . He has been a slow development but Mr. Regan & Mr. Billings [faculty members of Groton School] both said he had an excellent mind, Mr. B. adding that he was going to speak even better than James & that his thought was original & exceptional. Also they would grieve to have him leave as he is the best oar on the crew! He did remarkably on the gym team on Washington's birthday scaling the wall alone etc. & I think it has been good for his morale, as I've never seen him in such good spirits or apparently so anxious to fall in with other people's wishes! I think he is even considering the plan of going abroad with somewhat less antagonism than usual!
   They plan to finish the legislative session by the end of March which will mean Father gets to Warm Springs by the end of April but I am concerned that he is not getting his water power bills in till so late & fear the Rep.[ublicans] will say he is not giving them time to discuss them. Of course he has had a great deal to do but I wish he had concentrated on the big issues & let some of the other things go. . . . Isn't Hoover clever to put a democrat

in the one dept. which will be constantly under fire the next few years? If he does enforce prohibition they'll be sore with a democrat & if he doesn't it will be a democrat's fault!

I do hope you are enjoying every minute of your trip. . . .

Love to Curtis & a world to you dear,

Devotedly,
Mother

March 2d

". . . One has to know how to slow down, . . ."

Carlton Hotel
St. Moritz, Switzerland
March 12th, '29

Mother darling—

I was overjoyed to get your letter of Feb. 24th [this letter crossed Mrs. Roosevelt's of March 2 in the mail]. It must have caught a slow boat as it didn't get here until 2 days ago! . . .

The skiing has been really wonderful, & in spite of being a beginner, I have grown to really love it. We have taken some quite difficult ski trips together with a guide. We climb on skis with a strip of seal skin (the Campo kind) . . . Then one zigs-zags down. One has to know how to slow down, stop abruptly, & turn left or right quickly, to do any skiing here, & believe me we've worked like the devil, & had many a spill learning. As a matter of fact, we have over done a little. Last week Curt was miserable with a slight fever . . . & didn't get his pep back for 5 days. They tell us the altitude here has a lot to do with it, & that we should have just rested for 2 days to get used to it. I caught cold somehow, probably because everyday I came in my undies were wringing wet! And here I have been in bed with the grippe for 3 days. The Doctor says there is nothing to worry about. I have no "pneumonia or plursey" as he puts it! My temp. today has stayed consistently at 99.⅘, & the Doc. thinks I'll be normal tomorrow. My cough is much better—my sinesses are bothering me most now & the Doc says my head will be stuffed for 2 more days. The hotel was supposed to close here yesterday. . . . However, as I couldn't go out they have allowed us to stay on here in solitary splendour. . . .

Don't worry about my cold, as you know I would always cable you immediately if I or Curt were really ill!

A heart full of love, & take care of yourself for me,

Anna

March 12th

". . . must be a typical old aristocratic European family. . . ."

Hotel Bristol
[Vienna]
March 24th, '29

Dearest Mother and Father,

We have fallen in love with Vienna, and are having quite an interesting time here. We had a letter of introduction to a Countess Hoyos, and she and her family have been very nice to us. I think they must be a typical old aristocratic European family. The old lady is Granny's age and very keen, but a stickler for the old customs and manners, and very much "grande dame." Her son and daughter-in-law seem to be more or less lost in this day & generation. They haven't much money, but he wouldn't know how to make any! The Diplomatic Service seems to be the most popular and almost the only branch of occupation open! They are delightful however, and know their history, and that of Europe down to the last detail. They, of course, want a king, and firmly believe it is only a matter of time before nearly every country in Europe will be a limited monarchy. They say Vienna itself is very Socialistic but the country districts are not. Of course, they are frightfully bitter over the way Austria was cut up after the war. Before the war they had a population of 56,000,000, and now they have only 6,000,000! The old Countess's second daughter married Bismark's eldest son. They think nothing of Emil Ludwig's book [a biography of Bismarck], and say that he himself acknowledged lately that after further research he finds that some of his facts are erroneous! Ludwig is a Jew & dropped the name Cohen, which was his family name, when he became a biographer! By the way, here in Vienna Jews are taboo. They are the only really wealthy people, and have the most beautiful houses & gardens in Vienna. However, the younger Countess said "We regard the Jewish question here as you regard your negro question in America!" It is considered frightful for a gentleman to marry even a Jewess of the best family. The Rothschilds were received at court so they are grudgingly accepted. It seems to me that the truth is they fear the Jews, who are clever & hard workers & very powerful & wealthy. They are very numerous & have a very large Society of their own. The younger generation of Hoyos' seem to be doing somewhat better for themselves. One boy, Count George, whom we know in N.Y., married an American girl, and is in the Investment Banking business. None of the girls in the family do anything & seem frightfully young for their ages, though very well educated.

Yesterday they took us out to Schonbrunn, and today we went to the old lady's "at home," and met Count ——— [blank is Anna's] who was Austrian Ambassador in Washington when we were there & remembers you both.

Today we went to see the horses of the Spanish Equestrienne School. This school is, I think, the last of its kind. The horses are of the old fashioned breed, either all white or all black, (mostly all white now) with high arched necks and long flowing white tails. They are all either stallions or mares & must have a good deal of Arabian blood in them. There are about 35 horses & about the same number of grooms. If a horse lies down a groom goes in immediately & brushes its mane & tail & the blanket! There is to be a performance on Tuesday & of course we are going!

Forgot to say that we were told that Hungary now calls itself a Royal Republic, and is trying hard to get Prince Otto, son of the late Emp. Charles to be their king. They say there is no chance of Austria & Hungary ever joining forces again. The President of Austria, as in France, is a nonentity & the Premier is the man in the public eye.

We think we like Vienna better than Paris. We are seeing as many galleries as possible, & hope to see at least one more of the summer palaces, probably Laxenburg. And, of course, we will go to the opera!

We leave for Paris the 28th arriving there the 29th. I haven't heard from Granny yet, but saw by the Paris Herald that she & Aunt Kassie [Sara Delano Roosevelt's sister] had landed. I have written her.

Two years ago tomorrow Sister [Anna's daughter] alighted in the world—to put it mildly! We will be thinking of her & will drink her health in a choice wine. Give her a squeeze for me.

Thanks loads for your 2 last letters, Ma. They were great & most gratefully received. I loved the snaps of Sister. She looks so fat & rosy & grown-up we neither of us could recognize her at first.

Hope all goes well with you both. Loads of love from us both.

Devotedly,
Anna

P.S. I still, at times, have the rottenest siness I think I've ever had, but am doing everything to get rid of it. It bothers me mostly at night unless I pillow my head way up!

A

Anna and Curtis were enduring an idyllic life in a big white house they had built on thirty-six acres of meadow and woods on Sleepy Hollow Road, in North Tarrytown, New York, overlooking Lake Pocantico, where, from a certain knoll on the lawn, one could catch a glimpse of the majestic Hudson River. Pheasants, wild ducks, herons and an occasional eagle enlivened the place. "Enduring" is the right word for it, because for Anna, at least, the life was boring and peculiarly tense. Her three servants—Katy, a cook-house-keeper, Mingo, the butler-chauffeur, and Frieda, or Nan-nan, the nurse, took care of just about everything, so Anna, without conviction of purpose, frittered her time at Girl Scout work, entertaining Wall Street associates and neighbors whom Curtis felt obliged to impress, and finally organized a party-arranging business with some friends which didn't last long. Meanwhile, the stock market crash of October 1929 cast dark prospects on Curtis' investment business, to result within two years in loss of the showy homestead and they moved into Anna's parents' town house on Sixty-fifth Street.

Anna's boredom had been broken by the birth in April 1930 of her second child, Curtis (Buzz), and occasional excitements that arose by virtue of being the governor's daughter. She had been stirred by her father's prominence ever since the first outburst of talk that he might be chosen by Al Smith for the run to succeed him, Smith having entered the 1928 race for the presidency. FDR, hard to find and playing hard-to-get in almost-phoneless Warm Springs, elaborately agonized over whether or not to run, putting on an almost convincing show. Twenty-two-year-old Anna, one of those taken in, is to recall, "Having dropped agriculture as an avocation, apparently I felt competent to offer political advice. I telegraphed Father, 'Go ahead and take it. Much love, Anna.' His answer, by wire, was: 'You ought to be spanked. Much love, Pa.'" She accompanied him much of the time throughout the campaign, later writing, "Never before had I had such an intense interest in an election night."

The first page of the following letter from Anna to Eleanor, ca. 1931, is missing. Yet the fragment that remains is sufficient for a rare glimpse into the difficulties between FDR and Eleanor, and the ways in which they—especially FDR—had learned to enlist Anna as a go-between. FDR had become extremely attached to Warm Springs, Georgia, and to his faith that its hot natural baths would contribute to his walking again. Eleanor secretly detested and openly avoided going there. She thought of FDR's trips South as "his time with Missy." Missy LeHand regularly accompanied him to a cottage he built at Warm Springs and for lengthy cruises aboard his houseboat *Larooco* off the Florida coast, supposedly to take care of his vast correspondence (which his files, maintained during these trips, show to have been far from vast, and mostly personal). FDR's mother, Sara, disapproved of this arrangement, although Eleanor cooperated with it and appears to have encouraged it; indeed, to be somehow relieved by it. Perhaps Eleanor feared competing with Missy. But it may also be true that FDR relied on going with Missy because Eleanor wouldn't go—in fact, she often resisted sharing a variety of places and times that he especially enjoyed. FDR is often perceived as something of a cad for the ease with which he supposedly used or ignored his devoted wife. A dramatically contrasting picture comes through this letter from Anna to Eleanor.

". . . he seems ever so anxious to have you. . . ."

North Tarrytown, N.Y.
[ca. 1931]

. . . Father's letter to me was mostly about trying to persuade you to go to Warm Springs for a week with him. He feels you are tired, & ought to "slow up"—he thinks you could get a substitute for your classes for 3 days—& he seems ever so anxious to have you go with him this Saturday. Pa thinks one week would "put you in fine shape for the winter." As this Saturday is so close, couldn't you arrange to go down to Warm Springs for the last week he is there, or for a week in the middle of his stay there? As I see you usually for meals—or as you or I run in and out of the N.Y. house, it is very hard for me to tell if you are tired. I had thought you were quite harassed—more than tired—about 3 or 4 weeks ago. But Mummy dear, if you are tired, *please* take it more easily—cut out a few of the meetings, & some of the speeches (which you swore last summer you were not going to make!) and if you think it would give you any rest at all to go to Warm Springs—do go. Pa seems to want you there so badly, too. . . .

Oodles of love,
Anna

CHAPTER III

June 19, 1934–January 17, 1937

On November 8, 1932, in the midst of national economic depression, hunger, despair and pervasive fear, Governor Franklin Delano Roosevelt of New York was elected President of the United States. A bewildered Eleanor Roosevelt became First Lady of the land.

Amidst the election night rejoicing of family, friends, news writers and partisans in the mansion at Hyde Park, a reporter for the *Chicago Tribune,* John Boettiger, who had tracked the Democratic candidate since the early days of the nomination, sought out Mrs. Roosevelt in the crowd and murmured a comment, which was really a question, but to which he expected no answer: "I wish I knew what you are really thinking and feeling."

"I was happy for my husband, of course," Eleanor would soon write, "because I knew that in many ways it would make up for the blow that fate had dealt him when he was stricken with infantile paralysis. . . . But for myself, I was probably more deeply troubled than even John Boettiger realized. As I saw it, this meant the end of any personal life of my own. . . . I had recently enjoyed a certain amount of financial independence, and had been able to do things in which I was personally interested. The turmoil in my heart and mind was rather great that night, and the next few months were not to make any clearer what the road ahead would be. . . . Only once did I try to solve some of the questions that seethed in my mind about what I should do when I lived in the White House. I tentatively suggested to my husband that perhaps merely being hostess at the necessary formal functions would not take all my time and he might like me to do a real job and take over some of his mail. He looked at me quizzically and said he did not think that would do, that Missy, who had been handling his mail for a long time, would feel I was interfering. I knew he was right and that it would not work, but it was a last effort to keep in close touch and to feel that I had a real job to do."

As Eleanor divested herself of Franklin as the image of hero-husband, Anna took him on as hero-father, an image dramatized by her witnessing night after night along the campaign-train route the prayerful hope invested in him by worshipful multitudes, by the perspiring attentions of reporters and power dealers, his aura lifted all the higher by the depth of the national crisis.

"Starting with the Democratic Convention in Chicago," Anna later wrote, ". . . I have to confess to feeling more exhilarated than at any time before or since—or at least that's the impression I have almost thirty-four years later. And this feeling was to continue throughout the campaign, and afterwards as we moved into that historical old mansion, the White House."

There was something else that fed Anna's exhilaration. The reporter from the *Chicago Tribune,* John Boettiger, and Anna had been drawn into a love affair with each other, a passionate one, the passion fanned by drafts of secrecy. Both lovers were bound in decayed marriages. Thus, in the moral setting of 1932, both were holding matches to political and social explosives. Since early summer, all through the campaign, Anna and her husband Curtis kept up appearances, largely for political reasons, of being a family. But they had been occupying separate bedrooms in the East Sixty-fifth Street house and were virtually estranged. It was already decided that Curtis would not move into the White House, but that Anna and the children would.

Eleanor, feeling "the end of any personal life of my own," was enjoying the dangers and delights of Anna's, even claiming a certain proprietary interest in it: "I used to tease my daughter by saying that I knew John before she knew him."

Anna and John apparently didn't meet until a month or so into the campaign. When the candidate's train pulled into Albany, not far from Hyde Park, John was miserably ill with an infected throat that caused him to be hospitalized. The candidate, sagaciously concerned for the health of a reporter from a Republican newspaper, sent an automobile after John on the day of his hospital release, with the insistent invitation that John recuperate in a guest room of the Roosevelt home at Hyde Park. By late summer, reporters were known to have stumbled upon the pair kissing between two cars of the campaign train. Reporters who would have no qualms about scandalizing a candidate's daughter were quite circumspect when the potential scandal involved one of their own. So the couple was oddly protected. During a seventeen-state whistle-stop swing in September, almost nightly in the compartment shared by John Boettiger and his reporting colleague, Ernest Lindley, there was a cocktail gathering of Boettiger and Anna, Lindley, Anna's brother Jimmy and his wife Betsey. (Prohibition was in force: the stuff of another political scandal if reporters were not among the perpetrators.) Lindley observed that Anna and John behaved like a committed couple.

On October 10, 1932, less than a month before Election Day, something of a profound and specific nature occurred between the couple. Perhaps the occurrence was in the nature of a pledge, a commitment to one another. Perhaps, as a son to be born of them speculated almost half a century later, it was the first time they made love. Whatever, the tenth of October became a special date in their lives, marked by an extraordinary exchange of letters on the event's first anniversary in 1933. John's letter, written first, discloses the romantic fire that blazed between them:

My Darling—

A thousand thoughts, all precious beyond expression, come to me now as I look backward over the year.

In a sense this is not an anniversary, Darling, for it seems that I have ever loved you, even as I always shall.

So full of the most glorious adventures with you, however, I suppose that this past year shall always live indelibly in my memory, Darling, and if I could live it over and over again, as I surely shall in that lovely vale of dreams, I would ask naught else.

I LOVE YOU, my Sweet, always and always and always.

Every day, every second with you has made you the more dear to me, and as we look ahead to the years before us, I pray that they may be laden with the greatest happiness for you.

What joys you have brought to me, and what I may have given to you, shall always, my lovely Darling, be the boon of my life.

And so, Beloved, this day's message to you, one that shall always be ever new and alive, and coursing through all of me, is—

I LOVE YOU!

Yours
John

The secretive signature on Anna's letter, to cross John's in the mail, is the initial for "Beetle," a nickname used only by John.

My Very Precious One

The day's work is just finished at 11 p.m., and this is the first chance I've had to sit down alone. But, Darling, you've been so constantly in my thoughts all day. Our Oneness and our Love seem, and are, so very close to me. This is an anniversary for us, Honey, because it seems to bring to life—at the magical thought that we've actually been each other's for a whole year—the myriad memories we have of our ever growing living LOVE, our many glorious adventures and experiences, and the almost breathtaking realization that during this year we have found through each other that dreams sometimes do come true—and for me have proved more wonderful than my wildest imaginings.

Darling, you have, and are, giving me *so* much happiness; and you have opened up a great many more, very lovely, avenues to life, which I had thought about, and guessed at—and a year ago, didn't really think I wanted to go any further!

And Honey, your happiness means more to me than I can possibly tell you. Oh, my Sweet, unless we had that Oneness and instantaneous response to each other's touch, moods and thoughts, we would never have known that marvelous feeling of soaring in the clouds, just the two of us, replete with happiness.

Honey Darling, you'll have to forgive me—this morning with YOU, and your oh, so precious letter which I read right after lunch today, have made me a bit scoofy! Right now I want to take your head between both of my hands and cover your face, your ears, your neck and your hair with kisses—then lie down with your arms around me with my head in its favorite spot on your shoulder, snuggled into your neck—and slowly let that feeling of you steal over me, till I'm full to the brim of YOU, and US, and our LOVE.

I'm really so full of you just now that I'd probably burst if I were really with you!

Sweetheart, you *are* everything in life to me, and I LOVE YOU, with all my heart and soul, now and for *always*.

Your,
B.

Thirty-two-year-old John Boettiger was tall, serious of face, reserved, impeccably dressed, a portrait of self-assurance and success in his craft. Assigned to covering a favored presidential candidate, he was on his way to the most honored of reportorial niches, White House correspondent of a major newspaper. He had made a conspicuous mark as an investigative reporter, having unraveled the complex involvement of a fellow *Tribune* reporter who was shot dead in brazen gangland style in Chicago's busiest commuter railroad station. The story was recast by Boettiger into a well-received book, *Jake Lingle, or Chicago on the Spot.*

Self-confidence or the lack of it—the impressive show of it to cover lack of it—are beyond simple explanations, and John's sense of incompleteness at lacking a college degree or for being the son of a mere bank clerk did not explain the fears that lay tautly controlled beneath his sure exterior. He was to reveal, perhaps for the first time so directly and in writing, his life-binding secrets in an extraordinary letter more than ten years after meeting Anna, written from war duty in North Africa from which he knew he might not return. It was a letter of advice to his four-year-old son to be imparted at an appropriate time. It admonishes bluntly: "Think well of yourself. I labor under a definite inferiority complex, which tortured me as a child. I struggled against it, and maybe some will say I 'over-won' the battle, but *I* know I'm not an egotist, and never could be. But I try to give others the thought that they can have confidence in me, whether I have it in myself or not. This may seem like deception, but one never knows how well one can do a thing until he ventures it and he may never venture it unless he sells his ability to handle it to the people in control." As the advice goes on, the self-revelation, intended or not, goes deeper: "I hope you will always remember how completely Mummy and I love each other. Neither of us has ever known or heard of a love as perfect as ours. . . . You are the personification of that love, and since history records that children born of great love (in or out of wedlock!) are specially gifted, you might be said to eclipse all other human beings in that regard!" He turns from his deep faith in romantic love to what his son, one day to grow up and be trained in the psychological arts, is to describe as his father's "enduring, anxious, and often depressing doubt of his own adequacy as a man": "In your relations with the other sex, be *careful.* . . . Get to know them well, study them, but try very hard to keep your emotions, especially your biological urges, rational and introspective. Get experience with women before you marry one, or even before you think of marrying! . . . [Mummy] and I made grave errors in our first marital ventures. I think it has made us dearer to each other to have suffered, and seen the hell that bad marriages can bring, but I believe we would have loved each other with utter perfection anyway. In other words, don't get eager for any woman enough to marry her, until you (and she) have tasted enough of life, *and of each other,* to be certain. . . . Learn to dance early and well; it will help to buck any unnatural shyness with girls. I was horribly shy in this respect, and it plumped me into a marriage which was a flop from the very beginning. *Don't do that!"*

During the famous and stormy First Hundred Days of the New Deal in 1933, the President of the United States executed a duty not especially noted by political historians. He called Curtis Dall to the White House to inform him that Anna planned to seek a divorce. The President, not helped one bit by the chair of immense power from which he broke the news to his son-in-law, detested the task. He had always been terrible at breaking bad news face-to-face. His daughter, however, found it not only painful, but impossible to face the disapproval or anger of men important to her life. She asked Pa to do the job and do it he must. Soon the family friend and attorney, Harry Hooker, drew up a separation agreement that was agreeable to Anna and Curtis.

In the 1930s, only one state, Nevada, consented to grant easily obtainable divorces (in fact, made a minor industry of this permissiveness) on grounds less disgraceful than proof of adultery or displaying in open court the black and blue marks of physical beatings. Nevada favored its "residents" (of six weeks or more) by dissolving marriages on the ground of "mental cruelty." Translated, that meant the creation of an innocuous lie—and six weeks of enriching the local economy by purchase of lodging, food, entertainment and the lawyer's lapse of commitment to truth.

In mid-June, 1934, Anna secretly journeyed to Chicago where she and her two children boarded the Pacific Limited for Reno. Arrangements for her seclusion and comfort had all been made—secretly.

But not secretly enough. Reporters at the station circled and lapped at her, eager for any morsel of confirmation of rumors that divorce was the object of her trip West. Anna said nothing, her eyes imparting only terror. The train conductor and porter were under strict orders that no one was to be permitted to knock on the door of her compartment. In midafternoon, Anna, finding the confinement unbearable, went to the club car and listened idly to a baseball broadcast. The waiter was instructed to be watchful that no one disturbed her. Dinner for herself and her children was carried to her compartment. Late in the evening, as the train pulled out of Carroll, Iowa, twelve hours after its Chicago departure, a maid penetrated the protective barrier, no doubt spurred by some monetary encouragement, bringing Anna a note from a reporter of The Associated Press. Weary of the loneliness, weary of the posture of silence which was not her natural inclination, she told the maid to send the reporter to her door.

"I see I made the papers again," Anna said wanly. She was wearing a dark blue silk dress with white trim at the neck and wrists. Apologizing for her weariness after a sleepless night and long day caring for Buzzie, who was ill with a cold, and trying to entertain Sistie, who was immensely bored, Anna admitted that, yes, she was on her way to Nevada to establish legal residence and that, yes, the trip was in connection with ending her eight-year-old marriage. No, she had not retained an attorney nor made specific plans for a divorce proceeding. Yes, she had leased a house at Lake Tahoe, but did not know what kind of residence it was. It had all been handled through an agent.

While suddenly willing to talk, Anna remained in torment over what to say, as though direct words might force her to look squarely at matters she was not yet ready to look at squarely: "It's rather hard for anyone to say he or she is going to Reno to *get* a divorce. We may want a divorce, but there are any number of things to consider. It's easy to start out—but rather hard to carry through." Although consenting to answer questions, Anna was suddenly irritated at the questioner: "There's very little reason why the private life of *anyone* should be exposed to the glare of publicity. But I guess I'm up against the same thing Elliott was when he was divorced and remarried [the previous July]."

Anna and her children climbed down from the train at Truckee, California, where a lawyer, Samuel Platt, rushed them into a motorcar, leading a small caravan of reporters they could not shake, to a log house overlooking Lake Tahoe at Cal-Neva, Nevada, less than twenty feet from the California state line. For the legal requirement of six weeks, this was to be home.

From this point on, and for the next twenty years of correspondence, the letters that follow are preponderantly—for long stretches, exclusively—Eleanor's to her daughter. We know from Eleanor's letters that Anna wrote often and in detail, but the letters are not to be found. Surely, Eleanor had not casually thrown them away, because Roosevelts do not throw away *anything* in the nature of family mementoes, at least not the generation up to and including Franklin and Eleanor Roosevelt. Eleanor followed the practice, however, upon receiving a newsy letter from one of her children, of sending it on a "round robin" among her other children. In the course of these rounds, it appears, Anna's letters have dropped out of reach.

"*. . . & don't take these days too hard. . . .*"

49 East 65th Street
New York
Tuesday [June 19, 1934]

Darling,

Your letter came yesterday & I was glad to know the first part of the trip went off well, the papers had told me the A.P. had caught you & forced you to talk. Poor child! You were so tired when you left & with Sisty & Buzz all night & all day you must have been dead & that must have been the last straw. . . .

I know just how you feel about getting started. At least there is a goal in the offing & I am glad the first plunge is over. Granny sent for Harry [Hooker] yesterday p.m. & didn't want me to know so I called him this morning & made a suggestion which I think may help with Curt & also be better for the children. He is lunching with Curt tomorrow & I said to tell him that at any time that he would be having the children if it was inconvenient to take them, he could come & stay with us & you would stay away. Harry felt he would feel it was recognition & it would facilitate life & his situation with his partners if he could say he was going to stay with us & it would be better for the children than carting them around. I hope this seems wise to you as I couldn't consult you. . . .

I'll see John [Boettiger] next Friday before I leave so I can tell you how he looks. I think Hick [Lorena Hickok, a former news reporter who had become a close friend and frequent companion of Eleanor] & I will get to you about the 16th or 17th, so write me where the ranch is. . . .

All my love dear one & rest & don't take these days too hard. Remember even disagreeable things come to an end!

Much love
Mother

". . . then sneak away & drive up to you. . . ."

Hyde Park
June 25th [1934]

Anna darling,

What a dreadful time you had, it seems too dreadful & must have seemed unbearable. There is one consolation however that all the photographers & news hounds seem to have had no luck in disseminating their news for you've been out of these papers except for the small notice Friday that you'd gone to the ranch & Hick writes after two days you were out of the Colorado papers. . . .

I am sending in a separate envelope to Sisty & Buzz, two egg cozies a woman in Tivoli [a town near Hyde Park] made for them! I doubt if their eggs need to be kept warm but they are rather funny & may cheer a few moments! . . .

I plan to fly from Chicago to Sacramento on the 10th or 11th & stay with Hick in a little house a friend will lend us in Colfax [California] for 4 or 5 days, then sneak away & drive up to you. If there is room on the ranch & the Dana's will have us as paying guests grand, otherwise is there somewhere not too far away I could stay inconspicuously? I'm sure I can get away from newspapers & I thought we'd stay from the 16th–19th with you if that is convenient. . . .

I've lost my heart to Ruth [Elliott's second wife], she is sweet & dear with Elliott & I think they are safe. Perhaps it is too soon, they may settle into indifference but somehow I feel they won't. . . .

A cable from Granny says she landed safely, met by Amb. staying with him, going to Cliveden to Lady Astor on Sat. & then on Monday to Scotland so she must be well!

Father left tonight [on a voyage through the Caribbean and the Panama Canal en route to Hawaii] & was most interested in your news & sends love.

I will see John [Boettiger] in Washington Friday, if he is there so I can write you how he seems before I leave. . . .

We'll be motoring to Washington early Thursday & when Father leaves Sat. a.m. we will leave for Reedsville [West Virginia, near a self-help housing project called Arthurdale which especially interested Mrs. Roosevelt]. Any wire to the White House will reach me at once as I will wire them every night where I am, I'll be, & letters should be addressed to Nancy Cook c/o Gen. Delivery, Norris, Tennessee July 4th & Drake Hotel Chicago on the night of the 8th & 9th in my own name.

A world of love darling, you are a grand person & I am proud of you. Love to Sisty & Buzz & a hug for you.

Mother

"... Dear, dear, what excitements! ..."

The White House
June 29th [1934]

Anna darling,

. . . Curt insists that the children must go to the Wilmot's but apparently has no desire for them after Aug. 15th. So they will I hope be settled at Hyde Park as he told Harry he would be glad to come up & see them there!

John [Boettiger] came to dine last night & I had a little talk & then we drove for a half hour this morning. He told me some things to discuss with you & he doesn't want you to delay any longer than you have to on the way home! He said he was lonely, but I told him that was a good sign! He is fundamentally happy & there hasn't been a thing in our papers about you since the first few days so he is delighted & dreads the last splurge less. I'll see him in Chicago & bring you the latest news. He looks well & I feel safe about you two also.

. . . Pa's speech was good I think, what did you think? He is not leaving till Sunday night. . . .

F jr. just blew in from Wilmington & asked if I'd been reading the papers! His engagement was announced to Ethel Du Pont but he says they are not formally engaged & won't be & he'll finish his education! Dear, dear, what excitements!

. . . I am a little weary of adjusting everybody, offices, secretaries, desks, so I'll be glad to get out on the road next Monday & I can hardly wait to see you.

My love to Buzzy & Sisty & regards to Katie. . . .

Mother

". . . I'm getting lots of protests . . ."

Boone Tavern
Berea, Kentucky
July 6th [1934]

Dearest Anna,

I think I sent the kids cards from Asheville. . . . I've tried to stay out of the papers but fear it hasn't been very successful. I haven't been bothered much tho' today just one village met me with the fire truck & escorted me thro'. No one in town knew what all the noise was about but the firemen enjoyed it!

We had two nights in Asheville & learned a lot about weaving. Mr. Leahy the head of the Biltmore Industries insisted on sending homespun suits, (that is the cloth for a suit) to all the family & I chose a kind of red which I think you will like for you. Norris [Dam] & the T.V.A. is a thrilling thing. I hope you will come when Father goes in Nov. for it is worth seeing. Crossville where we went today, before coming here is an interesting homestead development . . . A mountain boy or girl 16 or more may come here & earn their way thro' & they may learn to read if they haven't had a chance before! I've met a lot of grand people on this trip, the world certainly should move forward.

I'm getting lots of protests on my radio [broadcasts] from manufacturers of other beds & bedding! [the First Lady's radio sponsor was a mattress manufacturer] . . .

Devotedly
Mother

". . . Washington is natural & safe . . ."

> Hotel Blackstone
> [Chicago]
> July 9th [1934]

Darling Anna,

Just a line because it is late & I am a bit weary from dodging news photographers (quite unsuccessfully) broadcasting, etc.

It was grand to find your letter & John here when I arrived. He came in last evening & looks better & is enjoying himself. I telephoned this evening & he will have his old teeth out on Thursday & it all seems simple. They must have been poisoning him. . . .

As soon as I see Hick I'll write you whether to meet me the 16th or 17th. She may want an extra day in Colfax & we can stay with you till the morning of 21st if convenient & still have 4 days in Yosemite & 2 in San Francisco & there to drive to Portland.

I hope Curt lets you keep the children & we must plan so you can see John as soon as possible. I tell him Washington is natural & safe or Hyde Park but we'll talk about it. Bless you dear, a world of love

> Mother

———————————

Eleanor's traveling companion, Lorena Hickock or "Hick," had, in the two years since they met, become the closest person in Eleanor's life, more dear than anyone was to realize until Eleanor's death. Between 1934 and 1940 the two wrote to each other nearly every day they were apart, and the volume dropped off after 1940 only because the two saw each other more regularly. The quantity of letters is not the only measure of the intensity of their friendship.

"I felt," Eleanor wrote one night after Hick's departure for a trip, "a little as though a part of me was leaving to-night, you have grown so much to be a part of my life that it is empty without you. . . . Oh! darling, I hope on the whole you will be happier for my friendship."

A journalist since 1913, Hick was assigned to cover Mrs. Roosevelt during the 1932 campaign. The two women won each other's devotion so quickly that in 1933, Hick, feeling a loss of objectivity, resigned from her assignment and from The Associated Press, and joined the New Deal. On the payroll of the Federal Emergency Relief Administration, she traveled widely and provided confidential firsthand reports to Mrs. Roosevelt (officially, to Harry Hopkins, relief administrator). She was later to hold posts with the Democratic National Committee and the 1939 New York World's Fair and to write books for teenagers about the Roosevelt family. Hick's habits were scarcely the kind one would expect to win the fondness of Mrs. Roosevelt. She enjoyed drinking sprees with her friends. Built like a squat barroom bouncer, Hick perpetually dangled a cigarette from her lower lip, its column of smoke deflected from the eye by gusts of profane speech. Frequently she incensed other friends of Mrs. Roosevelt by addressing the First Lady as "darling" and "dearest" at inappropriate moments of social gatherings. Some friends permitted themselves to wonder about Eleanor and Hick what they had previously wondered about Eleanor, Marion Dickerman and Nancy Cook. While not mentioning Hick in this regard, son James later wrote frankly in his book *My Parents:* "It has been suggested that there was some sort of unnatural relationship between Mother, Marion and Nancy. I was close enough to them to say there is nothing whatsoever to this. It's true that they were very close. In fact they shared Val-Kill. They shared it to the extent that the linen was embroidered with the initials EMN (Eleanor, Marion, Nancy). . . . I think the situation satisfied a need for companionship each of them had. They were among the first women's libbers, I suppose—at least they seemed determined to prove they didn't need men. I don't think Marion or Nancy ever married. They may have resented the fact that Mother was married, but if so they were consoled because it was a flawed marriage. I do not believe there was ever anything sexual between them. From what I saw, friendship was all they felt they needed. . . . Father never interfered with Mother's friendships. He felt she was entitled to hers as he was to his. It was part of their arrangement."

". . . when I found I was followed . . ."

[Colfax, California]
Thursday [July 12, 1934]

Anna darling,
    We'll be over on Tuesday & meet you beyond the Soda Springs Hotel at 10 a.m. We do have to drive slowly, chiefly because Hick is nervous!
    Gee! What a time I've had with reporters in Chicago & on the way but this a.m. when I found I was followed I pulled up on the side of the road & told them I'd wait till they phoned their editors but if I had to be followed I'd leave any state I was in & go home & I wouldn't meet Pa who might be a bit annoyed! We invited them to breakfast in a coffee shop in the nearest town & there I waited till their editors got up & they were told they could go home! So far no one has found me here. We're in a house way off the road which belongs to a friend of Hick's who owns a T.B. sanitarium & they send us in our meals! It is up in the pines & lovely & we ought to have peaceful days & make our exit unnoticed. John looked better when I left & was happier I think. We had a grand evening with Martha & Chuck & a good talk yesterday. Goodbye dear till Tuesday, I won't write again. Hick sends her best love.

Devotedly
Mother

We'll stay till Sat. or Sunday whichever seems best to you.

". . . I've grown to love you like one of my very dear ones . . ."

[Colfax, California]
Friday July 13th [1934]

John dear,

I haven't yet seen Anna & won't till Tuesday but your wire has just come so I am sending this to Tommy [Malvina Thompson, Mrs. Roosevelt's secretary] to send over to you. I am so glad all went well [with having his teeth out] & I know Anna will be relieved. . . . This not being together thro' bad times is particularly bad, isn't it?

The trip coming out was horrid, papers had it & tho' I wouldn't be photographed or interviewed it seemed so ungracious not to go out & say "hello" to the people who had come out to see me. I did at 3 a.m. in Salt Lake because the Gov. & Mrs. Blood were there & he got the photographers to go & I felt if people were there at that hour I must go out. . . .

I suppose Anna had a bad day yesterday & they'll watch there for they have all guessed I was going there so I decided to wait till Tuesday & stay with her till Sunday. I hope they won't know till I leave & then she can give it out!

Hick & I are in a little house way off the road, on a hillside facing west & the sunset last night was glorious. We sleep & eat out & this afternoon we're going where I can get a walk & swim. What more can one ask? The days are hot but the nights cold & Hick's two friends seem nice & I have lots of time to write & read & think. It really is glorious!

I loved seeing you in Chicago, John dear. I've grown to love you like one of my very dear ones & I'm grateful beyond words for the happiness you've already given Anna & I trust you for the future.

I'll write you after seeing Anna just how she is. Bless you dear boy, take care of yourself.

E.R.

". . . August is not far away . . ."

[Near Reno, Nevada]
[Between July 17 and 22, 1934]

John dear,

This is a hard time for both you & Anna but from the standpoint of health Anna is beating you out. She is sunburned & hard & looks rested & the place is so beautiful & the real people around have been good to her so I think on the whole things are well with her. We've talked of many things but come back always to you. Before long she will be with you & we think the Gray's [Maude and David Gray; she was Eleanor's maternal aunt] are the safest bet for a peaceful holiday for you both. I wrote Maude & should get a wire from her.

I hope the teeth have stopped hurting & that you are going to feel much better without them.

August is not far away so here is to happy days before long.

Much love to you,
E.R.

". . . I said you'd take sandwiches to the rocks when anyone . . . appeared unexpectedly! . . ."

Chazy Lake [New York]
Aug 17th [1934]

Anna darling,

. . . Why not ask Curt to put the children on Sept 4th on a train for Poughkeepsie. . . ? Then you could meet them there, John could be at the cottage, you could settle them. . . .

I'm going down from here on the 25th & John can come as my guest to the cottage whenever he wants & no one need know, if he arrives a day or two ahead of you all the better. Let me know tho' so I can arrange with Nan [Nancy Cook]. . . . I said you'd take sandwiches to the rocks when anyone had to come or appeared unexpectedly! . . .

You & John must have a holiday in Sept. & if one thing doesn't work we'll work out another.

A world of love to you & love to John,

Devotedly
Mother

In October 1934, the second anniversary of that unrevealed event by which Anna and John marked the commitment of their love, John literally asserted the "losing" of himself to the sweep of romance. This extraordinary letter informs us of the high-charge and romantic extravagance that flowed between Anna and John. It also helps us sense the magnetic source of Eleanor's sudden preoccupation and involvement with her daughter's romance. It is of an intensity that Eleanor never experienced, yet clearly had dreamed about; of a kind that she obviously would never now have, yet could experience through her daughter. So, for Anna, the romance was a double fulfillment: excitement over the love for its own sake, and capturing at last her mother's full attention, empathy, approval and emotional involvement.

There was no clear reason to doubt that both John and Anna were in Washington at the time of this letter, that John is choosing to write as an appropriate means of expressing the passions that threaten at once to drown him and set him afire.

My beloved—

Today I am dwelling on days gone by, and glorying over them, and dwelling, too, on days to come, and losing myself in a future world so beautiful that I tremble with the joy of it.

You, my Darling, are the treasure of my past and the all of my future, and in writing to you my thoughts for OUR day, I find them crowding each other so that they challenge the putting them down on paper.

O, life is so utterly precious with you in it, my One! I thought I was living before that first day when I held you in my arms, and learned how blessed is love, that day whose anniversary quickens my heart so today. But I never lived till you came into my being. . . .

Will you stop now, as I have done a dozen times since starting this letter, and let your thoughts drift back? O, my Sweet, doesn't it leave you breathless and very happy?

Then came other days, my Love, full of the loveliness which has enriched my memories—OUR memories—beyond compare.

Days under the pines, when the miracle of your great understanding heart was shown to me.

Days in the snow, with a biting wind whipping color to your cheeks.

Long days in the sun, gorgeous loafing lazy days.

Days on horseback, holding hands as we rushed on, laughing with joy.

Days of quiet, of long talks in which we explored each other, and found so to the very brim what we've always sought in companionship.

And days when we explored people, and things, and happenings, long perfect evenings alone—when perfection meant only that we might be alone.

Days and nights, when the urge to binge was strong in us and we went "on the loose", and loved it so!

Days of peace and solitude on a rock beside a stream that rushed noisily enough to banish all else but US. We shall never forget OUR rock, my Darling.

Impatient days when things conspired to separate US, but even those days rich because nothing *could really* separate US!

Darling they seem like a million days, so many are their joys. I love them all. . . .

I want so to hold you fast in my arms, today of all days, to hear you say it has been so sweet to you, too, and to plan with you for the days to come.

But comforted am I with the thought that this shall be our last anniversary apart.

I LOVE YOU, my Precious One, with all of me. I am yours,
yours alone, for always.
I LOVE YOU! LOVE YOU! LOVE YOU!

Your
John

(I have loved writing this. It has seemed almost as though you
could hear me. O, I'm *happy*, Darling!)
I LOVE MY BEAUTIFUL *ANNA*.

J.

Anna had been enduring menstrual difficulties and a Washington physician
had recommended a hysterectomy. Anna did not trust the opinion.

Eleanor, in a rare assertion of a certain kind of courage, accompanied FDR
on his annual Thanksgiving visit to Warm Springs, where she tried grimly to
enjoy herself—but fell short. Eleanor's aversion to cocktails, and the faintest
sign of the dipsy effects thereof, are not hard to understand. Her father,
whom she adored, was sacrificed to his need to drink before Eleanor attained
her tenth birthday. On her mother's side, her Uncle Vallie was a peril and
disgrace, having been known on occasions of rampaging binges with his
friends, to fire shots at neighbors out the window of Tivoli, the Hall family
mansion. And then there is her brother Hall, seven years her junior, virtually
one of her own brood of children, who drank all through his youth and drank
heavily still. Eleanor never stopped worrying about him, and Hall appears to
have thrived on her mothering.

Thus, a disproportionally confused, guilty reaction to a minor incident at
Warm Springs:

"*. . . I'd give the world & all to be out of the way. . . .*"

Warm Springs
Monday Nov. 19th [1934]

Anna dear,
I am sorry to hear you are having a bad time again & it is as well to go to
Johns Hopkins but I hope they won't be as panicky as the Washington doctor,
for I think you will gradually straighten out & I don't like those operations at
your age.

I will probably fly home in a day or two. I'd like to leave at once but I
injudiciously told Father I always felt like a spoil sport & policeman here & at
times elsewhere, because I lost my temper last night. He's been giving Nan a
cocktail every night & for two nights it went only a little to her head but it
was so strong last night that she not only talked incessantly much to their
amusement but couldn't talk straight & I felt he did it on purpose tho' he
swears he didn't. Anyway he needn't make them so strong & the others could
all have two or three if necessary. I felt revolt physically from anyone in that

condition & that made her unhappy & yet I hate to be the one to keep her from taking anything so I'd give the world & all to be out of the way and aside from the fact that I'd like to be where I could have an eye on you young lady! Father says however if I leave before I have to he will feel hurt so! I'm an idiotic puritan & I wish I had the right kind of sense of humor & could enjoy certain things. At least, thank God, none of you children have inherited that streak in me, it is as well to have some of Father's ease & balance in these things! . . .

A world of love to you,

Mother

Toward the end of a bustling White House day—a day that saw President Roosevelt present to Congress an arresting and comprehensive program to guarantee minimal human welfare "from the cradle to the grave," called Social Security—the First Lady descended the White House stairs to join the annual reception for the Supreme Court. At midnight she was to board a train to New York where, in the second-floor library of the family home at 49 East Sixty-fifth Street, at nine o'clock the next morning, Anna was to be married to John Boettiger. Somewhere in the course of the evening, Mrs. Roosevelt squeezed out time to write the following letter to her about-to-be son-in-law. She signs it "L.L.," for "Lovely Lady," an endearment devised by John, which he uses constantly as his salutation to Mrs. Roosevelt—clearly pleasing her.

". . . live so you keep the precious thing you now have . . ."

The White House
Thursday eve.
[January 17, 1935]

John dear,

I won't get a chance to talk tomorrow so this is a last word of motherly advice. You know I shall always want to help you both to be happy but never let me interfere & remember that Anna is I think rather like me, she'd always rather have the truth even if it is painful & never let a doubt or a suspicion grow up between you two which honest facing can dispel. I love Anna so dearly that I don't need to tell you that my willingness to let her go to you speaks much for my trust & love of you. Bless you both, live so you keep the precious thing you now have, have patience in the daily risks of life with each other & enjoy life together & with those you love.

My love to you

L.L.

Just before the marriage, John resigned from the *Chicago Tribune*, feeling he could no longer report on the Roosevelt White House with appropriate detachment, let alone with the anti-Roosevelt bias required by one of the nation's leading anti–New Deal newspapers. On the recommendation of Joseph P. Kennedy, chairman of the Securities and Exchange Commission, John became executive assistant to Will Hays, president of the Motion Picture Producers and Distributors of America, the famous "Hays Office," best known as the movie industry's agency for self-censorship. John and Anna rented a small apartment at 112 Central Park West, New York, leaving Sistie and Buzzie at the White House to finish the school year. They reunited in early summer at a larger New York apartment, a duplex at 2 West Fifty-third Street, rented from one of the Rockefellers. Anna kept in touch with her mother mostly by telephone during the year until a Christmas Eve letter from Eleanor that is a measure of how vastly Eleanor had permitted her feelings and affections to become visible compared to, say, a dozen years ago.

". . . if anyone says much I shall weep . . ."

> 1600 Pennsylvania Avenue
> Washington, D.C.
> Xmas eve 1935

Darling Anna,
   Perhaps I needed to have you away this Xmas to realize just how much it means to have you & so I think I'll try to tell you in these few minutes before dinner just how much I miss you. The dogs & I have felt sad every time we passed your door, it was hard to decorate the tree or get things distributed at the afternoon party without you & I dread dinner tomorrow night for so many of your friends will miss you & if anyone says much I shall weep for I've had a queer feeling in my throat whenever I thought of you. Anyway I am happy that you & John are together for I know you will be happy so please give him a hug for me & tell him I am grateful for him & for what he means to you every day of my life. Kiss Sis & Buzz & tell them everyone has asked for them & we miss them very much.
   I will be looking for you all on Friday & when I go to church tonight I'll pray for long life & happiness for each & everyone of you who mean so much to me & may I always realize what a blessed person you are dearest one.

> Mother

". . . Tomorrow we arise at 4 . . ."

> Grayville [Illinois]
> June 15th eve. [1936]

Dearest Anna,
   . . . Tomorrow we arise at 4 leave at 5 to go to a mine & go down with the miners! . . .

> Mother

". . . I'm sorry for them if they get in . . ."

Eastport, Maine
July 24th [1936]

Darling,
. . . It is cold here & beautiful. . . . Granny finds walking so difficult that she does leave one alone! We listened to [Republican presidential candidate Alfred M.] Landon's speech over her radio last night, not well delivered & in spots it faded out but it was effective if you didn't say "how." I'm sorry for them if they get in & after all the promises have to do just about what has been done. . . .

Mother

". . . if he wanted to be King . . . they'd fight for him! . . ."

Hotel Muehlebach
Kansas City, Mo.
Sunday Nov. 14th [1936]

Anna darling,
. . . I hope now the work & excitement [of the 1936 presidential election] is over you are going to get a little rest.
I've just written Pa to say goodbye & to tell him that Tommy is exhausted physically & emotionally answering telephones, wires & letters all telling stories of what has been done for them & how they feel for Pa. Darling, if he wanted to be King or dictator they'd *fight* for him! It is terrifying & yet it must thrill him to know how many people he has put on their feet. A rather grand, gaunt looking detective who was with us last night said to me "I was lost in '33, didn't believe in the country or in anything. I'm 53, I've worked for the public all my life & never been late to work once & I've been a Rep.[ublican] didn't vote for Mr. R. in '32 but in two years he had me. He gave me back my courage & I've got back all I thought I'd lost & this year I *worked* for him!"
The lectures are going better. I felt I was poor at first but the last three have been better. Only 6 more. We get home the 21st but I may stop off to lunch with Earl [Miller] & possibly spend the night but that is improbable for he will most likely have other guests. . . .

Devotedly
Mother

". . . first night on a new subject & I tremble! . . ."

The Stevens Hotel
Chicago
Nov. 16th [1936]

Darling,

It was grand to find your letter here & I am so glad you spent the week end with Pa. I'm sure he enjoyed it tho' I surmise he was pretty busy.

I am so glad Will Hays was nice with John & can hardly wait myself to hear the ideas for the future. Give him my love & tell him I'm back of anything you two darlings want to do!

I certainly hope Buzz & Sis both keep free from colds from now on & I don't think much of inoculations! What a lot of doctors one must see to make sure one's children grow up physically sound! . . .

Colston Leigh [Mrs. Roosevelt's lecture agent] seems to be satisfied even if I wasn't & even I think the last lectures have been better & so does Tommy. Tonight is first night on a new subject & I tremble! . . . Tommy is typing & sending to Mr. Bye [George T. Bye, Mrs. Roosevelt's literary agent] our 4th installment [of what was to become the first volume of Mrs. Roosevelt's autobiography, entitled, *This Is My Story*]. I hope it is interesting. At 2.30 the W.P.A. [Works Progress Administration] women come in & I give them 1 hour on projects then "My Day" [Mrs. Roosevelt's syndicated diary column] to be written & Louis Ruppel [a newspaperman] for tea. Dinner with Rabbi & Mrs. Mann in whose auditorium I speak tonight. Then speak & night train to Detroit. . . .

My Far Rockaway meeting on the 23d is a lunch meeting so I'll come in about five p.m. & get a glimpse of Sis & Buzz & you & John if you are there. I promised to have Hick for dinner that night alone. She thinks I'm an ogre because I'm insisting she write now while it is fresh the story of her four years investigations! Of course she may be in Washington & if so I'll wire you for perhaps we could dine together.

A world of love

Mother

Counting on lunch Tuesday anyway.

John Boettiger in many ways enjoyed his job with the Hays office, shuttling between the moguls of New York and the stars of Hollywood. But he felt out of place in public relations, chafed to return to the world of genuine news. The autumn of 1936 brought an exciting opportunity: an offer to become publisher of the *Seattle Post-Intelligencer*, a major West Coast daily. Moreover, the offer included an editorial job for Anna, too.

The considerations were not simple. The *Post-Intelligencer* (or *P-I*), was an important link in the chain of newspapers owned by William Randolph

Hearst. The entire chain was vocal in its opposition to Roosevelt's reelection. Apparently Hearst, a careful student of political expediency, had decided, following Roosevelt's landslide, that some link to the New Deal—to President Roosevelt himself—was in order. John would be unique among Hearst publishers and editors, guaranteed by a three-year contract of the authority to direct "the editorial [and] business policies of the paper." Anna would become an associate editor "as a contributor to women's pages . . . and in connection with all matters of interest to women." Her salary would be an impressive $10,000 a year, John's a far more substantial $30,000 a year, plus a bonus if the paper improved its financial condition. The *P-I* was losing money, was slipping in both advertising revenue and circulation, and had been shut down by a strike initiated by the Seattle Newspaper Guild.

Receiving White House approval, Anna and John seized the opportunity and transplanted themselves and Anna's children to Seattle.

In late fall the President journeyed to Buenos Aires for the Inter-American Conference for the Maintenance of Peace where he was shocked by the unexpected death of Gus Gennerich, his bodyguard since Roosevelt became Governor. Gennerich had been a New York City motorcycle policeman. FDR liked Gus enormously and trusted him completely. No one matched Gus's skill in shifting Roosevelt from wheelchair to automobile almost invisibly. He also provided other important family services, such as guiding the Roosevelt sons during "speakeasy" days to the right saloons where they would be least likely to scandalize their father.

"Earl," who begins to appear frequently in these letters, was another bodyguard, not FDR's but Mrs. Roosevelt's. Speculation over many years about the relationship between Earl Miller and Mrs. Roosevelt was to be frankly discussed one day by her son James:

"I believe there may have been one real romance in mother's life outside of marriage. Mother may have had an affair with Earl Miller. . . . I believe it is important to realize that . . . Victorian as mother may have been, she was a woman, too, who suffered from her self-imposed separation from father."

James recalled Miller as "an extremely handsome and physical man," a boxer, a horseman, and a state trooper. When Miller became Mrs. Roosevelt's bodyguard, continued James, "his fellow officers originally teased him about being assigned to 'that old crab,' but she took an interest in him, her warmth won him over, and when others saw how he felt about her they stopped kidding him about his 'awful assignment.'

"Mother was self-conscious about Miller's youth, but he did not seem bothered by the difference in years. He encouraged her to take pride in herself, to be herself, to be unafraid of facing the world. He did a lot of good for her. She seemed to draw strength from him when he was by her side, and she came to rely on him. When she had problems, she sought his help. He intervened on her behalf when Uncle Vallie went on a drunken spree at Tivoli, for example. He became part of the family, too, and gave her a great deal of what her husband and we, her sons, failed to give her. Above all, he made her feel that she was a woman.

"If father noticed, he did not seem to mind. Curiously, he did promote a romance between Miller and Missy, but that did not last. Miller, who'd had an unhappy first marriage, later married a cousin of his first wife, and that ended the gossip about mother and him. But this was not a happy marriage either. He was divorced in 1934.

"All the while, Miller had continued to see mother and frequently was a guest at Val-Kill. He saw other women too, and she encouraged his romances. He married a third time in 1941, though he continued to see mother regularly. This marriage was a failure, too, I believe. Maybe because of mother. Their relationship deepened after father's death and ended only with mother's death.

"From my observations, I personally believe they were more than friends and that mother was more than, as she was described, 'an aunt' to him. Joseph Lash in his excellent book, *Eleanor and Franklin,* glosses over the relationship as though to protect her reputation, but I believe this is a disservice to her, a suggestion that because of her hang-ups she was never able to be a complete woman."

". . . Pa answers no radios . . ."

> 1600 Pennsylvania Avenue
> Washington, D.C.
> Sunday [December 6, 1936]

Anna darling,

. . . I came up to Earl's yesterday morning & it has been so peaceful & restful. . . . We took a walk in snowy fields this a.m. which was hard exercise for me as I am pretty much out of condition & now he has gone to get Nan at the station as she is coming up for the night & we go down early tomorrow when he goes to Val-Kill. . . .

Pa answers no radios so we have as yet no date for Gus' funeral. I dread their return, everyone is going to miss Gus[,] & Tommy & I most of all, tho' of course from the standpoint of physical discomfort Pa is going to miss him terribly.

Darling, be sure to let me know how to telephone you & John Xmas morning & the hour in *our* time so I won't make any mistake. I'd give a lot to hear your voice right now & I miss you sadly, but Earl & the quiet here have helped a great deal! My dear love to John & ever so much to you dear one,

> Mother

In the following letter, Eleanor was surprised and somewhat haughtily "amused" that FDR decided to add James to the White House staff as a presidential secretary. When Eleanor made a point of saying, as she did here to Anna, that she "made no comments" and "I am saying nothing these days," she knew quite well that she was expressing herself to her husband eloquently. In her autobiography Eleanor wrote at about this time of her "Griselda mood" in which she "shuts up like a clam," how it annoyed her husband and almost everyone else, and that she knew it.

". . . A pacifist in the War Dept. is funny . . ."

1600 Pennsylvania Avenue
Washington, D.C.
Dec. 16th [1936]

Darling,

Pa & Jimmy got home last night & this is just a hurried line to tell you that both look well & rested. J. says Pa was much upset about Gus but he thinks he tries not to think about it & J. has a state policeman he's sending down to try out. James himself is coming down to act as Sec. on Jan. 15th. They are taking a house, he says he has about $25,000 a year he can count on from accounts coming in so he can pull out for 4 years & let John [Sargent, his insurance agency partner] carry the business. They are taking a house. I was amused & surprised but made no comments. I am saying nothing these days & Pa has no time to be talked to except on matters of business! J. told me & if true I think it diverting, they plan to make Harry Hopkins Sec. of war to reorganize the Dept. till Congress creates a Dept. of Welfare or whatnot when Harry will go in there! A pacifist in the War Dept. is funny, now isn't it? . . .

I'll go to N.Y. tomorrow evening, to Todhunter Friday a.m. See the kids off at 3.30 have the tree [Mrs. Roosevelt's expression for attending a Chrismas party] at the Women's Trade Union League & go to H.P. [Hyde Park]. Have the tree there Sat. late afternoon for the place go up for Sunday with Earl & be back here Monday p.m. to have the gridirons widow's party in the evening. I am not going away again for a long time! Be sure to let me know when to call on Xmas. I long to hear your two voices & I miss you both more than I can say. All my love to you both

Mother

". . . I may be able to make you a cocktail. . . !"

Hotel Statler
Boston
Saturday Dec. 26th, 1936

Dearest Anna,

It was just grand to hear both you & John yesterday. I had been trying for you all day & almost given up. I loved the bowl with holly which came to me in Washington from you both & also the things I found in my stocking. I'm wearing the jade pendant & the book [of] cocktail recipes will go to N.Y. & I may be able to make you a cocktail when next you appear! Thanks ever & ever so much. . . .

Perhaps I'll make it from Texas after my lecture trip in March. I want to see your house when you get settled for I like to be able to see you in my mind's eye when I'm thinking about you.

I know Xmas was dreary for you this year & it was for me but from all I hear the kids had a good time. . . .

> Devotedly
> Mother

". . . Xmas & New Year have been so odd . . ."

> 12 Otis Place
> Boston
> Jan. 1st, 1937

Anna darling,

It was so good to hear your voice & John's last night. Xmas & New Year have been so odd this year for me & tho' I've been so sorry not to be with the kids I think I would have missed you two even more if I'd been with all the others!

I think F jr. is really better & I am glad to have seen so much of Ethel. She is a sweet child but there will be much to learn, however, there is a practical streak there which may save many a situation!

This is Mr. Filene's house [of the department store family] & he is away; His secretary, Miss Schaedler, is a most interesting person & I've enjoyed being here with her & I think Tommy has also.

The book begins in the April Ladies Home Journal & I got $50,000, less $5000 to Mr. Bye & the same to Tommy for her work as I don't want it said she did it on Gov. time. I asked that ½ be paid now & ½ when it is all in to divide income tax. I invested ½ of what I got in fact ⅔ of the first and part for income tax & the rest for current expenses on apt. in H.P. etc. . . .

I love you both & will write when I get back to Washington.

> Devotedly
> Mother

". . . I think she just forgets. . . ."

> 1600 Pennsylvania Avenue
> Washington, D.C.
> Thursday night [January 15, 1937]

Darling,

. . . Elliott says Granny has tried Ruth to the breaking point because she *always* talks about Betty [Elliott's first wife, whom he divorced in 1933]! Of course I think she just forgets. . . .

F jr. left today & I hope he is sensible. He still has the bug floating about. . . .

> Mother

If anyone symbolized to Eleanor Roosevelt the sadness of learning to accept human frailty, it was her younger brother Hall, whom Eleanor described in the next letter as arriving for dinner at the White House in a "lit" condition. In a sense, Hall was her only sibling, since another brother, Elliott, Jr., older than Hall but younger than Eleanor, died in his fourth year. Like Franklin Roosevelt, his distant cousin and brother-in-law, Hall attended Groton and Harvard, where he was a superior scholar as well as a notable charmer. Those qualities seemed bound to direct him to a life of accomplishment, glamour and fulfillment.

But like his father and uncles and grandfather, Hall lost his way in a search for pleasure, concealing his uneasiness in compulsive drinking.

For Eleanor, every encounter with Hall—the deep affections and troubled concerns he stirred in her—activated childhood memories of her father, of whom she was one day to paint a most romantic and unrealistic portrait in her memoirs. To her, he personified affection, the gestures of love, overflowing with promises to provide it someday soon, but rarely showing up to fulfill his promises. Broken promises, unrealized love, the wasted potential of lives close to her—these, to Eleanor, were the wages of drink. The connection lay too deeply in her to be reached by simple appeals to reason that there's "no harm in just one—or two."

Without a sense of what Hall and his weakness touch in Eleanor, we cannot reach for a proper sense of her pervading apprehension, sorrow and of distrust of the reliability of men who become significant in her life.

". . . I went on fast & hope she forgot . . ."

1600 Pennsylvania Avenue
Washington, D.C.
Jan. 17th [1937] Sunday

Darling,

I'm just about to go over the chart for [Inauguration] seats at the capitol on Wed. I discovered last night, no cabinet wives or children had seats! Granny talked to me on the phone this morning for ten minutes on the subject of Mrs. Crawford, Mrs. Weekes & family & Mrs. Hoppin having seats & she is bringing Aunt Kassie to stay! Elliott jr. is being christened *Tuesday* at 4 & when all is over I think I shall sit down & have a good laugh or a good cry I haven't just decided which!

James & Betsy are bringing 7 with them for supper tonight.

. . . Hall came in "lit" for dinner last night & left before dinner, I think having realized his condition. I was annoyed & we were left 13 but this p.m. he came contritely & he says he's going on the water wagon which I devoutly hope is true.

The kids send their love & I love you & John more than you know.

Devotedly
Mother

CHAPTER IV

January 20, 1937–July 27, 1939

". . . Well, another 4 yrs begins. . . ."

[Inauguration Day, second term]
1600 Pennsylvania Avenue
Washington, D.C.
Jan. 20th [1937]

Darling,

I must write you a line before going to bed because I've missed you & John so much all day. We drank your healths tonight at dinner & I sent you a wire because it seemed as tho' I had to let you know how much you were in my heart. You would have been proud of Buzz taking off his cap whenever Pa did & standing by him all thro' the parade. Sisty looked sweet too & tonight Marion gave her before Pa & me her prize, a tie clip. She also has a really lovely bit of pottery she made to take to you.

We were all fairly wet but Pa & I drove back in the open car! I never sat down from 1–6.40 & shook about 3000 people by the hand at lunch & tea & then went to a lovely concert tonight but oh! my feet ache! Otherwise I'm not tired & I am so glad it is over. Granny is here for the week end. I don't know if Aunt Kassie & Harry [Henry Hooker] are staying or not. . . .

Curt wants the children at 5.30 on Sat. & the Secret Service man will be with them. Mdlle & I will await them at the train. I'll wire you after they are off & please let me know when they arrive how they are.

Well, another 4 yrs begins. I thought Pa's speech very good, what did you both think? It is a new job & a hard one however. For me, some struggle for a personal life, an effort to do some good because of the position & a continuing effort to make Pa's life as far as the mechanics go easy so he can have what he wants materially & not think about it. I'm a bit weary as I think about it but I guess I'll live through it! I love you both a great deal. . . .

Darling bless you always,

Mother

"*. . . I could cry that I did not hear you . . .*"

1600 Pennsylvania Avenue
Washington, D.C.
Jan. 21st [1937] eve

Darling,

It was grand to get your wire this morning & I could cry that I did not hear you on the radio but we were driving home. Agnes Leach told me at lunch today that you had Father's quality of voice & ability to project your personality & she was much impressed by what you said also & said the announcer said nice things about you also.

I kissed the chicks for you & we counted the days tonight till they would see you. They seem happy here. . . . I think Mdlle lets Buzz turn a bit too much to her but that will change when they are back with you & John.

Mother

Eleanor missed New York, where she could attend theater, see friends, and "go about without having much attention focused on me." James was now occupying the family New York house, so Eleanor rented a small apartment for herself and Tommy, her secretary, in a Greenwich Village building owned by her old friends, Elizabeth Read and Esther Lape. Later, her brother Hall took a small apartment in the same building. "It was a great contrast to the White House," Eleanor wrote, "and I think for that reason I enjoyed it."

"*. . . I can earn my living that way . . .*"

20 East 11th Street
New York City
Tuesday Feb. 24th [1937]

Darling,

. . . I've just been on my annual pilgrimage to Cornell & besides my speech this year I took up my inauguration dresses at the request of the Student

Council & modeled them in the fashion show. I've decided I can earn my living that way some day if necessary. . . .

Mother

". . . I am grieved at my poor judgment . . ."

20 East 11th Street
New York City
March 3d [1937]

Darling,

. . . I know how weary you & John must be but I hope the circulation increases steadily. I like the paper, it gives more news than any I come across in places outside the very largest cities.

. . . It was a full day . . . & had Hick to lunch to say goodbye before going off on this lecture trip. . . .

I'm enclosing $50 for each birthday. You can probably get them a good chest of drawers which will go with Buzz's furniture. Anything you don't spend for the kids can go in their bank account. . . .

Granny plans to go abroad with John [Anna's brother, about to turn twenty-one] & take a car in Italy to Paris & she also plans to go to you the 23rd of April. How much spare room have you dear? She will take Jennings [Granny's chauffeur].

Pa is both nervous & tired. The court hue & cry [the Supreme Court packing controversy] has got under his skin. I thought stupidly his little outburst of boredom on meals was amusing & human & used it in my column & it was taken up by papers & radio & over the ticker & Steve [Early, press secretary] & Jimmy got hate letters & were much upset & Pa was furious with me. James came & reproved me & said I must distinguish between things which were personal & should not be said or none of them would dare to talk to me & he thought I should apologize to Father. I did before McDuffie [FDR's valet] Monday night before leaving as I couldn't see him alone & Pa answered irritably that it had been very hard on him & he would certainly say nothing more to me on any subject! So it has become a very serious subject & I am grieved at my poor judgment & only hope it won't be remembered long. Will I be glad when we leave the W.H. & I can be on my own!

A world of love to you all & much to you darling.

Mother

". . . the plain clothes men sat in the beauty parlor . . ."

The Baker
Dallas
March 21st [1937]

Darling,

I am so sorry you have had such a horrid time & do refrain from using that arm. Nothing is worth that horrible nagging pain. I am so glad last week was the best one the paper has had & hope it keeps on.

You did not mention getting my check but I hope it reached you. I think, once my income tax is off my mind that I can give both you & Elliott a little check which may make the trip East to F jr's wedding easier. You will know by May anyway. . . .

Monday, Mar. 22d Little Rock [same letter continued]

. . . Tommy was worried because it was Palm Sunday & I gave a lecture at a school at 10 but I let them out at 10.55 so they could go to church! Elliott & Ruth arrived about 12.30 & Tommy took them to the movies after lunch while I discoursed till four! We got off at 4.30, got there at 6 & saw the kids. Baby Elliott had learned to crawl & their Great Dane is too cute with those children. The servants were out so Ruth was getting supper & "Peter" ate a good part of a very substantial salad but we had plenty left. They are all very sweet together & they would love you & John to fly that way on one of your trips & I think you would enjoy it. We got on the train at 9.30 & went to bed leaving orders to be called just before getting in here. When they called we got letters asking me to go out on the platform at 7.10 & wave to aeroplanes escorting my train in & that 4 ladies would bring breakfast to us *on* the train! We were dressed by 8.13 & got off at 8.15 so you can imagine I apologized to everyone but we got the bath & breakfast after it here! Then we had our hair washed etc. after a press conference & the plain clothes men sat in the beauty parlor with us. It is really cozy but Tommy just wrote Mrs. Helm [Edith, Mrs. Roosevelt's social secretary at the White House] that she was glad we hadn't decided on a turkish bath. . . .

I'm glad to know about your rooms. When I come, may I have the one next to you & John? I like a shower! . . .

A world of love to you darling,

Mother

". . . 'How would you educate a daughter' . . ."

The White House
April 1, 1937

Dearest John:

There are several things which are concerning me very much. I had planned to try to come out as a surprise to Anna and keep it quiet. I was going to leave on the 4:45 p.m. plane on Thursday the 27th, and arrive in Seattle at 9:30 a.m. Friday morning—28th. That would be P.C.A. and N.W.A. if that means anything to you.

I can not leave here before that because I have my radio broadcast on the 25th.

I have just heard from Mama that she is planning to leave on the 29th. I do not want to be out there at the same time, but I see nothing to do about it unless you think I had better tell her that I can not go at any other time and it seems a pity for us both to be there at the same time and that perhaps she could delay her going. If you think it is better to let her come along, it is all right with me. . . .

The radio people have suggested that Anna and I do a broadcast together for which they will pay Anna $300 which would include any expense to her. . . . The subject is : "How would you educate a daughter for the twentieth century." Broadcast Wed. May 5th. Fly back Fri. May 7th. . . .

I am so excited at the thought of seeing you all I can hardly bear it!

L.L.

". . . Granny says she is not going . . ."

Villa Margherita
Charleston, S.C.
Wed. eve. April 14th [1937]

Darling,

This trip has been really beautiful & I think Hick has enjoyed it except for a few rangers in the park! I hadn't planned on any hikes because I knew she was working in an office all winter but we did walk 4 miles to see some wonderful trees & she bore up nobly. The Great Smokies are lovely & would be wonderful for a week of climbing afoot or on horseback if ever I can find anyone who likes it! June 10th–16th will be a better time tho' when all the rhododendrons & azaleas & mt laurel are out. . . .

What kind of clothes shall I need? Coming by air I can't take much. . . . Granny says she is not going now so I think she will wait till autumn. I am very glad. . . .

I think I shall hug you all till there is no breath left in any of you!

Mr. Bye is very happy over my last installment but I have the very last two with me & they are poor & I can't get them in shape which is annoying. It must be done before I go West! . . .

Mother

". . . Believe it or not, I flew the plane . . ."

Seattle Post-Intelligencer
July 2nd. [1937]

Darling:

Since we left Chicago we have had a most restful time, sleeping ten hours every night and doing nothing but read back numbers of the P.I. The train is now seven hours late because there was a washout on the line yesterday and we had to be switched to the Northern Pacific tracks for many hours. This line seems to be having bad luck lately. The president of the road wired us his regrets at the delay and at lunch time we were informed that we were to get a free meal this evening!

Our day in Detroit was interesting. . . . On Thursday morning we motored to Dearborn . . . and Mr. Fords museum . . . From the Greenfield Village horse drawn carriages we climbed, or rather folded ourselves into Mr. Meigs little plane and took off for Battle Creek. Believe it or not, I flew the plane most of the way and enjoyed it immensely. First I used only the hand controls then only the feet controls, then both together. After a bit of experimentation I "got the feel." The weather was smooth which helped. . . .

We took off from Battle Creek in a rain storm and the air was much rougher, with a stronger wind. In this I found it much more difficult to keep the plane on an even keel. Mr. Meigs explained to me how to spill the wind from under my wing, but even using both the controls I had to concentrate to keep my course and also keep on an even keel! He also made me keep my course by following the air map. . . . As we neared Chicago the visibility became very poor. As Mr. Meigs was not too sure how long it would take us to reach his home field, he turned around and landed in Lansing, Ill. to fill up our gas tanks in case of emergency. As we neared the Chicago municipal airport he pointed to one big transport which had just taken off, and just then right ahead of us there loomed another big one. He nosed his plane down two or three hundred feet and in less than a half minute the transport zoomed over us. . . .

I told Mrs. McDuffy [Lizzie McDuffie, maid and wife of FDR's valet] that while the children were at Hyde Park I wanted them to have certain hours in the day when they would read, sew (for Sis), write letters, etc. I suggested that on hot days the children come in from play at noon and not go out again before three-thirty or four. Even when the days are not hot they should go in at noon and do something quiet until lunch time, then do something again for an hour after lunch. I am rather anxious that they should not feel that Seattle is the only place where they have responsibilities and work to do. I am even wondering if Duff could not let Sis make her own bed every morning, or at least have them dust their rooms every morning. At home during school time they each have to dust their rooms every Saturday mornings and Sis makes her bed. I know that Duff started Sis on some kind of sewing while they were at H.P. before going to Armonk, but I would love it if you could keep an eye on it, see that she keeps at it (or at anything in the way of handiwork), and encourage her. Buzz needs encouragement and suggestions and discipline to make him write a little something every day and read to himself. He loves to look at pictures but is still a bit lazy about actually reading. Sis, too, should do some good reading this summer, and both children will have no time for anything of this type except during July at Hyde Park. I feel very guilty asking you to keep an eye on all this! Last summer they followed a definite program but this summer they will only be home a week before school starts.

Did I tell you that Cousin Laura [Delano] told us that she had seen the children and had gathered the definite impression that they did not like Seattle. She says she asked Buz how he liked Seattle, and that Buzz' only answer was that there was lots of slush there and not snow for coasting. She said Buz refused to elaborate, and Sis maintained a grim silence!

Well, darling, this has turned into a book, but I still feel that I had far too little time to talk to you, and I always think of so many things I'd like to tell you *after* I've left you!

I love you so deeply and always hate leaving you so terribly. A world of love to you from us both,

Anna

"*. . . Heard about Amelia over the radio . . .*"

20 East 11th Street
New York City
Saturday a.m. [July 3, 1937]

Darling,

How I hated to see you two go off yesterday! I see by the paper the A.F. of L. are defying the [Newspaper] Guild so you will plunge right into that situation. Poor children! I hope you sleep Sunday but I fear you won't. . . .

Well, I drove home after leaving you. . . . Tommy, Henry [Osthagen, an engineer and frequent companion of Tommy's] & I went to the old Lafayette for dinner. I simply couldn't eat! I came back & worked till midnight. Heard about Amelia over the radio & felt even lower. [Amelia Earhart, reported down in the Pacific during her second attempt at an east-to-west around-the-world flight.] I do like her & I'll miss seeing her if she's gone but perhaps she'd rather go that way. Life might not have held such a happy future for her.

The radio also announced that Mrs. Clark [John Roosevelt's soon-to-be mother-in-law] said while Anne & John were not officially engaged there was an "understanding." I screwed up my courage to suggest just as he was sailing that I hoped just for this summer *both* would fee' free. I left Granny comfortably settled. . . . She said she might return via Seattle. I won't come out till Oct. or late Sept.! . . .

It has been grand just having you two somewhere near for a bit & whatever happens I'm happy about you two. . . .

Mother

". . . This sounds rather like an essay . . ."

4315 Semple Street
Seattle, Washington
Saturday [July 10, 1937]

Darling:

That week near you was so very short and passed so very quickly and hecticly—but I did love it. It's a funny fate that sends us two three thousand miles away to live and work!

As I wired you we found plenty of labor trouble awaiting us here. I've come to the conclusion our hardest job here is probably to keep our sense of perspective! We had luncheon the other day with an English couple, a Mr. and Mrs. Huxley, who asked us many questions about labor troubles in this city. Finally Mr. Huxley turned to me and said, "But, you're not really worried about the labor situation in the U.S., are you?" I said no, that I knew we were going through an inevitable and evolutionary period which was bound to tax the patience, senses of humor and perspective and common sense balance of a great many people. . . . Our immediate troubles to keep this paper open and make a success of it are very apt to loom large and out of all proportion if, because of continual pressure we forget to keep in mind the larger picture of what is going on not only in this country but almost all over the world. This sounds rather like an essay of some sort! But the reason for it is that I've been really interested to watch John and me in this situation from a psycological [sic] view point. We returned here, having talked to many individuals and groups in all the cities we went to, with the same old zest for making a success out of the old paper, playing square with those who work with us, and building through the paper a more generally alive and aggressive community. Then: The day we arrive The Star, an evening paper, is closed down by a jurisdictional labor dispute, and are informed that we will be the next to go! Our whole staff was in a terrific uproar because they had heard on one side that Mr. Hearst was closing the paper and on the other that a strike would close it. John made seven speeches, and I followed along, in our different departments during one day, to correct some vicious rumors, and to try to bolster the morale. It is true that we have to make some drastic economies because of the demands of the Hearst management to put the paper in the black at the earliest possible moment, and this will unfortunately mean letting out a few employees. But it will not mean cutting the salaries of those who stay. The Guild is apt to raise a rumpus over this. The Star is reopened, for the time being at least, and the jurisdictional dispute is by no means over. Dave Beck of the Teamsters is trying to stall an election by the N.L.R.B. [National Labor Relations Board] in an effort to secure a majority in the departments on the papers he feels should come under the teamsters union. The C.I.O. [Newspaper] Guild has made many promises to these departments and for the present probably has a majority and therefore wants an election at the earliest possible moment. Their own ranks are none too secure, though. For instance, the Guild has just slapped a large assessment on all it's members, in addition to regular dues, to take care of it's members who are on strike, and to pay a salary to it's president who is one of our reporters and is on leave without pay so that he can devote his time to union activities. Many Guild members resent this burden, especially the majority in our editorial staff who are none too keen about the C.I.O. affiliation, and who only joined the Guild just before it's convention in St Louis. The Guild brought the present situation about by going after members in the departments where the Teamsters feel they have jurisdiction, so they of course feel they must fight to the bitter end. The Teamsters have held sway here for a long time and for them too it is a matter of fighting it out to the end. so—we sit on a volcano, wondering when the time will come when we will be the goat! I don't think that either side is anxious to throw people out of employment, but each side is fighting for a "cause" and says they are willing to suffer anything to attain their ends. The immediate result for us—aside from the worry of wondering whether we will be closed—is that we have an awful time getting anyone to concentrate on the job of getting out a newspaper! Our work is practically doubled, and, as I said before we have to sometimes remind ourselves that we both have pretty good senses of humor and that they should by no means be ignored! Just between us, one of our worst problems is that we have some pretty dumb and un-understanding executives at the head of some of our departments. For instances, John made a very good speech in the Circulation Dept. where we have had considerable trouble, and ten minutes after we left the Dept. the head man fired four girls, with out any explanation. Another bad situation exists in our composing room where the executive seems to be universally hated by everyone. This man rules his Dept. very well economically speaking, but seems to believe in treating people more like dogs than humans. Both these executives have been with the paper for about fifteen years, and if we take on new people we must take other Hearst people— usually the poorest as they do not wish to come as far away as Seattle.

I'm not at all sure that C.I.O. organization is going to work out on newspapers, though it may if the leadership is rational. Our own Guild leadership is of the type which will stand up in a meeting and say that John is a sweater of labor and is only interested in lining his own pockets and therefore not to be trusted. Old fashioned Fourth of July oratory was nothing compared to what some of these boys and gals pull with heat and fire and quaverie voices!

Again for your private ear—wouldn't it be grand if Mr. Hearst felt that he must close down this paper and a local Santa Clause came along and opened a new paper and offered us our present jobs? No more expensive eastern management, inheriting of old and sour situations and no more inability to hire the people you feel could do the work best!

Aside from all this—both kids are fine. Buz lost quite a lot of weight when he had intestinal flu when we were away, but is putting it back again fast. They know that they are going with Curt to stay with the Wilmots and seem quite satisfied. . . .

MONDAY

Yesterday John and I took the entire day off; rode horseback in the morning for two hours, played two sets of badminton at home in the afternoon, and went swimming with the kids in Mr. Gray's pool afterwards.

John and I are seriously thinking of taking a two weeks holiday when the kids go to Curt. If we can arrange it we will go on the train with them as far as Glacier Park . . . where we were two summers ago. It all depends, of course, on whether things seem to be quiet enough here. . . .

I am so very sorry about Amelia—but you may be right that she would rather go in this way. I just hope that whatever happened, happened quickly.

Connie's note was a howl—so enthusiastic about us all—and telling me that she had stopped at the corner of 5th and 65th street the day of the wedding to ask the policeman some information about a bus, and told him that she was on the way to the wedding. The policeman then said, "Then you may see Mrs. Boettiger and please remember me to her." I imagine it's the man who's been there for years and whom we all know!

I am so hoping that you are having a peaceful, happy time in your own house. I can't imagine you idle but it should be a busy-ness with no rush attached to it.

All my love always, darling,

Anna

P.S. It's such a comfort to be able to blow off to you in this fashion—and I hope you can bear it! Don't forget to write about your talk with Heyward Broun [Heywood Broun, columnist and head of the Newspaper Guild] when you have your columnist picnic.

". . . I wish one didn't feel one had to do things . . ."

Val-Kill Cottages
Hyde Park
Thursday July 22d [1937]

Dearest Anna,
    Time flies for me doing little chores here so I can imagine how it flies for you. So far I see you've kept your volcano under control. In cutting expenses have you cut the women's pages out? There was more of your stuff in the Sunday paper but the Sat. one seemed to have none & I wondered if to take it out of the red you had been obliged to cut it out.

Heywood Broun couldn't come last Sat. . . . I am supposed to go to a picnic at Mrs. Broun's on Wed. but I may not go for I hate leaving here & I've been doing a good deal of gadding. . . .

There are endless things every day to do about the house & the workmen to watch & I do ride & swim. . . .

I finally got down to work & dictated an article today for the Reader's Digest but it is just the first draft. However it is a start.

Tomorrow night Hick comes & Saturday I motor her to Jean Dixon's [an actress and friend of Lorena Hickok] at Gloucester then Sunday I go to Cousin Susie in Newport & home Monday stopping to see Elizabeth & Esther on the way. I wish one didn't feel one had to do things for I'd be just as happy to stay quietly here!

Hall called up today & he's been elected V.P. of a N.Y. investment corp. at a "magnificent" salary he says, will be living there & wanted to come up this Sunday but has postponed it as I won't be here. He sounds on the crest of the wave. . . .

Devotedly
Mother

". . . I would never tell him I even noticed . . ."

Val-Kill Cottages
Hyde Park
July 30th [1937]

Dearest Sis,

Tommy, Nan & I went to Heywood Broun's on Wed. for a picnic & I had a nice talk with him. He told me he & many people in the Guild felt they had bitten off more than they could chew & writers should not be bound by same rules as other groups in a paper. He hoped the Editorial Writers would remain unto themselves with just a friendly understanding with other organized parts or groups in a paper. He said Mr. [John L.] Lewis [head of the CIO] had laid down no rules as to their affiliation with CIO & would[,] he felt sure[,] accept whatever they decided. A referendum was now going on but whatever the results [Broun] hoped we would all be patient. A young organization had stupid leaders in localities such as your Seattle boy but these things would gradually be improved & resigning would hurt them. I liked him [Broun] better than ever before & I disliked Westbrook Pegler [a columnist noted for his personal attacks on the Roosevelt family, and particularly Mrs. Roosevelt]. . . . I would never tell him I even noticed what he wrote! [Harold] Ross, the editor of the New Yorker was there & I had never seen him & wished I could talk to him for he looked interesting.

Now dear, how about the neuritis? Did the X-ray of teeth show anything wrong? I hate you to have this. . . .

What did Arnold charge you for clothes? I want to give you 2 or 3 dresses & will gladly pay the whole bill. I've got a line on a 2d hand movie & projector at Eastman's which they say is good as new, just turned in by someone who always gets the latest model. Do you think John would like it for Xmas & would he mind it being 2d hand? What do you & the kids want this year? . . .

Two articles are written for Reader's Digest but one is returning for a bit of amplifying. . . .

Earl came yesterday & brought 3 friends to supper. He stayed the night & went home today. Hall comes tomorrow or Sunday & brings a young lady!

I succeeded in getting to Cousin Susie last Sunday unrecognized & left Monday morning without having upset her household in the least! It was a triumph! . . .

Devotedly
Mother

". . . in consequence I won't go to his house. . . ."

Val-Kill Cottages
Hyde Park
August 5th [1937]

Darling,

I think it would be swell for you to do the [attack] on the naturalization bureau. Everywhere they seem to be the same. When I used to go with people in N.Y. for the Women's Trade Union League, I used to boil & a story such as you could write would do a lot of good & I don't see that it could do Pa or the administration any harm. This is nothing new it goes on in all administrations. I wouldn't be worried about testifying on the people you fired. That is your job you've done what you had to do & I can't see why you or Pa would be embarrassed. . . .

Pegler's last article on Pa & civic morality made me mad tho' I wouldn't let him know for the world. However, in consequence I won't go to his house.

I am very glad you are having a thorough examination & I am most anxious to know the results. I hope nothing much needs to be done but remember if anything has to be done & you & John want my moral support I can come at any time.

. . . Pa may go out sometime to Bonneville Dam, he hasn't said anything but I think he has wanted to see it again.

Hall came up last Sunday with a young lady, not *the* young lady. He looked well & loved the place. He's taken the apartment under me in N.Y. & I am to furnish it by Sept. 1st. In three months his divorce decree becomes final. Then we will see whether he marries again at once or decides to remain free to flit! . . .

I am swamped with peoples' manuscripts & can't get time to do my own writing! I did two articles & I think I must redo them but I hope someday I'll get the knack of more fiction type of writing.

I took Nan & Betty to a League of Women Voters meeting today. We all took things for lunch & then I spoke. I really like being back & doing these small group things & it is awful to say but I could so happily settle down here & have a garden & be busy in the house & in a small community! Mamie & James [new servants] are going to work out I think. They go to N.Y. one week end a month & last week Tommy & I had a grand time cooking. . . .

I forgot to tell you that Elliott said he could get Earl a pass on the American Air Lines to the coast & back & said he'd be glad to show him his ranch & have him there for a day or two so Earl is thrilled for he has never been out & only flown once when he went to Chicago [Democratic Convention in 1932] with Pa. . . . What a lot of fun people who have never had much get out of things, don't they?

Well, I must go to bed, bless you darling. I love you dearly.

Mother

". . . Pegler is after all of us again tomorrow . . ."

4315 Semple Street
Seattle, Washington
Saturday eve. [August 7, 1937]

Darling,
You'll be glad to know that we plan to leave this coming Monday afternoon for a 2 weeks vacation. We chose a place called Moore's Inn on Lake Chalan [Chelan], about 250 miles east of here. . . . We chose this place not only because the fishing is supposed to be excellent but also because the altitude there is about 1200 feet & the climate is hot & sunny in the daytime & cool at night. This last—the climate—should cure my arm. At least we sincerely hope so! We will have our own little cabin with a bedroom, sitting room with fireplace, & bath, & we get our meals in the central Inn.

I'm taking some "shots in the arm," into the bloodstream, now, as the Doctor feels it best to try this before going after the wisdom teeth & tonsil tissue as he is not at all sure that they are causing the pain. He says it is a mild type of arthritis—not the type that deforms, but the type that attacks the nerves. Anyway, it is really better this past week.

There are several things that Heyward [Heywood] Broun said to you which don't seem logical to me in the light of events. I can see that patience is greatly needed in any young organization, but I cannot see the reason for not making a beginning in the improvement of one's leadership. If Mr. Broun believes as he says that writers should not be bound by the same rules as other groups on a paper & should remain unto themselves with just a friendly understanding with other organized groups on a paper—then why doesn't he communicate these thoughts to his local units? On so many papers all over the country writers are resigning from the Guild, forming separate unions. It seems to me that Mr. Brouns present policy & leadership is endangering the whole union movement for writers. Here is a good example: Victor Watson, the ex-A.P. man who was fired by A.P. for union activities & then taken back thru N.L.R.B. & is now Vice-president of the national Guild, & head of the W.P.A. Living Newspaper, is out here preaching that the Guild is *not* organized to protect their working conditions & pay, but to fight employers as a class. Mr. Watson came into a meeting which the Guild had with John to present their objections concerning the Guilders who were fired during our "economy wave." John brought up Harry Bridges [CIO longshoremen's leader] statement to him that employers were d——— fools to try to meet with employees on a fair & square basis as labor should trust no employer & the latter as a class should not exist. Mr. Watson answered that the Guild felt there could never be a friendly relationship between employer & employee & that the Guild was in a war to the death with employers. Watson, in other words, coming directly from headquaters, has done more than ever to split the ranks open more bitterly, & I feel sure, to hurt the Guild's future. They're almost all a bunch of scattered brained, mentally undigested, theoretical youngsters with no leadership except that presented to them by such people as Bridges & Watson. Mr. Broun would have an awful time instilling any common sense in his leaders out here & an equally bad time persuading the big majority of writers on our staff, for instance, that he himself had common sense! John & I have a terrible feeling that Mr. Broun had his tongue in his cheek at least part of the time he was talking to you. Don't forget it would be a big blow to the Guild if you resigned! [Mrs. Roosevelt, as a columnist, was the Guild's most prominent member.]

Sunday

The kids & Katie leave this evening [for the East] & we *do* hate to see them go. As they, too, are feeling a bit low at the prospect, John suggested we have a little party at supper. So I've bought snappers & favors & some things to amuse them on the train, & we'll try to make the leave taking as cheerful as possible. Curt wired he expected to meet them at the train but if he wasn't there they were to go to the Blackstone Hotel & wait for him! Their address c/o Wilmot Camp—Plum Lake, Sayner, Wisconsin.

We can hardly wait to start off ourselves tomorrow afternoon & are holding our fingers crossed against any Guild upset. Our address until the 23rd will be Moore's Inn, Moore, Wash.

As far as we know now there is no chance that we will be going east during Oct. so we *do* hope you can come out here unless it will make things too rushed for you at home. Don't come later than the 1st two weeks in Oct. as the flying might not be so good after the snows start. Maybe I'm just being overcautious on dates—but I *don't* like winter flying! . . .

Anna

P.S. Almost forgot about the camera & projector. I *know* that John would love them for Xmas, 2nd, 3rd, or 4th hand! It would be a wonderful present, but such a big one that I think you should give it to me too. After all there are 2 items, so we'd each have one!

Pegler is after all of us again tomorrow [the *Post-Intelligencer* carried Pegler's column, so Anna saw it in advance]—really more vicious than ever. I'm so glad you handled him as you did at the Brouns!

So much love,
A

". . . 'They' want Pa to take a trip . . ."

Val-Kill Cottages
Hyde Park
August 12th, 1937

Anna darling,
I hate the arthritis, but I'm glad it is the kind it is for that is acute & does get cured!

I'm copying part of your letter & sending to Heywood Broun & will send you his answer.

Also, next week I'm having sent from Washington to Buzz at *home*, a cute picture of a squirrel for his room. I hope Curt met them & how glad I will be when they get home again.

Now for some exciting news. "They" want Pa to take a trip in the country, & as I thought, he wants to see the dams so as soon as John [Roosevelt] goes back to college we start, that will be between Sept. 21st & 26th. We spend 2 days in the yellowstone. (How I wish you & John could meet us there!) Then Bonneville Dam & on to you for a day & Pa hopes you will both, & perhaps Sis & Buzz, go up for two days thro' the Olympic Peninsula & the Nat. Park there. . . . Tommy will have to go & is delighted at the chance to see you & your home. . . .

I've got some good articles contracted for this coming year but I've done so little work this summer that I'm ashamed. . . .

Mother

". . . that's impossible. We have no clothes. . . ."

Moore, Wash.
Aug. 16th [1937]

Darling,

Hell—Fire—and Brimstone! The phone rang last evening—had been ringing all afternoon while we were happily scrambling from crag to crag & snaring unwary little trout. Mr. William Randolph Hearst calling *Mrs.* Boettiger. "This is W.R. We want you & John to come down to Wyntoon as soon as you can." "But, W.R., that's impossible. We have no clothes." "What's that you say? Where are you? I can hardly hear you. I'll send a plane for you." The upshot is that we leave hear either tomorrow afternoon or Thurs. a.m., depending on when we can get a boat—spend Fri. in Seattle, & leave for Wyntoon in Mr. H's plane on Sat. morning. You can imagine how much we love to bust up our privacy! I told Mr. H. we would go down next week, but after talking it over we realized that as John had told him we were on vacation that he was just asking us out of the goodness of his heart & would probably be hurt at my casualness. So our address from the 21st to the 29th will be c/o W. R. Hearst—"Wyntoon"—McCloud, Calif.

A letter from Katie says they are comfortably settled at the Wilmots & that all goes well except that Sis has to be held in check to keep her from telling Curt what she thinks of him!

Your exciting letter of the 12th came yesterday. We'll certainly meet you (kids, too) at Bonneville & Yellowstone if we can possibly make it. . . .

I must stop now if this is to catch the boat. Will write soon again.

All love from us both,

Anna

". . . Not a very high mental average but on the whole . . ."

Wyntoon
Wed. [August 25, 1937]

Darling:

This is a fantastic spot in many ways. It is probably one of the most beautiful untouched forests in California; and this is where W.R. has built (& still is building) a Bavarian Village along the [illegible] banks of the rushing Shasta River. The house we are in is "The Cinderella House", & W.R. lives in "The Brown Bear House." The stories are painted in vivid colors on the outside of the houses. A mile down the river is the place his mother used to own. These buildings are done over quite elaborately, but not out of keeping with the setting (at least on the outside). In one of these houses is the huge dining-hall, living rooms, study, kitchen, pantry, laundry, etc. with guest rooms upstairs. The other house also has guest rooms, the projection room, & a game room. Here is the average itinerary for a day: Breakfast anytime between 9 & 11. After breakfast until lunch at 2.30 swim & lie out in the sun around the pool. After lunch play cards or some game indoors, until about 5. 5 to 8 ride horseback, walk, fish or play tennis. 8.30 or 9 dinner. 10.30 or 11 movie or card games. Midnight, 1, 2 or 3 a.m. to bed. There are always anywhere from 15 to 30 guests consisting of members of W.R.'s & Marion's [Davies, a movie star and Hearst's mistress] families, movie people, the family dentist, Hearst newspaper & magazine people, an Austrian Prince, & always a number of people, whom W.R. & Marion either know themselves or thru someone else, whom they feel need a vacation or are just down on their luck. Not a very high mental average but on the whole a pleasant, easy going, mostly rather spoiled group.

John & I vary the above itinerary by taking a couple of horses & going on an all day fishing trip, or coming back to our room after lunch & reading & snoozing & writing letters, or coming to bed right after dinner. Even doing this last never gets you to bed much before midnight somehow or other!

The neuritis is heaps better. In fact I have had no pain at all for 5 days—since we got here. I'm taking full advantage of the hot sun.

John tried to get W.R. to "talk shop" with him yesterday as we both felt we should get back to Seattle & to work this coming weekend. But W.R. said he'd decided that this was a good place for my arm & that we both needed a rest & that he'd talk to John when he felt these aims had been accomplished, & then proceeded to start a discussion on China! So the up-shot is that we plan to leave here on the 31st—a week from yesterday.

. . . The first couple of days here I had an awful time adjusting myself because I had so loved being completely alone with John for that week on Lake Chelan, & resented being put back into the "polite society harness" again! But my sense of humor & my real interest in the people & the place finally asserted themselves, & now I'm quite enjoying it. And W.R. is right— it is a wonderful climate to be in after the almost continual dampness in Seattle. Someday I must tell you about such details as the cookoo clocks, the huge old porcelain stoves, the occassional piece of utterly incongruous furniture, the "court jestor"—& many others! There is very little drinking. Those who want it must take it in their rooms. Only occassionaly are cocktails served before dinner, & wine is served with dinner & beer with lunch if you ask for it. The females wear pajamas or dinner dresses in the evening & the males white flannels or a business suit. During the day a wash dress, shorts, slacks or bluejeans are in order.

I'm writing Pa in the next couple of days to tell him how glad & happy we are that you are both coming to Seattle. Do you think Pa will be spending a few nights there? We can easily put him in our room with McDuffy in your room, you & Sis in her room & John & I on the porch upstairs. The latter is just as comfortable as a room, is heated, & has 2 double beds! You, we hope & pray, will be able to stay on with us until you absolutely have to get back to N.Y. Tommy could stay at the hotel until Pa has to go & then move out to the house. Or if I let Mlle. go there will be an extra bed in the house. It is so hard to make a final decision about Mlle. The children are terribly fond of her, & having her has been a help to me while the work was so heavy. But she is not good for Buzz, is a big expense, & has *not* taught the children how to talk French. My plan is to tell her I do not need her any more when the children are settled into their school lives again—probably about the 20th of Sept.

We send you all our love—& are terribly excited at the prospect of seeing [you] in not much more than a month!!

Anna

". . . I don't see how anyone can contemplate marriage with anyone so peripatetic! . . ."

20 East 11th Street
New York City
Wednesday [September 17, 1937]

Darling,

. . . Mrs. Clark [mother of Anne Clark, twenty-one-year-old John Roosevelt's new fiancée] announced the engagement but Johnny was reasonable & said they would not set a date for the wedding. I hope he will get at work first but I suppose he'll want to get married & take a trip before settling down & of course in that case they'll have to have an allowance.

Pa may have to give up going west if the international situation looks too serious but if he does I think I will fly out anyway & spend a few days with you & come home via Elliott for he sounded rather anxious to have me. . . .

Thursday Hyde Park

I just talked to Pa & we leave Wednesday about one & he is wiring you about joining us as he could give me no definite information. . . .

Hall . . . is in the apartment below mine but is still constantly on the wing.

I don't see how anyone can contemplate marriage with anyone so peripatetic! . . .

To my surprise Betsy is not coming on the trip, I think on Pa's suggestion!
. . . Granny seems happy in Paris & well & says she only does *one* thing a
day.

I think this is all the news so my dear one goodnight. Love to you & John &
the kids & prepare to be hugged to death when we meet.

Mother

". . . I could be happy in it alone! . . ."

Val-Kill Cottages
Hyde Park
Saturday night [October 16, 1937]

Anna darling,

It seems a long time since I was waving to you & I always hate to leave you
but in a way I was glad to leave the crowd. . . .

Two unpleasant things happened. James★ got thrown from a horse, a new
one. . . . Number two, Johnnie had a collision in my car on the hill beyond
the brook with Joan, driving Nan & Marion's chevrolet! My car was damaged
$95 worth, theirs only about $15, but what annoys me is that John didn't wire
or even leave a note for me about it. Of course my car is back & seems o.k. &
the insurance people were notified but I think I might be told! . . .

My house seems nicer than ever & I could be happy in it alone! That's the
last test of one's surroundings I think! . . .

Mother

This collection of letters is sprinkled with dots indicating passages omitted.
A good many of these excisions are to eliminate "diary" passages: listings of
travel schedules accomplished and to come, forwarding addresses, arrival
times, names of people encountered along the way.

Yet the composition of Mrs. Roosevelt's life cannot be sensed without
getting a feel for the density, the energy, the variety and sometimes the
breathlessness of her travel schedule. The first paragraph of the following
letter is offered as a representative example of dozens removed.

Among traveling First Ladies, Mrs. Roosevelt is unique in her refusal to be
accompanied or chauffeured by the Secret Service. The head of the Secret
Service insisted, as a compromise, that when she was driving alone, Mrs.
Roosevelt must carry a revolver. With great distaste, she consented. One day
she asked Earl Miller to give her target practice "so that if the need arose, I

★ See letter of Oct. 20 [1937] for clarification.

would really know how to use the gun. After considerable practice, I finally learned to hit a target. I would never use it on a human being, but I thought I ought to know how to handle a revolver if I had to have one in my possession."

In one city where she was scheduled to lecture, the mayor, no admirer of Mrs. Roosevelt, threatened to arrest her on arrival for violation of a local law against carrying firearms. Called from the White House by her son James, she explained that since she wasn't driving on her tour, she didn't have the gun and wouldn't be arrested. Still, the Secret Service soon equipped her with a badge as a "special agent" of self-protection, entitling her to carry a gun in her luggage. She never had occasion to use it.

". . . a strenuous week & must go to bed . . ."

> The Lawrence
> Erie Pennsylvania
> Oct. 20th [1937]

Sis darling,
    Your letter of the 14th came this morning via H.P. Washington & the N.Y. apt.! . . . While I wait to go to my lecture I'll start this! I did two lectures Monday for pay, last night I went to Newark for the Women's Trade Union League (a labor of love & a long one!) & this day Tommy & I journeyed from 9 a.m. to 6.25 p.m. & now we've had a bath & dressed, eaten something & at 8 the gentlemen (a rabbi) calls for us[,] at 10.30 back to the train, a rush across N.Y. tomorrow between 9 & 9.30 & the train to Washington. . . .
    I'll do the paragraphs you want but I think my contract bars me from writing for papers so we'll have to get around it by my writing you a letter & you can then incorporate what you wish in an article of your own & I trust your ingenuity to do the necessary thing in the headline! Ask John if to protect you I have to speak to Carlin [George, manager of United Feature Syndicate, distributor of Mrs. Roosevelt's column, "My Day"] first & wire me if he thinks so.
    Must go[,] finish tomorrow!
Thursday night, Oct 21st back in Washington
    . . . Johnny wrote me about my car & it finally arrived a little late! . . .
    Darling, it was Mamie's [a servant] husband James who got thrown from the horse which he was trying to exercise! You see I wanted to try & get a horse who could eventually take Dot's [Mrs. Roosevelt's ˙aging mare] place. . . . George has trained a nice white boy who lives in Pete's old house & works for me in stable, garage & garden. He rides both horses but we've decided James never will, so while he helps in the stable he is not to ride again. I've tried the horse twice but he is a good deal of horse for me I fear however I haven't given up yet. . . .
    I think F jr. is working hard & that he & Ethel are leading a sensible life. . . .

I've had a strenuous week & must go to bed. Bless you dear, my love to John & the kids & a heartfull to you.

Mother

Among other brief news items, Mrs. Roosevelt reports in a sudden sentence and detached air in the following letter that her secretary and constant traveling companion, Malvina Thompson, is about to be divorced. Years later, Anna was to say to me: "The people who worked with [Mother and Father] had to be just as if they had no lives of their own. I think both of them unwittingly and unknowingly even to themselves never realized—it never occurred to them—that these people lived their lives through them, and had nothing of their own. The same is true of Mother's Miss Thompson. She never—for years and years and years—had a life of her own. . . . She was an attachment."

". . . I hope I get a series later . . ."

1600 Pennsylvania Avenue
Washington, D.C.
Dec. 10th [1937]

Darling,
. . . Since I got back on Tuesday I've been doing heavy work on many fronts! Luckily my time, in N.Y. last week & a day & two nights spent with Earl in Albany (absolutely peaceful) & Sat. & Sunday in H.P. at the cottage, was on the whole healthy & not wearing. I'm just beginning to be exhausted but next week I hope to get time to ride & a bit more sleep.

I am much disturbed about the piles, you can't go on losing blood but I hate the operation for piles inside, it is so very painful. Darling, I wish you'd come to N.Y. & go to the Dr. F jr. went to who does not operate. All the doctors go to him you know. I'll pay for your trip, you can stay in my apartment & I'll pay the doctor. It will be hard to leave John I know but I think he would prefer it to that operation. Please think it over carefully & I'll make all arrangments & send money for train or air as you prefer.

Sisty [now ten years old] will have to learn that we have to work for anything that is worthwhile in this world! . . . I suppose Buzz [now seven] will reach a difficult phase as she works out of one but he may be easy. . . .

I think you & John are doing such a swell job on the paper & I hope you can keep it in the black. I know what it means in work however & I'm only thankful your column is easier for you to write. . . .

I did a radio last night, just one for General Foods. I hope I get a series later but we had to turn down a cigarette & a chain store one. . . .

Cousin Susie has had 2 nurses for a week with a case of shingles. . . .

Tommy is . . . getting her divorce here in the District as a new law makes it very easy & harmless.

I must go & shake hands with 500 more ladies!

My love to John & hug the kids. Some parcels have gone to you, others follow. I do miss you so much darlings always but especially at Xmas, however will call you about 10 a.m. which ought to be 7 with you.

I love you dear

Mother

". . . Pa seems fine however! . . ."

1600 Pennsylvania Avenue
Washington, D.C.
Thursday a.m. [early February 1938]

Darling,

I wired yesterday because I hadn't heard for what seemed to me ages & I wanted to know how you got thro' your period & if you were leaving & where you were going. I'm glad it is Tucson & that Isabella [Greenway] will be there. I hate you to be down to 60 again [apparently a percentage of a normal hemoglobin count] & are you likely to have a tough time every period? . . .

Earl has been ill at my apt. there since Tuesday. I'm really worried about him but I think his trouble is being unable to find peace & no one can do that but the individual themselves.

Tommy has been miserable ever since Xmas & is still far from well. I can't *send* her away because she'd be unhappy. I'd like to take both Earl & Tommy & go to Sarasota & be near Maude for a week the end of Jan. but I'd have to back out of a two days trip to "Farm & Home Week" at the Kentucky University with Elinor Morgenthau [a Hudson county neighbor and friend, and wife of Secretary of the Treasury Henry Morgenthau] & I'm afraid she'd never forgive me!

Missy also has been miserable so you can see the household is none too brilliant. Pa seems fine however! . . .

I'm enclosing a little present to you both for the wedding anniversary. May you be happier every year & stronger in health & in love,

Devotedly
Mother

All the Roosevelts were concerned about the deterioriating health and mental state of Harry Hopkins, the New Deal's relief administrator, whose wife Barbara had died, leaving their child Diana motherless before her fifth birthday. James and his wife Betsey took Diana into their home. With increasing frequency Harry and Diana stayed at the White House and soon, on the President's invitation, they were to make the White House their home.

". . . I'm getting really good on make up. . . ."

1600 Pennsylvania Avenue
Washington, D.C.
Sunday night Feb. 13th [1938]

Darling,

I've been trying to write every day but life down here has been so hectic & just getting thro' the mail has kept me up every night till two & three a.m. Last week end at H.P. with Anne & Johnnie & Earl I went to bed Friday & Saturday at 9.30 which is about all that has kept me going!

Tommy is much better & I think if she rests at H.P. while I'm at Cornell this week she'll be really fine. . . .

I'm so sorry you've had a bad period & fear from your staying over that it has been an unduly long period with great loss of blood. It is discouraging & means you'll have to be careful every period till they find something to control it. I hope John hasn't been so worried about you or the paper that he hasn't been able to get all the possible good out of Tucson. Give him my love & tell him I wish I could be with you both tonight. . . .

James . . . says Harry [Hopkins] seems to him to come along very slowly. He sits & looks at his wife's picture for hours & can't be roused, & then is too gay. I'm sorry for little Diana. . . .

Missy has been ill again & I'll be glad when Pa gets her to Warm Springs in March! Hick has been ill with a very bad throat & Earl is better but planning to take 2 weeks sick leave next Saturday & go to Florida which ought to cure him. I am the only really healthy person I think in these parts! . . .

I'm getting really good on make up. You won't know me!

Bless you darling & love to Isabella.

Devotedly
Mother

". . . I'd like to adopt them both, . . ."

1600 Pennsylvania Avenue
Washington, D.C.
Sat. eve. Feb. 26th [1938]

Anna darling,

I had a long talk with Isabella over the phone & felt I knew so much more about all you had been thro'. You & John had a bad ten days but I hope it won't be so bad again. When is the next period?

How happy the kids must be to have you home again! I'm sending you a check $10 for each to put in their bank on their birthday & $5 for each so you can get some little things they want for me to give them. I'm sending each a pr. of blankets from N.Y. so keep if they arrive. Also if a package comes to you from the Kenwood Mills please keep for May 3d [Anna's birthday]. . . .

Little Diana is pathetic, today Harry sent her a dress & such a pathetic post card. I'd like to adopt them both, it must be so hard for him to have the future so uncertain. . . .

Our last entertainments are done & Pa is happy. His five days at H.P. were a great rest & he stood the last reception much more easily in consequence. [FDR insisted on standing with the aid of leg braces at receptions, which was extremely tiring.] . . . I hope to fly & reach you the 20th . . . & leave the 26th for Boise where I speak. I then fly to Warm Springs. . . .

The world situation keeps getting more confused but I don't think there will be a war, which is wishful thinking.

. . . You might see Uncle Hall before long as he *says* he's starting west next Tuesday. . . .

Mother

Increasingly, Eleanor was feeling left out and her pique shows in the next two letters. Nobody had explained to her the significance, if any, of a plan for Betsey to accompany FDR to Warm Springs when all the family knew that the marriage of James and Betsey was under severe strain and they had talked of separating. The fondness between FDR and Betsey, in fact, triggered Eleanor's annoyance on another level. Anna was one day to tell me that her mother "was apprehensive of anyone whom she felt got too close [to FDR]. Betsey would come in and sit with Father. And this would annoy Mother because she felt that Betsey was trying to usurp some sort of position with Father. But in a way that she was perfectly open about it. She'd say, 'Betsey thinks she *owns* him, you know.' It was just *annoying* to Mother. Betsey would come and say, 'Pa says he wants so-and-so after dinner.' And Mother's feeling would be, 'Well, Pa should have asked me himself!' The same thing happened when Harry Hopkins and his [new] wife Louie [the former Louise Macy] moved into the White House. I found this out from Tommy. Louie would arrange dinner parties and seat the table. My mother would be home. This would annoy the pants off her. She had no feeling personally about—this had nothing to do with Father. But this was her *position*.

"Now Missy, I don't think Missy ever did this. You see, this is where Missy was a very, very astute little gal. She didn't threaten Mother. And later, during the war when John Boettiger was overseas, this is one of the difficulties I had when I moved into the White House."

The second letter extends an undercurrent of bitterness: "Today he telephoned, the first word from the W.H. since I left!" As though to protect the integrity of her suppressed anger, Eleanor fails to mention to Anna that "today" is March 17, the Roosevelts' thirty-third wedding anniversary, no doubt the reason FDR called, and a date that at this point apparently stirred more warmth in the husband than in the wife.

". . . I don't understand it all but it seems very pleasant all around . . ."

> 1600 Pennsylvania Avenue
> Washington, D.C.
> Saturday March 5th [1938]

Anna darling,
   Your letter was a great satisfaction. . . . Another month will tell much, do wire me how the period goes. . . .
   James is doing 2 weeks with the Marines. When he returns there is a chance that Bets may go with Pa to Warm Springs. I don't understand it all but it seems very pleasant all around so I shouldn't worry I suppose! . . .
   It will be so good to see you darling & John & the kids & really *talk*. I am positively hungry for you. . . .

> Mother

". . . first word from the W.H. since I left! . . ."

> The Biltmore Hotel
> Los Angeles
> March 17th [1938]

Anna darling,
   If the flying weather is good I will land via United at 7.40 a.m. Sunday. Tommy takes a train Sat. night & arrives Monday a.m. about 6.40! I am getting very much excited at the prospect tho' I'm so busy on this trip I haven't had time to breathe! . . .
   Father wrote & sent you & John his love, & today he telephoned, the first word from the W.H. since I left! All seems well but he's having a wisdom tooth out tomorrow. . . .

> Devotedly,
> Mother

". . . I've written Sis & Buzz telling them . . ."

> Val-Kill Cottages
> Hyde Park
> July 3d [1938]

Anna darling,
   I can't realize that you are back in Seattle. Your visit was all too short & rather like a dream & I've been so busy ever since that I am just beginning to realize how much I miss you & John. I do hope I'll get out in October for I

can't bear not to know your house & be able to see you in it. Have I got the address & telephone no.?

. . . Shirley Temple is coming Sat. for a swim & picnic . . . so I've written Sis & Buzz telling them & a line to Curt just asking where he wants me to send for them. . . .

The Swedish Crown Princess & retinue came Friday p.m. & I was late to receive them. She was very nice & so were they all. Dinner was nice, we had a movie after it which helped. The picnic yesterday was nice, they liked hot dogs & left afterwards & this a.m. Pa got off. . . .

It is cool & I have no official engagements for 6 weeks! . . .

Mother

Curtis B. Dall & Co.
52 Broadway [New York]
July 6, 1938

My dear Mrs. Roosevelt:

Thank you for your note of July 3. Sistie and Buzzie and I have just returned from a quiet holiday week-end. . . . I will have them ready to return to Hyde Park on Friday, July 8, at four o'clock. . . .

Sistie tells me that there is going to be a picnic this Saturday for Shirley Temple, and if for any reason you are going to be away, may I express the friendly hope that you will carefully arrange so that there will be no pictures taken for publication or distribution in connection with this picnic. Such publicity would obviously be good for Shirley Temple, but I believe it would not be good for Sistie and Buzzie.

With best wishes,

Very sincerely yours,
Curtis

CBD:MD

July 8, 1938

Dear Curtis:

I will have the children called for at four o'clock.

When Shirley Temple is on a holiday it is the desire of every one that no publicity photographs be taken and you can be sure that none will be taken of the children. You are no more anxious to avoid this than we are.

Sincerely yours,

[no record of sig-
nature form used
by Mrs. Roose-
velt]

". . . honestly but not in great detail & he & Sis seemed satisfied. . . ."

Val-Kill Cottages
Hyde Park
Wed. night July 13th [1938]

Darling,
Curt's letter makes me boil. I never read anything so self satisifed & self rightous. . . . I enclose a letter he wrote me which I thought pretty cheeky & a copy of my answer. I would like to see what you write him but I confess I could not be very conciliatory. I never mention him to the kids for I would find it hard to be nice! They seem very happy. I read to them today while Sis sewed & Buzz lay on my sofa from 12.15–1 then we went & picknicked. . . . This p.m. after Sis & Buzz had read to themselves & Buzz had done some writing, they drove up with Tommy & me to Tivoli. . . . On the way up he asked when I first saw him & I said I was in the room when he was born & he said "how are babies born" so I explained I hope satisfactorily to you, honestly but not in great detail & he & Sis seemed satisfied. I was amused by your dream but you needn't worry[.] I love having the kids to do things with. . . . We swim every p.m. even had 15 minutes today tho' we got back late. . . .
I hope you & John are having a grand time with Pa. [FDR had traveled west to campaign for Democratic congressional candidates.] He said he'd telephone me Thursday night so I may hear about you & Elliott & Ruth. The newspaper accounts sound hectic & I'm glad I'm not along. . . .
Ethel, F jr. & I had a long talk & I like her & he seems so young! I've not heard a word since they left but will write tomorrow. . . .

Mother

". . . perhaps that generation will fulfill Granny's wishes . . ."

Val-Kill Cottages
Hyde Park
Sunday, July 24th [1938]

Anna darling,
The kids seem well & happy. They dragged me to church this morning because Mr. Wilson [Rev. Frank R. Wilson, rector of St. James's Church, Hyde Park] had promised to let them go up & see where the church bell hung! They are good as gold. Duffie says they *both* make their beds. . . . Buzz considers Dot his horse while he is here! They seem to have a real feeling about the place perhaps that generation will fulfill Granny's wishes & some of them live here! . . .
Did I tell you that the book of the first 18 months of "My Days" will be out the end of August? I am reading the final manuscript now. I don't see why

anyone should be interested but the publisher thinks it will sell & it has one advantage it won't be expensive.

I've had a great many Washington groups here & never an idle moment so I can't say I've found it restful! I think I'll do something else next summer. . . .

Devotedly
Mother

Mrs. Roosevelt remained miffed that FDR was not sharing his knowledge of Jimmy's marital crisis. In July, Jimmy checked into the Mayo Clinic at Rochester, Minnesota, for treatment of a gastric ulcer. Here Mrs. Roosevelt informs Anna that he is to reenter after Labor Day for what will turn out to be surgery.

". . . I've learned to stand on my hands in the pool . . ."

Val-Kill Cottages
Hyde Park
Tuesday night Aug. 22d [1938]

Anna darling,

. . . I feel as tho' neither of us had written for a long time but I know how driven you feel by work & social obligations because I feel the same way! Much of my time has gone too into swimming & riding but the dead line is nearing for some articles & the preparation of some speech material so I think exercise will have to go by the board for a while. . . .

I hope the children are home & I long to hear how they are. Tell them I've learned to stand on my hands in the pool & get my legs up straight!

Pa looks very well & had a grand trip. He's enjoying it here too tho' the stream of visitors never let up. I'm running both this house & the cottage & I think all is going well. Pa goes back to Washington Sunday or Monday for a week & I'll go back to the cottage but I must spend three precious days next week going to Cousin Susie & Tommy must go to Washington to see about her divorce. . . .

Betsy arrived here today & looks well but seems strained in manner. Pa still has said nothing to me about James! The latter goes to Rochester right after Labor Day Bets says. . . .

That is all the family news! . . .

Mother

Can you match your pearls out there or shall I bring yours back here when I go out?

Eleanor has learned (presumably by telephone) that Anna is pregnant and has sent a note of congratulations to John. He replies:

". . . this new joy which we didn't plan, . . ."

Seattle Post-Intelligencer
Aug. 27, 1938.

Dearest L.L.

Just a line to let you know how supremely happy I am, too! I think that the very fact that we didn't plan it at all, but just had it happen to US, makes it all the more exciting,

This is how I feel about it—

Ever since I laid eyes on Anna certain happy fates have attended my existence. One thing after another happened to me. I was extricated from a terribly unhappy situation. My work improved and I got ahead. My point of view on many things changed and brought greater philosophic enjoyment of life. Every second of the time I have been completely in love with Anna and just inclined to pinch myself ever so often to make sure I wasn't dreaming. I still do!

Now comes this new joy which we didn't plan, actually resisted because we were not sure we wanted to divide ourselves any farther. We wanted freedom to devote ourselves pretty generously to each other.

But now I feel that it is just another stroke of that happy fate and I'm fairly explosive with joy. Anna is a louse, however, and won't let me tell a living soul about it. I'm SURE the PI will be scooped on the story, also!

Loads and loads of love. . . .

Yours,
John

". . . & can hardly wait now. . . ."

Val-Kill Cottages
Hyde Park
Aug 30th [1938]

Dearest John,

I'm so glad "it" happend. Take good care of Anna & you may be sure that I'll be praying that the happy fates which have attended you & Anna so far will keep right on with you. Both of you deserve it.

I'll be out to see you in early November & can hardly wait now.

FDR is very well. A possible war in Europe is a constant cloud on the horizon however. . . .

I wish I could hug you now, instead so many loving thoughts go to you John dear for the present & the future.

L.L.

"*. . . but I rather think that will never come! . . .*"

> 1600 Pennsylvania Avenue
> Washington, D.C.
> Sept. 26th [1938]

Anna darling,

I saw Granny yesterday & she seems more rested & very happy to be going to spend a week with you. I hope you come through alive! We are telephoning her tomorrow afternoon. . . .

Father & the State Dept. are in constant communication [about the Munich Conference] & the tension in the house is great. He has had a cold in his head but seems recovered. Everyone near the coast has had a terrible time in the hurricane & there has been much loss of life as well as property. Johnny says the Clark's house stood but every boat in the harbor, but one which went to sea, was lost. There was sea weed on every window, every tree gone & the garden like a plowed field. Providence is still under water & no trains on the New Haven. I am supposed to lecture in Springfield, Mass. on Thursday but fully expect to hear it is called off. . . .

This is the end of the summer & I am a little depressed by it. There has not been the quiet & peace I wanted but I rather think that will never come!

Much, much love to you all & take good care of yourself dear,

> Mother

"*. . . does not seem to be our business . . . and yet . . .*"

> Val-Kill Cottages
> Hyde Park
> Monday, Oct. 3d. [1938]

Darling,

It was wonderfull to get your letter of the 25th. yesterday. I am very glad you take a nap whenever you can and don't worry about letters, send a wire now and then. The worst part will soon be over, and it won't be very bad till the last months. I think you will find keeping busy, if you don't overtire yourself is a help right through. Would you like one of my very loose tea gowns with flowing sleeves to wear in the evenings the last few weeks? If so, I'll bring it out with me in November.

I hope Granny is feeling well and that she can refrain for the week she is there from trying to plan your lives! She seems to me to be aging fast but she still takes so much interest in us all that she would be glad to direct our actions even in the future!

Pa's second message was grand and so well timed. I feel of course that Hitler having acquired all he wanted this time will begin again to get the next thing he wants when he is ready to do so. Therefore we have only postponed a war unless we are prepared to let Hitler and his ideas dominate Europe. It does not seem to be our business really and yet I wonder if we can remain uninfluenced by the growth of those ideas. If you and John have time to read the little book I sent you by Thomas Mann I'd like to know what you both think about it. I would like to get an opportunity to talk to him [Mann] in the light of recent events, for he stirred many questions in my mind.

The hurricane and high seas on the coast have left devastation behind them. I spoke in Springfield Thursday night and we saw what flood and wind blowing one hundred and twenty miles an hour had done to them. Portland [Maine] where we were on Friday night got very little of the gale. Saturday in Rhode Island we saw the worst of the damage.

Sand dunes and beaches gone and with them houses, bodies are still being found but identification is difficult and many will always be "missing". One can only be glad it did not happen before Labor Day, when so many more people would have been in their houses or cottages. Some of those old villages have lost all their old big trees, and the woods are blown flat. . . .

Hall says he is flying on Thursday with a german pilot and plane to Europe and will be back in five days. Since I think these thrills are all that make life interesting to him I don't think one can object but I will be glad when he is back. . . .

Mother

Nashville tomorrow. Washington Wed. night. Thursday Philadelphia. N.Y. Thursday night & Friday night & back to Wash. Sat. Pa returns Sunday or Monday.

". . . if I go to to one snooty group I should go to a working group, . . ."

Hotel Fontenelle
Omaha
Sunday, Oct. 23d. [1938]

Darling,

. . . Too bad Granny had to get on all her worries. She told me she wanted help about the [Hyde Park] place and wanted Jimmie to assist but I told her I thought Father would want to be consulted and would not like her to ask any one else. She said Pa was too busy but I pointed out that he always has time for whatever really interests him and presumably this would. She demurred and I think I know the reason, she is trying to tie someone in the next generation to the place while she is alive because she is so afraid it will not continue in the family. I wish she would not worry about my friends for I think she has reached an age when she should not bother about any one she does not like. Too bad Curt had to tell Sis that he never liked me but after all in the end children have to make up their own mind's as to whom they like and dislike. Now that I know you have told Granny about the baby I will write her and then she will feel free to talk about it when she wishes. . . .

I'd be glad to talk to the Women's University Club but I wonder if we want to give up our precious time on this trip? How would it do for me to go when I am there in April? Also if I go to one snooty group I should go to a working group, don't you think?

I wouldn't give up my trip to you for anything. This trip had to be made to pay the Dec. income tax installment and cover Xmas expenses. . . .

James has not said one word to me about his plans since I left him, he telephoned me once, and wired the day after my birthday and that is all I've heard so I'll know more after I see him.

My love to John and the kids, and a great, great deal to you dearest.

Mother

". . . I . . . learned how to use make up . . ."

20 East 11th Street
New York City
Saturday Jan 22d [1939]

Darling,

. . . I hope by now you are improving physically & John mentally! . . .

Earl has been here sick for ten days but I think he's going to let me drive him & his car up today if he feels well enough. . . .

The T.V.A. decision [by the Supreme Court, upholding the constitutionality of the project] made Pa very cheerful this a.m. & he also felt his talk with the automobile people was very successful. He looks older this winter & seems to me to mind the social things more.

I bobbed my side hair yesterday & learned how to use make up . . . & find it a great care & time consumer! . . .

Mother

". . . He thinks England & France go this spring. . . ."

1600 Pennsylvania Avenue
Washington, D.C.
Friday, Jan. 27th [1939]

Darling,

. . . Father is very gloomy about the international picture, thinks Spain lost to Franco which means Hitler-Mussolini domination & then he thinks gradual infiltration into S. America & inevitable closing in on us. He thinks England & France go this spring. It is not cheerful. He was beaten by one vote in the Senate on the W.P.A. cut & [Vice president] Jack Garner was responsible. I almost wish they [WPA supporters] would demonstrate at the Capitol but they won't, they will write to me & I won't be able to do much from now on. . . .

I'll bring Tommy with me & I should be with you in two months from yesterday so don't let the baby beat me to it. The crib goes the end of this month. . . . The mattress is in it. Do you need a hairpillow, slips, sheets & blankets? If so I'll get them. Will you buy yourself a bath tub & scales from me & let me know what I owe you? I think everyone else will give you clothes.

The winter has been busy but I came down so late that I've stood it well. Have only been to Hyde Park one week end & work here nearly every night till 2 & 3 but don't even look tired yet.

. . . Henry [Osthagen] is nearly over his operation which was painful. . . . Tommy has been torn between feeling she ought to be with him & should not leave me & her work & she has moved & is not settled & all in all I thought she'd have a nervous breakdown yesterday! . . .

All my love to you,
Mother

Sara Roosevelt, the President's mother, had been visiting the White House and, as was her habit wherever she went, had taken over.

In March, Anna gave birth to John Roosevelt Boettiger, the first and only child of her second marriage.

". . . a little prayer to live thro' the 11th . . ."

1600 Pennsylvania Avenue
Washington, D.C.
May 31st [1939]

Anna darling,

. . . I got home from Tennessee at 11.30 a.m. to find Missy in my room much excited. She had told Anna McGowan some little things that were wrong in the rooms, & Anna told Mama & there were reactions. Then Pa was annoyed every minute & developed sinus Tuesday & went to bed with a temperature of 100½ tonight after dinner. . . .

I say a little prayer to live thro' the 11th . . . [when Sara's visit to the White House ends]! Pa says he'll tell me Monday if we leave for the west June 15th or July 15th. . . .

Mother

". . . I look up while I write to enjoy it. . . ."

Val-Kill Cottages
Hyde Park
Sunday [July 17, 1939]

Anna darling,

I love the kodaks & look at them daily & can hardly wait to see you all.

Ruth [Elliott's wife] wired me that *temporarily* their finances were better but Father was to tell me if anything was settled & I haven't heard. I don't feel able to cope with high finance so did not go to Washington to give advice. Everyone is saying how well Elliott comes over the radio [he is now a commentator] & I must make a practice of listening but haven't yet. . . .

Wed. night Hall had two men here, one drunk like himself, & one sober, & they all discouraged me so with their views on business ethics as regards labor that I was almost willing to send them home in their cars but decided to persuade them to stay the night to prevent suicide! Zena [Hall's wife] said 3 of them were nearly killed (Hall driving) 4 times on the way up! I went to N.Y. Thursday with Earl & it was a relief to drive safely! . . .

I am getting quite a bit of exercise this Summer & I feel well. Seeing Earl here or in Albany now & then is nice & I wish you could see how lovely the sunsets are reflected in our small lake. I look up while I write to enjoy it. . . .

Father gets here Thursday or Friday for 4 or five days & I move to the big house & we have many guests for this coming week end. . . .

Mother

". . . haven't seen your column in ten days . . ."

[En route to Seattle]
July 27th, 1939

Darling,

Here we are on the train on the way home from Wyntoon. We imbibed lots of sunshine, went horseback riding, fished and swam during the six days we were there; so should have benefited in spite of the nervous strain which is always present for me. We learned definitely that W.R. would like to have us stay on in Seattle, but that the General Management would like to get rid of us because they do not like the fact that we have freedom that no other Hearst paper enjoys and are definitely New Deal. I think that W.R. rather enjoys watching what will happen to one of his papers run as is the P.I. but not so, the G.M. They hate the New Deal (even more than W.R., if that's possible!) and it galls them no end to realize that the P.I., under its present management is doing far better than it has ever done since Hearst bought it. John insisted he must have a contract; Hearst said he "thought that would be all right"; but Joe Connolly, now head of the General Management of the newspapers, remained silent. We believe that Connolly will try to postpone any decision about us until the latest possible moment—hoping for some break which will give him an excuse to go after us with W.R. At present he has no legitimate excuse—our advertising lineage is gaining steadily and our financial position is improving steadily. Anyway, we think we will bide our time and make no further moves for a new contract for another six weeks. Taking everything into consideration—children, salary, generally upset conditions in this country and abroad—we think that we will be better off for the next couple of years if we can go on where we are, under the same conditions of editorial freedom. If we are refused this freedom we will of course have to quit and search for work elsewhere.

According to yesterdays paper Pa has decided not to come to the west coast until the end of September. Do you really think you will make the trip then? . . .

We haven't seen your column in ten days, so feel lost for news of you! We send you two heartsfull of love, darling, and hope all goes well with you. A big hug from me, too.

Anna

CHAPTER V

September 11, 1939–New Year's Eve, 1943

On August 21, 1939, came the stunning news that Germany and the Soviet Union had agreed to sign a nonaggression pact. On September 1, Nazi bombs thundered down on Polish cities.

". . . We can't go on with ever recurring wars . . ."

1600 Pennsylvania Avenue
Washington, D.C.
Sept. 11th [1939]

Darling,
 . . . I feel sick about the war & want so much to do something that looks beyond toward building a better peace. We can't go on with ever recurring wars in a modern world. I'd like to talk to you about an idea I have but if it gets by all the critics you'll hear about it soon. . . .
 A world of love to you darling,

Mother

 Mrs. Roosevelt's "plan," which did win the tentative approval of the President and other "critics," was to go to Europe for the Red Cross as prelude to a large-scale refugee relief effort that she would head in partnership with former President Herbert Hoover. Hoover first earned his world reputation by organizing relief for hungry refugees of World War I.

As matters turned out, Hoover, still bitter over his election defeat by Roosevelt, refused to call on the President to discuss the plan. The surprising progress of Hitler's "blitzkrieg" through country after country soon caused Secretary of State Cordell Hull and Norman Davis, head of the American Red Cross, to veto a war-front journey by Mrs. Roosevelt. They felt the risk was too high of the President's wife being captured as a prisoner of the enemy.

". . . papers in these little towns don't mention his movements! . . ."

Hotel Woodworth
Robinson, Illinois
Sat. Sept. 23d [1939]

Anna darling,

I am thrilled that you won't need the money & that you want me. I kept from the 1st to the 8th free in case you did. Unless Pa has some special reason to the contrary I'll leave from N.Y. Sunday, Oct. 1st. . . .

I don't think Father intends to go West but you never know!

. . . The "powers that be" promise me some word about my plan next Tuesday but Mr. Hoover declined to head it up. A tale which I will tell you about. Please try not to get too weary. This is a long pull I fear with anxious times ahead & you & John should take care of yourselves.

Granny is pathetic & has taken James & Betsy's troubles very hard. I'll telephone her when I go back & I hope Father went up for this week end but the papers in these little towns don't mention his movements! . . .

Later Sunday a.m.

Just got a Chicago Herald *[sic]* Tribune [Colonel Robert R. McCormick's *Chicago Tribune,* which had once employed John Boettiger to cover FDR, was zealously anti-Roosevelt.] & read Walter Trohan's story which tells me Pa is at H.P. He says they were viewing the hole for the monument which Pa is building to himself out of government money which is hardly a truthful statement but he has to do it poor man! . . .

Give Sis & Buzz my love. People ask me about them everwhere! I am dying to see "little" John who must be a monster! A hug to John & all my love to you dear,

Mother

". . . domestic things have faded . . . from his mind . . ."

> 20 East 11th Street
> New York, N.Y.
> Friday Oct 20th [1939]

Darling,

. . . I enclose my lecture itinerary & a general schedule for the next month as I seem to be going to move about a good deal!

Pa is so engrossed in the war that domestic things have faded a great deal from his mind but I'll try to talk a bit with him this week end.

I lunched with the Labor Dept. people last week & find Frances [Perkins, secretary of labor] very jittery about "reds." The Dies [House Un-American Activities] Com. is getting on all their nerves I think.

> Much, much love darlings all,
> Mother

". . . so full of the war & the library & whatnot . . ."

> Dinkler Hotels
> Birmingham, Ala.
> Sunday, Oct 29th [1939]

Anna darling,

I saw Katie in N.Y. last Tuesday. . . . She said Ivan [Katie and Ivan are Anna's live-in household helpers] had heard from John & you had your contract & expected to be indefinitely in Seattle. . . .

Pa told me Curt only came to ask if he engaged in an export business to S. America who wld be the proper person to talk to in Washington. They talked of nothing personal Pa said. It seems obviously just an excuse for a visit & a picture.

Are you pleased with your contract? Do write me the details. Are salaries the same & are you as free?

Pa agrees wholeheartedly when you say we must not neglect domestic affairs but he is so full of the war & the library [for Roosevelt's presidential papers at Hyde Park] & whatnot that I don't know how much he is thinking about them. Perhaps when "Neutrality" is out of the way [pending in Congress was repeal of the Neutrality Act] he will be freer in mind.

This is the most strenuous trip we have ever taken. Every night on a train but it has been interesting so far. Ann Arbor & Youngstown especially. The woman who runs the lectures here bores me & so I've only done what I had to do & therefore I am getting some letters written! . . .

> A world of love to you
> Mother

The enclosed book on Ohio I thought the children might enjoy.

Participation of young people in public affairs had long stirred Mrs. Roosevelt's interest. Lately, this had taken a form of her sympathy with and assistance to the American Youth Congress, a federation of many national and local youth groups ranging from liberal to Communist. Many Youth Congress positions coincided sufficiently with Communist positions as to fuel widespread attacks on Youth Congress members as "Communist-dominated" and "fellow travelers." These attacks deflected attention (as they were intended by its enemies to do) from Youth Congress demands for job creation, student aid, an American Youth Act, and against Nazi and Fascist aggression.

Most recently, many Youth Congress leaders had abruptly switched from a militant anti-Nazi position to one of sudden "antiwar" noninterference in Europe upon the unforeseen signing of the Nazi-Soviet nonaggression pact. (A Leftist song to proclaim the abrupt new position chorused: "Franklin Roosevelt / told the people how he felt / And we damn near believed what he said; / He said, 'I hate war and so does Eleanor / But we won't be safe till everybody's dead.'") Representative Martin Dies of Texas, chairman of the House Un-American Activities Committee, who had catapulted himself into front-page prominence and power through the simple, dramatic means of scatter-shot accusations of Communism and of "looking for a Red under every bed," subpoenaed Youth Congress leaders to a committee inquisition in November 1939. Until then, the White House, disturbed by the circus antics of Dies, had largely refrained from open collision with his committee. With the committee's assault on the political expression of young people, however, Mrs. Roosevelt asked the President's permission—and readily got it—to turn up totally unannounced as a member of the audience at the hearing, surprising the committee and the news corps. She made a conspicuous gesture at the midday break of inviting six of the Youth Congress leaders to the White House for lunch and later for dinner and an overnight stay. Her sense of theater was triumphant. The committee suffered a stunning loss of nerve, questioning its witnesses with uncharacteristic gentleness and fairness.

That evening, after dinner in the White House family dining room, the youth leaders praised Eleanor's courage. Aubrey Williams, head of the National Youth Administration, privately admonished the youth leaders, "Don't let her down. It will break her heart."

Three months later the war situation and new domestic political alliances changed the Youth Congress's relationship with Mrs. Roosevelt and the administration. Russia had invaded Finland, charging that the tiny country was threateningly overdefended; FDR favored a loan to Finland to finance her fight for independence. The "Popular Front" of liberal-Left alliances on domestic issues split clean in two over sympathy for Finland versus sympathy for the Russian invasion. Youth Congress leaders and followers divided similarly, the majority of the leadership siding with the Communist position, against Finland—and against the Roosevelt administration.

Certain commitments, however, had to be honored. Months ago, the Youth Congress had scheduled a "pilgrimage" of some four thousand youth delegates to Washington in January 1940 to press for the American Youth Act and to hear speeches by a glittering array of government and public figures, mostly arranged through Mrs. Roosevelt's influence. The high point of the pilgrimage was to be an address on the White House lawn by the President himself. Although events made clear that the pilgrimage was to become a rally against FDR's foreign affairs position, the White House reconfirmed the President's—and Mrs. Roosevelt's—commitments to appear. Indeed, in the days before the inpouring of youngsters to the District, Mrs. Roosevelt organized a committee of congressional wives, reluctantly headed by the spouses of Vice President John Garner of Texas and Speaker William Bankhead of Alabama, to phone wives of government officials in search of guest beds for delegates. When these fell short of housing needs, she and George Allen, a District of Columbia commissioner, kept dialing until they lined up five hundred contributions of bunks from hotels, a welfare institution and a nearby army camp.

Through a Saturday-morning drizzle, the delegates paraded to the White House lawn where, from the South Portico, the President was determined to give the young ones a sharp spanking. They had a right to advocate change, he assured them, but under a different form of government "this kind of meeting on the White House lawn could not take place." That is not the assurance they had come to hear. They politely applauded his accounting of New Deal accomplishments for all the needy, including the young, grimacing slightly at his promises to do more "as fast as the people of the country as a whole will let us." Then abruptly swinging into what he really had on his mind, he offered the soggy delegates a "final word of warning": They ought not pass resolutions on subjects "which you have not thought through and on which you cannot possibly have complete knowledge." The belief among many of them that a loan to Finland would be "an attempt" to maneuver the United States into an imperialistic war is "unadulterated twaddle." A low-key surge of boos and hisses rose from the sea of umbrellas, and was quickly smoothed by other delegates responding in dismay, *"Ssshhhh!"* If the President heard the wordless exchange, he didn't show it. It was "axiomatic" that Americans favor such a loan since ninety-eight percent of Americans sympathized with the Finns, the President pressed on. To think that such loans might provoke the Soviet Union into declaring war on the United States was simply absurd. Regarding the Soviet Union, whatever one may have hoped would come from their social and economic experiment, that country was "a dictatorship as absolute as any other dictatorship in the world." The boos rose again, and again were quelled by the shock and hushes of other delegates.

Washington was not accustomed to emotional expressions directly to Presidents. Columnist Walter Lippmann described the young audience as "shockingly ill-mannered, disrespectful, conceited, ungenerous, and spoiled."

At the final session of the pilgrimage, on Sunday evening in a packed Interdepartmental Auditorium near the White House, Mrs. Roosevelt appeared for an extended period of questions and answers, the questions submitted in writing and selected by Youth Congress leaders. Her queenly stature and dignity embellished by a corsage of orchids presented by the youth leaders, she spoke slowly, surely, with an air that was slightly maternal but never condescending. When one of her early assertions stirred a suggestion of boos and hisses and a counterresponse of approval, she dismissed both with the stern instructions: "I want you neither to clap nor hiss until I have finished and then you may do whichever you like." She acknowledged the solicitude shown "poor little Finland" by the likes of Herbert Hoover who had had nothing to say about other victims of aggression, particularly Axis victims. "I agree with you that a stand should have been taken when Ethiopia was attacked. I agree with you in your sympathy for Spain. I agree with you in your sympathy for China and Czechoslovakia." The pitch of her voice rose slightly, her tempo stretching for emphasis: "But I also have sympathy for Finland."

Why, asked a question that spoke for most delegates in the immense hall and for those back in the localities who sent them, why was the administration cutting the budget for social legislation while allowing the budget for war preparations to rise? "I'll tell you why," came the blunt, still maternal response. "You will notice that even with the pared-down budget, Congress cut it further, which is an indication that *you* have not been *busy* forming public opinion in *your* communities, because Congress is responsive to *you*."

To a "question" that asserted—again expressing an apparent majority of her audience—that "we want jobs and education in America, not an M.A. in Flanders fields," she answered rhetoric with a personal statement that visibly touched her listeners: "You are not the only ones who don't want war. I don't think there are many older people in this country who want war, and certainly none of us who know what war is like." The President was among those, she declared, who knew what war was like, and her listeners should not forget "that we have four sons who are just the ages to go to war. Do you think that the President wants war? But nobody knows what they may face when the world is going through a cataclysm. I could agree with you right this minute that I don't want war, but I don't know what you might say under different conditions six months from now."

At the end of an hour, the audience rose for an ovation, surely more in tribute to the person than for her answers, which she had not tailored to what they wanted to hear. "The nation probably has not seen in all of its history," wrote Dewey L. Fleming in the *Baltimore Sun,* "such a debate between a President's wife and a critical, not to say hostile, auditorium full of politically minded youths of all races and creeds."

"... but I won't for the sake of family peace! ..."

Golden Beach [Florida]
Feb. 21st [1940]

Darling,

... I felt as you did about Pa's speech to the Am. Youth Congress, tho' I wish they had had better manners about it! ... Many of them the youngsters are inclined to believe well of Russia but that is because they are so afraid of all propaganda & feel Russia in Finland may be a victim of that. . . . I found them *not* communist except for a few city groups, & not concerned about communism which was forced down their throats at every turn but deeply concerned about getting a job & finding out how they could help themselves & each other in their respective communities to do this. Pa lost their support & will have to win it back. I'm enclosing two things for you to read & return to me. Frances Williams gives you the feeling of the leaders in the Congress. The other letter I'm going to give Father because it is so fair & she is so evidently one of his followers. I'd like to show him yours but I won't for the sake of family peace! . . .

I had a bad snowstorm going to Cornell this year & being down here is a great contrast. I'm getting a good tan & doing nothing social. Henry [Osthagen, Tommy's companion] & Earl are having some friends for cocktails today & yesterday Tommy, Earl & I went to see "Grapes of Wrath," otherwise I've lived on the beach in a bathing suit. . . .

Devotedly
Mother

". . . He is a prima donna but . . . amusing . . ."

The Ahwahnee
Yosemite National Park
Friday night, April 5th [1940]

Anna darling,

. . . It was, as it always is a joy to be with you & John & the kids. . . .

The lectures went well in L.A., Long Beach & Redlands but I didn't think I did so well in S.F. last night. We went to a marvellous Chinese place for dinner & I think I ate too much! I went to tea first with [the writer] Alexander Woolcott [Woollcott], & tho' he was very nice & very amusing perhaps I did too much! He is playing on up the coast & will be in Seattle & don't miss his play, it is one you will both enjoy & he is going to try & see you both. He is a prima donna but a generous & amusing one. . . .

Mother

". . . the civilized world is crumbling round one . . ."

1600 Pennsylvania Avenue
Washington, D.C.
Friday May 17th [1940]

Darling,

. . . I never told Abbott Simon [a national officer of the American Youth Congress] or anyone else you would arrange meetings for him. He is the boy you saw here & he loved Johnny! He is intelligent, rather aggressively argumentative but I do not think a communist tho' I think radical. Jewish, well to do family & wife the same so not realistic. I am fond of him & felt that it would be good for him to talk with you & John & you could have him meet any people you felt he should meet. He does talk "back" at times! . . .

What a life I have been leading! It really isn't decent to work so hard but the civilized world is crumbling round one so it is as well to he busy! . . .

Pa is gloom personified about Europe & doesn't think he'll leave again. Hitler says he will win in 7 days & Pa murmurs 30 days! Lord Lothian [British ambassador] & 2 Eng. women are coming to dine tonight & I don't look forward to a cheerful evening.

Jimmy was here the other night (Tuesday) & looked well. He was gloomy too saying he could of course be called soon & he wished he could feel we knew what kind of peace we wanted & insist before doing anything on cooperation but I don't think there will be anyone left in Europe by way of a government with whom to cooperate. Just the U.S. & Hitler!

I've just been given a walking horse from Tenn. I hope I like it but haven't yet seen it as I've been too busy to ride. . . .

Devotedly,
Mother

". . . What you think or feel seems of no use or value . . ."

1600 Pennsylvania Avenue
Washington, D.C.
June 4th, 1940

Darling Anna,

Your letter of the 30th came yesterday & I am so sorry about John's arm. I hadn't seen it tho' Pa had so this was my first news. . . .

You are right that the world makes personal things seem unimportant. I think we must continue our normal lives, doing what we can as well as we can & preparing ourselves to face whatever the future holds in store. Living here is very oppressive because Pa visualizes all the possibilities, as of course, he must & you feel very impotent to help. What you think or feel seems of no use or value so I'd rather be away & let the important people make their plans & someday I suppose they will get around to telling us plain citizens if they want us to do anything. . . .

Pa is working very hard, is worried & short tempered but I think remarkably well all considered.

I'm having a lot of young people (Youth Congress & other) to talk with Pa, Harry Hopkins & Sidney Hillman [of the CIO] so they will feel they have some share in knowledge of conditions & defense plans. They may not believe it is for defense but I think they should be given a chance to hear. . . .

Devotedly
Mother

". . . I hope I'll never think I am of any importance, . . ."

The White House
Wednesday June 26th [1940]

Anna darling,
　. . . I have been in N.Y. almost more than here on this Refugee Children's Committee. I think men are worse than women on committees & they do think more of their importance. I hope I'll never think I am of any importance, it makes one so stuffy!
　. . . An interesting letter from Maude [Gray] describing war preparations. They have bought a cow & laid in a stock of candles & prepared a shelter in the cellar for everyone.
　I've got to get on with a short book but I can't find time to think it out. . . .
　The republican convention seems so "usual" & the times so "unusual" that I find it hard to reconcile the two. It looks to me as though Great Britain might sue for peace & what will the terms be for them? France is crushed & I dare not write the Laboulaye's [the French diplomatic family the Roosevelts had known since World War I]. What will be Hitler's next move? S. America or the U.S.A., economic or military, & will Japan be acting with them in a concerted plan? It looks that way just now.
　What a sad world, but we can still enjoy life & I love my porch at night. . . .

Devotedly
Mother

For two years the nation and the press had been alive with speculation as to whether a President, for the first time in American history, would run for a third term. The speculation intensified as the 1940 Democratic Convention approached, and no strong alternative candidate emerged. "On several occasions," Mrs. Roosevelt was soon to reveal, "I asked him if he did not think he should make a definite effort to prepare someone. Franklin always smiled and said he thought people have to prepare themselves, that all he could do was to give them opportunities and see how they worked out. I felt that he, without intending to do so, dominated the people around him and that so long as he was in the picture, it was very hard for anyone to rise to a position of prominence. Finally, however, I came to realize that, after all, this was something that people had had to do many times before and that no man could hand another more than opportunity."

While the prospect of a third term sorely divided the Democratic party, stirring the reluctant opposition even of its national chairman and Roosevelt lieutenant, James A. Farley, a clear majority of delegates, persuaded by the imminence of American involvement in war, demanded a third term. No Democrat but Roosevelt, they were convinced, had the stature to win.

Roosevelt was determined to trade on his strength for his choice of a vice-presidential candidate, Secretary of Agriculture Henry A. Wallace. To most delegates Wallace was either too little known, too ineffective, too "soft-headed," too liberal or too inexperienced a campaigner. The last of those feelings, if true, was of major importance, because Roosevelt, in consenting to run, asserted that the war emergency would prevent him from leaving the White House to campaign.

The Chicago convention was in pandemonium over the vice-presidential battle. Roosevelt, remaining at the White House, was in danger of losing control of it—even while threatening that he would refuse to run if Wallace was not accepted. Urgently, Jim Farley and Lorena Hickok called Eleanor at Hyde Park, appealing for her to fly to Chicago immediately. FDR consented.

One of her first maneuvers in Chicago was to dispatch Franklin Jr. to find Elliott. Elliott had widely announced his intention to nominate, as vice-presidential candidate, Jesse Jones, head of the Reconstruction Finance Corporation. In perhaps the only instance of a Roosevelt parent instructing a Roosevelt offspring what to do or not to do politically, Mrs. Roosevelt urged—in effect, commanded—Elliott to do no such thing. A reporter got to her side and asked whether she was happy about the President's third nomination. "Happy!" she scolded. "I don't know how anyone could be particularly happy about the nomination in the present state of the world. It is a tremendous responsibility to be nominated for the presidency."

That gave her the theme for her speech, which she had had so little time to think out. Whoever became President, she told her vast, hushed and grave audience, faced "a heavier responsibility, perhaps, than any man has ever faced before in this country. . . . You cannot treat it as you would an ordinary nomination in an ordinary time. . . . So each and every one of you who give him this responsibility, in giving it to him assume for yourselves a very grave responsibility because *you* will make the campaign. *You* will have to rise above considerations which are narrow and partisan. This is the time when it is the United States we fight for."

She did not mention Wallace, but clearly, dramatically, her speech was a plea for support for the President in every way—including his unpopular choice of a running mate. "She has done more to soothe the convention bruises," wrote the reporter of the *New York Daily News,* "than all the efforts of the astute Senators. Thanks to her the roll call began in a fairly dignified atmosphere."

Wallace won, but only barely. Editorials across the country, even by opposition newspapers, and letters and phone calls that poured in on her upon her return to Washington, were summed up in a letter from nonpartisan Senator George Norris, called the "dean of American progressivism." Just when it seemed, he wrote, "as though the convention were going to 'blow up' [and] the battle for righteousness was about to be lost, you came on the scene, and what you said in that short speech caused men of sense and honor to stop and think before they plunged. . . . You turned a rout into a victory. You were the Sheridan of that convention. . . . That victory was finally realized is due, in my opinion, more to you than to any other one thing. That one act makes you heroic."

". . . You have grown to be a part of that job . . ."

Seattle Post-Intelligencer
July 19th, '40

Darling:
  I've listened to the Convention with such a mixture of emotions—and your
speech practically finished me last night! By that I mean that you did a
wonderful job. Your sincerity and high-minded purposefulness rang so true in
every word you said. And, at the same time, I couldn't help the thoughts
which crowded in, warning me of the strain and stress to come—on top of the
strain and stress of the past eight years.
  I was so happy to hear the tribute you paid Jim Farley, because, from little
pieces of gossip I've picked up here and there, I have gathered that people like
Tommy the Cork [Thomas L. Corcoran, a young adviser of FDR], Harry
Hopkins and a few others have been very rude and open in their criticisms of
Jim; at the same time giving the impression that they had Father's backing in
their feelings about Jim. It seems to me that this campaign is going to be very,
very difficult if Jim doesn't run it. I like Frank Walker [treasurer, Democratic
National Committee, during 1932 campaign], but he'd be like a babe in the
woods in that job. Jim is certainly not a man of deep vision, but he has proven
himself to be a genious at political organization. So, I'm still hoping against
hope that Pa can persuade him to run the campaign. Could Pa get any of his
high-up-in-the-Catholic Church friends to bring a little pressure to bear on
Jim? I'm afraid there'll be a good deal of political chaos if Jim doesn't
somehow handle his many organizational followers. I regret to say that I
think the reason that most of these organizational followers are so devoted to
Jim is that they feel that Jim will deal with them in orthodox fashion in giving
out patronage; and they fear that New Deal leadership may drop them from
the patronage list.
  Pa's speech was very moving, too, and sounded a note of patriotism which
rang very clear and true. It seemed to me that he also showed very clearly the
need for experience in handling the difficult tasks ahead, and his own
confidence in his policies as carried out this far, coupled with his statement
that there is still a long way to go, should do much to keep up and further
build the confidence of the voters. Somehow, when he first started to talk last
night he sounded a bit weary, to me; but as he went on his voice regained the
same old ring of strength and conviction. His job is so immense that it is
really frightening to think of. You have grown to be a part of that job in the
eyes of most of the people—which puts such a terrific burden on both of you
that all that the rest of us on the sidelines can do is to hope and pray that you
stay strong and well.
  We will do the best we can to help things along in this neck of the woods,
as campaign plans are shaped up. And if you or Pa think of anything specific
you want us to do—just yell.
  About two weeks ago we acquired a 25 foot motor boat and are having
loads of fun with it. This week-end we, and Sis and Buzz are going off on a

fishing cruise. I can't begin to tell you how much healthful benefit John, all three kids and I have derived from our new place. We all spend a great deal more time out of doors, and with the help of the tennis court we've managed to get plenty of exercise.

Did I tell you that Sis and Buzz have their own vegetable gardens? What with their gardens and ours we are eating only our own vegetables these days. We are going to can string beans, corn and tomatoes.

Sis and Buzz are leaving here on Aug. 2nd with Tom Carmody (Secret Service man), his wife and neice and nephew, to spend two or three weeks on a wheat ranch in eastern Oregon which is owned by Mrs. Carmody's brother. . . .

Anna

"*. . . liberals . . . insist on being individualists . . .*"

Seattle Post-Intelligencer
Aug 25th, '40

Darling,

. . . It must indeed have been a mixed summer for you, and I don't wonder that you have found less time for letter writing. It seems to me that its a grand thing that you've been able to see so many people this summer because there is so much confusion of thinking and ideas even among liberals, that you are, I know, a tremendously reassuring influence!

Conscription seems to be the main stumbling block among women. They are afraid of such things as an army bureaucracy; a fear that only those who are conscripted will have a chance to secure jobs in private industry, or will at least have a better chance; a fear that military training will assume such importance in the minds of people as a whole that military influence will gradually seep into the educational system in the schools; and a general fear that this present bill will merely be the forerunner of other military training bills. Among those who are not just blindly fearful of conscription is a feeling that they could agree to a years military training if they knew there was also to be compulsory training for other young people in trades, professions, industry, etc. This last point seems to me to be so tremendously important. And yet, there is no general publicity on the subject. These different youth agencies can make recommendations until they are black in the face and it won't do any good in solidifying the thinking in this country unless it is handled concretly by someone of real importance in the administration—insuring it some front page stories. Among those who think at all is the eternal question of what will happen to our social and economic system when the armament program is completed? [Drew] Pearson and [Robert S.] Allen [authors of a widely syndicated Washington column] have already printed a story saying that some of the big companies upon whom some of the defense program depends are holding up operations and refusing to go ahead until they find out how heavily they are going to be taxed—how much profit they are going to be allowed to make. So, profiteering is another big topic of discussion.

I know you hear all these questions all the time—but I'd sure like to know what answers you give to some of them! . . .

As for politics out here, . . . this week things seemed so desperately unorganized that we called Ed Flynn [former Bronx party leader whom FDR selected to replace Farley as chairman of the Democratic National Committee] on the phone. He asked us to write down all that we had told him and send it to him at the hotel where he is living. This we did. We have hesitated before to write anyone frankly, naming names, because we always have the fear that a letter may fall into the wrong hands and in some way be harmful to Pa. But, this time it seemed the only thing to do. We naturally did not try to tell Ed who should run the campaign in this state—but did give him the low-down on our impossible national commiteeman and state chairman, and offered a suggestion which is by no means perfect, but should be helpful politically—and the man is a good organizer.

Right now we are working behind the scenes to get the liberal groups organized. Its a tough job because liberals, or progressives as some of them insist on calling themselves out here, insist on being individualists to the exclusion of all realization that they must get together on a program in order to be able to put it over! The Commonwealth Federation in this state has gone completely "Commie". Those who have broken away are full of bitterness, to the extent that they would love nothing better than a good public tarring and feathering ceremony! The C.F. still has a few C.I.O. unions, but is gradually dieing out. The others have no leadership—and that is what we're trying to get. They are also the group whom Solicitor General [Francis] Biddle came all the way out here to speak for, today. By the way, I think Biddle is one of those whom F. Jr. would find very interesting, and who should be able to teach F. much along the line of liberalism.

Biddle made a good speech and did very well answering questions afterwards. BUT—you might put this but in Ed Flynn's ear: Tell him to request that all speakers sponsored by the national committee, limit their talks to 30 or 40 minutes. Biddle spoke for a full hour. He made out a good case in excellent lawyer fashion—full of "evidence" and quotes. But he's not colorful enough or fiery enough to hold the attention of an average audience for an hours time. In fact, I'm pretty well convinced that most audiences can remember more of what they are told if it is simple, direct and as short as possible. Biddle has lots of personal charm and is good at meeting people.

I'm awfully glad you're trying the experiment of going to N.Y. headquarters twice a week, because your experiences throughout the country should be of inestimable value to Ed Flynn. I'm hoping, however, that there will be no publicity or very little about your work there, for it seems to me that through your column you can answer more questions in the minds of people, and in a non-partisan way, thereby doing more good than you can through too much partisan work. Of course, [a] certain type of publicity about your working at headquaters would only stimulate interest in your column and might, therefore, be all to the good. But, I'm not much good at guessing ahead as to how the Republicans will try to "get you", so all we can do is hope for the best!

We saw Jimmy's anti-Nazi movie [brother James was now in the movie business] at a pre-view, and were tremendously impressed by it. I think it gets across the idea that its not the people we must hate, but the system. Its hard to guess how popular it will be and therefore how many people it will reach, but it certainly is the best way I can think of to try to show people what life would be like under that kind of system. The fact that you are introducing it lends it weight, and you do a swell job—Madame Movie Actress! John and I only wish that they had not made you up quite so much and that they had not "directed" you so much, because you have so much individual forcefulness, charm and showmanship you've developed for yourself, that we thought you'd have been an even better "salesman" on your own!

I haven't heard a word from Rommie [Romelle Schneider, fiancée of James] or Jimmy since he got sick, so hope that no news is good news. . . .

You may be amused to know that on the same day Willkie made the accusation that W.P.A. roles were being padded, I started receiving kicks from a hundred odd women who have just been kicked off the Seattle sewing project. I'm looking into the situation as best I can—but I never cease to wish that the administration of W.P.A. could be worked out so that such huge blocks of people didn't have to be thrown out with such suddenness—and with explanations which are always way above their heads.

The kids had just two weeks at the ranch and loved it. Sis had to make beds, clean rooms and wash and dry dishes with the other two girls and Buzz had to split fire wood, help milk the cows and feed the stock. There was plenty of time left, however, for horseback riding and swimming. As the children in the ranch family are all older, Sis and Buzz came home having learned considerably more about the "facts of life"—some desirable and some not—but all to the good I think in the long run!

. . . Johnny has become a naughty sadist! If you are reading he will take great pleasure in either knocking your paper or book out of your hands or biffing you over the head with the nearest hard miscle—and he's an excellent shot! Yesterday, he was discovered standing by our little cocktail tray and cramming hors d'oevres down his throat at a remarkable speed for a young man sixteen months of age. Two days ago he stole our nose drop bottles and threw them in the ash can. At present he has successfully secreted your last letter to me. Altogether, he's just a rascal! He has quite a temper and protests loudly when he is disciplined, but the storm is over in just a few minutes—and he's laughingly off on his next escapade! . . .

We all send you loads and loads of love, and a very special hug from me.

Anna

The previous letter and the next two reveal the continuing need of Anna, at thirty-four, to search out ground on which she can win her mother's approval as an adult. That desire seems to generate the heavily political and somewhat flattering tone of the previous long letter from Anna. In the next, Mother politely brushes aside the politics in favor of "personal bits." Anna's response—a letter almost as long—contains nothing but "personal bits."

"The Norwegians," whose arrival is noted in the following letter, were the members and attendants of the royal family of Norway. They were among several royal families of Europe who established residence in the United States to escape the occupation of their countries by the Nazis.

". . . beds for everyone & no one has been hungry yet . . ."

Hyde Park
Friday night, Aug 30th [1940]

Darling,
Your letter of the 25th was most interesting politically tho' I preferred the personal bits! Johnny must be adorable & I long to see him, tho' I hope he treats me with respect. Sis & Buzz must have gained much from the Ranch. The powers that be think I should go West in Oct. & just happen to be at some LaGuardia meetings on the coast but not speak myself. . . .

Pa is thrilled over acquiring the naval bases [from Great Britain, in exchange for some "over-age" U.S. destroyers], considers it the biggest thing since the acquisition of Louisiana & says he may go in a week or so & visit them which will be a week's trip. Good for him but I tell him he must explain to the people first or they will say "Ah! ha! time for a pleasure jaunt but not for campaigning!

I'm going to answer your conscription questions in my column someday next week. . . .

All the Norwegians arrived yesterday, & 3 Roosevelt nieces (Hall and Dorothy's) children. Harry Hopkins came, attracted by royalty I surmise & I asked Harry Hooker who always basks in such environment. One extra Norwegian child, Mme Osgaard's little boy, was not expected nor was the valet but I found beds for everyone & no one has been hungry yet I hope! The planning is terrible however & it is time consuming! They stay on for a week or more but we leave on Sunday. . . .

It is late dear, so goodnight. Love to all & a big hug for you,

Mother

". . . new nurse for Johnny . . . white, and only 22 . . ."

Portland, Ore.
Sept. 24th [1940]

Darling:
. . . John and I are spending four days here going twice a day to a Dr. Benson, trying to find out what causes our clogged noses. They now think it

may be a minor "strep" germ, so are now growing the cute little babies under glass, and will inoculate us with them tomorrow. Anyway, we go home Thursday afternoon.

You should have seen Sisty going to her first dance, last week! . . . Sis was scared to death for 24 hours ahead of time; made us wash and curl her hair especially for the occasion; and called me on the phone at the office, the afternoon before the party, begging me to get her a "swing" skirt and button-down-the-front sweater, for the occasion, as that was what the other girls were wearing. All her instructions were carried out to the letter—and, needless to say, she had the time of her life!

Did I tell you that I have a new nurse for Johnny? She is white, and only 22 years old. But, so far, she's a tremendous success. She makes Johnny mind, say "thank you", "no thank you", "you're welcome", and ask for things like his toys and food, by name, before he gets them. I must say that it takes intuition and good guess work to understand Johnny—but he no longer whines or grunts or yells or grabs as he was getting into the habit of doing. Big John would undoubtedly deny that "his" baby ever did such things! . . . [The new nurse] took the entire household training course at our W.P.A.–N.Y.A. [Works Progress Administration–National Youth Administration] center (through which I got her), and, to my joy, told me she thought this course the finest and most practical she had ever heard of. I just hope she continues to be as perfect as she now seems! Another great help is that Katie and Ivan think she is swell.

Both Buzz and Sis are thoroughly satisfied with their new school. I am thinking of putting Buzz into a manual training class at the Y.M.C.A. on Saturday mornings, as his coordination is not too good. It happens to be the only one I can find in the city. But before sending Buzz there, I have to sell the idea to John as he has a constitutional dislike of Y.M.C.A. boys!!

Sis is also taking ballet dancing once a week to try and help her get through the rather heavy, awkward stage she's in now. Then every other week she takes a ball-room dancing lesson. So, adding all the activities together (not to mention our local Symphony concerts, movies and what-nots) our young family seems well enough occupied! . . .

We both send you heaps and heaps of love—and can hardly wait to see you! A special hug from me.

Anna

". . . One never knows what the vote will be . . ."

Val-Kill Cottages
Hyde Park
Sunday night Nov. 3d [1940]

Anna darling,

I have lived over in thought many times our days together & being with you & John always makes me happy for the whole family seems to be on such a firm foundation of mutual respect & love.

F jr. seemed a weary & rather dispirited young man when I saw him at headquarters yesterday. We had little time to talk but he enjoyed being with you & I'll hear more when he gets here tomorrow. . . .

I've been to Washington twice for a day each time. Done a lot of political chores, yesterday, for instance I went to N.Y. & did 5 meetings! All enthusiastic. One never knows what the vote will be till it is counted however! I wish you were going to be here on election night. I often think of John [Boettiger] & his look at me & remark on election night 1932! Harry Hooker [the family lawyer and friend] is coming up, the Morgenthaus [Henry Morgenthau, Jr., Dutchess County friend and neighbor, was secretary of the treasury] will be here with their boys. Only F jr & Ethel & Johnny & Anne will be here of the family. Mrs. Helm is here, Earl & Joe Lash [a leader of the student movement to whom Mrs. Roosevelt had taken a special liking] are coming for the night & countless others to hear returns! Henry Osthagen came up on Friday & is staying over & I think Esther Lape may come for the night if Elizabeth is feeling pretty well.

Mrs. McAllister [Dorothy, of Michigan, director of the women's division of the Democratic party] & her daughter & Geno Herrick [Genevieve, a Washington journalist, who became a friend] spent last night here so you can see something is always doing!

I thought Pa's speech in Cleveland last night was grand & nothing that I've heard from Wilkie [Willkie] can touch it. Pa gets here tomorrow morning & goes the rounds of local campaigning as usual. I have a picnic for the last N.Y.A. [National Youth Administration, a student-aid agency] boys from Woodstock. . . .

My love to Sis & Buzz & Johnny. Someday I hope to see enough of that young man so he is not afraid of me. . . .

Devotedly
Mother

". . . I'm really afraid of Wilkie [sic] *& his backers[.] . . ."*

Stevens Hotel
Chicago
Nov. 15th, '40

Dearest Anna,

. . . I wish you could have been home at H.P. for election night. F jr. & Johnnie worked hard with Pa all night. I had a stand up supper at the cottage for 40 or 50 at 7.30 & everyone except Granny & Pa & Missy came over so they were quiet till 9.30. People kept coming all night & of course more village people than you have ever seen. We did not carry the town however, only our district as usual & Ham Fish [Hamilton Fish, conservative Republican congressman from Dutchess County] was reelected tho' he only won by 10,000. The small popular vote is strange I think & there is no use minimizing what money & high pressure advertising can do & I think they mean to do it for these next four years. I believe, therefore that much better organization & publicity must be done by the [Democratic National] Committee & all independant groups & Father must build Wallace up if he is to succeed [presumably, if Henry A. Wallace were to succeed Roosevelt as presidential nominee] in 1944. I'm really afraid of Wilkie [Willkie] & his backers[.] So many sinister stories have been coming in which I'll tell you sometime.

I spent last Sunday in the 65th Street house clearing out storerooms & what dirt & what junk! Tommy & Joe Lash worked with me all day & we lunched in the restaurant you & John & I used to dine in now & then. We've offered the house for rent but I fear it would cost a bit to put it in order. Granny wld like to use it if it isn't rented so I shall have it cleaned, put back what furniture we have & you will be able to stay there in Jan. if you wish. How I look forward to Jan. I hope you can make the Inauguration & when you know your plans I will try to spend the days in N.Y. & Boston with you. . . .

I go down to N.Y. Sunday to see Earl who sails Monday, the 25th for a four week's navy cruise as reserve lieutenant. I hear rumors James [now a Marine captain], is stationed on an Island, do you know if it is true? He hasn't written. . . .

We started this lecture trip last Sunday night & it has been very easy & I think the lectures have gone well.

I've just been asked to answer Herbert Hoover's article in Collier's so I must stop & read it & decide if I want to do it. Do read Ernest Hemingway's book [For Whom the Bell Tolls, a novel of the Spanish Civil War], horrible but so well written & a great book I think.

. . . I'm not looking forward to the next four years but we'll see each other spring & fall at least!

Devotedly
Mother

". . . Horror on Pa's face & then: . . ."

Hotel Statler
Boston
Sat. Feb. 15th [1941]

Darling,
. . . We have a grand one in Johnny [Roosevelt] & Pa. I went to West Va. by the night train last Sat. to speak Sunday p.m. & return by night train. Johnny called me Sunday night & was much peeved because I wasn't home & got Pa & the following conversation took place:—

Johnny: I can't get Ma, she's never home. Will you take down the arrangements about the baby?
Pa: Delighted
J: Please call tomorrow morning the Didie Co.

Pa: The what?

J: The Didie Co.

Pa: Who is she?

J: Oh! you are old fashioned, the diaper Co. They have to have several days notice.

Pa: Hasn't the baby any diapers? We have a stove & they can be boiled here.

J: Oh! no Pa. We don't do things that way now.

Pa: Very well, I'll call. How many do you want?

Consultation with Anne then:—

J: One hundred and forty.

Pa: (horrified) 140. Has the baby got kidney trouble?

J: Oh! no Pa. He's perfectly normal.

J cont. He uses 20 a day[,] 140 a week!

Pa: I see! I'll call in the morning.

Pa went to bed chuckling over the morning conversation to be: "Hackie [Louise Hachmeister, in charge of the White House switchboard] get me the Universal Didie Service." "Yes Mr. President." Connection made. "This is the President of the U.S. Please deliver on Thursday morning at 9 a.m. 140 diapers." "Oh! Yea!" In the morning a message from the Sec. of State & diapers sink out of mind. I come Tuesday or rather Wed. at 1.45 a.m. Army & Navy reception over[,] long & encouraging talk with Mr. Wilkie [Willkie] who thinks England can & will hold out[,] finally bed & a pretty happy feeling. I go in to say goodnight & remark: "Anne won't get in till Thursday a.m. instead of Wed. I had a wire about milk." Horror on Pa's face & then:

Pa: I knew that, John telephoned me about didie's on Sunday night[.] Will you see to them in the morning, he wants 140!

Then an account of the conversation as I've given it to you above. I hope you laugh as much as I did. It appears that Johnny never smiled! . . .

I found a model miners hospital in W. Va. the men contribute $1 a month, collected by the companies as union dues or rent, & for it they receive any amount of hospitalization & their families, including parents if they live with the man are cared for also. No extra charge for operations, special care or medicines is made! . . .

The Communists & the Youth Congress are after me in real earnest now & on the other hand Mr. Pegler took me neatly apart the other day. Mr. Carlin wrote him he thought his column was a bit rough but I think it shows I must be steering a fairly middle course! . . .

F jr. has been called to service but asked for a deferrment till he takes his bar exams early in March. He thinks he will be in about April. Johnny has not been called yet & is promoted to manager of the Winchester store [of Filene's, the Boston department store] in May.

I'll be back in Washington tomorrow afternoon & hope to find your stuff to read.

Give my love to Sis & Buzz. I hope you liked the Inauguration medals, they were done by Joe [Jo] Davidson. I sent one for you & John & one for each child.

My love to John & all my love to you dearest,

Mother

". . . Mr. Alexander Woolcott . . . spent 2 weeks in the house while playing in 'The man who came to dinner' . . ."

The White House
Wed. Mar. 12th [1941]

Darling,

. . . Johnnie [Roosevelt] . . . had a large cist taken out where the little extra bone is at the end of the spine. He spent a week in the naval hospital but was quite well when I left Thursday last. Mr. Alexander Woolcott [Woollcott] who spent 2 weeks in the house while playing in "The man who came to dinner" wrote me he'd seen Johnny Sunday a.m. & he seemed quite well. He was most anxious to get back on his job but both he & Anne are worried for fear he will get called in the draft & wonder if he should volunteer in the navy supply corps. I'm offering no advice for I don't know what he should do. How I hate war & all it does to people's lives even at this distance! . . .

Pa can't leave till the 17th but I hope he leaves that night for a cruise. He was tired when I left but I'm sure now the lend lease bill is through that he will feel much better.

Did you see Pegler's column on attacking me the other day? Someday I think I'll satisfy his curiosity & show him my list of charities! . . .

Devotedly
Mother

I haven't heard yet about F jr's bar exams but he expects to be in the navy April 1st. James has not written either about his wedding.

The Roosevelt family was directly caught up in preparations for war ahead of most other people. Before December 7, 1941, all four Roosevelt sons were in the service, either in the active reserve or on active duty. In the letter that follows, Eleanor, like any bewildered mother containing her fears over what it may mean reports Franklin, Jr., sailing off for active naval duty. Her oldest son James is in the Marines and Elliott in the Army Air Forces. John has been commissioned an ensign in the Navy.

Few families in the United States were to undergo the anxieties of the

Roosevelt parents upon the outbreak of war. Four able-bodied, combat-age sons in a single family were rare enough, and all four young Roosevelts soon found themselves under dangerous exposure to the enemy: James, as a volunteer with the famous "Carlson's Raiders," a Pacific island-hopping commando group; Elliott, originally an air intelligence officer in Newfoundland, flying reconnaissance missions in unarmed photographic planes under heavy fire, rose to a combat brigadier general, commanding a wing of more than 250 planes and 5000 men, winning the Distinguished Flying Cross; Franklin became executive officer of the destroyer *Mayrant,* dodging torpedoes from Iceland to Minsk, enduring a bombing in the Sicilian invasion, and winning the Silver Star for carrying a critically wounded sailor to safety under heavy fire; John, serving aboard the aircraft carrier *Hornet* in the Pacific war zone, won the Bronze Star and the stripes of a lieutenant commander.

The high position of their parents clearly did not shelter the Roosevelt sons from dangerous assignments. Each requested combat duty and their father, the commander in chief, was careful to ensure that his position of power did not protect them. In fact, assigning officers appeared to go out of their way to shield themselves from accusations that they reserved soft and safe jobs for the sons of the President.

". . . The situation with Harry, Missy & Pa is . . . a very close corporation . . ."

> 1600 Pennsylvania Avenue
> Washington, D.C.
> May 15th [1941]

Anna darling,

. . . F jr. . . . sailed 5 a.m. Sunday for Norfolk. Ethel was at the big house with Joe [child of Franklin, Jr., and Ethel] & she is just starting on another baby due Xmas & Ruth who has been here with Elliott & left today will also have one next Jan. War time you know! I expect Anne will soon be telling me the same tale. Saturday, I . . . went to the women's democratic lunch in Poughkeepsie. . . . Marion [Dickerman] blandly said she hoped we would keep our sense of humour about our nazis, I fear I interpret that as a slap at Pa for criticizing Lindbergh [Charles A. Lindbergh, the flier, had been accused of pro-Nazi sympathy] but I may be unfair! . . .

I found Pa had really been quite ill & Dr. McIntire [Vice Admiral Ross T. McIntire, surgeon general of the navy and FDR's personal physician] was worried because his red cells which should be up to 5000000 dropped suddenly to 2,800000. He has had 2 transfusions, iron, & his tummy is cleared up & his color seems good, his blood is back to 4,000000 & while he still is easily tired & *very* edgy I am sure he is on the way to being quite well in a few days. No temperature for the last 4 days.

The situation with Harry [Hopkins], Missy & Pa is funny. It is a very close corporation just now. So far I've told him nothing [presumably about observations on her most recent trip] as I didn't think he was well enough to accept any disagreeable facts.

Granny went up to Toronto for a moneyraising lunch. Isn't she amazing? . . .

I had such a lovely time with you all & you are all so sweet to me that I love to live over again all my time with you in my thoughts. . . .

Mother

In early June 1941, the President gave a party for the White House staff in the State Dining Room. Toward the end of the dinner, Missy LeHand, looking strangely drawn, told her assistant, Grace Tully, that she felt ill. She refused, however, to go to her tiny apartment on the third floor before the Boss left, which he did at about 9:30. A few minutes later Missy slumped to the floor, unconscious. Dr. McIntire rushed her to her room. The signs of a stroke were unmistakable. Her left arm and leg were paralyzed. Her speech was gone.

On June 22, Missy was taken to Doctors Hospital, chiefly because the constant vigilance and care she required were difficult at the White House. After a few weeks there, at her request, she was taken to Warm Springs, where both rest and medical attention were available.

In 1927, when Missy was twenty-nine years old and attending FDR while he was struggling vainly to learn to walk again in the cottage at Warm Springs, she had suffered a sudden and puzzling illness. Grace Tully one day described it to me as "a little crack-up." That long-past occurrence is the only known background of Mrs. Roosevelt's comment in the following letter that Missy's "mind went as it does." For what condition Missy had been "taking opiates" (insomnia?) is also unexplained and the belief that she "had a heart attack" is not corroborated in any other known record.

"... I'm not staying just seeing her settled. . . ."

20 East 11th Street
New York, N.Y.
June 12th, '41

Anna darling,

. . . Missy is very ill again. She's been taking opiates & had a heart attack & then her mind went as it does, so now we have three nurses & the prospect of some weeks of illness before we get her straightened out. Pa has a slight sore throat but nothing to worry about tho' he spent yesterday in bed. He sounded better when I called him last night. . . .

Granny was laid up nearly three weeks & narrowly missed a stroke so I'm going to take her to Campo this year so I'm glad to have the I.S.S. [International Student Service] group there to give me a little more incentive for going! I'm not staying just seeing her settled. . . .

Ivan can have a job as messenger in the Treasury whenever he comes but of course the salary won't be high! I think they usually run from $1260 to $1320 a year. . . .

Devotedly
Mother

I should say that Pa has been *very* well till yesterday's sore throat.

". . . more cots & pots & pans & china & glass. . . ."

Campobello Island
Sunday June 22d [1941]

Darling Sis,

. . . Pa has had another throat or rather a low temperature which they say comes from a low grade infection but they don't know what it is. I telephoned every day since I've been here & today begged him to have an outside doctor & he said he would tomorrow. Missy was taken to the hospital today & has been worse for the last few days & that may be at the bottom of much of the trouble. I hope she gets well but it is complicated with change of life.

. . . Elliott has landed safely back in Newfoundland & now is preparing for a mapping trip which should be over in August if all goes well but I shall be most anxious till he's back. . . .

If Ivan lets me know ahead at H.P. when he wants to go to work I'll let Henry Morgenthau know & give Ivan a note to the right person at the Treasury.

Poor Sisty I hope all went well & uneventfully on her trip with Curt. Buzz is still too young to feel it much. Let me know how it came out. I can imagine John was none too happy with Curt around. . . .

There is much to do here to get this house ready for 30 young people [the I.S.S. visitors] & 5 constant staff with occassional visitors! We've fitted them all in but I go to St. Andrews tomorrow to get more cots & pots & pans & china & glass. I'm having a nice time though. Tommy loves it here. . . . We've hot weather (it must be awful at home) but beautiful & gorgeous sunsets! . . . I will be going back to Washington now & then to see Missy & if Pa isn't well of course I'll have to stay a while but I hope he'll come to H.P. & stay. . . .

Devotedly
Mother

Eleanor, summering at Campobello, perhaps did not know the nature of the "cruise" upon which FDR was about to embark in this first letter. He would probably not have written her about it by mail nor spoken of it by telephone. It was the first of many major wartime trips FDR was to take under the cover of unprecedented security.

On August 3 he sailed out of the harbor of New London, Connecticut, on the presidential yacht *Potomac,* going through the Cape Cod Canal, making quite a show of the President enjoying a pleasure jaunt. As soon as the yacht was out of sight of land observers and newsmen, he transferred to the U.S.S. *Augusta* and headed north for a four-day secret rendezvous at sea near Argentia, Newfoundland, starting August 9. Aboard the *Prince of Wales* was Winston Churchill. They were to negotiate the Atlantic Charter with its famous list of "points"—joint declarations of the principles of postwar order, emphasizing human freedom, justice, security and access to raw materials and natural resources.

Eleanor's letter of August 10 appears to confirm that she, like the rest of the world, is in the dark. She has "no news of Elliott," who actually was accompanying FDR on the journey. The press, discovering that the President and the prime minister and their top military staffs had been unseen for days, had begun to speculate that something unusual was up. That presumably accounts for the last sentence in the letter of August 10.

". . . Pa . . . leaves tomorrow on his cruise . . ."

Campobello Island
Saturday Aug. 2d [1941]

Anna darling,
    . . . Pa had a good week end at H.P. with Harry Hooker as our only house guest. He leaves tomorrow on his cruise but of course does not come up here.

Granny is still in her room & I should not be surprised if this were the start of a more restricted, invalid life for her. She seems better however, & the nurse has fitted in well & relieves everyone of anxiety.

I shall be leaving tomorrow & making my way back to Hyde Park where I hope to have some fairly quiet weeks.

Tommy is well but weary & hopes to stay home for a long while!

I'm enclosing a note for John. He wrote such a cute note saying he hoped you never went away without him again.

A world of love darling.

Mother

". . . tho' I still believe . . . she will live for some time. . . ."

Val-Kill Cottages
Hyde Park
August 10, 1941

Dearest Anna:
    . . . We've been home since last Tuesday & it is very nice at the cottage. . . . I've done an article for Liberty, & one or two chores but mostly I've been home, & fairly lazy with a swim each day.

I left Granny comfortable with the nurse but I think she is failing fast, tho' I still believe if she is quiet she will live for some time. F jr. is off for some months on the coast of Newfoundland. I have no news of Elliott but he should be back soon if all is well. . . .

You know as much about Pa as I do! . . .

Devotedly,
Mother

". . . perhaps . . . I could take you all for a debauch . . . ?"

Val-Kill Cottages
Hyde Park
Sunday Aug. 17th [1941]

Anna darling,

I asked Tommy to send you the check as I certainly did want to give Buzz the same as Sisty. . . .

When I go out [to Seattle] perhaps there is some kind of place I could take you all for a debauch or would John die?

. . . I talked to Pa today & he sounded very pleased & said he got nearly all he wanted in the "points." I am so glad Elliott & F jr. were with him. He was on Elliott's arm at the time the official picture was taken. Elliott is now on his way to Iceland, or should be there if all is well. I do hope this is the last trip. . . .

Granny seems better & is enjoying the nurse. . . .

Devotedly
Mother

On the seventh of September 1941, a day that will live in memory at Hyde Park, without advance warning—there was no storm, no wind, no lightning—the mightiest oak on the Roosevelt estate groaned and toppled to the ground. Geologists were later to be called in to investigate. They were to explain that, because of a thin layer of earth over a rocky base, such occurrences in Dutchess County were quite normal.

The people around the Roosevelts—the secretaries, the Secret Service men, the household workers and gardeners—never quite accepted that judgment, preferring to rely on a more symbolic explanation. Barely five minutes before the great tree fell, Sara Delano Roosevelt, lying in her bed on the second floor of the mansion, gave up her last breath.

Later in the afternoon of that somber day, her only son, Franklin, was taken by a strong urge. He wished to go out among the trees and quiet roads of the place, driving in his little hand-controlled car—alone. He was not permitted to do so. Even at so private a moment, the Secret Service insisted that its agents must ride by his side and in a car behind him. Not even his wife, it appears, could relieve the loneliness of this poignant moment.

Three days later, immediately after the funeral, the President and First Lady entrained for the White House, she further burdened by her brother Hall's final surrender to alcohol. That night, weary but overflowing with thoughts to release, Eleanor wrote to Anna.

". . . but I just can't . . . Will you & the boys understand it . . . ?"

The White House
Wednesday night Sept 10th [1941]

Anna darling,

I've thought of you often & wished for you & yet been glad you did not come for these hectic days. Father wants you both to come when you can spend a long week end at least & I think he will pay for the trip as he wants to have you choose some inheritances so to speak.

The funeral was nice & simple, the casket in the library on the south side & only a spray of H.P. flowers on it. We drove to the churchyard & Father stood by the car through the interment service. Romaine [her name is actually Romelle], Anne & Ethel [wives of James, John and Franklin, Jr.] did all the cards on the flowers & the 3 boys all the arranging of seats & cars & ushering. Father has begun to forget all that was ever disagreeable in his relationship to Granny but he was not emotional & neither was anyone except Aunt Kassie [sister of Sara]. I kept being appalled at myself because I couldn't feel any real grief or sense of loss & that seemed terrible after 36 years of fairly close association. . . .

Early this morning I got Hall off in the Secret Service car with Zena . . . & he is in Walter Reed [Hospital]. I doubt if he ever comes out but I'll know more tomorrow after I go out & see the doctor. I won't leave if things look desperate but if it is a matter of weeks I'll go to N.Y. tomorrow night after Father's speech.

I fear I won't get west till next spring so please write me what you want for Xmas also in general whether you are interested in silver, china, any furniture from Granny's N.Y. house, rugs, pictures, books, linen or ornaments.

The will leaves ⅒ of the Estate to be divided in 6 parts. This will mean *about* $12,000 a piece. 1 share to me in trust to have income for life & then reverts to Father or all of you. You each get principal at age of 30 before that only income. Pa gets the rest. Of course it will take some time to settle. The N.Y. houses are on the market for sale now. Jennings says Granny wanted you to have one string of pearls & her fox furs. Some day they will go to you. I am going to try & sort papers & check books & clothes before Father comes back to the N.Y. House next Thursday or Friday & then to H.P. Deciding about servants etc. is going to be difficult.

Tommy & I are moved from the apartment [at 20 East Eleventh Street] into 49 [East Sixty-fifth Street] & the phone no. is RH-4-2143 if you should ever want it. . . . There will be room for any of you to stay & Georgie to give you breakfast & simple meals.

We left [Hyde Park] at one today & arrived [at the White House] at 8 & Pa went into conference at once on his speech [a radio Fireside Chat about

Hitler's aggression, in which he urges the nation, "When you see a rattlesnake poised to strike, you do not wait until he has struck before you crush him"], Harry [Hopkins] & Diana are living here this winter. She goes to boarding school in Alexandria. Harry looks very ill & I suppose will be off to Russia or Japan soon!

I can't feel much about Hall either, because he is so changed, & I just hope he won't be ill long or suffer much. His mind is pretty foggy as he's been drinking an average of at least 1 qrt of gin a day.

Pa sprang it on me today that I had better take Granny's room [at the big house at Hyde Park] but I just can't & told him so. Of course I know I've got to live there more, but only when he is there & I am afraid he hasn't realized that & isn't going to like it or understand. Will you & the boys understand it or does it make you resentful?

A world of love to you & John. Please tell the kids I'm heartbroken not to see them this autumn but it doesn't look possible just now. I forgot to tell you Cousin Susie is ill too & I may have to go there on Friday!

Love to the kids & a special hug for you darling.

Mother

". . . I think we have many days before us . . ."

1600 Pennsylvania Avenue
Washington, D.C.
Tuesday night [September 17, 1941]

Anna darling,

I've wanted to write—but been too weary. This watching Hall die & seeing Zena suffer is a pretty trying business. It is such an unattractive death, he's mahogany color, all distended, out of his head most of the time & his speech is almost impossible to understand. He moves insistantly & involuntarily so you try to hold him quiet & it is really most distressing though they say he does not suffer. Ellie [Hall's daughter by his first marriage] came yesterday but I sent her home today as he didn't know her. Sometimes he knows me even when he doesn't know Zena & I can quiet him.

I think Pa has taken Granny's death very philosophically & he's already forgotten everything dis-agreeable as I think I wrote you. He'll go on Thursday to H.P. to look after the Norwegians & I stay here for I think we have many days before us as Hall's heart is so strong. . . .

Give Sis this stamp & tell Buzz & Johnnie theirs will be along soon.

Love to John & to you & such a big hug.

Devotedly
Mother

". . . Always . . . I've wanted people to fight . . ."

> 1600 Pennsylvania Avenue
> Washington, D.C.
> Thursday a.m. [September 25, 1941]

Darling,

Hall finally died this morning at 5 a.m. & I am thankful[;] for since Sunday at 2 it has been a pretty harrowing experience & though he was unconscious there was a kind of reflex suffering & an unconscious struggle which was hard to watch when you knew he could not win. Always before I've wanted people to fight & there has been some hope, this time I longed for a peaceful end & at the last it was. I took Zena home to get her things & the dog & have brought her here & will take her to Tivoli where I will bury him & then try to get Zena to Hyde Park for a rest at the cottage. She was loyal & devoted & even now asks for nothing material. The funeral will be tomorrow here at 3 o'clock in the East room so Hall's friends can attend, then only Ellie & Henry will be asked if they want to go to Tivoli.

Father told me this morning to tell you at once that there are still negotiations going on & he might go to Alaska to meet the Japs. You & John are not to mention this to anyone. If he goes he would leave about Oct 10th & be returning via Seattle about Oct 21st & wld bring you back *free* with him. Anyway you better plan to come before 10th or after 21st just on the chance he goes.

Monday next I start with civilian defense but I've been learning plenty & the last few days Elinor Morgenthau who is going to help me has been studying too. There is no co-ordinated organization so I start first on my office, then on channels, which don't now exist to reach the communications & you will be hearing from me officially next week.

James & Rommie have been too sweet to me all this time & Tommy is her usual angelic & helpful self & Joe Lash who was here last Sunday was a great help & has continued to be such a thoughtful, sweet person from N.Y. I'm grateful to them all & to Elinor Morgenthau who has been very helpful. . . .

I wish you were nearer but when I do see you I'll hug you all the harder & love you all the more. . . .

> Mother

On Sunday, December 7, 1941, in the early afternoon, FDR was seated at his desk chatting with Harry Hopkins while awaiting a call from Secretary of State Cordell Hull about Hull's discussions with two emissaries from Japan, Kichisaburo Nomura and Saburo Kurusu. At 1:47 P.M. the President's phone rang. The call was not from Hull, but from Secretary of the Navy Frank Knox. The message was astounding: "Mr. President, it looks as if the Japanese have attacked Pearl Harbor!" The incredible report was followed by others: The Japanese attacked Guam, Wake, Midway, Howland Island and

Hong Kong, and there were unconfirmed reports that they also attacked Manila and Singapore.

As late as 3:00 P.M. Mrs. Roosevelt remained uninformed of the news and, in another part of the White House was writing a chatty, leisurely letter to Anna. In the middle of it she learned of the calamity. Surprisingly, she went on at some length with tidbits of Christmas shopping and gifting. Here is the letter in entirety:

". . . No word yet & it is after three. . . ."

> 1600 Pennsylvania Avenue
> Washington, D.C.
> Sunday, Dec. 7th [1941]

Darling,

Your letter was grand & I was so glad to have it. I'm working out my itinerary now & hope, weather permitting to leave Jan. 1st spend the day & night of 2d in Los Angeles working, the 3d & till p.m. of 4th in San Diego, reach San Francisco that night late spend 5th there working, & get to you p.m. of 6th, leaving again a.m. of 9th & reaching Fort Worth 10th, leaving there p.m. of 11th & getting home late that night.

Tommy will not be with me & it is all the time I can be away. I would like to meet State Defense Council people in Seattle & some key local defense council people but no big meeting, a chance to talk & question is preferable. I would like to see the 4 young ones who were at Campo & I'll send you their names & addresses or ask Joe to do so. If they feel I could do anything for I.S.S. I'd like to do it. That is all! The rest of the time I want to see just you & John & the kids. I'd like to talk to Sisty about the future, if you think it wise.

F jr.'s destroyer had a collission while convoying at night, & they had to put into Porto Rico for 3 days repair. [For many months the U.S. Navy had been furnishing convoy escorts for merchant vessels across the Atlantic. Several American ships were sunk by Nazi U-boats.] He is o.k. & was not the officer who had the watch. Pa "forgot" to tell me till today when I heard rumours from other sources & asked. Ethel expects the baby any day. I talked to her today & she sounds well & cheerful.

Elliott is supposed to arrive with two other boys this afternoon but no word yet & it is after three. Ruth is back in Fort Worth for good but the baby isn't expected till the middle of Jan.

The whole Adams family [of Mr. and Mrs. Frederick B. Adams, cousins of FDR] have been here over the week end & so nice & no trouble! At least I have no time for guests so they can't be any trouble! Mrs. Hamlin is staying here too for an indefinite period.

———

The news of war has just come & I've put in a call for you & Johnny as you may want to send the children East. I've talked to the mayor [Fiorello La Guardia, co-head with Mrs. Roosevelt of the Office of Civilian Defense] & all plans will change from now on. He'll be here tomorrow & go west to recruit for air raid wardens etc & get the west coast organized on civilian protection. I may go along.

The check I sent you was for defense stamps for the kids $5 more for Sis & $10 each for Buzz & Johnnie. I've given the same to all the others & I'll begin the rounds again soon.

I'm enclosing a check $20 for Buzz & $20 for Johnnie[.] Get them what they want & $15 for John's razor & I enclose a card. I sent Johnnie some blocks addressed to you from Abercrombie & Fitch. I'm sending Sis gloves & hankies but I'm not sure they are marked right in future they will be. I'll send her the microscope set the J. L. Guild subscription & the Geographic. We'll send Buzz the Jones book as soon as we can get it. His J. L. G. subscription goes on & "Young America." I'm getting John two films which will go in the package with other little things. I've got some things you don't need but I hope they'll fit & you'll like them, also the candles & lunch set. 4 silver candles will go soon from N.Y. that I have. I'm also sending you some sables of Granny's, is your cheap black fur coat worn out as I'd like to give you mine? I think I'll send Sis some less nice furs of Granny's too. Do you want a large table cloth & large napkins of Granny's or of my grandmother's?

I must go dear & talk to Father.

Much, much love,
Mother

"... Pa told me Churchill was arriving. ..."

1600 Pennsylvania Avenue
Washington, D.C.
Dec. 23d [1941]

Darlings Anna & John,

... I went up to Hyde Park on last Saturday & gave all the presents out & everyone asked for you all.

Ethel & the baby, born Sunday morning last are fine. He weighed 8 lbs 3 oz. We radioed F jr. but thought we could get no reply. Yesterday a.m. however a message came "Joe's daddy is safe & well, sends love & is sorry he couldn't be home for the big event" Signed Jay Vanderbilt & sent from Capetown!

Monday a.m. when I got back Pa told me Churchill was arriving. The house is full & very busy officially. Diana & a little friend helped me trim the little tree in the west hall so we would not interfere with officialdom at the other end of the hall. I have no feel of Xmas & so am filling no stockings this year tho' I have some things for Harry to fill Diana's. Harry looks badly & I wonder how long he can go on.

Elliott left last Sat. with his bombing squadron which was hard on Ruth. I think he is now in California bound out. James is still in California. We may hear some of your voices on Christmas morning.

I hope the day will be as happy as possible for you all. I shall be thinking of you & loving you *very very* much.

Mother

Enclosed is a little gift for you & John.

". . . but I don't want him to write the peace . . ."

1600 Pennsylvania Avenue
Washington, D.C.
Jan. 4th [1942]

Darling Anna,
I have so many thanks to write I don't know where to begin! First we loved our holly & I thank you & John & Sis, Buzz, & Johnny many times. It is nicer than any other! Then my lovely wooden candle holders will be beautiful at Hyde Park & my raincoat is a perfect size & has already been used. Pa did open your presents but I don't know if he'll ever thank you, he hasn't even opened piles of packages!
Tell John I loved his letter & I know nothing will ever come between us! . . . I liked hearing all your voices but I missed F jr. & Elliott & Xmas was a very sad day for me. I think Pa enjoyed all the officialdom & he did know that much of importance was being accomplished. I wish I could be less personal! . . . I can't help but worry about the boys . . . It just didn't seem as tho' anywhere around there was much personal feeling. We didn't bother about stockings & nothing seemed to have much zest but I suppose life must be like this till we return to peace! . . .
Keep the checks & spend on something you both want for your wedding anniversary. They come out of income not earned money & I'm giving away plenty these days so it is quite all right to give you both these little checks. I don't need anything! . . .
I like Mr. Churchill, he's loveable & emotional & very human but I don't want him to write the peace or carry it out.
Well, I must go to bed. A kiss to each member of the family. . . .

Devotedly
Mother

". . . no doctor on board so I was scared. . . ."

1600 Pennsylvania Avenue
Washington, D.C.,
Sunday [February 9, 1942]

Anna darling,
    . . . Betsy [James's former wife] will soon be Mrs. Jock Whitney.
    F jr. is home & Tuesday a.m. he had his appendix out. I'm so relieved he could stay & have it done for he's had several attacks at sea & the trips have been so hard & no doctor on board so I was scared. . . .
    Did you get the ring? I had it put in order at Tiffany's. You haven't cashed a $25 check I sent you. My love to all. . . .

Mother

". . . he seems to expect bombings this summer . . ."

29 Washington Square West
New York, N.Y.
April 27th [1942]

Anna darling,
    I've stopped payment on that old check & enclose another one now. I think the original one was to buy stamps for the three kids. . . .
    Pa has the gold bangles that belonged to Granny & he said you could have them but I don't know when he will get around to giving them to me.
    He's been busy on this message [to Congress on wartime taxes] which I think is fine only I hope net income allows deductions for all charitable purposes! I feel he is more content with the way the war is going, tho' he seems to expect bombings this summer in N.Y. & Washington & perhaps Seattle.
    Nearly everything is out of 47 & 49 [East Sixty-fifth Street]. This apartment is settled & I think very comfortable & there is light & sun & I hope air even in summer! I'll begin now everytime I go to H.P. to sort linen & silver & I'll send you what I can of linen. . . .
    The papers reported Elliott in Cairo & spoke of him as a major. I hope he got the promotion. He wrote his piles were bad & bleeding constantly & he'd have to have the operation on his return. . . .
    I've been doing a lot of talking around here in between moving. That seems to be all the war work I can do so now I've offered to speak for the Treasury.
    Earl is staying here because there are no quarters at Floyd Bennett Field yet, so I've told him he can have men from far away once a week for supper. . . .
    A world of love to you darling, from your devoted,

Ma.

". . . never was much on Mother's Day . . ."

VIA WESTERN UNION

SEATTLE

MAY 5, 1942

MRS. FRANKLIN D. ROOSEVELT

THE WHITE HOUSE

WASHINGTON, D.C.

WOULD YOU BE WILLING TO HELP OUR WAR BOND DRIVE
SERVICE MOTHER'S DAY CEREMONY NEXT SATURDAY NOON BY
MAKING A MINUTE AND A HALF TRANSCRIPTION ON AN ORDI-
NARY PHONOGRAPH RECORD AT ORDINARY SPEED? AM TOLD
ANY BROADCASTING STATION CAN DO IT BUT IT WOULD HAVE
TO BE SHIPPED AIRMAIL BY THURSDAY MORNING.

LOVE

ANNA

VIA WESTERN UNION

THE WHITE HOUSE

MAY 5, 1942

MRS JOHN BOETTIGER

THE POST INTELLIGENCER

DARLING I HAVE REFUSED TO TAKE PART IN MOTHERS DAY
CELEBRATION IN NEW YORK AND NEVER WAS MUCH ON MOTH-
ERS DAY AND COULD NOT THINK OF ANYTHING TO SAY WORTH
SAYING. TERRIBLY SORRY

DEVOTEDLY

MOTHER.

". . . Elliott dropped from the sky today . . ."

1600 Pennsylvania Avenue

Washington, D.C.

May 7th [1942]

Anna darling,

I thought of you so much on your birthday & wished I could be with
you. . . .

The house [Hyde Park] is being cleaned & is full of unpacked things from
N.Y. but Pa says they will like to picnic & he takes the Norwegians [Crown
Prince Olaf and Princess Marta, whose country had been overrun by the

Nazis, were visitors] to look at a summer home in Stockbridge [Massachusetts] on Sunday. They can't go to the sea shore this summer for fear of being shelled! Harry [Hopkins] will go up too, he's gained 10 lbs & seems very perky. F jr. had a blood infection some kind of "itis" that eat up the white corpuscles & he had jaundice with it. It is a new obscure ailment about which they know little or nothing but they say in 6 weeks his blood should be normal again.

Elliott dropped from the sky today just 45 hrs from Liberia to Washington. He has some kind of dysentery but they completed their mission & he has 18000 films with him. The plane fell to pieces when they made their last landing & they just got in. I'm thankful to see him but he looks thin.

The Peruvian president is here tonight & Pa just had a stag dinner for him. He brought Pa 30 pieces of old Indian pottery 4th century after Christ. . . .

The N.Y. houses are empty but rugs, linen & silver still have to be gone over at H.P. & I hope to do it the last Sunday in May with Pa. . . .

The N.Y. telephone number [at the Washington Square apartment] is Algonquin 4-2822.

. . . I've just done an article for American magazine that comes out in the July number & have finished the script to go with the book of photographs of the U.S.A. They are lovely & I hope what I wrote will go with them adequately.

. . . Write when you can.

Devotedly
Mother

". . . He did not appear . . . but has wonderful reasons . . ."

29 Washington Square West
New York, N.Y.
[Monday] May 11th [1942]

Anna darling,

Yesterday was such a grand day that I longed for you & John & the kids to be here with us. Elliott & Ruth couldn't get up till late Sat. so F jr said he'd come down to see them & we stayed here. Elliott & Ruth came down about 11.30 liked the apartment & we waited for F jr! We had lunch & he appeared at 2.45 & had to be fed! We listened to Churchill & they stayed till five so we had a grand talk & then they went off to a party together. F jr. is supposed to meet me at lunch [today, Monday] & then to come back here for the night & go with Earl to Floyd Bennett field at 6.30 am.

Later He did not appear for lunch & is not here for the night but has wonderful reasons & swears he'll be here at 6.15 a.m.! He is better but they've told him to be careful till June 1st & I wonder how careful he'll be! Elliott has had dysentery but luckily they are giving him a little leave & I think he'll soon be well. Africa was a shock to him, he can't get over the disease & filth & how the natives have been exploited. He brought back 18,000 plates & they photographed everything they went after. Almost had to come down in the desert the last day. One engine nearly dropped off 850 miles from base over the desert but it froze & hung by hair & they limped in with all landing gear gone & after landing Elliott said the plane practically fell apart. Weren't they lucky? It took him only 45 hrs. from Liberia home. . . .

I'm enclosing 2 stamps I took in change for the kids & a lock of your baby hair which John might like! I found it in an old envelope!

My love to John & the kids & a world to you,

Mother

I go to Boston tomorrow & Buffalo Wed. Washington Thursday & the week end in Miami . . . & the Farm Security Camps & I'll be back in Washington on Monday next.

". . . I forgot the President of Peru. . . ."

1600 Pennsylvania Avenue
Washington, D.C.
Tuesday May 19th [1942]

Anna darling,

. . . Elliott did come home with dysentery but he went home & when he got over dysentery he was to be operated on for piles. I wired Ruth yesterday but have had no answer as to how he is. He looked thin but not really ill. F jr. is here & out till all hours tho' he still looks badly. He ought to go back to duty June 1st & since his boat is *now* on the other side he wants to fly over, & probably will! . . . Pa says Johnnie will get sea duty on a destroyer probably soon. Poor boy!

We've had the Dutch [royalty] for a night, all the [Philippine President Manuel] Quezon family for a night & in June await the King of Greece. President Quezon was interesting & seems loyal. I forgot the President of Peru. Mr. Manuel Prado is very charming & he is now examining production. . . .

I'm rather tired because I have nothing to do these days, so I asked Pa tonight if I could do anything but it appears I can't so I guess I go to H.P. the 13th & enjoy my leisure! . . .

Mother

". . . this haunting fear day and night . . ."

Washington, D.C.
June 21st. 1942

Anna darling,

We have had a lovely visit from Jimmy and Rommie. A week ago Saturday word came that James was being sent from Midway with first hand accounts of the fight. I called Rommie and being forbidden to mention any names or facts had some trouble making her understand that I thought she had better come on here in case James was on a bomber and couldn't travel with her. Luckily she heard from him, however, and they came East together arriving after much delay on Monday evening. The reports are very interesting but sad because we are losing grand men because of inferior equipment and we are still faced with the necessity of shipping to every part of the world about 80% of our production. Our loss in ships is of course not yet announced but luckily the personnel was very largely saved. Our loss in aviators is very heavy and some of the accounts of those who came down and were rescued in their little rubber boats are really extraordinary.

James is very thin though he looks well. The doctor told him if he lost another five pounds he would have to be transferred as it was probably largely due to the heat. Naturally he doesn't want to leave his "raiders". He expects to leave on Wednesday to go back to Hawaii and about July they move to New Zealand and when the push starts they will be used to take the Solomon Islands and on from there. I like Rommie better and better, but she is an obstinate puss, and when Pa made Jimmy go to Hyde Park Friday she stayed in New York with the Sergeants. We all went to New York on Wednesday afternoon, and Pa went to Hyde Park that night. I had everyone including the Sergeants to dine and we went to a funny but rather rough show called "By Jupiter". Then to the Stage Door Canteen which is the most popular place in town with the boys. All the actresses perform and wait on tables and dance and they have achieved a miracle, namely the coloured boys guarding New York are allowed and coloured actresses act as hostesses. So far there has been no trouble which speaks volumes for the tact and good behaviour of all concerned. . . .

I came back here on Friday as I had a meeting, and Jimmy and Rommie arrived Saturday morning. Looking at him, it was hard to realize where he had been such a short time ago and where he would soon be again. I took the two to the airport this morning and saw them off with a lump in my throat. How glad I will be when this war is over and those we love just run the normal risks of living! I don't mind taxes or discomforts in transportation and I think I can take with equanimity changes in my way of living but this haunting fear day and night for so many that one loves is a difficult adjustment.

I hope I can continue to earn enough to keep the apartment in New York and the cottage because incredible as it will probably seem to you I feel just as much a visitor in the big house as ever, and while I can run it I can't live in it.

Churchill is here and Tobruk has surrendered. A serious situation for it looks more and more as though the brunt of future fighting must be on us except in Russia if they continue to be able to hold and in China. Even in these places they are dependent on our production. Somehow one wonders how Germany holds out in spite of all her preparation.

I'm here till Wednesday then I have two speeches in New York and Thursday Tommy and I go to Hyde Park. Pa comes Friday with all the Norwegians and the King of Greece. The latter stays only one night. . . .

Johnnie is very sad because he applied for sea duty and he is at the destroyer base in San Diego whereas he hoped to be on a plane carrier. Anne is expecting a baby next December and they are very pleased. . . .

Mother

". . . one feels very guilty about taking any . . . vacation . . ."

Mercer Island, Washington
July 4th [1942]

Darling—

Like a sap I've waited to write you this line until it must be posted in a Canadian port & therefore may be subject to censorship!

Believe it or not—on 4 days notice we decided to take a ten day vacation cruising with the Donoghs on their boat. With Sis & Buzz in camp, it seemed the best time to go. . . . Somehow, one feels very guilty about taking any sort of vacation these days. On the other hand, common sense certainly points toward the need for good health. Dr. O'Shea, needless to say, is tickled to death to get me out of town, & I'm tickled to death to get away from his "shots" for a while!

Last week John & I were speech-making for 2 days in Spokane. . . .

The last few weeks were hectic enough to make Johnny look up at me most wistfully one evening & ask: "Is mummy going to stay in this house for just a *little* while?" I almost wept because we had to leave for Spokane that same evening!

. . . The war is certainly not cheering, & its definitely impossible to be completely calm & relaxed when one knows of the continuing loss of human life & the chances that this will be a terribly long struggle. Sometimes when I start thinking of Jimmy & the other boys I have to make my mind move on to something else! I guess we can only hope & pray & do what we can to make sure that the results of the blood shed will be a more satisfactory existence for those who are left when the firing ceases. The sad part is that it seems to me there are still too many people figuring that the end of this war will give them their chance at last to get rid of the New Deal & the radicals, while on the other hand the dangerous radicals are working & planning for the day when our war factories & plants close & they can enlist mob sympathy. In other words, there are still too few sane, fairly unselfish & far-sighted people!

. . . Almost forgot to tell you that our radical, pacifist [housekeeping] couple left us. He got a job in a reform school. It pays less but he's happy! As a result I found entertaining house guests & other visiting firemen quite strenuous! I've now acquired a cook who is a doctor's widow. She's a bit on the ancient side but seems very nice & cooks well. I also acquired a practically decrepid [sic] 2nd maid—nice, but I fear she'll never be able to pass the soup without baptising us. Palsy is fast descending on her. Both these treasures were in the house just 24 hours when I left on this cruise, so I typed out for them all sorts of minute instructions which I hope will result in a much needed thorough house cleaning.

We go into a port every day so that we can telephone home. Otherwise, we can only pray that all stays quiet on this coast for the next 10 days & that we stay clear of those floating mines we've been warned about! . . .

How is Pa? Is he getting any restful moments at Hyde Park?

Is Missy still at the W.H. & how is she? . . .

Anna

Here is one of those letters between mother and daughter that conceals—no doubt innocently—an insight into larger-scale history. It also provides a delicious morsel of evidence of FDR's devious mind, which so often infuriated his critics, on occasion served his country extremely well, and never ceased to intrigue his biographers.

Beneath the grand design of military strategy in the Pacific and Europe, a fierce political struggle consumed the three leaders of the Western alliance, Roosevelt, Churchill and Stalin. While American and British forces were still assembling and girding for the mammoth campaigns that lay ahead, Russia was under the worst imaginable siege. The vital industrial city of Stalingrad on the banks of the Volga took such poundings by incendiary bombs of the Luftwaffe, that a newspaper, so reports say, could be read at night forty miles away. "The vital thing now," Hitler ordered his generals, is "to concentrate every available man and capture as quickly as possible the whole of Stalingrad itself and the banks of the Volga." On the same day, Moscow ordered the besieged citizen-defenders of Stalingrad to "barricade every street, transform every district, every block, every house, into an impregnable fortress."

The relief Russia needed was an invasion of Europe from the west—a second front to split the power of the Nazi war machine. The Soviet press gingerly hinted that "some British leaders" were not entirely free of the taint of Munich. Extended, the hint was that Churchill was far from eager to relieve Russia's stress: Let the Germans and Russians slaughter each other without unseemly involvement of English-speaking forces. In contrast, Roosevelt's commitment to destruction of Nazi Germany was uncompromising. He could not, however, press the issue of invasion from England any faster than Churchill would agree to go along.

In September 1942 Roosevelt's last election opponent, Wendell Willkie, announced a world tour. Roosevelt received him at the White House and outfitted the Republican leader with letters to heads of state and a large serving of inside information. Days later, in a newspaper column dispatched from Moscow, Willkie displayed the temerity to horn in on this international political struggle by publicly urging a second front to save Russia. Clearly annoyed, Roosevelt, at a press conference, derided "typewriter strategists," yet oddly went out of his way to reiterate his support of Willkie's general mission.

Roosevelt's annoyance was to become the conventional observation in accounts of the period and biographies of both men for decades to come.

Yet here we have the first evidence that, in somewhat typical fashion, FDR may have purposefully prodded Willkie into his "temerity." He frequently set ıp others to voice an "opposite" position from his own public one to help ɔuild pressure that might "force" him to make a compromising shift he ɑlready knew he wanted to make. One easily imagines at their White House meeting, Willkie expressing the urgency of a second front, and the President, with or without revealing his true intention, encouraging Willkie: "Why don't you put that in one of your columns? You have a perfect right to say it. ıt's a free country."

". . . I dined with Pa alone tonight & he says . . ."

> 1600 Pennsylvania Avenue
> Washington, D.C.
> Friday night Oct. 9th [1942]

Anna darling,

I hated to leave as always but you & John are always my best time. You send me away refreshed & reassured for you meet your problems with such honesty & courage. I think the kids must turn out alright in spite of your discouragements for I believe example is worth all the precept in the world.

. . . I dined with Pa alone tonight & he says he was pleased to have Wilkie [Willkie] speak as he did & they hope for a second front soon! When? brings no real response.

. . . I got down here today [from New York] & have just had a party for the [all-soldier] cast of "This is the Army." The boys seemed to have a wonderful time.

Now I must go to bed. Kiss all the chicks & my dearest love to John & to you.

> Devotedly
> Mother

". . . She can't get over this informal household, . . ."

> Mercer Island, Washington
> Oct. 14th [1942]

Darling Mum,

. . . I have searched this town for a smallish clock with a loudish alarm to no avail. The only kind of clocks with alarms are electric and they're a nuisance to pack. Also it isn't always easy to find an electric outlet where you want to place the clock. They tell me that all other clocks are out for the duration. Maybe there are some left in the east, nearer the manufacturing centers, but I hate to order by mail because then I can't be sure the alarm is loud enough. When Tommy gets back with you from the trip maybe she'll have time to make a few inquiries for me. All of which explains why you didn't get a package as well as a wire on your birthday! Also, you didn't give me any second choice!

Please try to find some way of letting me know where you are and how you are on your trip. [Mrs. Roosevelt was about to go to England.] Couldn't we arrange some sort of code system like Pa had on his trip? I would die if anything got out through straight messages which would be dangerous for you. At the same time I would like to half-way keep track! . . .

Everyone we've talked to, plus ourselves, thought Pa's Monday evening speech most excellent. There was much needed directness to what he had to say, and the people were longing for some "straight from the shoulder".

You gave us a terrific thrill when you wrote what you did about being with us—mostly because we've always thought of you as being *our* biggest tonic and stimulator. Somehow, and no matter how long we have been separated, there is a "click" when we get together, and a continuous clicking until we have to part once more!

Regarding Granny's Fisher fur—it is so hard to know what to say. Right now neither Sis nor I need furs. None of the girls who are Sisty's age wear furs—mostly because the climate is too mild and dress-up occasions too few. I still have my old fox which the Agnews gave me for the 1932 inauguration, and a white fox like yours which I've never worn and Granny's long brown stoll [sic] which is pretty worn. Sis has Granny's short brown stoll of mink. I also still have my childhood ermine stoll and muff and a black sealskin muff. The old Chinchilla I had died a natural death as the skins rotted. I don't even know what a Fisher fur looks like. If you think it would survive a few years of moth balls I love to have it—for either Sis or myself—with the idea of doing it over later on according to the styles of the future. If, on the other hand, you think Ruth or Anne or Rommie could use it right away, it would certainly be too bad for me to "save" it. Ethel, I imagine, has all she needs. . . .

You may be amused to know that my job at Johnny's cooperative nursery school is to collar John once every week-end and get him to help give a thorough housecleaning to the school room and playroom! This job is in lieu of helping the teachers one morning each week as most of the other mothers do. I start this coming weekend, but am not quite sure yet of my ability to corner John! . . .

Believe it or not, I've acquired a second maid. She can't get over this informal household, having last worked for the Boeings who employ a man housekeeper, butler, valet, personal maid and all the trimmings! When Mrs. Williams told her that you made your own bed when you were here, and tidied your room she almost passed out with incredulity! Nevertheless, she is well trained and endowed with good old Norwegian efficiency, and I'm hoping we can at least keep her for a breathing spell.

There's no more news—and I love you very very dearly.

Always devotedly
Anna

". . . a chance to live in the apartment a day . . ."

29 Washington Square West
New York, N.Y.
Oct. 20th [1942]

Darling,
      . . . I'm glad you didn't find the clock for Elinor Morgenthau gave me one
& the alarm will never have any effect on my slumbers! I'm wiring you
tomorrow a.m. if we get off as we now expect at 10 a.m. It was put off this
a.m. because the weather was bad tho' it has been a beautiful summer's day
here!
      My column will come out daily & the W.H. will send you any special
news.
      . . . [Tommy] hated waiting over & I've enjoyed it. Last errands done, & a
chance to live in the apartment a day & visualize what it may be like someday.
I think I will enjoy it!
      James is back from the Solomons. He may be in hospital a while & then the
marine training camp. . . .

Mother

". . . I quaked over this visit but they have been wonderfully nice . . ."

Buckingham Palace
Oct. 24th [1942]

Anna darling,
      I thought the kids might like a line from here! . . .
      I quaked over this visit but they [King George VI and Queen Elizabeth]
have been wonderfully nice & I've seen interesting people both nights at
dinner. I had tea with them alone & their two daughters, really old fashioned
nursery tea around a set table. The oldest girl [Princess Elizabeth] reminded
me of Sisty as she is about the same age tho' neither so tall nor so pretty!
Elliott came to dinner, we had a movie & talked till two a.m. He looks well
but is in for a long, hard pull I fear & I am not very happy about certain
things. He is impressed with the work of the women & the effort of every
man, woman & child in civilian work. . . .
      At three the King & Queen took me & Tommy followed with the Lady &
Gentleman in waiting & we visited St Paul's, the City, Guild Hall, Stepney
(small shops & slums) all badly blitzed & finally a large air raid shelter which
at one time housed 12,000 people & where about 300 old people sleep each
night. The column will have told you all this but I can't convey the wanton
destruction which fills you with horror.
      Henry Morgenthau came in to see me here at 6.30 & gave me many
suggestions of what to watch for on my tour which begins on Monday. . . .

These two days haven't been so bad & I hope Tommy has enjoyed them. Tomorrow morning I must get the low down on her feelings! . . .

Mother

". . . we can't have the telephone round up this year . . ."

Hyde Park
Dec. 21st [1942]

Anna darling,
I've just been told that we can't have the telephone round up this year so I hope this will reach you for Xmas. I shall be praying that you all have a very happy day together & that another year will bring us a happier world in which all of us can feel that we are building up instead of destroying. I shall feel sad not to hear all your voices, I'd have missed Elliott & Frankie anyway but it would have been grand to hear the rest of you & that has come to mean all of Xmas to me. The rest is a pretty heavy chore to be carried alone in spite of all Tommy's efficient buying & wrapping, but what has to be, has to be I guess! . . .
Tommy, poor dear, has the shingles & suffers a lot & so I left her in Washington & hope she'll get better soon because the work is heavy.
I saw Mme. Chiang [wife of Generalissimo Chiang Kai-shek] on Saturday & I am growing very fond of her. She is a wonderful person.
I also saw Cousin Susie & must see her again Wednesday because she is so miserable. It must be awful only to enjoy the company of doctors & do as little & enjoy as few people as she does. I asked her to come to Washington but she won't move from 76th St. . . .

Devotedly
Mother

". . . Pa took my breath away . . ."

1600 Pennsylvania Avenue
Washington, D.C.
Jan. 2d, 1943

Anna darling,
. . . I'm sure the kids were happy, they don't anticipate disasters. I wake up in the night, & imagine every horror & can't go to sleep again. . . .
Pa took my breath away too by his magnificent gifts to the grandchildren but he'd bought no [war savings] bonds so got his whole quota this way.
Tommy is better but still bothered with a pain from the shingles. I suppose she needs a rest but she won't take it!

. . . No word from Frankie except a wild story that he led a landing party a little while ago which I can hardly believe.

Much, much love darling,
Mother

———————————

In a manner that Eleanor would not have expected, the war invaded the marriage of Anna and John Boettiger.

John, the complete romantic, so inseparable from Anna, so fused to her that he always capitalized the word "US," signing his letters, "Your 50%er" or "Your Other Half," shocked his wife with news that he craved to go off to war. He was forty-three years old, far beyond draft age. He held an important job that contributed to the national war effort. If he left it, how could Anna keep hers? For what would she stay in Seattle? What would her life be about? What was he trying to prove? Why unnecessarily smash their home?

Their trouble seemed to run deeper than his patriotic urge, rooting earlier than Pearl Harbor, and its reasons more puzzling. "All we know for sure," their son wrote decades later, are "the increasing worries she had about John beginning around 1940," and the reappearance of "a pattern of depressive experience that my father had known periodically for most of his life. . . . Returning now at a critical time in his marriage and his working life, that endemic distress must have begun to evoke a natural impulse to escape the pain. And that, in time, bode ill for his and Anna's future together."

John's dark moods, unsignaled outbursts, withdrawals from family and work, caused Anna to consult their physician, Dr. O'Shea, who suggested that John seek the help of a psychiatrist. John rejected the step as unthinkable, regarding psychiatrists as fakes whose trade should be practiced, if at all, on the crazed.

In earlier pages, particularly in letters to his infant son, we have already caught intimate glimpses of insecurities and fears that haunted John, and of the shells he carefully fashioned to conceal his fears. Now for eight years, so in need of believing in his own worth and significance, this man had basked in the reflected light—what his son was to call the "derivative power and prominence"—of being husband to the daughter of the most powerful and magnetic figure in the world of power.

The perils of deriving too large a measure of one's self-esteem from another came home one night in January 1943. Anna and John prolonged a Christmas visit to the White House to await the return of FDR from his dramatic conference with Winston Churchill at Casablanca. On his first night home, the President, alone with his daughter and son-in-law, ignited them with vignettes of the high drama, freshly experienced, vividly told.

In a later letter to Anna, John re-created the tantalizing moment. He exclaimed to FDR: "I'd give my eye teeth to go along on a trip like that."

That couldn't be done, the President said regretfully.

For each of these historic trips, the President had arranged the company of one or more of his sons.

"Why not?" the son-by-marriage boyishly pressed.

Without warning, from out of the dark, came the fatal thrust: *"Well, you are not in uniform!"* (The italics and exclamation point, it's worth noting, are John's, written months later.)

The President may have intended a far-from-personal fine point in White House public relations. John, however, prickled with the shame of rebuke by the nation's commander in chief. The shabby threads of his civilian suit exposed him as less than a man.

"I won't say that one remark of his did it," John later reminded Anna in his letter, "but it went farther than any or *all* influences that did make my mind up."

Before returning to Seattle with Anna, John got off a letter to an influential military man he came to know when covering Washington—General Dwight D. Eisenhower, now in North Africa. Eisenhower was building a staff for major operations ahead, and perhaps John could be commissioned and join it.

Anna recited encouraging words—and bit her lip. "My main trouble," she later said to John, "was that from the moment you wrote that letter to your friend in North Africa, I began to suffer acutely. I seemed to know all too accurately what it was going to be like when you left. . . . There was nothing I could do to get 'the ants out of your pants'—without running the possibility of hurting US permanently. . . . Uppermost in my mind was a dread that if I tried to adamantly dissuade you from going into the army, you might sometime regret it so much that you would feel down deep inside of you that I had been wrong. . . . Maybe I was wrong not to have told you all I was thinking and dreading—but I just couldn't."

Before leaving Washington, apparently she conveyed some of her dread to her mother.

". . . & the women are always held by 'appendages'! . . ."

> 1600 Pennsylvania Avenue
> Washington, D.C.
> Sat Feb. 6th [1943]

Anna darling,

The days slip by so fast that you & John must be nearly home. I hated to see you go for I know that having John consider going off ends something very close & precious which you two have had & one can't help feeling these days that happiness hangs by such a slender thread any move may tear it apart. Yet always men have had the urge for adventure & fared forth & the women are always held by "appendages"! . . .

> [letter incomplete—lacks signature]

"... *Many women working & enthusiastic* ..."

> 1600 Pennsylvania Avenue
> Washington, D.C.
> Feb. 9th [1943]

Darling,

... Sunday, we spent 3 hrs at the Naval Hospital [in Boston] & then I went to see Missy [in her hometown of Somerville, Massachusetts]. She doesn't seem to me much changed & I could see no improvement in speech.

We reached Portland at 9 p.m. & were taken at once to see the night shift at the shipyards. Many women working & enthusiastic about their jobs. 8 a.m. Monday off to Camden, Maine & it was beautiful. Not too cold & a clear blue sky & sun on the water. I christened the barge & myself! Back to Boston & the midnight to N.Y.

... Tommy stood up well under all this & sends her love.

James wired yesterday so I called him from Boston & said goodbye. He sounded very down & I couldn't be very cheerful either. ...

I miss you very much.

> Mother

"... *Pa is a little afraid of Mme. Chiang* ..."

> 1600 Pennsylvania Avenue
> Washington, D.C.
> Feb. 21st [1943]

Anna darling,

... John won't hear for a while I imagine as I imagine Gen. Eisenhower is having a bad time just now. I can't bear to think of the boys we've lost. ...

Mme. Chiang [wife of Generalissimo Chiang Kai-shek] arrived here last Wed. p.m. & she did a wonderful job in Congress but it tires her very much & arranging for her is not easy. I like her so much & I think I am going to China soon, perhaps next summer or early autumn.

Tommy has been much bothered by a kind of acute neuritis in her left leg & left hand. She takes shots every day & I hope will soon be better but she doesn't sound enthusiastic about long trips!

My visit to the WAAC'S [Womens Auxiliary Army Corps] last Sunday & Monday seemed to be a great success but it was very cold. They are being well trained. I spoke at two universities & had big audiences tho' I have no idea how much they agreed with me!

Pa is a little afraid of Mme. Chiang & yet he likes her I think. She stays till the 2d I imagine when she goes to speak in N.Y. ...

> Mother

". . . She . . . wants to nail them down & they squirm. . . ."

1600 Pennsylvania Avenue
Washington, D.C.
Feb. 28th Sunday [1943]

Anna darling,

Pa has been feeling rather miserable since Wed. tho' yesterday & today he's had no fever & he never had over 100.2. Dr. McIntire thought he'd eaten something but I don't think he knows! This afternoon he's up & just now talking to Mme. Chiang. In a queer way I think the men are afraid of her. She is keen & drives for her point & wants to nail them down & they squirm. Tommy doesn't like the nephew & niece & I don't think she quite likes or trusts her but I think it is because she feels an oriental is inscrutable! I like & trust her but perhaps I'm wrong. They leave tonight & I wonder how she is going to stand the trip. We went to Mt. Vernon last Monday & she liked the house & grounds & said the fields might be in China & the little outbuildings made it a little like a Chinese compound. We had a Cabinet tea in the afternoon & she talked to Pa in the evening & listened to his broadcast. I, of course went to the Democrat dinner & drove around town for 15 minutes in the middle to observe a blackout, with the Commissioners. I liked Pa's speech [opening the Red Cross fund drive], how did you & John feel about it?

Tuesday, I flew to N.Y. & saw F jr. at the Navy Yard but couldn't get on his ship as it was about to go in dry dock so we went on the Iowa & saw Capt. McRae. That ship is enormous. I had tea & cocktails for the officers & wives & left them all in the apartment when I left at 6.40 for the airport. . . .

Wed. Mme. Chiang had a press conference with me & in the p.m. we had one with the magazine press arranged by O.W.I. [Office of War Information]. Mme. C. had pictures taken on the lawn, some alone & some with me & I've ordered enough of those together to give each of you kids as I thought it might be historically interesting. The V.P. & Mrs. Wallace had a lunch for the wives of all the South & Central American representatives & I think if I kept on travelling steadily, I might cover the places I am asked to visit! Dick Neuberger [conservationist-author and future senator from Oregon] was here today & wants me to go over the Alaskan Highway & see the soldiers this summer & if you & I & John could go, I might try to do that.

Thurs. Fri. & Sat. I was in N.Y. & the column will have told you what I did. I do love getting to the apartment & away from the strain of the W.H. tho' I was busy all the time. . . . I had tea with Cousin Susie who is just discovering rationing & thinks it terrible! . . .

Have you & the kids seen Walt Disney's "Saludos Amigos"? It is delightful. . . .

Has John heard anything yet? I don't suppose so for the Gen. [Eisenhower] must have been busy. I'm thankful things are better. Stalin's speech seemed to me arrogant & unwise but I suppose it was for home effect & I confess that Joe Stalin's [obviously an error; she probably means Joseph P. Kennedy] openly saying that he feared Russia & hoped the Russians & Germans would kill each other off seems to me to justify Stalin's attitude. We can't take it for granted that we are the only trustworthy people in the world & we must believe in other people's intelligence & good intentions if we expect them to believe in us. That doesn't mean that we need to be weak either. . . .

> Devotedly
> Mother

". . . I don't mind spending hours on people I love but . . ."

> 1600 Pennsylvania Avenue
> Washington, D.C.
> March 14th [1943]

Anna darling,

Tommy, I hope, sent you what looks like a final itinerary & I hope it doesn't appal you. I'll get to San Francisco but I may not get back to Los Angeles after meeting Father because my income tax is so large & I spent more than I should last year so I'll have to be saving this year!

Father says it isn't time to go to China & Russia now & he hopes I believe to meet Stalin & Chiang this summer in or near Alaska (& we might go along) & wants to do so before I go to their countries.

Eden [Sir Anthony Eden, British Foreign Secretary] is here now. Last night Pa had a long conference & tonight an informal but distinguished dinner is being given. Pa seems pleased with all that they discussed. . . .

Dorothy Roosevelt [a distant cousin and contemporary] has been here 4 days & had 2 friends staying & people in for all meals till I grew a bit weary of them all! It is horrid of me. I don't mind spending hours on people I love but it seems such a waste when you don't care much.

I begin to feel we'll soon be together only a little over two weeks off & I am looking forward to a big hug! My love to John & the kids. I hate to miss everyone's birthday. A world of love

> Mother

For more than two months—January to March—John Boettiger chafed at the silence from his old friend Eisenhower. As his impatience mounted, so did Anna's tension. She remained torn between the devotion of a traditional woman to her husband's wants and ambitions, and her continued resistance to his insufficiently explained urge to go.

In March, John flew to Washington to force matters to a yes or no. He arrived at the White House during a small dinner for British Foreign Secretary Anthony Eden. The President greeted him ebulliently:

"Have you taken your physical?"

Wondering why the President would want to taunt him at such a moment, John replied that he yet hoped to. The President turned proudly to his guests and announced that General Eisenhower had requested John's services—in the army, in North Africa! Eisenhower had stipulated, however, that John was not to serve on the general's personal staff, lest political critics charge favoritism for a First Family member.

"I can't tell you," John wrote Anna, "how perfectly wonderful your Father has been! He has just about overwhelmed me with kindness and help! . . . Never has he gone so far in *wanting* to do things for me!"

Earlier in March, General George C. Marshall, army chief of staff, observed to the President that John's background best suited him as a civil affairs officer—one who helps govern occupied territories. John was commissioned a captain and was assigned for several weeks of indoctrination at the Army's School for Military Government on the campus of the University of Virginia in Charlottesville.

"*. . . [They] . . . thought it meant at least a year . . .*"

Hotel St. Francis
San Francisco
Thursday [April 8, 1943]

Anna darling,
The days in Seattle were nice & I enjoyed Sunday very much. I'm glad John knows what you are up against, it makes it simpler in the long run. . . .
Johnny [Roosevelt] has word that he may go soon & Anne is much upset & seems to feel it is Pa's doing & yet I remember when John asked to go to a carrier. They've just moved & are comfortable & it was expensive & Anne thought it meant at least a year so it is hard. The world really is pretty bad for all you young things! . . .

Mother

"*. . . Men are always little boys . . .*"

Ambassador
Los Angeles
Easter Sunday [April 26, 1943]

Anna darling,
. . . I'll always be on hand these next few months I hope when you need me. Men are always little boys I guess & strange mixtures! . . .

Devotedly
Mother

". . . Pa now thinks I can go . . ."

29 Washington Square West
New York, N.Y.
Monday May 31st [1943]

Anna darling,

I've been hoping for news but if none is in Washington when I get back today I'm going to telephone you & then send John a cable. The move into Europe should start soon & I think John would like some news before the excitement becomes so great no personal wires get over.

The weather at H.P. was wonderful & the country lovely & Pa seemed very happy & slept 10 hrs both nights. He got there Friday a.m. with the Crown Princess [Marta, of Norway] & Mme. Ostgaard & Harry Hopkins & Tully [Grace Tully, FDR's secretary since Missy's illness]. I got there for lunch, as I spent Thursday at Arthurdale [a rural self-help housing project in West Virginia]. I stayed at the Cottage as I had just opened it. . . . We all had tea at Pa's [Hilltop] cottage Sat. p.m. . . .

Pa now thinks I can go . . . to the S. West Pacific about August 10th & I think I will go alone. I don't like to take up space unnecessarily & Tommy I know isn't keen about it. . . .

Dr. McIntyre [McIntire] is West this week & I hope will bring back some real news of James. I've had very little so far.

Dot [Mrs. Roosevelt's favorite horse at Hyde Park] is looking very thin but Natomah still looks well & so does Badger. The three horses the Army is loaning us seem nice & a four year old mare is pretty & very gentle.

Earl & Simone [Earl Miller's third wife] & the baby come to me for 5 or 6 days on the 20th. Queen Wilhelmina [of the Netherlands] is coming a Sunday soon & I hope she decides soon!

Love to the chicks & a big hug to you darling,

Mother

". . . with specific instructions from Mr. Hearst . . ."

[The carbon copy of this letter is damaged. Bracketed fragments of words in the fifth and sixth paragraphs are surmised from context to be the missing fragments. B.A.]

June 1, 1943

Dearest Mum:

Enclosed are some Hearst-ish colored so-called news stories which I would like some authentic information about. We ran both of these stories in the Post-Intelligencer, and you would be simply amazed at the mountainous sheaves of material of this sort which comes in over our wires every day. Much of it comes with specific instructions from Mr. Hearst as to where he wants it run.

I feel that for the present anyway I can handle his campaigns to have the war concentrated in the Pacific and against communism in Russia, in this country and in France, but I don't have the information to answer the charges being made by the Dies Committee concerning the War Relocation Authority, nor the background of the reasons for the special House Investigating Committee which is looking into the O.P.A. [Office of Price Administration, the wartime price control agency] setup.

Here on the paper, I am running into arguments that too many communistic individuals and groups are backing the grade labeling program of the O.P.A. and that, therefore, the O.P.A. must be wrong.

Is there any way that you can get for me a satisfactory reason as why the War Labor Board delayed for ten months its Boeing wage decision. About two and one-half to three months ago the Boeing workers walked out for a day to hold a protest meeting. The decision then came very fast. I am still being asked this question from the standpoint of whether the War Labor Board is as efficient as it should be, and would just like to have some background knowledge.

Could you also find out something for me regarding the thousands [of] acres, including several towns, which the Army has taken over surroundi[ng the] town of Pasco, Washington. I understand that some sort of huge Du Pont [pro]ject is to go in there and of course, I am not asking for any military [secrets.] On the other hand, there is a rumor going around that sixteen or sevent[een] thousand negroes are to be moved into this district and many groups in [the] state are just waiting the chance to protest. No one seems to know whe[ther] the negroes will be civilians or soldiers. All of the normal inhabitant[s of] this huge area have been ordered out.

. . . What is the administration's policy concerning "doub[tful"] Japanese? Naturally, this question is an extremely hot one out here.

Lots of Love,
[Anna]

"*. . . read your letter to Pa last night . . .*"

The White House
June 7, 1943

Dearest Anna:
I read your letter to Pa last night and am getting from the War Labor Board, the background for the Boeing decision. It was a decision which effected the whole industry and Pa thinks that was the reason for the delay. However, I am sending you the facts.

I am getting a memo from the War Relocation Authority and will forward it to you. I can tell you, however, that as far as food goes in those relocation camps, the only true statement is that they do get it from the Army Quartermaster Corps. They do not get the same food as the men in the Army, they get the same rations as other people. The day I was at the camp in

Arizona, there was no sugar, no butter and no coffee. They had fish and a green vegetable for lunch and again for supper. Strange as it may seem to some people, the Japanese do not like coffee—they drink tea.

Pa says that the OPA labelling is the same old fight and that gradually through the years, legislation has been passed which obliged people to put the amount on a package. The housewife has always been the one who was fooled. The packages looked the same in size, but Bill Smith's package would contain one ounce less than Bill Jones'. The advertisers hate labelling and are opposed to it because it cramps their style. The competition between poor manufacturers of food-stuffs and other goods and the good ones is so great that they all join together in opposition to labelling because it would mean they would have to tell the truth about everything we bought. As to its being communist individuals and groups who back a good labelling program, that is just the usual type of nonsense. The old Consumers League started on this years ago. When Tugwell [Rexford G. Tugwell, an early presidential adviser] was assistant secretary of Agriculture, in order to help this program along, he had a wonderful exhibition which I think was here when you were in Washington. Don't you remember the story of the hair dye which was used and which blinded a woman and disfigured her because the contents were not properly labelled? There undoubtedly are some groups that are classed as communist groups who are back of this, that is the kind of accusation that is always made.

Pa says the Pasco, Washington thing is some of the most secret work of the Army and they had to put it as far away as possible from other places. That is why this place was chosen and it displaced comparatively few people.

Pa says the tale about the Negroes is just bunk. . . .

I think the things taken out of Galbraith's book on advertising are, of course, all absolutely true. A free press is not maintained by free advertising. In fact, as you know, advertising has frequently controlled the press. Advertising which isn't honest, and it frequently isn't, should be controlled by the government and that is why in certain important things, the government should vouch for the truth by the labelling on a package or a garment. . . .

[Mother]

———————————

Out of the darkness of John's departure, one ray of excitement for Anna had been her anticipation of working at the newspaper on her own authority—for the first time in her life, nurturing and testing her own professional abilities, without trading on her father's prominence or her husband's position as publisher.

To substitute for John, Hearst had appointed Charles Lindeman as acting publisher. Perhaps Lindeman was uneasy with Anna's accustomed free-form authority as associate editor (and Mrs. Publisher); perhaps with the liberties the Boettigers had taken with Hearst's normally anti-Roosevelt editorial policies. In any case, John had scarcely waved good-bye when Lindeman proceeded to "clarify" Anna's position, virtually "clarifying" her out of any autonomy whatsoever.

Reticent to heap the details upon John—now adjusting to a strange military existence in North Africa—Anna unburdened to her mother, seeking support, and getting it.

"... it won't be a failure, just a strategic retreat! ..."

> Val-Kill Cottage
> Hyde Park
> Saturday night June 12th [1943]

Anna darling,

... I think you are having a dreadful time & I think all the men [of the Hearst management] have been pretty two faced with you & John all these years. I have complete contempt for Charlie Lindeman, why didn't he "clarify" the situation when he & John & you all were with W.R.? Well, you are a wonder, if you succeed it will be wonderful & if you have to give it up it won't be a failure, just a strategic retreat!

I know just what you mean about John's letters. Somehow, they can't give you a warm, close feeling when they have to be so guarded. . . .

Saturday Queen Wilhelmina comes & I have to stay at the big house. There is quite an entourage & they'll be here till Tuesday. . . . The 1st I come up again with Pa & the norwegians & I leave the night of the 4th. . . .

Mme. Chiang gave me a small jade ring for you the last time I saw her. She says jade stands for steadfastness.

Not a word from Elliott or F jr. & I do hope all is well. . . .

> Devotedly
> Mother

I sent John [Boettiger] a cable & a letter.

"... Every [day] I live I become more convinced ..."

> Tumbling D.W. Ranch
> Franktown, Nevada.
> Thursday, July 8th. [1943]

Anna darling,

... Having a job when everything goes haywire at home is bad, but under the present situation it must be awful. Lindeman sounds very fishy to me. How is he to do the job of printing all the things you don't like and still keep you satisfied by being tactful.

This is rather a lovely spot. . . . This afternoon in fear [and] trembling I shall try a ride. Tomorrow I shall probably not be able to sit down.

I have a nice room with a porch where Trude [Pratt, Joseph Lash's wife-to-be] and I sit much of the time. I had a press conference this morning as they heard I was here and it was as well for a rumour was about that you were here getting a divorce and if I had not scotched that John might have had a disagreeable shock in Africa. I carefully said I had just stopped for a few days rest and was not visiting anyone in particular.

I'll be with you soon now. I have some interesting things to tell you about Jimmy and Rommie. Every [day] I live I become more convinced that the human animal is the most interesting study in the world. There is never anything predictable about people even when you think you know them. . . .

Devotedly,
Mother

". . . It is a secret but Churchill . . . come[s] here the 12th. . . . I leave . . . the 17th . . ."

Val-Kill Cottage
Hyde Park
Sunday, Aug. 1st [1943]

Anna darling,
   . . . I left Washington last Monday night. I loved seeing Elliott but I felt Ruth was entitled to him as much alone as she could have him & you know fundamentally we think so little alike on many things that tho' I love him, I have to be careful when with him & that means that short visits are better than long ones! I hope they'll come here before I leave however.
   . . . Thursday night, I called Pa & before I had a chance to speak he announced "Frankie is all right." He had known since the night before but had forgotten to call me or Ethel! Five men were killed & six wounded on board & I'm sure F. will feel badly & I'll be happier if we ever hear from him because he may have some after results.
   It is a secret but Churchill, his wife & daughter all come here the 12th. Pa was here Sat. & left in the p.m. in high spirits to fish in Lake Huron till the 8th or 10th, then he returns to Washington & comes here the 12th. I leave . . . for S.F. the a.m. of 16th[,] [then] 11 p.m. the 17th for the trip [to visit armed services hospitals and bases in the Pacific]. I should be back Sept. 17th or 19th, is there a chance you might be there with Sisty? All seems settled & I'll send you an itinerary when I get it & then we'll hope all goes well & I do a good job.
   . . . Today Walter Reuther [a rising young leader of the CIO-United Auto Workers, later to become its president] came for the day. He is much the most interesting labor leader I've met & I hope you meet him. He spent 2 yrs. with a younger brother bicycling around the world & earning their way. He's been to such out of the way places as Baluchistan [in Pakistan], worked a year in Russia & they averaged spending .50 a day on their travels! Now he's dreaming dreams of the Postwar World & you would find him interesting. . . .

I've begun to write my extra columns for the days when I can't file, 4 are done but I suppose I should write ten or twelve or fourteen!

I must go to bed. Write when you can. . . .

Mother

P.S. Did you get any cable from John?

Shortly after Eleanor Roosevelt departed for her historic month-long tour of Pacific war bases and hospitals, the following letter from John Boettiger arrived in her White House mail and was opened by Tommy.

The letter was deeply disturbing—to Tommy, to Anna, and both knew it would be to Eleanor when she returned. The letter's length, its relentless repetition and often bizarre rationalizations bespeak John's brittle state of mind—and his dismay at having left Anna's side, voluntarily. An extraordinary emotional dependence had been evident between them since their first love letters. John's side of that dependence explodes here in full force; but alas, less splendidly than in earlier days.

John's certainty that, despite an ocean of physical separation, he and Anna "FEEL each other's thoughts" is not accurate, as we learn in Anna's letter to Tommy (and, indirectly, to Eleanor) that follows. Clearly Anna is worried about the state of his mind—and his misreading of hers.

". . . you above all people understands US as no one else. . . ."

AMGOT—15th/ARMY GROUP
APO 777—Postmaster NYC
August 13th, 1943.

Dearest LL:

I have just received your letter of July 18. . . . You didn't say a great deal, but from what you wrote, and from between the lines of [Anna's] letters, I believe I know the situation.

I want to give you some very brief chronological information, because it appears that Anna and I have separately reached the same conclusion, and I think it is important (for the future) that we all realize that independently of each other we arrived at that point. Of course, I believe firmly that we are so much a part of each other that our subconscious thoughts constantly speed back and forth, and while we don't have the black and white facts of what goes on, we FEEL each other's thoughts. I can write plainly to you in the full confidence that you above all people understands US as no one else.

. . . On Monday I sat down and wrote to Anna my thoughts on my general situation, my reactions to what I have been able to accomplish thus far, and comparisons on what I could be accomplishing were I continuing my work before entering this phase.

I wound up by expressing the view that I still could be of much greater service, ALL AROUND, were I to get into a situation where Anna and I could work together. I pointed out that it didn't really matter where that was, London or Rome or South America or Washington, but that I wanted desperately to bring it about. Neither of us is giving to the war effort, separately, what we could give jointly, and I fully realize now what a tragic error it was, in every way, to attempt anything differently. This being true, it seems to me, as I set it down in the letter, that we ought to try to do something to correct the situation. As to the method, quite frankly I haven't any specific thoughts, except one which I will get to later in this letter. If she could obtain an assignment which would bring her to some point abroad where I might be permanently assigned during the war, it would be grand for us, altho difficult because of the children. It might be simpler from the pssob [the family's bawdy abbreviation, of uncertain translation, to denote advantages and costs of being the President's son-in-law] end of it, also, but it is really quite complicated and I don't think it would work. Many things would have to be done at both ends of the picture.

. . . I received a long letter from Anna dated July 12 and July 13, in which she discussed the problem, but more from a defeatist point of view, and possibly with the thought that nothing could be worked out. But she KNOWS, from my letters, that things haven't worked out over here in such a way as to make me feel I am making anything like the sort of contribution I had anticipated, nor anything like the service I was giving, and still could give, under other circumstances.

Then I returned to my post yesterday, and was overjoyed to find 21 letters and two cables from Anna, and the letter from you. Up until that time I had gotten NOTHING from her except a few V-mail letters which were quite non-committal and unrevealing. I haven't yet read all of her letters, but I have read enough to understand the whole picture, and I don't think there is any sense at all, from any standpoint, for us to continue in a frustrated way, IF there is something that can be done about it.

So far as I am concerned, were I unattached, and with no particular feeling that my experience and past work has fitted me for certain things, nothing could give me greater pleasure than to follow through with the work I am doing. It is exciting, interesting. But great heavens, there are greater responsibilities on my shoulders than to seek excitement. It may be difficult for you to believe that I had a completely different picture of what my contribution might be over here, but I did honestly feel that I could give a bigger service, and if I didn't feel that I wouldn't have, COULDN'T have, come. As it has worked out the bigger job hasn't developed, and in all frankness, I can see the reasons for this. Part of it is pssob, but there is also rank, and there is also the fact that the army is vastly different from business and works differently.

I don't want to imply that I have flopped on the job, and at the risk of seeming immodest, I think I can say that I have fitted in well, have been well up on the operational end of my work, and that my colleagues and senior officers would say I had performed creditably. But sizing it all up after three months over here, and a month in active service doing the job, I can see most plainly that I can never achieve the degree of contribution in this field which I could do elsewhere. This much of it entirely on my own single contribution.

But when you add to that the plain fact that Anna and I can do so much more as a *team*, it does seem tragic to *waste* our resources.

Now I realize that we are only two minor people in a huge world, which will flounder along somehow regardless of what happens to us two, and I am also aware of the complicating factors which would be involving [sic] in approaching the matter. But I do want you to know the whole picture, because I know how precious one half of that team is to you, and I know too of your devotion to me.

Maybe we will simply have to grit our teeth and live through it. As you say, war will leave its mark on both of us, but so far as I am concerned, I will not change fundamentally, nor ever have my whole-hearted loyalty and fidelity and COMPLETE devotion to Anna changed in any respect. I am sure you know that. I know she will never change in the same fundamental respect. But I am gravely worried that she will suffer so, physically and mentally, as to make that mark of war you speak of actually wreck the future.

Now that is something which we cannot, MUST NOT, permit to happen. I believe there are times when these personal problems must weigh heavier in the scales than petty political problems, and I speak advisedly when I say petty. I mean to say that there will not be any adverse reaction of sufficient importance to really matter if something is done to correct this situation.

I happen to know that a Lieut. Col. Hammond, brother of Bud, went to N. Africa and after a month or so of active service, was ordered to Washington on the civil affairs staff of Gen. Hildring, who is in charge of that department. I know that my intimate knowledge of problems which have arisen here in the field, and at headquarters, would make me valuable in the same way, perhaps even more so than in Hammond's case.

Is there any reason, from any viewpoint, why some such thing shouldn't be worked out? I am asking this as a question, because I am many miles away, and alone, and of course have discussed it with no one. Will you think about it, from all sides of the picture, the present, the future, discuss it with Anna, and then if you want to and can, take whatever steps are indicated. As I have thought it out, over all these months, something should be done, and I say to you frankly I want it done.

I have to assume full responsibility for the situation, and I do so, ruefully. I should have had more sense, more comprehension. War does queer things to people's thoughts and emotions. Certainly I have learned a lesson, and a lesson which may be terribly bitter and even ruinous as time goes on. If amends can be made, I will be ever so grateful, but I do want you to know I realize I have no right to ask it for myself. I did it with my eyes supposedly open, and I ought to be old enough and experienced enough to have weighed the possibilities. I just wasn't! I ought to be permitted to add that I was led by at least one other person (over here) to believe it was my duty to do this, and that I could make a real contribution. That person just didn't have the facts upon which to make a decision, and I should have known that, too.

Well, there it all is. I hope you won't think too badly of me. I am counting on you to help decide what is right, and to insist on such a course being worked out. Whatever may transpire, I will always be doing my level best, in my job and in my conduct, to try to live up to the great blessings which God has given me when he gave me these years with Anna. I know my unworthiness, all the more these days, but I'm a-tryin'.

This has been such a long letter that I'd better chop it off. I do want you to know that mail is a real problem. I am up at dawn to write this because an officer is bound for the other side, where this letter can be mailed. There are facilities here, but they are indirect, and will delay transmission a long time, to a point where we have always waited until we encounter an officer going over.

I don't think there is any excuse for mail being delayed so wretchedly in delivery to us, but it is one of the misfortunes of war, I guess. The mail I received yesterday has been laying around on this island for at least two weeks that I know of, but I couldn't locate it. I believe it will get better immediately, but there are plans for me which will start the same mail difficulties all over again. So don't try to give me reactions with the thought of getting my opinions. I have written plainly enough here so that you know how I feel, and I am content to rely upon your judgment and Anna's. Whatever you do will have my fullest assent, as I am sure you know without my need to say it.

If it is ever possible—which I doubt—I will have a talk with the same friend I originally wrote to, and see if he has any suggestions. I don't think he will have; in fact, I am rather certain he couldn't do anything in any case, unless it would be to arrange for me to be ordered to a convenient post where the *team* could function. But that would have to be in this theater, and I can't see how that would be practicable.

I haven't mentioned a certain person with heavy responsibilities, but you and he know I am always thinking of him, and I have not been unmindful of him in my thoughts expressed here. I have tried to say things in a discreet way, which accounts for a somewhat cryptic style. I'm sure you understand!

Physically I am very well indeed, have the appetite of a horse, sleep well though not many hours because of the pressure of work, and for that work I am deeply grateful for obvious reasons. I will have MUCH to tell you all whenever I do see you.

My love to Tommy and my grateful and devoted love to you always, Darling.

Yours,
John

". . . God knows I'm not enjoying this separation business. But, . . ."

Seattle Post-Intelligencer
August 30, 1943

Tommy dear:
 . . . So far, all of the newspaper accounts I have seen of mother's trip have been friendly. This morning we ran her first column explaining about her trip. I hope she won't run into too many difficulties in getting the column written and filed from now on.

. . . Now as to John. I'm so glad you read the letter he wrote to mother. Yesterday I received the letter he wrote me in the same vein. . . . His present feelings make me sad as God knows I'm not enjoying this separation business. But, I have written him previously and will again, that I don't see how we can get together until hostilities are over in Europe. After that, there may be a chance that he can get a transfer or that I can take Johnny and get some sort of a job over there, either in the reporting field or in Lehman's [soon to go into business as United Nations Relief and Rehabilitation Administration] outfit. And, of course if the war in Europe lasts into next summer, there is always the chance that he may get a leave. But, this I would doubt. John's letters, written since his first one to me on this subject and which arrived way ahead of the first, acknowledges that the three children present great difficulties. Also, from what he's written, I think he realizes that if he hadn't gone into the army he might have felt that he had missed something, and not been happy with that situation either. So—its just one of those Godawful war problems! I don't think that any mention of all this should be made to F.D. at present. I do think that John could put in a request, through regular channels over there to be transferred to the Military Govt. division in the War Dept.—but not until he has had 8 months or so of active duty abroad. At that time, it may be necessary to take it up with F.D. as there is always this business of Army and Navy officials who are afraid to do anything regarding members of the family for fear it will be construed as special privelege.

Tommy, save this part of this letter for E.R. . . . Also, I'd appreciate it if you had the time to give me your own thoughts. It is so true that I have no one out here with whom I can discuss the thing completely openly. In fact, you and Ma are the only ones I know of!

. . . Love from us all to you—and an extra bucket full from me.

Anna

". . . but Pa would do nothing about bringing John home . . ."

White House
Monday, Sept. 27th [1943]

Anna darling,

Your letter, enclosing John's came this morning & I think you have done the right thing & I will write him. If he gets assigned somewhere possible for you to join him then we can ask Pa for a little special influence & you'll have to turn the kids over to me for a time but Pa would do nothing about bringing John home or getting him to a place where you could join him. . . .

I'm glad you liked the Guadacanal cemetery column, it was a moving sight. Joe [Lash] was fine, tho' atabrine makes everyone a bit yellow. . . . Of course he longs to come home & get married but like many others he must wait & pray & work! . . .

I doubt if it would do much good to have anyone talk to Harry [Hopkins] or Pa about the trip but I find Judge [Under Secretary of War Robert P.]

Patterson told Mr. [Bernard M.] Baruch [a financier, established informally as an "adviser to presidents"] I did a wonderful job & that will help. Pa asked me more questions than I expected & actually came over to lunch with me Saturday & spent two hours!

I am still weary but slowly getting rested. . . . Much love darling,

Mother

I found this check in a pocketbook of Granny's. Have you carried it all these years?

"*. . . Anna wrote . . . that we couldnt expect [FDR] to understand (as you would), . . .*"

Oct. 19, 1943

Dearest L.L.—

I have just come from a visit with Henry [Morgenthau] at the General's HQ and he has agreed to carry this back to you. We are both going up to the front tomorrow morning and he is leaving afterward, so I am jotting down my latest thoughts to you before going to bed for a few hours.

It was good to see Henry, but he was so weary that I couldnt get much out of him about family matters. I left him in his regal bedroom at the palace, about to go to sleep under a *crucifix,* so he ought to rest well! Maybe I'll get more out of him tomorrow.

He told me you had hinted to him I was not happy out here. I have always felt Henry was a loyal friend so I told him the truth and the facts. He had no suggestions and I rather gathered he felt there was nothing which we could do.

Maybe he is right, but as I said to him something may turn up which will make it perfectly natural for me to take an army job which will let me work with Anna. At that, and as well as Henry knows us, I gathered that his reaction might have been, inwardly, that I was not being "sacrificial" and (though he said nothing directly) that these aren't times to consider personal relationships.

I tried to make it clear that if I were permitted to do a job of sufficient importance to justify the sacrifice, I should not complain, and also that I felt there must be a job somewhere in this war effort—over on this side or at home—which Anna and I could do more or less together. But as I say I dont think it registered with Henry. I dont know whether you expressed your own opinion to Henry on the subject. He said no more about your feeling than that you had said I wasnt happy here.

I am sure that you and Anna have talked it over and probably a letter from you is on the way. Naturally I am keen to know your reactions.

I did tell Henry that he should not disclose my feelings to F.D.; that if he wanted to he might tell him what my General (the AMG Commander who was here also and who apparently said some pleasant things about my work) had to say about me and to let it go at that. Anna wrote me that she felt it would serve no good purpose to take the matter directly to F.D.; that we couldnt expect him to understand (as you would), and that it would just serve to lessen his feelings toward me.

I do hope earnestly that you dont look on me as one unwilling to suffer and face danger and rough living. I havent risked my skin foolishly, of course, but I have been in the thick of things and I have enjoyed the excitement and thrill of it. I came ashore on the beach at Paestum with the assaulting troops, was the first AMG officer of Fifth Army to land in Italy, dodged machinegun and bomb fire from German planes during that first day and the next several days. I slept on the ground with not even a blanket, and in the first ten days, which as you know, was touch and go on our side, I was up with the forward HQ of the Army. One night we moved our HQ at midnight when German tanks broke through our lines and came within 1200 yards of the HQ. Those were days I'll always remember with a thrill and I'm glad to have had them, because come what may, I know no one can say I couldnt "take it." Incidentally, some of the news correspondents wanted to tell the story about me, but for some unfathomable reason AFHQ has had a rule ever since I landed in Africa last May that my name is not to be passed by the censors. It must be part of the PSSOB jitters, but it seems rather senseless to me. It explains why nothing has been printed out of this theatre concerning my movements. I plan to ask Butch to find out the reason for it.

On this job with Fifth Army I do feel I have done more than with the Eighth. My present C.O. is Col. Edgar Erskine Hume, a regular Army man of the medical corps. He is a great guy, has done a swell job in Naples, and I am devoted to him. He has given me responsibilities far above my rank, and the other officers, in AMG and the other units of the Army, have *not* frowned on a Captain doing jobs of higher rank. Every day I sit in on conferences where only Lt. Col's and higher ranks participate.

All of which I'm afraid is a bit of bragging, but I dont want you to think I'm in a funk. I just cant sell myself on the idea that what I'm doing is the best contribution to the war effort. I still feel that Anna and I both can do a bigger job if there is any way for us to find a good one we can work at together.

I am slated to go on into Rome, which ought to be a great experience. What will follow that I dont know. Maybe Anna could come over to Rome for the Red Cross. I realize that would involve many things, but I know a husband-wife combination (both in the Red Cross) with Fifth Army. I wouldnt want to go into a Red Cross job, of course, but probably there will be continuing Army jobs in Rome.

Let me say again: I'll be a good soldier. Don't worry about *that*. I dont want to tear down what Anna and I have built up by having a scandal break around us. If it cant be done *right*, it shouldn't be done at all. Anna wrote these thoughts to me, and I agree with her 100%.

But both of us *know* we can work better, more effectively, together. And we love each other more than any two people ever have before.

She is coming to you for Christmas and maybe something will break for us. If not, we'll carry on. The only thing I am really worried about is what all of this will do to her. The P-I gang has let us down. I wish she would either set her foot down and allow no Hearst propaganda in the paper, or quit the paper. I know its easy for me to say this, but damn hard for her to actually do the thing on the scene. I am content to let her decide that issue, but I dont want her to stay on holding the job for me, or anything of that sort.

Well, darling, I've rambled on and on. I've got to get up before light and I'd better duck under the covers for a little while. Will you send this on to Anna? It carries a world of love to you both. You know I would give up anything I have for her, go to the ends of the earth, do anything, to make up for my grievous lapse—to make her happy.

Always your devoted
John.

". . . help does not go to those who do not help themselves! . . ."

White House
Tuesday Oct. 26th [1943]

Anna darling,

Didn't I ask you long ago if you were superstitious about wearing opals when they are not your birthstone? I meant to but you've not answered. The one valuable thing given me on the trip was a large opal in Australia, it is beautiful & I've had it simply set so it can be a pendant or a pin. I want to give it to you but not if you would not wear it & I'll keep it for Xmas anyway!

I loved your letter on Sisty & hope you told her why she could not have my little check as I think she should clearly understand that help does not go to those who do not help themselves!

Pa needs underclothes & I've got him 6 sets but am told he should have 24! Why don't you kids give him the remainder or else [FDR's new chief secretary, Grace] Tully might pick out a book he's earmarked & you could send her a check for amount you want to spend. Tommy wld like good soap or toilet water I think. Trude the same, or maybe some linen. I would like some shower curtains for H.P. or if you all got together some standard sets of books or new H.P. china. Much that I have is getting chipped & cld be used in playroom. I'd rather have china or pottery that can be easily filled in. Harry Hooker a book or ties I think. Now, was I ever so good? . . .

Pa told me tonight Granny's estate would be settled as of Jan. 1st. He said he hoped then to live on his income. He gave the kids bonds out of principal (sale of N.Y. houses) & would continue similar gifts as so much was lost in inheritance taxes.

If there is a railroad strike you had better try to get off sooner! I don't see how they could tie up everything however as public opinion wld be outraged.

I got back yesterday & found Pa better but still not really well. . . .

Devotedly
Mother

In a surprisingly unguarded note, Eleanor wrote Anna a note about FDR's highly secret departure (naming day, place and even identification of the ship, commanded by the President's former naval aide) for Cairo where he was to meet Churchill and Chiang Kai-shek. (From Cairo he and Churchill flew to Tehran to meet Stalin.)

As matters developed, "all females" were not "out." Madame Chiang Kai-shek attended Cairo, and so did Churchill's daughter Sarah.

". . . but I fear all females are out! . . ."

White House
Sat. Nov. 6th [1943]

Anna darling,

. . . Pa's up at Shangri-la [now Camp David] trying to get a last rest & a visit with [Princess] Martha & some others & he's off Wed. I think for Norfolk & goes over on the Iowa, Capt. MacRae's new boat. I'll read him your desire but I fear all females are out! . . .

Much, much love.

Mother

". . . & may they be with us next year. . . ."

29 Washington Square West
New York, N.Y.
Nov. 24th [1943]

Anna darling,

. . . The rumor that Elliott was a prisoner kept us all wondering Monday but I guess it had no truth in it. . . .

I'm just back from Boston. Johnny's ship the "Wasp" is enormous & the commissioning ceremonies went well today. My heart felt queer as I looked at all those young faces 3200 on board!

Goodnight darling. I'm weary. May we all be thankful that those we love are safe tomorrow & may they be with us next year. Bless you all.

Devotedly
Mother

The Roosevelts had a family custom of leaving notes of special personal wishes on the pillow of the recipient. Apparently that was the form of delivery of the following short letter, for Anna was East with the children for a visit of a planned few weeks that had included a Hyde Park Christmas.

". . . contrast between great companionship & the present blank . . ."

White House
New Year's Eve [1943]

Anna darling,
This is just a little line for you to carry with you thro' the coming year. I know how empty life seems, how purposeless & how deeply lonely. The contrast between great companionship & the present blank is what makes it so hard to bear.

I can hope & pray that the coming year will bring your John back & you know that both of you are never out of my mind & heart. God bless & keep you both & give you health & strength for this ordeal.

All my love, admiration & devotion to you dearest one.

Mother

CHAPTER VI

March 10, 1944 – May 19, 1945

Anna's year-end visit had led, without serious forethought, to a great change in her life, and indeed a change for both her parents. She was to describe it with striking casualness:

"In December, 1943, Father returned to Washington from the Cairo-Tehran Conferences. With no preliminary talks or discussions, I found myself trying to take over little chores that I felt would relieve Father of some of the pressure under which he was constantly working.

"After a couple of weeks I asked Father if he'd mind if I resigned my job on the newspaper and stayed on to help him."

As matters turned out, Anna was to reside at the White House for the rest of her father's life—until April 1945. She was not only to witness peak experiences of history but to become a daily working part of them.

To ease his experienced statesman's apprehension about giving her a free, intimate involvement in every corner, every moment, of his daily secrets—wartime, political and personal—Father set one stipulation: Anna was not to keep a diary of any kind. Chroniclers are to be forever saddened that she obeyed that instruction faithfully. Everyone in the inner circle recognizes that no one since Missy LeHand had ever been admitted closer than Anna to the center of Roosevelt's magnetic field. Yet:

"In my work for him I never had an official job or title or salary. Father and I never had any discussions as to what my job or jobs should be. Actually, they grew like Topsy, because I was there all the time and it was easy for

Father to tell someone to 'Ask Anna to do that,' or to look at me and say, 'Sis, you handle that.' So 'Topsy' quickly grew into a full-time job."

Anna's decision to resign her Seattle post became even more fortuitous when on January 24, 1944, John Boettiger arrived in Washington for assignment to the Pentagon's military government headquarters. He too took up residence at the White House. The family was reunited. Anna continued:

"It soon became apparent to me that I couldn't write fast enough to take accurate notes on some of the things Father would ask me to do. Complete accuracy was of the greatest importance. So I taught myself shorthand at night, when the day's work was done.

"It was immaterial to me whether my job was helping to plan the 1944 campaign, pouring tea for General de Gaulle or filling Father's empty cigarette case. All that mattered was relieving a greatly overburdened man of a few details of work and trying to make his life as pleasant as possible when a few moments opened up for relaxation."

Years later her son John was to speculate, "My mother—for the first and only time in her life—was acting out her most vivid childhood dream: to be her father's companion and helpmate, even his lifeline."

But from another standpoint—regarding her mother—living in the White House was a minefield of potential explosion. The tension becomes apparent by contrasting Mrs. Roosevelt's *public* account of the time, written for her memoirs, against Anna's private recollection in conversation with me.

"Anna's presence," writes Mrs. Roosevelt, her admiration perhaps blended with traces of envy—and relief, "was the greatest possible help to my husband. Ever since Miss LeHand's illness . . . there had been gaps which could have been filled only by someone living in the house. Now Anna filled them. She saw and talked to people whom Franklin was too busy to see and then gave him a digest of the conversations. She also took over the supervision of his food. . . . She brought to all her contacts a gaiety and buoyance that made everybody feel just a little happier because she was around."

Eleanor was painfully aware of the President's own need for the "gaiety and buoyance," something she knew she could not provide—and everyone in the official family knew it. Grace Tully, his new chief secretary, frankly recalled that on some mornings in the office he would confide, "Eleanor had a lot of 'do-gooders' for dinner and you know what that means." Rex Tugwell commented: "Really serious talk at table was avoided if Roosevelt could manage it. Eleanor, so humorless and so weighed down with responsibility, made this difficult." Judge Samuel Rosenman, FDR's chief speechwriter: "She was invariably frank in her criticism of him—and of his speeches. Sometimes I thought she picked inappropriate times . . . perhaps a social and entertaining dinner." Grace Tully: "On one occasion of a dinner party cross-examination by Mrs. Roosevelt, I recall Anna speaking up jokingly: 'Mother, can't you see you are giving Father indigestion?'"

"She pushed him terrifically, this I know," Anna allowed, trying to give me a picture in sympathy with both contenders. "But you can't ask somebody to be your eyes and ears and then not—"

What increasingly concerned Anna was her father's health. She began to question the competence of his personal physician, Admiral Ross McIntire, beyond his skills as an ear, nose and throat specialist. Did he ever look far beyond Roosevelt's ever-troublesome sinuses? "I wasn't married to a physician then as I am now," she said to me in 1967, "but I didn't think McIntire was an internist who really knew what he was talking about. I felt Father needed more care, more general care. Since then, of course, we've learned that he had arteriosclerosis even before the Casablanca Conference, but nobody recognized this. This was not Father's fault or Mother's fault, but you've got to realize that these two were brought up in a generation when you just *didn't talk* about what's wrong with you physically. I can remember going to Mother at that time, after Casablanca, and saying, 'I think Father has to have such and such and I've already talked to Dr. McIntire.' She said, 'Well, dear, I agree with you, I think this is very important.' Of course, by then Bruenn [Dr. Howard G. Bruenn, a heart specialist] was in the picture. But there were no anticoagulants or whatever then, and I don't think there is the slightest doubt that Father must have had times when the blood was not pumping the way it should through one hundred percent of the body. I saw this with my own eyes, but I don't think Mother saw it. She wasn't looking for him to be any different. Father wasn't interested in physiology—that was all there was to it. But neither was Mother interested in physiology. She seemed to be cerebrating one hundred percent, *all* the time.

"She couldn't see why, at a moment when he was relaxing—I remember one day when we were having cocktails. This is upstairs in the Oval Room. A fair number of people were in the room, an informal group, nobody important. I was mixing the cocktails. Mother always came in at the end so she would only have to have one cocktail—that was her concession. She would wolf it—she never took it slowly. She came in and sat down across the desk from Father. And she had a sheaf of papers this high and she said, 'Now, Franklin, I want to talk to you about this.' I have permanently blocked out of my mind what it was she wanted to bring up. I just remember, like lightning, that I thought, Oh, God, he's going to *blow*. And sure enough, he blew his top. He took every single speck of that whole pile of papers, threw them across the desk at me and said, 'Sis, you handle these tomorrow morning.' I almost went through the floor. She got up. She was the most controlled person in the world. And she just stood there a half second and said, 'I'm sorry.' Then she took her glass and walked toward somebody else and started talking. And he picked up his glass and started a story. And that was the end of it.

"Intuitively I understood that here was a man plagued with God knows how many problems and right now he had twenty minutes to have two cocktails—in very small glasses—because dinner was served at a certain hour. They called you and out you went. He wanted to tell stories and relax and enjoy himself—*period*. I don't think Mother had the slightest realization."

I ventured a conversational risk, wondering aloud to Anna whether these tensions at home might account in part for FDR's cultivation of Eleanor as his traveling eyes and ears—to get her out of the house and out of his hair. Was it possible he had "a certain eagerness to have her go"?

"Well, listen," Anna responded instantly, "I always suspected this. Neither of them, obviously, would ever tell me whether they were reluctant or eager, but I think without a doubt that it was more peaceful. . . . So that this was—I don't know whether you want to call it an accommodation or what."

For whatever the motive, on March 4, 1944, minutes after an East Room church service commemorating FDR's first Inauguration, Mrs. Roosevelt and Tommy Thompson departed for a 13,000-mile plane trip of military posts in the Caribbean area. "My husband," she writes for public perusal in her memoirs, "had insisted that I take this trip. He thought that because the war had receded in that area the men stationed there felt they were in a backwater and chafed to be where they could do what they considered a more important job. Nevertheless, we had to have men there to guard and watch for submarines because there was so much traffic to Europe, Asia and Africa. Franklin wanted them to realize that he knew and understood the whole picture and believed they were doing a still vitally necessary job—that they were not forgotten, even though they were not on the front line."

Eleanor and Tommy visited Guantánamo, Cuba; Jamaica; Puerto Rico; Virgin Islands; Antigua; St. Lucia; Trinidad; Paramaribo; Belém, Natal and Recife in Brazil; La Guaira; Caracas; Curaçao; Aruba; Barranquilla; Canal Zone; Salinas; Galápagos Islands; Guatemala; Havana, Cuba.

"... the Army can't persuade the dear religious groups! ..."

[San Juan, Puerto Rico]
Friday night, Mar. 10th [1944]

Anna darling,

I feel very far away tho' we have scarcely been gone a week. . . .

Guantanamo [Cuba] & Jamaica must be hard for the men. They see planes in & out daily. They have no people they want to be with around & yet they can't get home for a leave. In themselves the places are beautiful & for a visit there is much to interest one. People are different, vegetation & animals are varied but soon one is accustomed to it & then, no danger, no fighting & no families allowed makes it seem very hard. The U.S.O. can't sell beer & in town it is the one place for the men but of course they go to horrible dives & drink dreadful stuff since they can't get beer at the U.S.O. & the Army can't persuade the dear religious groups!

The weather is fine, not hot. Being here with the Tugwell's [Rex Tugwell was governor of Puerto Rico] has been pleasant. Someday I want to return as a plain tourist to the little hotel on St. Thomas. I didn't get there today but they told me it was good. In both Porto Rico & the Virgin Isles the food is double in cost for the people. Rice their main diet costs 10 cts a lb. as against 5 cts in the old pre war days. Grace Tugwell has started milk stations for the 2–7 yr olds & they look healthier for a good morning meal daily & school lunches are almost universal but the numbers of children are impossible to believe till you see them.

Tommy bears up uncomplainingly tho' our morning starts conform to tropical habits & should call for an afternoon siesta which we never get! . . .

I hope John is still home. I think of you both all the time & hope for the best.

A big hug to you darling.

Devotedly
Mother

". . . I always think he will forget to mention . . ."

Natal [Brazil]
March 15th [1944]

Dearest Anna,

I wrote Pa last night but I always think he will forget to mention to you that Tommy & I are flourishing. . . .

The sun makes the days pretty hot & Belem [Brazil] was very damp. The islands seem to have more breeze at night. I've seen hundreds of boys here & we inspect Brazilian installations as well as our own. I pinned all kinds of decorations on a squadron of Navy fliers this morning in a moving ceremony. They are the squadron who came to bomb the subs in Jan. & they went after the group of subs which was causing so much trouble in the spirit of kill or be killed. Out of 120 men about 40 were killed but the seven subs were all sunk. . . .

I have some Brazilian flags for little Johnnie Boettiger but so far we have not seen many thinks [sic] that one could buy.

If transportation is once developped here there are limitless possibilities & our co-operation seems genuine. They like our men & we seem to get on.

Love to John & much to you dear,

Devotedly,
Mother

". . . Tommy is grand . . . But I rather think she'll need a rest . . ."

Flying from Recife back to Belem
March 17th [1944]

Anna darling,

Your grand letter of the 9th reached me in Natal. . . . I am so glad John is lecturing & you'll have his birthday together & I'm hoping he'll still be there on my return. . . .

Tommy is grand & will furnish all the light touches on our return but I rather think she'll need a rest for she doesn't stand heat well & it has been hot! The schedules have been full! Of course I know she won't take a rest! I gave her your hug & your spank.

We've visited both Brazilian & U.S. Army, Navy & Air & I've had a press conference a day (translated) & sat thro' 3 dinners struggling with a gentleman who knew "a little French." I wish I knew Portugese & I wonder if one could learn Spanish & Portuguese simultaneously. I can read their letters & papers pretty well. The dinner last night was formal & large & the decorations were orchids in such profusion that I shall never again consider them rare! I think most of the men like my visit & feel friendly, of course now & then an officer has asked what the political implications are! . . .

Devotedly
Mother

". . . He won't like the latter but it may be good for him. . . ."

Flying fr. Br. Guiana to
LaGuaira [Venezuela]
March 19th [1944]

Anna darling,
    Enclosed is a letter from Elliott. Show to Father if you think wise. It takes my breath away for one wld think divorces & one's 3 children were a mere incident not to be mentioned! I've ordered the magazines sent regularly [to Elliott] & I'll pick out some books & send in the middle of each month. I'm also subscribing for him to the Sunday Times & PM [a liberal New York daily newspaper]. He won't like the latter but it may be good for him. I've an idea Elliott may cut loose & live in China or Russia but I may be wrong. I'll be sorry but I guess there is a streak of unruliness in some of us.
    . . . The war will have to end soon for I find one night stands less & less inviting & the smell & feel of things that are always damp & washed in brown water, will never appeal to me. Tommy is a God send but no one can do your job for you!
    We visited both the Army Air base & the Navy Base yesterday & had a 2 hr flight over the country in between. We missed seeing the highest falls in the world as the fog envelloped the mountain but the sight of the starry sky & steaming jungle was like a look at Dante's Inferno. There is lots to be done in these countries but no weaklings will do it. . . .

Mother

". . . I don't want it but I don't think I can sell it. . . ."

Hyde Park
Sunday July 30th [1944]

Anna darling,
    First, do you want a jacket or short coat made out of Chinese sables? Ritter says they are worth 8 to $10,000. Mme. Chiang sent it to me & I don't want it

but I don't think I can sell it. As it is no one could wear it so it would have to be recut & you would have to go & choose a style & have your measures taken. . . .

Devotedly
Mother

". . . I'd better get the fur coat made to fit me . . ."

[At a conference of war leaders]
The Citadel
Quebec
Tuesday, Sept. 12th [1944]

Anna darling,
The Churchill party comes to H.P. & Pa thinks he'll get there with them Sat. a.m. & they'll stay till Tuesday a.m. He can't decide yet about [Princess] Martha. . . .
Since Mme. Chiang is here I'd better get the fur coat made to fit me & let her see me in it & then you can get it refitted later!
The ladies [Mrs. Churchill and other wives of Quebec conferees] have little to do but it is pleasant & restfull. Conversation at meals is interesting, this old barracks turned luxurious house is charming & has great atmosphere. I've not been so luxurious in years. Tommy & I worked for an hour this a.m. & she came to the big dinner last night but the rest of the time she's pretty lonely I guess.
Love to John & ever so much to you,

Mother

Two days after the unusually simple 1945 inauguration ceremony, Roosevelt left—with Anna in his party—for an elaborately secret sea voyage to Malta, thence by air to the Crimea, for the war's climactic meeting with Stalin and Churchill—the Yalta Conference.
Fastidiously concealing any disappointment and resentment that Eleanor may have felt at not being invited, she wrote in her memoirs: "We discussed whether I should go, and he said: 'If you go, they will all feel they have to make a great fuss, but if Anna goes it will be simpler. Averell Harriman [U.S. Ambassador to the Soviet Union] will bring his daughter down from Moscow.' Thus it was decided."
Five years after Eleanor's death, I asked Anna, "Do you think she was hurt?"
"Yes, I'm pretty sure she was. Of course, I was so terribly anxious to go that this wasn't half the embarrassment that it was to have those papers thrown at me, when he said, 'Sis, you handle these.' I wanted *desperately* to

go, you see. But I also knew that if Mother went, I couldn't go." (Anna laughed with faint guilt.) "The other thing was that Harriman and Churchill were bringing their daughters, and there would be no wives. So I sort of fell in with this, just blocked it out for my own purposes very selfishly."

While the party was en route to Yalta, Eleanor got caught in a storm of resistance in the Senate against confirming the nomination of Henry Wallace as secretary of commerce. Her irritation with Franklin—perhaps still over the noninvitation to Yalta—is reflected in her letter to Anna about Wallace. The background: To compensate in part for permitting the Democratic Convention to dump Wallace from the vice presidency, Roosevelt offered Wallace any Cabinet job he wanted. Wallace, the experimenter in chicken breeding and wheat varieties and the New Deal's first secretary of agriculture, surprised everyone by choosing the Department of Commerce. In a way, this was a relief to Roosevelt, who had kept Jesse Jones in that job as a sop to conservatives. Now he had an excuse to get rid of Jones. The President wrote Jones frankly that "Henry Wallace deserves almost any service which he believes he can satisfactorily perform. . . . It is for this reason only that I am asking you to relinquish this present post. . . . There are several Ambassadorships which are vacant. . . ." The yowls from Jones's friends and Wallace's enemies in the Senate were so fierce that the White House had to cable FDR for a personal demand that Wallace be confirmed.

Another irritation at Yalta: Temperamental General Charles de Gaulle was miffed, not having been invited as one of the war's major leaders. Roosevelt offered to meet de Gaulle in Algiers on his way back from the conference. The general huffily—and publicly—declined. The incident earned a crisp comment in Eleanor's letter of February 19.

". . . I was sorry we had to bother him . . . but . . ."

> 29 Washington Square West
> New York, N.Y.
> Friday Feb. 2d [1945]

Anna dearest,

It was wonderful to get your note & I hope by now the interesting part is in full swing. Too bad Pa had a head cold but I'm glad he was better when you wrote. I was sorry we had to bother him about Wallace[,] but if he [FDR] continues to show so much less interest in him [Wallace] than he did in the State Dep. people there is going to be a great feeling that he nominated him just to have him beaten. . . ."

The weather you described did not make me envious. . . .

Your little Johnny ran a bit of temperature & the doctor called it "flu" but he seemed better yesterday. The dogs miss you but are well. John is very lonely, but spends much time when home with Johnnie & says he is getting rested. They will be happy to see you back. . . .

Much, much love to you dearest,

Mother

". . . & all is well in the country. . . ."

> 1600 Pennsylvania Avenue
> Washington, D.C.
> Feb. 13th [1945]

Anna darling,
    All is well with both your Johns. . . .
    I'm so anxious to know how you feel about Russia.
    The reaction to the report from the conference is grand & all is well in the country.
    . . . It should be a triumphant home coming.

> Much, much love
> Mother

". . . but you will get more criticism . . ."

> 1600 Pennsylvania Avenue
> Washington, D.C.
> Feb. 19th, 1945

Dearest Anna,
    Johnny is still in bed with this loose cough & a fluctuating temperature. I'd been [sic] inclined if I were you to get at the cause if it is possible to discover. John seems well but both of them miss you.
    In a week & two or three days you should be home. The Nat. Women's Press Club want you for lunch & to speak to them. My press conference wants to have you at once at a special conference. Tommy is sending you the letters & I told them I had no idea what you would want to do. I think it would be very interesting to hear what you saw & what your impressions were & it might be good for the country to see it through your eyes but you will get more criticism & you may not feel it worth while. Pa may have some ideas too!
    I'm going up to N.Y. on Thursday morning & back Sat. evening & then we will just be awaiting your arrival. It will be wonderful to see you & I hope both you & Pa get a rest on the way home.
    The DeGaulle thing is unfortunate, the man is a fool.

> Much love dear,
> Mother

On March 1, 1945, Roosevelt addressed Congress with his report of the conference at Yalta. Explaining that he is wearing "ten pounds of braces" on his legs for the first time in his public career, he asked the indulgence of his audience as he spoke from a sitting position. Many in the audience before him—and among the millions who soon saw him in movie theater newsreels—were shocked at his loss of weight, the slouching frame, dark shadows beneath his eyes, the foreboding aura of a deep weariness. His voice, for twelve years a clarion of strength and optimism, was muffled, consonants indistinct and thick. While many were alarmed, there was no clear sign that Mrs. Roosevelt was permitting herself to be aware of the dramatic decline in the President's physical health. For that matter, most of the official family fastidiously maintained their unawareness. The man who embodied strength and power to them—to the world—could not be seen except as invulnerable.

"I knew," Mrs. Roosevelt was to write in hindsight, "when he consented to [address Congress] sitting down that he had accepted a certain degree of invalidism. . . . I was pleased when he decided to go to Warm Springs where, as I said before, he always gained in health and strength. He invited his cousins, Laura Delano and Margaret Suckley, to go down with him. I knew that they would not bother him as I should have by discussing questions of state. . . ."

The President also asked Anna to go, but she had to stay in Washington. Little Johnny, about to turn six, came down with a serious gland infection while Anna was on the Yalta voyage, and he was then taking penicillin (a radical measure in 1945) at Bethesda Naval Hospital.

Roosevelt was accompanied, among his official party, by William Hassett, a scholarly, somewhat poetic presidential secretary. Hassett is the only one on record among those close to the President who permitted himself to ponder the gravity of the President's condition. Standing one night before the tall columns of Georgia Hall on the grounds of the Warm Springs Foundation, Hassett unburdened himself to Lieutenant Commander Howard G. Bruenn, the young cardiologist assigned by Rear Admiral Ross T. McIntire, the surgeon general, to watch over the President almost daily starting in March 1944. A few minutes afterward Hassett reconstructed the conversation in his diary:

"Tonight had another talk with Howard Bruenn about the President's health. I said: 'He is slipping away from us and no earthly power can keep him here.' Bruenn demurred. 'Why do you think so?' he asked. Told him I understood his position—his obligation to save life, not to admit defeat. . . . I told Bruenn I had every confidence in his own skill; was satisfied that the Boss was the beneficiary of everything that the healing art can devise. I couldn't suggest anything which should be done differently, but in my opinion the Boss was beyond all human resources. I mentioned his feeble signature—the old boldness of stroke and liberal use of ink gone, signature often ending in a fade-out. He said that not important. Reluctantly admitted the Boss in a precarious condition, but his condition not hopeless. He could be saved if measures were adopted to rescue him from certain mental strains and emotional influences, which he mentioned. [Hassett's atypical, careful vagueness in his wording of the preceding sentence may be as he originally wrote it, or perhaps he cleansed it between its writing and publication. Dr. Bruenn was soon to make clear to me (and was one day to repeat to Dr. James A. Halsted, Anna's third husband) that he meant Mrs. Roosevelt. She phoned from Washington at least once a day to press the President on causes that stirred her at the moment, or with the pleadings of delegations that incessantly besieged her.] I told him his conditions could not be met. . . . We said good night with heavy hearts."

On the morning of April 12 at the White House, Mrs. Roosevelt gave one of her regularly scheduled press conferences, a practice she had undertaken at the suggestion of her friend Lorena Hickok. No previous First Lady had spoken regularly to reporters about public matters. Mrs. Roosevelt announced she would accompany her husband to San Francisco for the founding of the United Nations.

At three o'clock—two o'clock at Warm Springs—Mrs. Roosevelt received Charles Taussig, an adviser to the United States delegation to San Francisco. In her sitting room on the second floor of the White House he solicited her help in clarifying the President's interpretation of United Nations trusteeships. She promised to call her husband about it, then was distracted by a signal from Tommy, with an air of uncommon urgency, to pick up the phone.

The voice was Laura Delano's—from Warm Springs. The President had fainted. Mrs. Roosevelt asked terse questions, careful to guard the subject matter from Taussig. For all anyone could tell, she might have been talking to Anna about Johnny's sore throat. Moments later came another call from Admiral McIntire. Gracefully but rapidly, Mrs. Roosevelt concluded the conference with Taussig. McIntire told of a phone report he had just received from Dr. Bruenn. He was not alarmed, McIntire assured her, but suggested that Mrs. Roosevelt prepare to fly with him in a navy plane later in the day for Warm Springs. Should she cancel a speaking engagement she had in half an hour? No, advised McIntire, a cancellation followed by an unexpected trip might cause great comment.

Mrs. Roosevelt proceeded to the annual tea of the Thrift Shop, arriving at the Sulgrave Club, according to a society reporter, "looking unusually smart and in soaring spirits." She sat through tributes and an entertainment that seemed interminable. During a solo by Evalyn Tyner, a pianist, Mrs. Roosevelt was whispered a message that she was wanted on the telephone. A lady nearby observed that Mrs. Roosevelt gave "a quick start, obvious only to the persons immediately around her." She quietly left the table.

Mrs. Roosevelt described the moment: "Steve Early [presidential press secretary], very much upset, asked me to come home at once. I did not even ask why. I knew down in my heart that something dreadful had happened. . . ."

Early later told newsmen: "When she came back, Admiral McIntire and I went to her sitting room and told her the President had slipped away. She was silent for a minute and her first words were: 'I am more sorry for the people of this country and of the world than I am for ourselves.'"

In the next twenty-four hours those words were quoted by nearly every newspaper in America and most others around the world. People quoted them in the streets. Editorials were written about them. One columnist wrote a searching, speculative piece about her remarkable words: about Mrs. Roosevelt's accurate understanding, even under the pressure of personal shock, of FDR's position as a leader of the world, which transcended his position as head of a family. The impromptu sentence was taken as a signal of her greatness as well as of his.

The odd fact, Mrs. Roosevelt was to tell me a few years after the event in a tone of absolute certainty, is that she knew she never made the statement at all. It could not be a matter of her recollection failing her, she asserted. The words were called to her attention by admirers within hours after she was supposed to have spoken them, and they had the sound of utter newness to her. So perhaps they comprised a thought that Steve Early, an imaginative public relations expert, wished she had said. Or perhaps "her" thought was born in his mind with such poetic force that he thought he heard it spoken.

At 11:25 that night, after a five-hour journey by plane and auto, accompanied by Steve Early and Ross McIntire, the widow entered the simple white cottage at Warm Springs. Grace Tully noted that she appeared calm, perfectly under control. After embraces and exchanging condolences, Mrs. Roosevelt sat on the sofa and asked Grace, Miss Suckley and Miss Delano each to tell her exactly what happened.

When the turn came to Laura Delano, an aristocratic eccentric occasionally given to dyeing her hair purple, Mrs. Roosevelt got more of "exactly what happened" than anyone expected. For reasons that her companions were not able to explain, except that Miss Delano was a sayer of blunt truths and whole truths, she chose to include in her detail of exactly what happened that the portrait of the President, for which he was sitting at the moment of his collapse, was being done by Elizabeth Shoumatoff, a friend of Lucy Mercer Rutherfurd; that, in fact, the portrait had been commissioned by Mrs. Rutherfurd; and that, verily, Mrs. Rutherfurd, at the moment of the collapse, had been sitting in that window alcove right there, and had been Franklin's visitor, inhabiting the guest cottage, for the past three days.

Mrs. Roosevelt's supreme effort to control her shock was visible. After a time, she rose, walked to the bedroom where the President lay and closed the door behind her. For five minutes, she was alone with her husband. When she came out, Grace Tully noted, her face was grave, eyes dry.

At some moment in that hour, the stunned widow asked other questions of Cousin Laura—and received truthful answers: yes, Franklin had seen Lucy on other occasions in recent years; she had dined more than once with him at the White House; and yes, Laura and Daisy (the family nickname for Miss Suckley) were present at one of these dinners—and, most shocking of all to Eleanor, Anna served as its hostess.

"Mother was angry with Anna," writes brother James, "for participating in the deception of the final years. But what was Anna to do? Should she have refused Father what he wanted? She was not in a position to do so even had she wanted to. Accepting the confidence of Father, should she have betrayed him by running to report to Mother every move he made? A child caught between two parents can only pursue as honorable a course as possible. Anna could no more serve as Mother's spy on Father than she could as Father's spy on Mother. Anna suffered some private anguish, but she was as true as she could be to both our parents and she was blameless in this matter."

There is much that Anna needed to feel "blameless" about. She knew of a visit by Lucy to the President when he accepted an invitation in 1943 for an extended rest at Bernard Baruch's South Carolina estate, Hobcaw Barony. The President had been hounded by a lingering cold and persistent sinus pain. Baruch offered not only his hospitality, but some of his own precious gasoline ration tickets for Lucy to drive up from her home in Aiken. In addition to the White House visits, Anna knew that around Thanksgiving, 1944, Lucy motored down from Aiken to Warm Springs to stay for several days. In talking of these visits to me, Anna spoke readily—almost eagerly—not only out of a respect for history and truth, but with the apparent feeling that a little bit of truth, blown out of shape, had wronged her father. She described the resumed relationship as "an important friendship to both of them." It presented special difficulties to her, she added, confirming James's observation, because she was also concerned that her mother not be injured again. Anna said to me one day:

"Soon after that Thanksgiving 1944 visit to Warm Springs—you see, this is all *late* in his life—Lucy Rutherfurd told me something that, although she probably didn't know it, was very revealing to me about the kind of relationship it was. She told me, 'You know, your father drove me in his little Ford up to'—what's the name of that mountain where he loved to go on picnics?—'Dowdell's Knob.' And she said, 'You know, I had the most fascinating hour I've ever had. He just sat there and told me of some of what he regarded as the real problems facing the world now. I just couldn't get over thinking of what I was listening to, and then he would stop and say, "You see that knoll over there? That's where I did this-or-that," or "You see that bunch of trees?" Or whatever it was. He would interrupt himself, you know. And we just sat there and looked.'

"As Lucy said all this to me—Father was right there in the room—I realized Mother was not capable of giving him this—just listening. And of course, this is why I was able to fill in for a year and a half, because I could just listen. I remember, when we were starting out for Yalta, it was almost dusk. We sat out on deck watching. He started telling the history of various parts of Virginia that were going by. It was quiet, and at one point he said, 'That's where Lucy's family used to live. That's where they had their plantation.' This was so open, aboveboard, not hanky-panky or whatever you want to call it. That is why I think this whole thing has been blown up to such a—" In frustration she let the sentence hang there.

After the funeral train arrived in Washington in the early morning of Saturday, April 14, one of Mrs. Roosevelt's first acts upon returning with the President's body to the White House was to confront Anna over the daughter's now-revealed complicity. What James and Anna both say in the preceding paragraphs is essentially how Anna defended herself. The conversation ended in a chill that wouldn't easily go away.

About three weeks later Anna was able to bring herself to place a condolence telephone call to someone who she felt was entitled to such a call. She phoned Lucy.

For the rest of her life, not in her files but in a special folder in a special locked drawer of her desk, Anna kept a letter that came in reply to that call. Twenty-seven years after it was written, in 1972, at her home in Hillsdale, New York, Anna volunteered the letter to me—to read, to handle, to discuss with her, apparently seeking confirmation that the relationship between her father and this beautiful "other woman" was *all right*, that Anna's limited complicity with it was all right, that indeed it was, as she had described it, "an important friendship to both of them." But I was not to copy or quote from it.

Later I was offered full access to the extraordinary letter:

". . . He told me so often & with such feeling . . ."

Aiken
South Carolina
May 9th, 1945

Anna dear—

Your telephoning the other night meant much to me. I did not know that it was in me just now to be so glad to hear the sound of any voice—& to hear you laugh—was beyond words wonderful.

I had not written before for many many reasons—but you were constantly in my thoughts & with very loving and heart torn sympathy & I was following every step of the way. This blow must be crushing to you—to all of you—but I know that you meant more to your Father than any one and that makes it closer & harder to bear. It must be an endless comfort to you that you were *able* to be with him so much this past year. Every second of the day you must be conscious of the void and emptiness, where there has always been—all through your life—the strength of his beloved presence—so filled with loving understanding, so ready to guide and to help. I love to think of his very great pride in you & can still hear his voice speaking on a different note when he would say "Hello, Girl, how is Johnny." He was so distressed about his little grandson & so concerned about you and your terrible anxiety. He told me so often & with such feeling of all that you had meant of joy & comfort on the trip to Yalta. He said you had been so extraordinary & what a difference it made to have you. He told me of your charm & your tact—& of how *every*one loved you. He told how capable you were & how you forgot nothing & of the little typewritten chits he would find at his place at the beginning or end of the day, reminding him of all the little or big things that he was to do. I hope he told *you* these things—but sometimes one doesn't. In any case you must have known—words were not needed between you. I have been reading over some very old letters of his & in one he says: "Anna is a dear fine person—I wish so much that you knew her—" Well, now we do know one another—and it is a great joy to me—& I think he was happy this past year that it was so. He was so wonderful about all of the others too—& when after this last Inauguration I said how wonderfully well he had looked—like a flash he said, "but didn't you think *James* looked well." He was so thrilled when Eliots promotion went thro—& so proud that Franklin had his own destroyer to command. He was looking forward so to having a ball for Sistie at the White House, even though she might be a year or so too young to come out. He also talked of the difference it made having your husband there—& how really devoted he was to him & what a help he was in so many many ways. And through it all one hears his ringing laugh & one thinks of all the ridiculous things he used to say—& do—& enjoy. The picture of him sitting waiting for you that night with the Rabbi's cap on his extraordinarily beautiful head is still vivid.

The world has lost one of the greatest men that ever lived—to me—the greatest. He towers above them all—effortlessly—& even those who openly opposed him seem shocked into the admission of his greatness. Now he is at peace—but he knew even before the end—that the task was well done.

It is a sad inescapable truth that you will now suffer in the sum & measure of your love which was so great. No one can spare you that. Your husband will be your strength—& your children who need you so—but it must all seem meaningless & unbearable.

Forgive me for writing of things which you know so much better than I, & which are sacred, & should not even be touched on by a stranger. I somehow cannot feel myself to be that, & I feel strongly that you understand.

My love to your husband—and to you—Anna darling, because you are his child & because you are *yourself.*

I am very devotedly & with heartbroken sympathy

Lucy Rutherfurd

President Harry S Truman urged Mrs. Roosevelt to continue occupying the White House as long as it suited her convenience, but within twelve days she was out of it, gone to her New York apartment at 29 Washington Square West. Anna and John Boettiger returned with their children to Seattle.

Mrs. Roosevelt was seen doing ordinary things that New Yorkers do, even riding the subway. A young woman reporter approached her for an impromptu sidewalk interview. Mrs. Roosevelt brushed away the overture with the soon-publicized comment, "The story is over."

No clear clue is to be found of how deep was the chill between mother and daughter, or how long it lasted, or if indeed there was a particular moment at which it can be said to have ended. One might be tempted to read the chill into the letter of May 15 and its businesslike tone. But it should be noted that the letter is on a relatively businesslike subject about which the widow had been grinding out an enormous quantity of correspondence. The letter is typed, which means it was dictated to Tommy, which in turn means its author was in a formal frame of mind and was more interested in getting rid of it efficiently than warmly. The tone of another that follows almost immediately—May 19—again has the familiar feel of a lifetime of letters between mother and daughter.

". . . seeing that the people have to stand the whole time, . . ."

Hyde Park
May 15, 1945

Anna dearest,

The Roosevelt Home Club of Hyde Park sent representatives to see me today and they want to hold a Memorial Service on the 30th of May at the grave. They will make it short and it is to be at 10:00 a.m., starting with a short prayer by Mr. Anthony, two hymns by the choir and a short fifteen minute speech by some one who knew Father well. They want me to get some one from Washington or from New York.

I wonder if you could find out whether [Postmaster General] Frank Walker might like to come if you think he would speak interestingly enough, seeing that the people have to stand the whole time, and also that there will be a number of children representing each school. Perhaps Jonathan Daniels [FDR's last press secretary and son of Josephus, World War I secretary of the navy] or Felix Frankfurter [Roosevelt-appointed Supreme Court justice] or Henry Morgenthau might be good. Please ask any one you think would do and tell him that I will be delighted to have him spend the night before at the cottage. . . .

I hope all goes well with Johnny. My love to John and ever so much to you.

Devotedly
Mother

". . . I could get no meat . . . at home! . . ."

29 Washington Square West
New York 11, N.Y.
May 19th [1945]

Anna darling,

I hope you are not having rain daily as we are. I think of you taking Johnnie to the Isle's today & hope all goes well.

. . . I saw Cousin Susie yesterday p.m. & she still enjoys poor health.

I took [hired] a colored ex-service man last Monday & last night he took[,] i.e. stole my car & drove it to Goshen with 3 girls & 2 other men, all drunk, they smashed up, & 4 were killed & he & 1 man are in the hospital still unconscious! I thought I was being kind but next time I'll bond him! I'm insured but that won't restore people to life or keep him out of jail if he recovers. He was just a bad boy but it will give a bad name to all the colored soldiers. I'm trying to get another[,] to emphasize that it is an individual who went wrong & not a group but I haven't heard of anyone yet!

Just had dinner around the corner . . . as I could get no meat to eat at home!

My love to John & Johnnie. . . .

Devotedly,
Mother

CHAPTER VII

July 29, 1945 – March 6, 1952

Within weeks after the President's death and Mrs. Roosevelt's departure for a presumed private life in New York, John Boettiger received his discharge from the army. On June 8, 1945, Anna, John and little Johnny headed for Seattle. Along the way they picked up Sis and Buzz from their boarding schools. All were eager to resume residence in the home they hadn't seen for so long, but life would not be the same. John and Anna would not go back to their employment with Hearst, who had asserted his intention of resuming full control, editorial as well as business, over the *Post-Intelligencer*. They had no complaint over a severance settlement worked out with Hearst: $40,000 to settle John's uncompleted contract, $15,000 to Anna. Added to their savings, the couple began a new life with a nest egg of close to a hundred thousand dollars. That sum, John calculated, if put up as risk, should attract other investors for purchase of a going newspaper. "We would not be foolish enough," John wrote to his brother, "to try to start a new venture—which would require all kinds of capital and involve risks of failure. . . . The problems of starting from scratch—minus good comics, good columnists, the AP, etc.—are pretty severe. . . ."

John Boettiger told a friend that he and Anna might start an advertising agency in the Pacific Northwest. In a letter to Eleanor, John confessed discomfort at the unfamiliarity of lacking "a flood of work ahead of me constantly," a "specific business responsibility" and a "clear cut program for our old age!" In past years he bathed in a kind of fulfillment at the celebrity status that descended upon him as the President's son-in-law, even though not feeling comfortable and secure with it. Now the source of that identity was gone as well as much of the attention that came with it. Even political leaders, who previously nuzzled up to the couple to sniff their derived fame, held them at a protective distance, apprehensive that either John or Anna—or both!—might run for public office on the strength of their names.

John's first move was a daring overture to Hearst to buy the *P-I*. Finding financial backers for the man who restored the paper to profitability would have been no trouble at all. But perhaps John had been too successful. Wartime and postwar prosperity had lifted the *P-I*—and virtually all newspapers—to such high levels of profit that Hearst's asking price appeared exorbitant. Indeed, John and Anna soon found that all existing daily papers were priced out of reach.

Thirty years later their young son, grown up to become a teacher and psychological counselor of college students, was impelled to reconstruct this critical period in his father's life. He portrayed his father as "evidently struggling against a powerful resurgence of those depressive tendencies that had begun to manifest themselves before the war. In origin, no doubt, they were very old tendencies related to the convictions of inferiority which he remembered torturing him as a child. . . . By late 1945 I think he was running scared. No one knows just what happened, or how, for he did not—could not—speak clearly, even to my mother, of the changes in his mind. . . . If there was a critical event, it was probably FDR's death, though had my father's last frantic publishing adventure succeeded, he might well have recovered his earlier balance."

". . . the lake seems the only answer! . . ."

Mercer Island [Wash.]
July 29th [1945]

Mummy darling:

The time has just flown since we got back from our trip on the 21st. All of our things from Hyde Park, Washington and the Seattle storage company have arrived, but much of it is still unpacked as we are still struggling to get a carpenter to put in shelves to take care of everything. Some shelves have been promised for this coming week, but promises don't mean much in this country where labor is still so short. . . .

Because of the lack of labor, Buzz [now 15] is learning from John how to do simple plumbing jobs and mend many different types of motors and do whatever carpentering is needed. So, all in all, we're having a very wonderful and healthful summer. . . .

Sis is going to Reed College, outside of Portland, Ore. this fall. It is a small college, but a very liberal one. Buzz goes back to Northwestern Military and Naval Academy. He has to be there by Sept. 14th, but Sis doesn't have to be at Reed until Sept. 28th. Johnny will start in 1st grade, at the island's public school, about Sept. 9th. Transportation for Buzz will undoubtedly be tough—but that can't be helped.

The P.I. still carries your column. The contract involving your column, as it stood when we left, also involved Pegler and [Drew] Pearson. We had to buy all three when we finally got yours away from the Seattle Times. If Carlin [syndicator of Mrs. Roosevelt's column] ever tells you that the P.I. doesn't want you, tell him to try to get you in the Seattle Star. It's not exactly a liberal paper, but more so than either of the other two. . . .

I certainly agree with you that Elliott should not borrow money to buy the place [a parcel of land in Hyde Park where FDR had built a hideaway he called Top Cottage, where Elliott now planned to farm] and your plan sounds like a most reasonable one—except that the executors might not want to agree to setting a definite price for 5 to 10 years from now (and Elliott might not want to either)—in case land values change radically in that time. In case the executors don't agree with your plan, wouldn't there be a chance that they would agree to some compromise whereby a large part of the land along the road could now be sold—still leaving Elliott all the good ranching and farming land, and plenty of rights-of-way? . . . If your plan goes thru, and Elliott is definitely working with you to run the place so that it makes a small profit, I most assuredly don't feel that any of the other 3 boys or I are entitled to any possible profits or income from the place. I don't see how any of the rest could possibly feel "unfairly treated"—unless we were actually putting some personal effort or money into the place.

I don't know what F., Jr. said to you about money—and which led to your asking me to tell you honestly how I felt you should "treat" whatever does eventually come to you as income. My only thought has always been that that income is yours to do with as you please. Of course, if you were the financial promoter type, speculating in a lot of wild-cat schemes and having to continually dip into principle to get yourself out of trouble—we might have something to worry about! But somehow, I can't quite visualize you grabbing the morning paper and nervously studying the financial page!

Also, I hope very strongly that when all the boys are home and the majority of the details connected with Father's will are settled, that you'll be able to be free of most of the business and financial worries you have had.

PLEASE stick firmly to your guns on the question of "Doc" [O'Connor, many years earlier FDR's law partner and lifelong friend] as chairman of the FDR Memorial Com.! I just feel, way down inside, that we'll all be unhappy in the long run if "Doc" heads that up. When is a meeting to be held?

I'm delighted Jimmy is home, and hope his "flu" is all gone by now. And gosh how I hope Johnny gets home soon! It does seem ages since he went to sea, and I know how much it will mean to Anne to have him home.

Everyone you meet out here seems to feel that the Japs will "fold" by Oct. or not later than next Jan. 1st. What thoughts do you run into on this? Not that I really think any of us can actually guess correctly! Also, what is the feeling you run into as to how Truman has done at Potsdam? Out here he did not make too good an impression—mostly, I think, because he had too much local publicity, with pages of grinning pictures. But, the feeling here is that he is doing a good job at Potsdam.

I'm happy you think so much of Faye [Emerson, a movie actress and Elliott's new wife], and that she's proving a comfort.

. . . Thanks a lot for the FDR Memorial stamps you sent us all. We're delighted to have all that come out. . . .

John is up at the pump house mending the pump, which, for the moment, is on the blink, leaving us without any water. I need a bath, having mowed the lawn for over an hour, and then done the marketing—but the lake seems the only answer!

We all send you worlds of love—and a big hug from me—which I do wish I could, at least once in a while, deliver in person!

Anna

P.S.—Be sure to give Tommy loads of love from us all.

". . . I lay awake all night thinking about it & then decided . . . [to] buy it. . . ."

29 Washington Square West
New York 11, N.Y.
August 4th [1945]

Anna darling,

Your letter of the 29th must have crossed mine. . . . There is not much general speculation here about the end of war in the Pacific & I wouldn't have any way of guessing[,] but I think it will last as long as the Japanese government can control its people & make them fight. Everyone feels Truman did well at Potsdam but the press & radio have complained about getting no news. I don't see how it could be otherwise. . . .

The trustees met. They decided to accept no offer of rental on the place but to sell *now*. I lay awake all night thinking about it & then decided that I would put *all* my personal capital in & buy it. It will probably cost more than I have but they will accept a mortgage for the balance since I have to pay 4% & otherwise they can make no investments bringing in more than 3%. It is as broad as it is long. Till I die I get all income so am just without any principal. Having bought I can then sell to a child (Elliott if he makes the money) or dispose of it as I wish at any time. If they sold now, there would be no place for grandchildren or any of the children to come if they happened to want to visit me. Father's tree planting plans would be ruined & his cottage dismantled. I don't want the job of running it[,] but it seemed wrong to shirk it. Elliott wants to help & still says when he can he wants to take over. If he doesn't in the end & I live a few years someone of the grandchildren may. I shall go at it slowly & try to run it as a business & in time it may produce a small income. I can't even put tenants off now under O.P.A. regulations! . . .

I dined with Jimmy Thursday night & Harry Hooker. "Doc" insists he must be chairman of the Memorial Com[mission] & agrees to have someone else chairman of the Com[mittee] to decide on what they will do. This will be the Executive Com[mittee]. Jimmy will be on that Com[mittee]. He hopes they will buy the little library in the village & run it in memory of Granny & her husband & Pa. The stamp collection will be sold. "Doc" to make arrangements. Jimmy to look after all securities with a good investment firm. Mr. Ickes [Harold Ickes, secretary of the interior] says he can't take the big house till Jan. [on behalf of the Department of the Interior, to whom FDR bequeathed it as a historic site if no member of the family wanted to occupy it] so I shan't know till then how many pensions I carry [for employees of the family property]. . . . Believe me[,] Rommie is a good business woman. She gave him [James] cards with all they wanted & described the silver & china & glass accurately.

   . . . The weather is fine & cool & I like the feeling of really getting this in order. . . .

   I've turned down an offer to be Chairman of the Nat. Citizens Com[mittee] of P.A.C. [National Citizens Political Action Committee, known as NCPAC, a nonlabor counterpart of the CIO-PAC, the political arm of the Congress of Industrial Organizations]. I'm trying to get 1 radio a week to do. I'm not going on any speaking (paid) trips & not travelling anywhere requiring a reservation till the war is over. I may go for A.F.S. [American Friends Service Committee] to Russia in April & to China a bit sooner. Mme. Chiang came to tea in H.P. & she expects the generalissimo in Oct. . . .

Devotedly Mother
(I started to sign "ER")

   ". . . Everyone we see is flabbergasted with the possibilities . . . of the atomic bomb. . . ."

August 6th, 1945

Mummy darling:

   . . . Last time I wrote you I meant to tell you that a very insistent lady by the name of Doretta Tarmon, of the New Masses [a magazine dependably voicing Communist party positions], insisted on seeing me when she was in Seattle about ten days or two weeks ago. She gave me a long winded description of the bad financial condition of the New Masses and the importance of it in this country, and then asked me for a financial contribution. After that she asked me if I would write an article for them on the press in this country and particularly what I thought the roll of the press should be. I told her that, after what she had told me, that no money I could spare would be more than a drop in the bucket, and then told her I would let her know later about the article. She gave me 3 copies of the New Masses— which I regret to say I haven't had time to read yet. Today, I got a letter from her, not mentioning the financial contribution but asking me to let her know if I had decided to do the article. What about the New Masses crowd? Wouldn't the anti-Roosevelt press (those who are trying to smear Father's name thru his family) immediately pick on anything I did for the New

Masses? Let me know as soon as you can where they stand from all angles. All Mrs. Tarmon kept reiterating was that they are the only publication which is doing an honest job of fighting Fascism in this country!

There is still nothing definite in the wind for John and me on the job score. We are looking into all the possibilities we know of for getting back into the newspaper game thru the back door, and there are two possibilities (as yet not probabilities) which may work out. But, it's a very complicated situation while the war is on and profits so great. Neither of us would be satisfied to be jobless indefinitely—even if it were possible financially for us to do so. . . .

It certainly must have been hell for you to have to decide what should be done with the place. I can so well understand your wanting to keep Father's top cottage and tree plantations. On the other hand, I hate to see you burdening yourself with the business of running the whole place. After you buy it in its entirety, can't you lighten your financial burden by selling off, in lots, some or most of the road front property—keeping only that road front which you need for rights of way? This would leave you all the good tree and farming land—and still leave you some high up spots which you could, if you wanted, sell to friends. It may not be too great a burden if you can find a good manager who has a good business head and also knows forestry and farming. Are the OPA regulations such that you can't put tenants out if you actually sell the property? . . .

Your own plans sound very, very interesting, and I do hope your trips, your radio and your office work out as you want. Also, I do hope Tommy gets an apartment for herself before fall. Everyone of us need some little spot where we can occasionally shut out even our best friends! . . .

Everyone we see is flabbergasted with the possibilities opened up by the use of the atomic bomb. I don't see how it can help but hasten Japan's surrender—particularly now that Russia is in the fight too. . . .

Anna

"*. . . So strange not to hear Pa's voice . . .*"

August 23rd, 1945

Mummy darling:

During those days between August 12th and 15th I wanted so very badly to phone you! As you said in your column, it did seem so strange not to hear Pa's voice over the radio. I just sort of felt during all those days that the true significance of the Japanese fold-up, the atomic bomb and the entrance of Russia into the war with Japan, were not brought home to the people as a whole with any sort of inspiration. Even the British broadcasts did more to make one feel the emotion of it all. I wondered whether Pres. Truman would call you and am happy he did. But, it wasn't enough! With the limited material that is printed out here, we may have missed some of the good things said. But, to us, your column has been the only clear and ringing voice "in the wilderness." Very apparently you did a very real service thru your column decrying the surging sentiment for immediate removal of all war-time controls, as Pres. Truman very decidedly changed his tune in a couple of days. Then, too, you have done a superb job on Russia—and, last but not least, a beautifully restrained but, oh so effective job of reminding people of Pa's work in the Russian situation and in the development of the atomic bomb. How is your column circulation going? Both John and I feel you are doing a wonderful job—and you have the good gift of writing simply and lucidly enough for the average person to understand rather complicated problems.

We had a lunch and dinner with Beanie [C.B.] Baldwin and ex-Gov. [Elmer] Benson [leaders of National Citizens PAC and, by 1948, they emerged as leaders of the Progressive party that nominated Henry Wallace, in opposition to President Truman and Thomas E. Dewey] while they were out here. . . . I'm afraid that Beanie and Benson weren't too encouraged about starting a National Citizen's Com. P.A.C. in Seattle. This state is still predominately AF of L, and the CIO here is still dominated pretty much by the same little group of Commies. In everyone's mind out here, the CIO-PAC is either one and the same thing as the Citizen's Com, or is too closely affiliated with it. The liberals, in this part of the country are badly in need of constructive (respectable!) new blood. . . .

We seem to have dinner guests practically every night—everything from arch conservatives to mildly liberals to rank radicals! They do come at seperate times!

. . . We all send you our love, darling, and think and talk about you so darn much. A specially big hug from me.

Anna

"*. . . [Secretary of State] Byrnes . . . isn't much beyond a nice feather pillow! . . .*"

29 Washington Square West
New York 11, N.Y.
Aug 27th 1945

Anna darling,

. . . My column circulation has been going up steadily until now I'm getting $300 or $400 more every month than I did in the W.H. I'm glad you & John think they are good. Someone took a test of readability & I came out [high]★ but the reason isn't so flattering. Lippman & Krock [Arthur Krock, another columnist of serious political analysis] require a college education to read & understand. A 5th grader can read me, so more people read me! Geo. Carlin was delighted but it is a rather doubtful compliment! . . .

Will you write me what you & John & each of the kids wants for Xmas? . . .

★Word is illegible, but the context clearly indicates this intended meaning.

Tommy really got a lot of good out of her vacation & now she has an apartment below me in this building. We are pleased & I'll use two rooms for servants & storage & pay part of the rent. . . .

I got upset over our stupid way of handling the end of lend lease. If our manners had been better the British couldn't have had so much cause to complain & I blame [Office of Economic Welfare director Leo T.] Crowley & Byrnes so I called same but he isn't much beyond a nice feather pillow!

May Craig [well-known Washington reporter] came on from Washington yesterday to tell me about her trip & her description of Dachau made me feel ill. The nurses there with our hospitals deserve some special recognition I think. Doris Fleeson [a newspaper columnist] has also been on & is writing a piece for the Sat. Eve. Post about me! . . .

Elliott & Faye are in Los Angeles & she's doing a picture. He can't be busy & I wonder if you asked him if he wouldn't go & see you. I'd like him to tell you about his troubles & I'd like your reactions to his state of mind & real desire to run the H.P. place. . . .

Devotedly
Mother

"*. . . far greater public service than all of the high-brow writers put together. . . .*"

Mercer Island, Wash.
Sept. 9th, 1945

Mummy darling:

At present John is off on a 36 hour cruise with Stanley Donogh and Bill Douglas (Justice)—a fishing cruise. And, I am nursing the household along as Sis came down 5 days ago with a tummy upset; the cook came down yesterday; Johnny came down with a cold the second day of school—and Buzz started a cold today!! Sis seems practically recovered today, and ditto the cook, and I think Johnny will be okay to try school tomorrow. So, I'm not too worried. Because we are a seaport town with direct connections with the So. Pacific and the Orient, there seems to be an epidemic of tummy poisoning going around. But, it is not a serious type, thank goodness.

Also, today, tomorrow and Tuesday we are running an ad. in the P.I. trying to get a couple to look after the household and place. And, as we have no downtown office all calls come in here. By the end of this evening I will have interviewed 4 couples. Two are still to come. But, the first two interviewed have children to bring with them. The white couple have a 2½ year old boy, and the colored a 10 year old boy. This presents a problem I hadn't thought of ! Anyway, it looks as if we'd get *something* out of our 3 days of ads! . . .

Mummy, you ought to be really proud of the test taken on your column on readability! After all, you *could* write the type of column which would be way above the heads of the average reader. But, I feel so strongly, that the fact that your column is understandable to the 5th grader on up, means that you are doing a far greater public service than all of the high-brow writers put together. . . .

. . . Isn't there some way that, in some states, the National Citizens PAC could have a different name? The fact that Sidney Hillman [of the CIO] holds such a prominent position with the Committee, is much against it in as pro an AFL state as this one. I have just learned they got Rabbi Cohn of this state to head up their committee here. He is in Seattle and is one of those rabidly in favor of opening up Palestine to all Jews. He has been after me to speak for them—on the grounds that the '44 Demo. platform called for this. I have an appointment with him tomorrow or Tuesday—but am going to steer clear of speeches on that subject! . . .

There has been some talk that John will be offered the head of Gov. Walgren's [Mon C. Wallgren of Washington] state reconversion committee. If it should come to a head, we would seriously consider it—as an interim, public-service job, until the newspaper situation opens up here. I would work with John, unofficially and in making speeches at meetings. The salary would be infinitesimal. But, we figure that if we truly believe in the potential growth of this part of the country, we owe some effort in making that growth realistic in peace time. Selfishly, it will keep us before a potential reading public in our own state. The hitch apparently is that Walgren has been told by some people that both of us are politically ambitious—and he wants no competition!

Yes, I would love the mink coat any time you want to send it. Are you sure you can't use it, or don't have someone you'd rather give it to? If you do send it to me, I am going to give Sis either one of two imitation fur jackets which I have worn quite a bit but which are still nice looking. That mink coat looked so nice on you that I really hate to have you give it up! . . .

John has just yelled that he is going to the post office, so I'll close in a hurry. A big hug, & so very much love,

Anna

"... *Fala is wonderful & enjoys life* . . ."

Val-Kill Cottage
Hyde Park
Sept. 13th [1945]

Anna darling,

. . . John's possible public-service job sounds to me a good thing to do if it is offered.

I'll send the mink coat early in Oct. I couldn't wear it. Black will always be more suitable! . . .

I've asked Tommy to send you a letter about a soldier in the St. Louis hospital who got polio overseas & if you are ever near there do go & see him. . . .

Pegler wrote one fairly decent column on Jimmy but today he attacks Pa openly & I would love to answer so it is taking much self control to keep quiet. Read it if you get a chance & remember how snidely he insinuates vast millions [in the estate left by FDR, which was of less than a million] & no thought for others in his employ. They [the family employees] are all receiving full wages & will be pensioned as Pa expected but it is best to say nothing. . . .

I doubt if you can separate N.C.P.A.C. from Hillman. He is the guiding force, the others can't function without his backing. . . .

I plan to come to the coast in Jan.[,] start at L.A. & work north. I'll stay awhile in S.F. for Tiny wants me to be with her when her baby is born & I'll do some lectures to pay for the trip. We'll go to you last for a couple days & stop one day in Portland for a glimpse of Sisty & then come home & get ready to go abroad in the Spring.

Fala [the family dog] is wonderful & enjoys life & I think I'll take the puppy soon[,] tho' how I'll manage them in N.Y. is a bit of a worry & what I'll do when Tommy & I both go away I don't know for Fala has no attachment to any employee! . . .

A world of love
Mother

"... I've written no letters! ..."

29 Washington Square West
New York City 11
Dec. 5th [1945]

Anna darling,

How could you think anything was wrong between us & I would not tell you? I've thought of you daily & rejoiced that we had had the time together but life has been literally so busy that I've gone to bed between 2 & 4 a.m. when I couldn't stay awake any longer & I've written *no* letters!

Thanksgiving was nice at H.P. but busy. The whole committee on choosing H.P. for U.N.O. [United Nations Organization, the original name of the United Nations] hd'qt's visited me in a.m. . . .

It was the day before we left H.P. that Tommy had Fala out on a leash & Blaze [Elliott's dog] had followed the colored maid down & jumped on Fala. He had gone for Scoop [nickname of one of Elliott's children] once & Elliott felt he could not risk keeping him. I felt badly for them but had to take Fala at once to the vet & leave him there. I was afraid he might not pull through but he is fine & I am to get him on Sat. Laura [Delano] has got me a lady Scottie 6½ months to give Scoop & Faye. Elliott & Faye have had a bad time, the dog publicity & then the vestry elected Elliott & Bishop Manning reproved them & said he would not allow him to serve. The Bishop gave it to the papers & that was unpleasant! . . .

Poor Tommy had a finger badly torn trying to rescue Fala & the doctor found she had blood sugar again so she has been miserable. . . .

Devotedly
Mother

In the search for a publishing venture, John's usual caution appears to have vanished with a proposition he and Anna considered in Phoenix, Arizona.

They found that buying an existing daily was too expensive. Starting a new daily required the ability to absorb staggering losses before breaking even—if it ever did. So John and Anna were attracted by a way designed to sidestep both those hazards—but with hazards of its own. In Phoenix, a city already outfitted with two dailies put out by the same conservative, anti-Roosevelt publisher, the Boettigers were offered the purchase of a small shopping news—a giveaway weekly—which they hoped to enliven with respectable editorial content and eventually convert it to a daily. "We have been invited," John wrote his brother Bill, "to start a daily newspaper in a western city. . . . There is no going concern, no plant, no presses—nothing." In fact, all there was of the paper, besides the value of its masthead, was an assortment of rickety furniture and a few old typewriters in a cramped, gray frame house on North First Avenue. Anna writes her daughter at Reed College: "Right now (or rather up to now) we have financed our newspaper by ourselves. If all goes according to the plans we've laid out, the newspaper will carry itself until we have to build a small plant and buy a press. This will mean borrowing money. And, we cannot expect any personal income from the newspaper for at least a year. . . . All of this means only one thing, and that is that we must all be very careful of every penny we spend." Mother advised daughter to seek out a job waiting on tables for pocket money.

A crisis that soon threatened the life of their new enterprise—and was to torment Anna and John for many months—was the postwar shortage of newsprint paper.

Early in December, Mrs. Roosevelt was chatting with Franklin, Jr., at her Washington Square apartment when her telephone rang. She became especially alert as the caller identified himself, saying, "Yes, Mr. President . . . No, Mr. President." As Franklin recalled it, suddenly her voice turned to a tone of protest, "But, Mr. President, I have no experience in foreign affairs. I don't know parliamentary procedure. I couldn't possibly do it. . . . All right, Mr. President, I will think it over."

"That was the President," Mrs. Roosevelt needlessly informed her son. She added with slight bewilderment, "He wants me to be a delegate to the United Nations Assembly in London next month."

The choice was entirely political—and Mrs. Roosevelt had no quarrel with that. Only a month before, Truman told the new secretary of state, James F.

Byrnes, that there were two people who were indispensable to him as political allies: Henry Wallace, because of his high standing with labor unions, and Mrs. Roosevelt, particularly because of her acceptance by black voters. He instructed Byrnes to find a proper—and conspicuous—position for Mrs. Roosevelt. While Byrnes was still sitting in the President's office after suggesting the United Nations appointment, Truman placed the call to her. A few days later, her nomination was approved by the Senate with a single dissenting vote, that of Theodore G. Bilbo of Mississippi, the Senate's most flamboyant white supremacist.

". . . All my plans are changed. . . ."

Thursday Dec. 20th [1945]

Anna darling,

. . . I'm glad you are going to look into the Phoenix proposition tho' you are so well settled in Seattle that I can't help hoping things pan out so you stay there.

I'm sorry Johnnie may get mumps but it's best to have them young. . . .

The corner cupboard has been on the way some days by Railway Exp. You'll have to fetch it when it arrives & I fear they did not prepay charges so I enclose a check. Father bought the cupboard when we were living in Washington in the R. St. house [1916–20] & then it stood in the hall at 49 till we sold the houses. . . . I rearranged my living room & it looks much bigger.

All my plans are changed & I leave on the 30th of Dec. by boat for England. I'm leaving Tommy here, she isn't well. . . . [Ambassador to Great Britain, John Gilbert] Winant will find me someone there. I'm going to write the column but nothing that the press is not in on where the conference is concerned but I think there will always be personal things which can be made interesting. I won't be seeing you therefore dear for quite a while. . . . They say we'll be gone from 3–6 weeks!

You will be relieved to hear that I had a physical check up & for my age I'm a remarkably healthy specimen!

I'll call you Xmas day between 12.30 & 1 our time.

I like Walter Kirschner [a wealthy acquaintance who kept offering to lend money to family members] but he has certainly adopted the family. I hope none of the boys take favors without doing the equivalent in work. He seems to me a bit exotic & I'd find easy intercourse difficult but I liked his niece & nephew who were there & I think he is genuinely kind.

Much, much love darling. Say prayers that I'm really useful on this job for I feel very inadequate.

Give John & Sis & Buzz & Johnny kisses for me on Xmas morning & tell John to give you a specially big hug from me.

Always devotedly
Mummy

". . . I'll just do my best . . ."

> [Aboard Queen Elizabeth]
> Dec. 30th [1945]

Anna darling,
  Just a line from the ship to tell you I am comfortable & tho' the responsibility seems great I'll just do my best & trust in God.
  I made a will since I've not yet been able to buy the place & am sending Tommy a letter of specific bequests to you which she'll put in the file.
  It seems that Boston (backed by the Vatican) & H.P. are the two choices for a permanent home [of the United Nations Organization]. That would change the picture on [the value of our Hyde Park] property considerably. . . .

> A world of love darling
> Mother

Mrs. Roosevelt devised a novel (for her) means of communicating with all the members of her immediate family while on the United Nations mission that she was certain would leave her scarcely a moment of spare time. She scribbled a detailed and almost daily diary of events and impressions, sending it to Tommy. Tommy transcribed it and sent copies to family members. Anna preserved her copies among precious papers—which indeed, these were one day to become.
  Mrs. Roosevelt's fellow delegates were Secretary of State Byrnes; Edward R. Stettinius, Jr., FDR's last secretary of state, who was now U.S. representative on the Security Council; Senator Tom Connally, Texas Democrat, chairman of the Senate Foreign Relations Committee; and Senator Arthur H. Vandenberg, Michigan Republican, ranking minority member of the Foreign Relations Committee. In addition, the delegation included five alternates: Representative Sol Bloom, New York Democrat, chairman of the House Foreign Affairs Committee; the committee's ranking Republican, Charles A. Eaton of New Jersey; FDR's Postmaster General and Democratic National Chairman Frank Walker; former Republican National Chairman, ex-Senator John G. Townsend, Jr.; and John Foster Dulles, foreign affairs adviser to Governor Thomas E. Dewey, 1944 Republican presidential nominee.
  After arriving in London, Mrs. Roosevelt was assigned to Committee III, which was to oversee humanitarian, social and cultural affairs. This committee—soon to become the active and influential United Nations Educational, Scientific and Cultural Organization (UNESCO)—was expected at first to be relatively bland and uncontroversial, and therefore a safe spot for the former First Lady.

Weds. Jan. 2nd. [1946]

  A curious New Year's Eve! I went to bed at 8:30 and was glad to be oblivious to the ship's roll at midnight. I did think of you all at home before I went to sleep and wished for each one individually a happier New Year than the last. I breakfast alone at the Captain's table each morning as the senatorial families do not arise and shine early. After breakfast I walked the deck and talked to a number of people. Then I set to work on the material we had been given and with time out for lunch, I read till I had to get ready to go to a party Mr. Stettinius gave for the whole delegation at five o'clock. More reading, dinner, more reading and ten-thirty bed. So far I have remembered to put my watch ahead one hour each night. Last night was bad, fog horn most of the night, heavy roll and much colder. I used my rug for the first time and was glad to have it. I know a few more things I forgot, a nail brush and I only brought two hair nets besides the one I am wearing which is already nearly in shreds. Tommy mail me two more. This morning I began to be busy seeing people—at ten o'clock Freida Miller came and brought me Frances Perkins memo which seems quite easy to understand. We talked till eleven and then went into the conference room to meet and have Mr. [Alger] Hiss of the state department go over the agenda with us. From twelve-thirty to one Dr. Bunch [Ralph Bunche, also of State] went over the questions of trusteeships with me. After lunch I went back to the conference room and Mr. Hiss, with some eight or nine others, went over the question of specialized agencies with me. Three to four-fifteen I read some more official documents and fell asleep occassionally. Then I went to have tea with Col. Gwynn's little group again. There the talk is good and I stayed till five thirty. On returning to my room I . . . had to hurry to get ready and go to the Captain's cabin for cocktails. The Senators and wives, Congressman Bloom and his man Friday, the Executive Officer and I made up the party. I like the Vandenburg's more than I do the Connollys ★ but I don't like any of them much. Senator V. is all upset over the atomic energy proposal but I think that is Secy Byrnes' affair and not mine. Here I had to pause and dictate two minutes of words which I am to say in a few minutes over NBC to the U.S.A.

. . . I've spent an hour and a half with the press getting a repetition of much that we had this morning from Hiss and Pavolsky. The latter is a smooth article, but Hiss, I am inclined to like. Now to bed for it is really twelve-fifteen by getting up time.

Friday, Jan. 4th. [1946]

Yesterday I was busy every minute I thought, but it was very similar to the day before. Today we had a morning session with the state dept. boys till 12:30, then a half hour with the people who are interested in seeing a health group called together. Lunch and the afternoon has flown. First a meeting with the girls of the secretarial staff. Then a photograph on the top deck of the whole delegation. Four-thirty tea with the executive officers of the ship. After that a visit to the ship's hospital and to the hospital for the soldiers being carried, in this case the patients are nine Dutch marines. Lastly a talk with our own marines. . . . I've refused an invitation to lunch next Sunday with Lady Astor. This evening I talked with Mr. Stettinius for half an hour and he

★Mrs. Roosevelt quite consistently misspells Vandenberg and Connally.

approves of such plans as I have so far laid out for myself in London. The tears came to his eyes when he spoke of Franklin and the ideas which he had talked over with him. I believe it is a sense of loyalty to F.D.R. which keeps him on the job. Went to hear the Senators broadcast at ten, but conditions, atmospheric, I suppose, made it impossible to get through. Now to bed.

I have been assigned a gray-haired Miss Norton from Boston. She did the columns for practice, though it is understood that on shore she works in the office.

Sunday evening, Jan. 6th [1946]

The columns describe the landing and drive to London and our luxury here, so I will only say that Sen. Connolly kept repeating: "Where is all this destruction I've heard so much about, things look all right to me." I started to point out bombed spots but soon found he just wasn't interested. They all went out to lunch today with Lady Astor and Adlai Stevenson went with them and he told me the Senators made much the same remarks to him. . . . John Winant came in and was sweet. It is hard to believe that whatever his financial troubles are that there is any lack of integrity involved. The tears came to his eyes in talking of Franklin. The rest of the evening was recorded in the column. At nine-thirty this morning Miss Cuddy came and she stayed until nearly one. We did two columns and I dictated some notes and listened to her phone some messages in order to judge what she would do. I think she will do all right, though she is not as good as the one who will be at the office, slower and not as accurate.

January 7th [1946]

Two letters from you today.

Breakfast here is eatable (Claridges). I take tea and toast in the morning. For the rest if I am not going to a friend, I eat at the Embassy canteen which is a four block walk. I have now from nine to ten to do all personal work, columns, notes, telephones, and beginning next Monday I will have to do personal stuff from eight to nine as we have a delegation meeting at the office every morning at nine-fifteen. It is a five minute brisk walk from the hotel but we meet on the seventh floor and the lift runs more slowly, and far less reliably than the one in our old apartment house here. Therefore, I must leave at nine sharp. At ten-thirty we must be at the general meeting place in a church house near Westminister Abbey, nearly a fifteen minute drive. Committee meetings will be there and we do not get back till late. This morning I began work at nine here. At eleven we met at 20 Grosvenor Square, which is our office building, for our first delegation meeting to decide on press policy. Senator Vandenburg is difficult. I was worried about independent action but he doesn't want to even listen to anyone else. On the boat he circulated a secret memo giving his objections to the wording of the Moscow resolution. He gave it to the press in confidence, he says, tonight it is on the front pages of New York and London papers. The Times man sent it in and says everyone knew about it. Ten minutes before a scheduled press conference at five-thirty, Mr. Dulles told Mr. Stettinius that he and Mr. V. could not go to a press conference where they could not answer questions, this had been agreed to this morning because Secy. Byrnes arrives tomorrow night and this should be discussed with him. After we had gone up, Sen. V. walked in and took some of the remaining press people up to his room. It seemed to me pretty shoddy behavior though I was in sympathy with parts of his memo. I think he is right that language should be clear. Mr. S. seemed to show up well, calm and no apparent anger.

To go back to my diary, our meeting ended at twelve-thirty. I went to my office and went over what had come in there, and at one-fifteen John Winant came to take me with him to lunch at the Churchills. They were charming, the only other guests were the First Lord of the Admiralty and Lady Cunningham. He was at Quebec.

I am on the "Humanitarian and Cultural Committee" and Senator Townsend is put on with me. At three in my office we met the technical advisers, got our home work, a weighty sheaf of several pages, which I still must read tonight. Arranged to meet at ten-thirty tomorrow morning.

At four I talked to both United Press people here for an hour. At five I gave a tea party for Mesdames Connelly, Vandenburg, Dulles. Lady Reading came, Dorothy Brown brought the Marchessa Roselli and Lady Salter rang up so I asked her. Ben Welles and his fiancee came in, and also Mrs. Blaisdell who is working for UNRRA, and I think I accomplished what I hoped and these ladies will see something of what the war has meant to England and they won't leave thinking this hotel is the way everyone is living. They will have to tell their husbands since together I fear they only dine in good society and visit the Clivedens which still exist.

At five thirty I was sent for to go to Mr. Stettinius's room and hear the bad news about Vandenburg and Dulles. Then we went to the press conference where all went well till the inevitable question came: "Where are the two Republican members of the delegation? Does their absence indicate a split in the delegation?" Mr. S. said: "Certainly not, you men who were on the boat know that is not so. I think Sen. Vandenburg is probably at a committee meeting." Then we left quickly.

My tea party was still going on so they seemed to have a good time. . . . Since my return . . . I've written several longhand notes. One [to] the Queen who sent me today a sweet note of welcome. I am sending home by slow mail carbons of all columns, letters that we should keep or you might like to see. Everything is ready for tomorrow morning and I must go to bed and read. It is 12:30.

January 9th [1946]

I didn't write last night because it was too late after I got back. . . . Miss Cuddy comes at 8:30 and apologizes for being late, when I just barely manage to drink my tea and get it taken away!

Yesterday morning I worked with Miss Cuddy till 10:30 and from then till one I attended a meeting in Mr. Stettinius' room, going over the people the delegation was to back for the various positions with the reasons for the choices. They now want [Paul-Henri] Spaak of Belgium for President of this session of the Assembly. The Big Five are not asking for any of the elective positions so as to avoid being thought to want too much domination! The British and ourselves would like [Lester] Pearson of Canada for Sec. Gen, but that will take Canada off the Security Council. This type of choosing runs through all the positions but all may change at a moment's notice so I won't tell you any more. . . .

Secy. Byrnes got in on time yesterday and Mrs. B. came with him. Mr. [British Foreign Secretary Ernest] Bevin called on him in the evening and he saw the Senators and Mr. Stettinius and all seems to be serene on the atomic bomb statement which stirred up such a rumpus with Sen. V. I am not sure the gentleman does not like a little newspaper publicity. . . .

I had dinner alone tonight, read a long memo on the refugee question which we must try to put off till the next part of this session, and still be prepared on if Great Britain insists on having it taken up. A new type of political refugee is appearing—people who have been against the present governments and if they stay at home or go home will probably be killed. Britain is supporting most of them and would like the expense shared—the budget for the job might run to double what is contemplated for the whole of UNO. I have a few more things to read tonight. . . .

January 11th [1946]

The columns today and yesterday were very full so I'm just sending this personal note and news. The sessions were short so I got home and found Maude and David [the Grays] here and we then had lunch together. They are unchanged and it is grand to be with them. They are, at least Maude is, hungry for news and very anxious that I at least go home that way, so I'll try. We had dinner and the evening together and David went home early and Maude to bed about 10:30 and now I've cleaned up my desk and am ready for tomorrow. . . .

A delegation of G.I.'s came today to ask if I could find out a definite policy for the 45 to 60 point men in this area so I agreed to write Gen. "Ike". I told them I wouldn't carry weight but I think I'll write the President too.

I'm liking old Sen. Townsend and I'm going to see his giant farm in Delaware some day!

". . . my presence seems to remind them all of him[,] . . ."

Claridge's
Jan. 11th [1946]

Anna darling,

I think of you all in the land of sunshine & hope it does Johnny a great deal of good. It rains daily here but is much less cold than last time & in this hotel we are very comfortable & the food is very good if very expensive.

I'm glad the kidney test was o.k. but watch such things. You are less rugged than your Ma. The old lady holds up very well under the load of work here & believe me it is formidable! Tommy will send you the copies of my diary letters which I try to send when I can't say it all in my column. It is bad not having Tommy or someone who knows the people with me & overworking new secretaries seems inevitable[,] but I am managing tho' some of the letters I sign make me smile, they sound like Senators or State Dept. officials!

My contribution to this meeting, beyond the fact that I am Pa's widow & by my presence seems to remind them all of him[,] is very insignificant. Perhaps when we get to work on our Com. I shall feel that there is more I can do. I've got on well with the delegation & I don't think they've tried to hide anything as yet!

I gave your messages to Gil [Ambassador Winant] & the Churchill's.

I'm writing much longer columns here as they asked me to do so for European papers which are buying it but it may be much cut at home so I mail the copies of full columns to Tommy slow mail & later you can all have copies if you want them.

Auntie Maude & Uncle David came today. They . . . are selling the Tivoli place for $7500.00. Maude is sharing my room & I fear I will keep her awake as I write late & get up early! . . .

A hug for you,
Mother

January 13th [1946]

I won't need any money from home, I imagine, as I find I have some in my account here with Baring's. I must have left it here since the trip I made with the boys. I can't take it out of the country so I might as well use it.

Yesterday was the first day of voting, which means that we just go and sit. I felt I had to go or something might come up and I would not be there for consultation. You know I don't like sitting and doing nothing. I wrote the President about the G.I.'s complaint which seems to me entirely reasonable.

I will only be with UNO through the second part of this session. The government only pays me the days I work and I only have a secretary while I am working. She will be of no use for regular work. Remember in getting someone that we will be away a great deal, or at least I will, since I want to do some lectures and go to the west coast soon, next if the session is not held till the summer I will go to Russia in the spring. If the session is held in April I will probably go to Russia in the early or late summer, which ever fits in best with Elliott's summer plans, as I do want to go to Campo with them and be at Hyde Park when the children are there. . . .

Maude has gone to bed. Tomorrow we begin meetings at the office at 9:15, so I leave here at nine. I have Miss Cuddy come now at one and try to do the column while I drink a cup of soup for lunch and go through the mail. If I can't get it done she has to stay till I get home and then I do it and send her off to get it passed and sent by messenger to U.P. . . .

Jan. 16th [1946]

Your nice long letter came this morning after what seemed like a long silence and I was beginning to worry. How long my letters were in reaching you!

I heard today that the Army does want me in Germany and now I shall plan to go to Ireland the day after the conference ends, spend one night, come back here and leave for Germany at once. The army will deliver me in New York. I am glad to be flying back but I'll probably send my big bag by boat with one of the others.

I am doing my column now from 8:30 to 9:30 every morning and if I don't finish I dash back and dictate while I drink my soup for lunch. The dinner last night was interesting as a sight, and I like Peter Fraser who sat one side of me but the old Belgian Ambassador sat on my other side and I never liked him when he was in Washington. . . .

I watch our delegation with great concern. Secy. Byrnes seems to me to be afraid to decide on what he thinks is right and stand on it. I am going to try to tell him tactfully that everyone has to get the things they need from us and that is our ace in the hole. We could lead but we don't. We shift to conciliate and trail either Gr. Britain or Russia and at times I am sure a feeling that we had convictions and would fight for them would be reassuring to them. Secy. Byrnes is afraid of his own delegation. He has held very few meetings and now we begin to need them and yet we have to ask to see him in separate groups. It isn't that he is leaving me out, for the others complain to me. . . .

London, January 17th [1946]

. . . I went to the Byelo Russian dinner and arrived at the end but I think they were very grateful that I went and understood why I could not go earlier. I said some pleasant things and got on well with them. I tasted Vodka and *don't* like it.

Home at 11:00 and have just finished the mail, rather light tonight and I think I'll get an extra hour of sleep. . . .

How is Elliott's book coming and has any part gone to the publishers. He promised to send me typed copy to read but it hasn't come.

January 27th [1946]

. . . Sen. Vandenburg is funny about his committee, says they won't agree to anything and he doesn't know how long he'll be here, but I think he does it to be important. . . .

At 3 Mr. Stettinius called a surprise meeting to go over again our position on Secretary General. Vandenburg's position is funny and I am interested in the way all the legislators react. I think not having strong convictions they doubt their ability to defend a position which they may take so they can not decide on any position and go on arguing pros and cons endlessly.

At 3:30 I gave my vote and left for a trip to see some new housing down near the docks and I got Mrs. Connelly, Vandenburg and Dulles to go. . . . I dined with [old family friend Sir] Arthur Murray. He read me a chapter in a book he is about to publish. It is about FDR and very nice. Then he told me how he saw the world scene and I was interested. He was active in Washington with Gray and Tyrrel (during first World War) and has been in Parliament and in business and more or less in touch right through the years. His opinion of Winston except for the period after Dunkirk is none too high. . . .

I'm not so convinced that Great Britain and ourselves must line up to keep the Russians in hand. I think we must be fair and stand for what we believe is right and let them, either or both, side with us. We have had that leadership and we must recapture it. . . .

January 29th [1946]

. . . A wire came from Louise [Macy Hopkins] this morning saying that Harry was failing rapidly and at about 6 the United Press called me to say he had died. I'm sorry they couldn't have had a few happy years. . . .

At 10:15 I had to go to a meeting with Stettinius who wanted to tell us the Security Council had chosen [Trygve] Lie of Norway for Sec. General. It was well done I think and we took the lead and though our first choice was Pearson of Canada, when we found the Russians wouldn't consent but would compromise, we proposed Lie. The papers should not be pessimistic, progress is being made here. Vandenburg and Dulles are largely responsible for pessimism, I think. These representatives of ours don't build friendship for us, they have no confidence so they are rude and arrogant and create suspicion. Honesty with friendliness goes down but they haven't the technique. Jimmy Byrnes' over-cordiality isn't right either. Why can't we be natural and feel right inside and just let it come out?

January 31st [1946]

Your letter of the 26th and 27th came today and I was glad to hear. I assure you when I don't write I'm just too busy and if I am ill I'll let you know.

Tomorrow we begin three sessions a day and I had to give up going to Maude as we have them Saturday! . . . They say definitely we'll end the 9th. Weather permitting I'll go to Maude Sunday and from there to Germany and then home. . . .

Yesterday was the usual pattern. 9:30 delegates meeting; at office, 10:30 committee meeting. Ate and dictated column, saw a doctor on national health organization, went to BBC and did two recordings, 1 for Infantile and one for Amer. Broadcasting program. Had tea for a Swedish woman and a Jewish refugee, went to Port of London Authority tea and Turkish Embassy. Freida Miller dined with me and I had all the women delegates here in my room. . . .

At 7:30 five soldiers who asked me to dine came for a drink and I got rid of them at 7:55 and was at the Norwegian Embassy at 8:30 for dinner in honor of Mr. Lie. Now the mail is done and I must go to bed.

February 2nd [1946]

I heard tonight that Stamford, Conn. was the favored site for UNO. The committee arrives Sunday, tomorrow night and rumors will fly fast and furious.

For two days I've had no voice. No cold, just no voice. I hope it returns by Monday night when I have to speak at a dinner.

I gave up going to Ireland and then we only had a morning session. Both of my secretaries are ill, however, so I was glad to have a quiet afternoon to get through the mail. . . .

I've been notified to mail in two extra columns to cover the return trip but they can be short ones. . . .

I was supposed to go to a buffet lunch but our driver couldn't find the place and I was so late I gave it up to come home and get today's column started and telephoned my apologies. Worked till 3:30, saw the King of Greece who didn't come the other day. Then a man from Luxemburg with a book, then Peter of Yugoslavia and his bride. The king looks (can't read word) [inserted by Tommy in transcribing hand script for family] and little Peter younger than ever. They all want to come to the U.S.

. . . I went to two cocktail parties in the hotel on getting back, one the San Domingo people and the other given by Frank Walker. At nine I went to the stage door canteen and back at the hall for 9:30 to midnight listening to speeches on UNRRA. Everyone agreed with Sol Bloom, praised his speech and patted him on the back and he was as pleased as a little boy and went off today to board the ship to-night and sail for home feeling a hero. I think he felt kindly toward me though he hated not being a full delegate. He is able but so many foibles! All these important men have them, however. I'm so glad I never *feel* important, it does complicate life! . . .

February 3rd [1946]

In reading the Times of the 31st, I saw a notice of McDuffie's [FDR's valet for many years] death. Will you send the enclosed note to Lizzie [Mrs. McDuffie].

My voice is a little better but none too good. I had breakfast at 9:15 and read papers, etc., till 12 when the Philippine delegate came to talk about his resolution on free press. We talked about his country too and I hope in some way I can help them. He left at 12:30 and then Senator Townsend . . . came to lunch. We then went to the service at St. Paul's for the delegates. . . . To my surprise they sang Cecil Spring-Rice's hymn which I think lovely. . . .

Soon I shall have Mr. Russell (United Press man who handles column) and Mr. Watson for tea. The latter has bought my column while I'm in Germany and Mr. Russell seems pleased. It will be my last visit from him. He has been helpful though he's given me a lot of extra work!

Mr. Stettinius comes to dine alone and I hope to learn a few things! I'm going to bed early. . . .

February 6th [1946]

I am sorry I couldn't get a letter off yesterday so here is the diary for Tuesday and Wednesday. Column 8:30. Delegates meeting 9:30, reported on refugee troubles and left for 10 a.m. committee meeting leaving Sen. Townsend with the boys in the delegation meeting which he loves. He joined me about 11. Committee was one long wrangle. Finally at one I asked for a vote, the Russians who always play for delay asked for a sub committee to try to get a resolution we could agree on. It is hopeless as there are fundamental disagreements but Peter Fraser is fair to the utmost. He asked if I would withdraw my motion and then appointed a committee. I was a half hour late for lunch with the Anthony Edens in the House of Commons. At 2:30 I opened a doll show. At 3:10 we sat down in the sub-committee at Church House and we got up at 6 having agreed on 25 lines. Then I went to the ceremony of the Women's Appeal which I hope got some play in the U.S. Was home at 7 and dined with the Grenfells at 8. At 10:45 when I was back and working, the advisers came down to show me a compromise paragraph they hope we might get agreement on. I finished the mail at 2:30 and was too weary to write.

At 8 a.m. we started on the column while I ate breakfast. No delegates meeting because the boys couldn't agree up to 11 last night in the Security Council and so they couldn't have a meeting at 9:30 thank goodness!

At ten we went to work in the sub committee again and at 12:45 the Russians and Yugoslavs on one side, the British, Netherlands and U.S. had agreed to disagree on all new points brought up! Lunch with Miss Bernadine for women delegates and some others. Plenary session at 3, election of judges and I was not needed. Left at four. Lady Cripps and her International Youth Group came[,] just six in the group. Gave me a memorial resolution to FDR and we talked till 5:10.

Dictated tomorrow's column till 5:30, was called for and went to staff meeting of UNRRA office in London. Talk and question till 7. Dressed, dined at 8 with Winant who has had bad flu and was up for first time. We had a nice time alone and I left at 9:45 and have now finished mail and am going to bed.

Tomorrow we are trying to meet with an even smaller group before the sub committee meets but I think we cannot agree. I will tell any of you who are interested what I have learned in these meetings. It is a liberal education in backgrounds and personalities but one thing stands out. Since the Civil War we have had no political or religious refugees fleeing our country and we forget to take it into account. No European or South American forgets it for a minute. Next it seems to take years of stability to make you look beyond your own situation and consider that there are human rights that operate for those who think in a way that you think wrong!

My voice is back and fine! . . .

". . . Everyone wants to see me, . . ."

> 29 Washington Square West
> New York City 11
> Sunday, March 3d, 1946

Anna darling,

It was so good to hear your voice & then to get your letter & wire. I hope you get newsprint. In roundabout fashion I hear that Mr. K. [Kirschner] is worried for fear you pay too much for the radio station & cannot earn enough. That business [radio] is new to you both so I hope you will be careful.

. . . It has been hectic since I got back. Everyone wants to see me, the mail is enormous & all the boys are in & out! . . .

Much, much love & a big hug,

> Mother

". . . I'm getting too old for this travelling . . ."

Anna darling,

If we miss meeting in the East I shall feel very sad for I don't see much chance again for a long time. . . .

What an idiot I was to come west to see you all! In the future I'm going to stay home & wait for you all to come & see me. I'm getting too old for this travelling anyway & I wouldn't go to Russia if everyone didn't seem to feel it might be useful just now, & the same will hold good later of China I fear, but then, believe me, my travel days are over! I hated the trip out here & am still deaf so the time really has come to stop! . . .

> Mother

". . . The crowds are almost reverent . . ."

> 29 Washington Square West
> New York 11, N.Y.
> April 15th, 1946

Anna darling,

Ever since you left, I have been so busy even in my few days at Hyde Park that it has been impossible to write & the mail is terrifying!

. . . I grieve over your long trials in getting newsprint. . . .

I'm glad you liked what I said at the ceremonies [marking one year since FDR's death]. It all seemed dignified & simple. Just the President & I went out to the grave & he laid his wreath & no other flowers but those from the greenhouse were there. Later the diplomats placed wreaths. Today I took a spray of lilies over from the family. . . .

Elliott & Faye have . . . an apt. on May 1st in the building on 5th Ave. & Wash. Sq. They are lecturing & doing recordings for a joint radio programme & life seems rosy!

Jimmy [asked to have] the portraits of Granny & her husband in the hall [of the Hyde Park home]. . . . No one took the Gilbert Stuart & I am glad. Last Sat. 700 visited the house & the papers say several thousand came on Sunday but no admission was charged that day to Dutchess Co. people. The crowds are almost reverent as tho' they really cared deeply. . . . Very quiet, & no laughter. . . .

Devotedly
Mother

Being the offspring of a popular former President can take over and run one's life as readily as being his active widow. In the years immediately following FDR's death, not only Mrs. Roosevelt but all of her children found themselves heavily engaged as trustees of Pa's place in history.

In these early post–FDR years virtually every decision that had to be made with regard to the FDR legacy required that the Roosevelt daughter and sons hammer out a "policy." As they were trained to do since childhood in family discussions around the dinner table, the Roosevelt children used each of these decisions as cause for vigorous exchange, difference of opinion, argument, sometimes distrust and injured feelings. Yet beneath their frequent battles and genuine hurts and resentments, there endured a foundation of affection and loyalty. Neither was a disguise for the other; both extremes characterized their complex family feeling.

The following, from Anna to Franklin, Jr., is an example of how family members were learning to think through the responsibilities of their "trusteeship."

". . . it's just 'way down deep.' . . ."

350 North First Avenue
Phoenix, Arizona
May 20, 1946

Dear Frankie:

It's taken me longer than I thought to answer your grand letter of May 8th—but I think you can imagine how swamped we've been with the details of moving, and with getting caught up with work. Our furniture starts arriving tomorrow, and by the end of the week we ought to be fairly well settled. Young Johnny is going to school until it closes next Thursday, and has already made enough new friends to keep him well occupied all summer!

By the way, don't, please, give any further thought to the things you apologized for. They were forgiven long ago—as you know. And now, I'm only interested in hearing from you that you've been through the medical mill and are your old self again. . . .

Now, about the movie of Father. . . . It seems to me all important that the immediate family should not only pass on every phase of the movie, but should also see to it that the movie company's research staff has all possible proper material available to it. I would doubt sincerely if this is possible until all of Father's papers, now in the National Archives Building, are sorted as to what goes to the government, what to the family and what is returned to certain people who wrote Father highly personal and confidential material. I realize that the "settling up" of these papers involves court action, but don't see why they can't be sorted by competent experts right now. I have a conviction that the executors could get people like Bernie Baruch to finance these competent people. I know, for instance, that right after Father died, Bernie offered to pay Isadore Lubin [U.S. representative to the International Labor Organization] a good salary for a few years, if the family should agree that the papers should be sorted immediately, and if they should agree that Harry Hopkins and Sam Rosenman wouldn't have the time to do it.

Another example of the type of material that should be collected and taken into consideration before a movie is made of Father is this: I had lunch, alone, with Felix Frankfurter, soon after Father died. Felix told me he had a complete file of every letter and memo that Father ever wrote him, and that many of them were revealing as to Father's thinking and planning. He said that Father would write him a letter on a specific subject, but that in the middle of the letter he would interject a paragraph which did not deal, alone, with the subject at hand, but dealt very significantly with his overall policies. He also pointed out to me that Frances Perkins had kept verbatim notes on all of her interviews with Father; that he had seen some of them and they are most significant. Henry the Morgue [Morgenthau] should have some things akin to this, and undoubtedly Harold Ickes has others. According to what Isadore Lubin told me, Bernie B.'s idea was that well chosen people should be paid to collect this material as well as to sort the papers.

All of this seems of paramount importance to me *before* a really good movie can be made.

Now, as to revenues from the movie. John [Boettiger] and I still feel as strongly as ever that the family should not receive remuneration for such a movie—or from it. I recognize Jimmy's and Elliott's and Johnny's feeling about making trust funds for their kids. And, I recognize that ours may be in plenty of need for such! But, we do feel so darn strongly, that we have no right to capitalize on Father's accomplishments in life. It seems to us that the greatest thing we inherited from him was a deep responsibility to see that the things he accomplished and stood for are presented constructively to the world, and are used to further his high principles for the good of the world. And, none of this is said histrionically—it's just "way down deep."

Practically, I can see that the family may have to incur expenses in connection with the making of a movie on Father. Trips to Hollywood, for those who don't live there; help in going over material and in giving advice, could all be construed as legitimate expense. But, none of this will ever amount to anything which will be tantamount to possible trust funds. In other words, I can certainly agree to the expense angle—but nothing further.

And, we do not like the idea of having Milton Diamond handle this movie for the family. It seems to us that it should be someone who is a close friend of the family and whose loyalty we can count on.

Further, rather than to have Jimmy and Johnny "notify five outstanding companies that we are ready to consider offers," it seems to me, that it would be much more dignified if they notified these five outstanding firms that we have already been approached by one outstanding firm to make this picture, and that it means so much to us, that we feel that if other firms are interested we should talk to them, too, and find out if others are anxious to make this picture. In other words, I don't agree to our seeking, as a family, to have this movie made. Also, we should be sure that these five outstanding firms have among their directors (of movies) men whom we are sure have the knowledge and understanding to make such a picture.

If members of the family should notify movie companies that they are ready to consider offers it is obviously a commercial interest on our part.

As to the MGM picture with Lionel Barrymore. John tells me that it was a definite policy of the motion picture industry to get a release from the family of any character being portrayed in a movie. If this release is not secured, the family have an excellent chance of winning a good law suit. In this case, the main thing is to stop the picture or have it corrected.

This is a H———— of a long book, but I've honestly tried to condense my answers to your letter. And, I'll be mighty interested to hear what your reactions are, as well as Mother's and the other boys.

Jimmy told us, when we saw him briefly at the L.A. airport, that you had sent him a copy of your letter to me, of May 8th. So, to simplify matters, I'm sending copies of this to Mother and the boys. Why don't we all "live next door" and really simplify matters!!

Lots of love from all of us.

Anna

". . . evidence of your ownership . . ."

350 North First Avenue
Phoenix, Arizona
May 31, 1946

Dearest L.L.:

Attached is a certificate, evidence of your ownership of two shares of Class A common stock of Arizona Times, Inc.

You know how grateful Anna and I are to you for joining in our enterprise and in making possible the whole financing program.

Devotedly,
[John]

Mrs. Franklin D. Roosevelt
Apartment 15-A
29 Washington Square West
New York, New York

"*. . . I don't want to see Father on the stage . . .*"

Val-Kill Cottage
Hyde Park
July 20th, 1946

Anna dearest,

Hours spent in the hospital, with what time I have in the apartment divided between doing mail, columns & seeing the inevitable people who turn up as soon as one goes to town, is not conducive to letter writing! As I wired you the operation [Tommy's, to remove her gallstones] was done successfully on Thursday a.m. We spent 2 days in hospital having tests & xrays made to be sure all was safe. She was in good condition & yesterday Dr. Whipple found everything so fine that he made her sit up in a chair for ten minutes. They believe this keeps the patient from embolisms & adhesions. She was still in great discomfort today & told me she would never have had it done if she had known how ill she would be afterwards! By the time I get down tomorrow to see her I hope she will feel a little better & by Tuesday there should be marked improvement. . . .

Sept. 23d I serve again on the Assembly & the President also put me on his Committee to study higher education. . . .

I think Diamond is ok to deal with the movie people but I'm not always sure he isn't working *for* them & not for us so I've become very explicit lately in writing. I don't want to see Father *on the stage* no matter who asks it. I liked Bob [playwright Robert] Sherwood's idea of a story of things he had done for people & occassionally cutting in a picture of him where he had spoken or done something . . . The other biographical picture I'm willing to let Diamond negotiate about & even glad to have material collected but no production for 20 or more years I hope. . . .

Mother

"*. . . Separate tables in the dining room . . .*"

Campobello
July 31st [1946]

Anna darling,

How I have wished that I could just put all of you on a magic carpet & wisk you here in a few minutes. The air would do you all good! . . . Tomorrow there are ceremonies & the unveiling of the Memorial to Father & Friday a.m. we leave.

Elliott & Faye & the children have been here a week & they love it. They want if we can work it out to go shares on putting it in order & then run it like a family club. Separate tables in the dining room & prorate expense. Granny's house would cost too much to put in order but ours we hope can be done. . . . All family could come at cost. Fred Adams says there is no sale value so I hope we can get all land etc. for $1500 & Elliott will go shares. . . .

I keep forgetting to tell you that I told the people on the atom picture they could only use back shots of Father & I won't approve any other. I also have said I would welcome a documentary of the period showing his work & results in nation & abroad but giving no impersonation of Father[,] only a real picture taken of him & a real speech which he made. The biography will be done someday & I'd be glad to see a company do the research & get material which may not be obtainable later but I want no picture now or for 20 or 30 yrs. . . .

Devotedly,
Mother

As the congressional elections of 1946 loomed, foreshadowing the presidential election of 1948, the Democrats' predilection for intrafamily squabbling had been elevated into a major, bitter, seemingly irreconcilable split. The left wing of the split, organized around opposition to President Truman's Cold War policy of sternness with the Soviet Union, was launching as its hero Henry Wallace, who had fallen out with Truman. The Left was flattered to have so distinguished a rebel voice, and Wallace was flattered by the attention as a potential presidential candidate.

Mrs. Roosevelt shared many of Wallace's reservations about Truman's policies. But she regretted Wallace's attack on a plan, proposed by Bernard Baruch, that would have emphasized caution in sharing control of atomic energy with the Soviet Union. In turn, Baruch publicly attacked Wallace. Among other concerns, Mrs. Roosevelt feared that the split would doom the Democrats at the polls—especially endangering the fate of Herbert H. Lehman, running for a Senate seat from New York.

". . . She feels I was most inconsiderate . . ."

Val-Kill Cottage
Hyde Park
Oct. 6th, 1946

Anna dearest,

. . . There has been much talk of your running for Nat. Committeewoman. Is it just talk or is your rival afraid & taking this way of forestalling your candidacy?

You haven't sent your Xmas wishes yet & time is growing short for me, tho' it may be that our hours won't be as bad as I expect when the Assembly begins! . . .

I think the Democratic rows on the high levels have pretty well given the Republicans the election this fall. . . . Mr. Baruch & Mr. Wallace have both been a bit foolish I think, but they all feel so important they can't wait to speak their minds! . . .

Cousin Susie on my last visits has been miserable. She feels I was most inconsiderate to have an accident [in August Mrs. Roosevelt broke two teeth and suffered bruises when her car was involved in a collision between Hyde Park and New York] & Henry [her husband] didn't consider her when he committed suicide & between us we've given her another nervous breakdown! Poor Henry! . . .

Devotedly
Mother

". . . one of his pals slips him MEAT! . . ."

The Arizona Times
Phoenix, Arizona
October 7, 1946

Darling:

This darn town has not succeeded in yielding any bright ideas for a suitable birthday gift for you! . . .

The main thing is that your Phoenix tribe wants you to know they will be thinking of you all day on October 11th. . . .

This is our third day of working in our new plant. . . . Our big press is about two thirds erected and should go into operation about Nov. 1st. Today is the first time we've come out with a Tuesday issue. . . . Last night we were down here until 1.45 a.m., waiting for the first press run, because we had some stereotype trouble.

Did I tell you that our couple, Oscar and Elsie left us for a better paid job? Anyway, we've now got a couple who keep us in stitches of laughter. He was a chef with the Harvey Restaurants for 17 years, and refuses to cook anything which "wasn't on the Harvey menu." He has no teeth, and talks a blue streak. BUT, he has had so much experience in buying meat for restaurants that he has butcher friends all over town, SO, twice a week, one of his pals slips him MEAT! It's the first we've seen in ages, and while not always good, it is still nourishing. Last night it was the grissliest beef stew we've ever eaten! His wife cleans very well, sets the table very badly, and is very pleasant. They both love children and dogs and are really good (so far) at handling both. They are fifty years old, have two grown children and a seven year old grandson; have never before done housework, but are trying it because they got tired moving around and wanted a home. The latter, they said they could not afford on their own with present day prices. All together we think we're very lucky and hope they continue to work out. . . .

An extra big hug from me.

Anna

". . . some people might buy wanting to be my neighbor. . . ."

29 Washington Square West
New York 11, N.Y.
[October 9, 1946]

Anna darling,

. . . I got the pen & pencil sets for Sis & Buzz this a.m. & they will be marked & sent to you from Abercrombie & I'll send you a card for each to go with my things later. I'll get Johnny the dart set & toy car & send from Schwarz to you. I'll order Buzz's handkerchiefs & get the desk caraffes for you & John & the black bags with shoulder straps for you & Sis. I'll send John also a little check to use toward riding shoes. I will also be sending your things I had marked for Xmas, they are not bought presents but I hope you will like them too. Did you get the jewelry of Granny's I sent?

I am afraid the Wallace controversy makes it hard sledding for any of our state Democratic tickets. Lehman might pull thro, but I feel shaky. Registration is high in the cities however which ordinarily would mean a democratic victory but since the meat shortage & cost of living is so high it may mean rage at the Federal administration! Henry Wallace is wrong on the atom bomb I think though I wish Baruch could have been more patient. . . .

I'm afraid Mr. Koons [lawyer for the FDR estate] is not wrong & the property will have to be advertised. I think the best way to safeguard the situation you fear is to let Elliott buy outright as he can but put a clause in sale that if he has to sell or wants to any time the other members of the family shall be given a chance to buy. Neither he nor I would want to lease & if it is sold to outsiders I shall not live there & told Mr. Koons, thinking some people might buy wanting to be my neighbor.

Beanie Baldwin was nice & sad & I don't think he's a communist[,] just afraid of being a red-baiter. I agreed to do just 2 things for them[,] speak [at] an N.C.P.A.C. ladies "School of Politics" & it is done. The other I may or may not do depending on developments. Won't work for I.C.C. [Independent Citizens Committee, a left-wing political action group]

I'm well, my ailments when I'm conscious of them are largely because of age! Tommy is better too.

A world of love to all & a big hug to you.

Devotedly
Mother

". . . Father is all full face & quite horrible. . . ."

29 Washington Square West
New York City 11
Jan. 19th [1947]

Dearest John,
    . . . Yesterday Mr. Kirschner came to tea with me & told me how pleased he was with your progress & that you would need more money & more advice but he was ready to rush to you if you didn't come here first. He's a generous soul & gave Wiltwyck [School for Boys, a training school for waywards and a favorite charity of Mrs. Roosevelt's] a breathtaking contribution! . . .
    I hope with you Sisty won't marry too young but I've hoped that many times in my life! You may be more persuasive than I was.
    I just pray you may come East in February & in April & I'm all agog at the prospect. I was going to give up this apartment April 1st but I'll keep it till May 1st so I can be here with you. . . . It will be better for me to really settle in H.P. & just keep a double room & bath in Tommy's apt. where any of us can stay but only in relays! . . .
    We saw the atom scientists picture & the part with Father is all full face & quite horrible. I have protested & may get out an injunction. Before April I should know if I own any land at H.P. Of course I won't give up this apt. till that is settled. Kiss Anna for me.

Devotedly
L.L.

". . . letters going back to Father's childhood. . . ."

[This letter is typewritten and apparently went to each of Mrs. Roosevelt's children other than Elliott.]

Val-Kill Cottage
Hyde Park
February 16, 1947

Dearest Anna:
    As you know, Elliott and I have been going through endless boxes of old letters and we find letters going back to Father's childhood. We have decided that a very fascinating book, showing the development, with photostatic copies of the letters in many cases, could be done with a minimum of story written around the letters, very much in the way that I did my Father's letters.
    Elliott will do the work and he will take the advance, but on the book we would like to write a foreword which all the children will sign, stating that

we felt this book would be not only historically interesting, but a satisfaction to many of the people who had been fond of Father, as they could see his development through his own letters.

If you are satisfied with the work when it is done and will sign the letter, we will make it a family project and anything over and above the advance would be divided equally among us.

Will you let me know how you feel?

Devotedly,
Mother

"... I must move the farmer & our cows & chickens & pigs ..."

29 Washington Square West
New York 11, N.Y.
Feb. 19th, 1947

Anna darling,

... I've been leading my usual idiotic existence. It has to stop but somehow once you are "in the swim" it is hard to pull out!

It is the Smith Farm [Moses Smith, a Hyde Park neighbor] which we intend to use for cows & chickens & a two family house that needs immediate work. No milk house & we must have one, small & built out of cinder blocks with a concrete floor for it has to be clean as we will sell cream & use skim milk for pigs & chickens. We have to buy a pasteurizer if we sell according to state laws. Mr. Koons told me yesterday that even tho' the Trustees have agreed to sell to me it won't be sure till the surrogate & the grandchildren's guardian approve. That consent may not be obtained till July & I must move the farmer & our cows & chickens & pigs out of the old farm as soon as possible. Incidentally to carry itself I must get a "big" start by April 1st. We can put the fields in cultivation anyway & Elliott is going up today to start getting estimates. . . .

I think it is wonderful Sis is doing well in philosophy. She should meet Dr. Chiang, the delegate from China on the Human Rights who talks continually of Chinese philosophy as it influenced European 18th century thought & I see blank looks around the table among the South Americans & Russian group who don't care much about ancient philosophy! . . .

Devotedly
Mother

"*. . . Buzz looks . . . like his Father but I hope that may change! . . .*"

Hotel Oaks
Chico, California
Saturday, March 8th [1947]

Anna darling,
Tommy & I have been wanting to tell you & John what a wonderful job
you have done with Sis & Buzz. There is complete security therefore poise &
calm. Buzz looks a bit like his Father but I hope that may change! He is the
nicest child & I can see what a satisfaction you must get out of his sense of
integration with you both & family responsibility. He . . .
March 9th Had to stop & go to dinner & then drove down here & found
your letter last night. I am furious at being here when you are in N.Y. I
believe I'll just stay home after this year & let all of you come to me! These
trips are an effort, their value is problematical, & I don't make anything
except expenses out of them! I imagine one reaches more people by writing &
I can do that at home!
Sis [now nineteen] was fine. Not shy at all & we both saw much of her &
the young man. He is a very nice, sensible boy & good for her I should
think. . . .
A big hug to you

Mother

By early October, Anna and John had built a plant and installed in it a huge
press, both heavily mortgaged. They started publishing their *Arizona Times*
twice a week, then three times a week. On May 1, 1947, their paper made its
bow as an evening daily. While appearing a glorious success story, actually
this fruition of John and Anna's dream was shrouded with trouble. The fund
of borrowed money was dangerously low for sustaining inevitable losses yet
to come. The strains of the challenge enlivened Anna but severely shook the
confidence of John, who was increasingly haunted by a lifelong sense of
lacking the proper stuff. The burden fell on Anna to prop up not only John's
self-confidence but their confidence in the marriage itself. She was visiting her
mother in New York less than a month before the paper's debut as a daily
when she wrote an urgent and remarkable letter to John:

[April 9, 1947]
My darling, you are about to board a plane for Seattle, where
you may be requested by one or two of our prospective investors
in our Arizona Times, to pledge my future inheritance as
additional collateral. I am only writing this note because I know,
from all you've said, that you do not agree with me that we should
do this.
On the contrary, I feel this way: You should bargain with the
buzzards up to the hilt (or to the limit of their telling "us" to go to

hell). After that you must give concessions that you deem necessary. *And,* of those concessions intail of money which I will inherit directly from Father's estate . . . then I *want* to gamble that inheritance in this project of ours. Why? Because I have unbounded confidence in YOU, and in "US" as a team. I fully accept the "dare" to "US" to succeed, and what's more, I love it!

Our children (and Johnny's training will be the same) have been trained to stand on their own feet, and I do not feel that . . . we owe them more than that.

Don't ever forget this trust and confidence I have in YOU! Above all—I LOVE YOU—but I also mean every word I've written above!

Your Anna

". . . I'm reading the old Jungle Book which I used to read to you . . ."

Campobello
July 19th [1947]

Anna dearest,

Here we are after a very long trip up. It was a caravan, truck, station wagon & my car. The children moved from car to car, Fala stayed with me & Frannie & a new 2 months old white Basque dog rode in the station wagon with 4 colored people! We spent the night at Ogunquit [Maine] & saw Faye [Emerson] in "State of the Union." She is very good but the part says all the things she would want to say so she can be herself! She arrives here tomorrow with 3 friends. The house is not in good order but it can be made very comfortable & sound in construction with comparatively little expense. . . .

I still don't know whether I go to Switzerland on Aug 23d but I have been asked to serve on the Assembly again & await Senatorial confirmation. . . .

We've had fog every night since we came & gray days but I hope it will clear tomorrow. . . . I've revised for the last time I hope the nine chapters of the book & tomorrow I start dictating new stuff. Fala seems happy but he did not enjoy the long trip. We still hope Frannie is going to have puppies. She looks very fat but we keep our fingers crossed till the 23d which is supposed to be the day. I'm reading the old Jungle Book which I used to read to you to Chandler & Tony [Elliott's children] & they love it.

One is so far away here that wars & rumors of wars seem to recede into the background & yet I am really discouraged over Russia's attitude on the Marshall plan & find it hard to understand. Elliott feels they think we won't come through but even that makes no sense to me for they are furnishing the reasons why we shouldn't! . . .

Devotedly
Mother

In the distribution among her children of many of their father's legacies, Eleanor gave a special plum to Elliott, who, at thirty-six, remained unpredictable, often troublesome—and whom, out of guilt over her confused feelings, Eleanor so often favored. She had given Elliott the valuable privilege of editing and publishing Franklin D. Roosevelt's private papers. Elliott obtained a contract to compile them into a series of books. He received an advance guarantee against royalties of $10,000, which appeared handsome, and which stirred distrustful responses in Anna and her brothers (although Elliott's explanation of where the money was to go cast the treasure in quite a different light). Elliott offered a plan (restated in detail in Anna's letter of July 21) for all the Roosevelt children who endorsed the book to share in additional royalties, if any. The siblings, distributed from coast to coast, wrote one another, feeding each other rumors of what Elliott was up to. John informed Anna that Elliott had assured him that "the only editorializing" would be "purely identification of characters that might appear in the letters" with "no effort to interpret Father's development." Franklin, now in law practice in New York, reported to Anna of hearing "from my private secret service" that Elliott planned a preface "in which he *interprets*" their father's childhood, and that Elliott planned to emphasize the influence of Grandfather James "and practically no mention of Granny, etc."

The apprehensions of the siblings finally came out in the open in the following letter from Anna to Elliott. She wrote it shortly before leaving with John Boettiger for Norway in a desperate attempt to buy a supply of newsprint to keep their daily paper alive. Elliott, hurt by Anna's tone, sought moral support from Mother. Protectively, Eleanor scolded Anna on July 28, before Elliott summoned up the directness to answer Anna himself the following day.

[Phoenix, Arizona]
July 21, 1947

PERSONAL AND
CONFIDENTIAL
Dear Elliott:

Thanks for your letter of July 14. I have enjoyed very much reading Mother's Foreword and your editor's notes for the first volume of Father's letters.

Tell Mother that I was terribly surprised and, naturally, very personally unhappy when I read in her column that you and she had already left for Campo—because I have Mother's letter before me which says you are all leaving for Campo on August 15. I do hate to think that I will miss seeing all of you both going and coming from Norway.

As long as I won't have a chance to see you for quite some time to come, there are a couple of questions which occurred to me after reading the galley proofs and your letter:

1. Will Jimmy and Franklin and Johnny and I have a chance to see the "brief historical and biographical notes" as well as the "short commentaries before each section" while the book is still in the galley proof stage in case comments occur to us which we would like to pass on to you?
2. The next to the last paragraph of your letter is not clear to me—probably because I may have missed intermediary family discussions. In case you don't have your files with you, it is as follows:

"If you approve, and your name is listed, 10% of the royalty received from the sale of this book will accrue to you and your heirs, less an advance which has been paid to me for the research required for the footnotes."

If all five of us children and Mother should each get "10% of the royalty received from the sale . . . less an advance which has been paid me" this means that 60% of the royalty received will be accounted for. What happens to the other 40%?

Also, can you let me know what percentage of the total will be deducted in the way of an advance for you?

I hope you don't mind my asking these questions, but I am sure you can understand my interest in the letters.

The weather has been really hot here the last few days and we have thought often of all of you at cool Campo.

In view of the above questions, I am not answering, until I hear from you, the letter I received from Duell, Sloan & Pearce, Inc., enclosing duplicates of the galley proofs you sent.

Lots of love to you all,
[Anna]

Mr. Elliott Roosevelt
Campobello Island
Eastport, Maine

". . . what a critical & almost hostile letter . . ."

Campobello
Saturday July 28th [1947]

Dearest Anna,

I was distressed to hear from Tommy that I had written you Aug. instead of July. We left home *July* 15th & leave here Aug. 14th or 15th. I think you & John will enjoy the trip to Norway if all goes well & I hope you will get the paper you need. . . . I am dreadfully sorry to miss you but of course none of us can make our plans when we live so far apart, & have them dovetail. . . .

Elliott gave me your letter to him to read & I hardly think you realize what a critical & almost hostile letter it sounded like. The "notes & historical data" are identifications of places & people, the research has been considerable to identify & put the letters in order. The publishers paid an advance but Elliott says it has already cost him more. We none of us know how these will sell. I suggested originally that they be published. I only divided the mail in the boxes (I still have a number to do). I hope you have received from time to time letters from yourself to Father, to me or Granny. Father's letters I gave Elliott, he did the reading, sorting etc. & all the work. At the beginning I suggested that all of us sign the foreword & each of us (outside of Elliott) receive 10% of net profit after advance as I liked to feel that we all had some share in the enterprise. When I found you were all unwilling or reluctant to sign I told Elliott to call the whole plan off but he persisted in the 10% idea. You must know that by the time letters are in galley proof there is no time for extensive changes & I can think of none that you could make since these are matters of fact which we have had trouble in finding out. They occured before you were born & when Father was not yet in political life. This volume ends with college.

Elliott has already put all his earnings of the past year & the money he borrowed from W.K. [Walter Kirschner] into the farm. After Oct. if you come East I hope you will come up to see what has been done. He will have more of an investment than I have in it & while we will be partners, he will own the major share. There are plenty of building sites for children or grandchildren should they ever want them. I hope it will be the one place where there are roots for a family needs that I think.

Good luck to you & John on this trip. A great deal of love to him & a special hug to you.

Devotedly
Mother

Elliott's letter to Anna of July 29, 1947, written from Val-Kill, assures her that his "commentaries" will only include historical and biographical notes and identification of people and places not made clear by the letters themselves. The $10,000 advance was to cover secretarial, research and travel costs—to Groton, Harvard, Campobello, Hyde Park and New York for personal interviews to obtain factual background, and for examination of school records and newspapers—and these costs, including the pay of five researchers and two secretaries, already amounted to more than $12,000. "So, you can readily see," asserts Elliott, "that I am not riding a free gravy train as your letter implies." Elliott concludes warmly with his concern and Faye's for the success of the Boettigers' trip to Norway, hoping against "any lessening of our close family ties" and looking forward to the chance to "talk to each other and understand each other's problems." Elliott states he "will be ready to give you and John any aid within my power when I can be of assistance in your enterprise."

". . . he was reluctant to show it to me. . . ."

Val-Kill Cottages
Hyde Park
Aug. 4th [1947]

Anna dearest,
   Your letter from the plane came two days ago & I am praying hard that you & John are successful. It seems outrageous that you can't get paper here. "The Daily Worker" [the newspaper of the Communist party] got it from the "New York Times," how about your trying them? . . .
   I saw your letter to Elliott only after we reached here. I think he was reluctant to show it to me. . . .
   We had much fog but now it is lovely here. The book *[This I Remember, second volume of her autobiography]* has gone ahead & when we leave we will send you new chapters to read.

Good luck & a world of love,
Mother

". . . there is to be another baby . . . I believe. . . ."

Val-Kill Cottage
Hyde Park
Aug. 20th [1947]

Anna darling,
   . . . I wired Mr. Baruch & asked him to send you some information for your broadcast as neither Elliott nor I could think of any material. Points in favor of free enterprise are the obvious urge of human beings to work harder for their own. Need of world now is production & we should utilize this urge in human beings. Our success due to natural resources but other resources must now be developed. . . .
   Elliott says you will get complete page proof on the letters very soon. Please read fast & send James & tell him to send Johnnie & have him return to F jr. Research has all been to verify facts & explain allusions. For instance who was "old rubber boots"? Elliott did not mean any other members of the family should have done work on the "letters", obviously only one person could. Three of you are too far away & F jr. is too busy.
   I go to N.Y. the 9th for the U.N. Assembly briefing. Except for Sunday I'll probably be there 8 weeks. Dec. 1st I must be in Geneva, Switzerland, & that will last till Dec. 19th. Could I have Xmas wishes now please as I must get everything done soon?
   Jimmy comes on Sept. 4th I understand & there is to be another baby as you know in Jan. I believe. . . .

Devotedly
Mother

". . . The Norwegians [don't] show much gratitude. . . ."

29 Washington Square West
New York City 11
Sept. 19th [1947]

Anna darling,

. . . I'm delighted that you & John like Van [Seagraves, Sis's future husband]. He made such a good impression on us too & yet I'm glad that he & Sis are taking another year at Reed.

It was hot here for the start of U.N., but nothing like what you recorded in Phoenix. I like [new Secretary of State George C.] Marshall to work with. I doubt my work in Com. III will be heavy this year so I ought not to get tired.

I shall pray that you get the newsprint. It does not seem to me that the Norwegians show much gratitude for all Pa's devotion to their Royal family in exile. The paper seems to me so very good & is read by the whole household including the kitchen!

W.K. as usual makes me mad. He wouldn't accept a 2d mortgage because I was not in it & I couldn't be because the land belongs to Elliott. He's all paid on interest & now he's taken the mortgage!

My letter was just to let you all know just what was done & how[,] since I felt all of you should know. I don't think Elliott meant everyone wasn't entitled to their 10% on the letters, whether they sign or not. The advance comes out first, then 10% to each child & to me & mine goes to the Memorial Foundation, the rest will undoubtedly go to the government in taxes. Elliott's share to the place. The original letters will of course go to the library. I hope Tommy has sent you your letters which I found? . . .

I'm glad you like the latest chapters & I'll mention that Pa & I paid the [White House Christmas] bills. I thought I had. . . .

I hate your having all this extra anxiety & hope it will soon be over. The darkest hour comes just before dawn!

Devotedly
Mother

". . . I love a fight against a reactionary monopoly, . . ."

The Arizona Times
Phoenix, Arizona
Sept. 27, 1947

Dearest Mummy:

Well, we [had] our talk with W.K., and nothing happened of any great moment. He said he thought that with business conditions as they are today, that we had very little chance of making a success of the paper, and that we'd be better off quitting now. When we talked about trying to sell it, he brightened up—because he saw a chance of perhaps getting some of his investment out. That was actually all that happened.

And, now we have just finished our talk with Charlie Ward, and his advice is substantially the same as W.K.'s. He feels there is a chance that newsprint prices will go up instead of down; that wages will go higher, and that prices will keep on going up for the type of equipment we need in our business. Therefore, he feels we should liquidate immediately if we can't make a quick sale—which he doubts if we can. John told him he was worried about future work, and he promptly said he could use John in his business, very well. Be that as it may, I think it does give John a feeling of an anchor to windward.

John has been terribly upset and pessimistic for a long time now, and I know he will be relieved to be out of it. He is not built to enjoy that kind of a risk when it's someone else's money he's gambling with. To me, it is more disappointing than I can tell you. I love a fight against a reactionary monopoly, and I hate to see the latter winning out in so many fields of endeavor in this country today—and particularly so in the newspaper business as it is really the chief avenue of information which the public has, and which they should be able to count on if our form of government is going to go on successfully—and, while most of the public don't know it, they have fewer and fewer newspapers in this country today which they can depend on to be truthful. The whole damn newspaper business has simply become "big business."

Well, we'll see Marshall Field [a Chicago newspaper publisher] on Monday, and I doubt if he'll want to buy us out because he's already so heavily invested in losing newspaper properties. . . .

I can't write any more—I'm really feeling pretty low.

Lots of love to you,
Anna

"You have given them hope again. . . ."

[29 Washington Square West]
[New York 11, N.Y.]
[October 10, 1947]

Dear Mr. Baruch:

Anna and John dined with me last night and told me of your very great kindness to them. I can not tell you how much I appreciate what you have done in lifting their spirits and helping them.

I hope you will be successful in getting together enough people to lift them over what I hope will be their last hump in the financing of the paper and that you will be successful in getting them newsprint, which after all, is essential if they are going to publish a paper.

I think the paper is good and I see it every week. I have a feeling there is a future in Arizona and that they have a future in this paper. Anna herself is such a dynamic person and both of them are so capable, I can not believe that they will fail if these first difficuties are overcome.

You have given them hope again and I know they will do their very best to be worthy of what you and Franklin's other friends may do.

John told me how you feel about my remarks on Wallace and the 1940 Convention. I think I did not explain sufficiently carefully and I will talk it over when I see you which I hope will be soon. I want any other criticisms that you have, as so often it is a case of knowing things and not expressing them well. It is very valuable to me to get the impact of what is written on someone else.

With my grateful thanks, believe me,

Affectionately,
[Eleanor Roosevelt]

". . . a paper like a farm has to watch all the little leaks . . ."

29 Washington Square West
New York 11, N.Y.
Oct. 20th [1947]

Anna darling,

. . . Mr. Baruch told me he had telephoned you that he had 400 tons of paper for you & he feels confident that with others he will get the financing. I've written John a note because I feel if he can get to feel he can succeed your battle is more than half won. You won in Seattle & you can do it here & now over a period of time & with good business management. I guess a paper like a farm has to watch all the little leaks to cut losses. Henry Morgenthau stresses that to Elliott whenever they meet.

Life has been rough on you for a long time but I hope the tide will turn.

I love you darling, & think you the finest most loyal human being I've ever known. God bless you & remember when you can rest again a home always awaits you all at Hyde Park.

Devotedly
Mother

The following letter gives the first clue to how deeply and seriously John Boettiger had sunk into pessimism, immobility and depression. Since autumn, the *Arizona Times* had been losing $30,000 a month. Writing to Buzz at the end of October about "our very dear but gloomy Pops," Anna explained what she would not say outside the immediate family: "Just like last spring, last summer, and long before that, he is *sure* the property cannot be made to pay. And, as per usual, we have spent hour after hour arguing and getting nowhere. It's very sad."

The disagreement was over more than the business decision of whether to carry on. Anna could not abide his pessimism, his fearfully black moods, insomnia and angry outbursts. Fearing for her own physical safety as well as his mental health, she begged him to seek the help of psychiatry, but he would hear none of it. Still hoping to save the paper—as well as herself—from his destructive turn, Anna worked on him to go away, to seek peace in travel and what rest he could find, to leave the care of their home, their son and their business to her. On December 1, 1947—the day before Mrs. Roosevelt wrote this next letter from Europe—the separation of Anna and John began. Anna took over running the paper alone.

If the storms raging in John were more than Anna could understand and handle, soon to come was additional explanation of a most excruciating kind. Perhaps with the intention of consoling her, one of their *Times* colleagues told Anna that John had been seeing another woman for some months before leaving. That others had known while she did not made the learning infinitely harder to bear.

This episode throws a new light on her comment to me in 1967 of how she emotionally sided with her mother's pain at hearing of her father's love affair with Lucy: "I remember my first reaction was that I was mad at Father for having at one time hurt Mother. Because I was a *woman*, you see. And this could easily happen to me." Now the drama, previously separated from her by a generation, had engulfed her.

The letter that follows also provides Eleanor's first mention of a man a generation younger than herself, Dr. David Gurewitsch, who was to become a presence in all her remaining days. They met in 1945 through Trude Lash, who had been a student with David in Freiburg, Germany. Cultivated, handsome and gallant, David became Mrs. Roosevelt's doctor. There was no sign of their becoming close friends until the end of 1947, after David had come down with tuberculosis and was ordered to recuperate in Davos, Switzerland. When he could not obtain a plane reservation, Trude prevailed upon Eleanor to pull strings. Due to go to Geneva herself for a meeting of the Human Rights Commission, Eleanor got him aboard as her traveling companion. The plane was fogged in at Shannon Airport, Ireland, for two days. In the dreariness of that wait, Mrs. Roosevelt read to David, brought him milk, mothered him, became his friend. From Geneva, she telephoned him at Davos frequently, writing him shortly before leaving: "Don't ever worry about being a nuisance. I've always liked you & was drawn to you since we first met & the trip just made me sure that we could be friends. I never want to burden my young friends & with all my outward assurance I still have some of my old shyness & insecurity & that is probably what makes you feel shy. I've really taken you to my heart however, so there need never be a question of bother again. You can know that anything I can do will always be a pleasure for me & being with you is a joy."

". . . all kinds of people go there for nerves . . ."

[Geneva, Switzerland]
Dec. 2d [1947]

Darling,

I have thought of you so much & hoped to hear all was well with the business arrangments & John's plans.

I enclose the Xmas check which I hoped to get time to send before I left but somehow did not!

Dr. Gurewitsch who came on the plane with me as he has to stay in Davos for awhile told me of a fine psychiatric clinic in Kansas City [presumably the Menninger Clinic in Topeka, Kansas]. He says all kinds of people go there for nerves & it is no stigma. I told him of John as a "case" & he said he should have a doctor's help, it might shorten the period of mental depression.

I wired Tommy today asking for news of you. We were much delayed en route & I arrived a day late but others were caught by bad weather too. . . . The two fog bound days at Shannon were peaceful!

All my love dear,
E.R.

". . . I am supposed to sell the U.S. . . . to Switzerland! . . ."

Geneva
Sunday, Dec. 14th [1947]

Anna darling,

A note from Tommy just come tells me of your trip to N.Y. & I hope the financing is set. I have a feeling great economy is in order & perhaps fewer columns. You are a wonder to carry all this & I take my hat off to your courage. It is doubly hard because of the emotional strain I know you must be under where John is concerned & I hope he can get some good psychiatric help & come back more quickly than now seems probable. Nevertheless, the next few months in which success or failure will be assured rest on your shoulders. You have the ability & the courage to meet it & I am deep in respect & admiration for you.

I hate to have missed you as I doubt if you will be East again but the unexpected does seem to happen.

The work here has been a constant drive & for that reason I will be glad when it is over. The place is beautiful & I find the snow covered mountains even more impressive than in summer. Food here is wonderful but everything except food costs more than at home & even food is not cheap. Bread is rationed & milk is scarce but Switzerland tho' more conscious of surrounding misery than we are is still a little self-centered, complacent & well to do community none too aware of her surrounding nations. These other nations struggle for existence & for freedom from dictatorship with the U.S. as their only hope & constant Soviet propaganda as their worst enemy.

I speak at a big meeting tomorrow night & from what everyone tells me I am supposed to sell the U.S. & the Marshall plan to Switzerland!

At 4.15 a.m. on Thursday, the 18th if all goes well we will leave by T.W.A. for the U.S.

. . . A world of love to you darling

Mother

". . . Darling, there is no use looking back. . . ."

Val-Kill Cottages
Hyde Park
Jan. 11th [1948]

Anna darling,

Here is a little wedding anniversary check. I hope there will be happier ones in the future.

John left this afternoon. I said little & I only hope what I said was right.

Darling, there is no use looking back. I hope you will have the strength & wisdom to put the paper on its feet & somehow I feel confident that you will. I think John will struggle & I hope the more difficult task of recovering a personal relationship which is once shattered can be achieved because of the great love you have known.

Sis & Buzz wrote such nice letters but I grieve to be away when Buzz hopes to come East in the spring, but I go about March 15th & won't be home till April 20th. They might like to stay here & I'm writing him that all will be in readiness. Will Van have a job before he & Sis marry? What do they want as a wedding present?

I'm going to Washington this week but I'll write at length on my return.

A world of love & admiration.

Mother

". . . the strain will show up when you begin to let down . . ."

Val-Kill Cottage
Hyde Park
Jan. 20th [1948]

Anna darling,

I haven't written because I could tell you nothing about John. He looks well. Elliott was to take him to Mr. [illegible] last night & if things shape up & he can get in to Russia I think that seems to intrigue him. Gen. Marshall said nothing to me & I thought I had better say nothing. Elliott will be back tonight or tomorrow & if he has anything to report I'll let you know.

John said Walter [Kirschner] & his friend were giving you trouble. . . .

You are a wonder to put up such a fight with John & keep the family happy over the holidays & keep the job on the paper going. Mr. Baruch told me he had not heard from you so write him how things are going & if you liked his testimony tell him so for he was very pleased when I called him about it today.

I think you are doing just right dear & I admire your courage, integrity & capacity. Cut costs where you can & rest when you can. You need it for the strain will show up when you begin to let down & are alone.

I hope Van & Sis get jobs & all goes well for them but Van better realize that he may not have a working wife for long! Of course I'll come to Sisty's wedding. I shall be anxious to hear what you do about the house. Moving now seems a terrible added chore.

Fala's grandson came to stay today & he's sweet but I don't know how Fala is going to like it for the young bore him!

Did you read Mr. Baruch's testimony? I thought it a blueprint the democrats should adopt & if they do Wallace will have a hard time [Wallace had decided to run for President as candidate of the Progressive party]. He will get many votes I think & achieve none of his objectives except perhaps to defeat Truman.

> All my love
> Mother

". . . give nothing out & . . . interest will lag. . . ."

> Val-Kill Cottage
> Hyde Park
> Jan. 26th [1948]

Anna darling,

. . . Tommy & Elliott & F jr. all think as I do that no statements would convince those who do not wish to be convinced. John is desperately worried for fear the world, & we, will think he is running out on you & his statements would be unconvincing. I think if he writes articles for the paper, the facts as they develop will be the best answers. If you or John are asked[,] stick to the same story but give nothing out & in the end interest will lag. Write what you wrote me to Mr. B. & he may be able to help with advertisers, he told me he would & I mentioned it to John who said his help would be harmful. . . . But if he [Baruch] knows what you are up against he may think of ways to help. Walter Winchel called Elliott yesterday & E. said it was your opposition giving out harmful rumors. B.M.B. [Baruch] can't be prevented from gossiping but he might make it useful if he understood what was going on. Walter Kirschner called me yesterday to say he heard I had called him which of course I had not done, but he talked to F jr. & told him he'd [Franklin] have to come out which F jr. will do I think if necessary. . . .

Elliott & F jr. Faye & Ethel seemed to get on well this week end, helping you & John is a unifying force tho' I always feel an explosion is not too far under the surface. . . .

I've never known such a winter, the snow is 5 ft. deep on some fields . . . !
I love it though & only grieve because Tommy gets so little joy out of the out of doors.

Tamas McFalla joined the family just a week ago & is completely a part of it. He's Fala's grandson & Miss Suckley trained him & gave him to me. He's 8 months & as friendly as Fala tho' a better watchdog. He sleeps with Tommy but walks with Fala & me & I feed both & all goes serenely tho' Fala still acts a little nose out of jointed now & then.

The book has been revised & I've written two more chapters & I try to do some work everyday tho' week ends it is impossible.

I feel sure you will lick your problems on the paper & if John just gets a job I hope all will come out well.

. . . All my love goes to you always,

Mother

". . . All I can do now is buckle down. . . ."

February 3, 1948

Dear Mom:

. . . I know that it is hard for all of you, from such a long distance, to realize how difficult it has been to see that this paper lives up to its financial responsibilities while it was being beset locally by all sorts of rumors day in and day out.

It finally got so the Advertising Manager and Assistant Publisher were being told openly by advertisers that they knew we were financially unstable and therefore not worth supporting, and that they had heard that John had left and was seeking a position in the East so that he could then move me and the family East. Our men could only reply that they knew nothing about this except that they had been told that the paper was in perfectly sound financial condition and that John was in the East on a business trip. But as these same people came back at them time and time again, it became obvious that their statements were not believed.

In addition to this, the whole situation has meant a loss to us in dollars and cents from an advertising standpoint, at least over the past four weeks, and some of the advertisers have acknowledged this. . . .

Time alone can tell what the final reaction to all this will be. And all I can do now is to buckle down to work harder than ever and hope with all my heart that John gets something which will give him a rest from responsibilities and yet prove of real interest to him.

I am so very, very appreciative of all that you've done to help out and keep things going smoothly in this difficult situation.

Maybe some day I can say thanks with more than words. I hope so!

Lots of love,
[Anna]

The rumors that Anna was instructing her salesmen to deny, that John had left the paper and had gone East looking for a job, were true. What seeped through his every application, every interview, was his pessimism, his despair, and a puzzling conflict that tormented him: No job that might be open to him was quite equal to his former station, and any job that might be good enough stirred his fears that perhaps he'd not be equal to *it*. So prospective employers, while perhaps flattered that a Roosevelt in-law came as a job seeker, were left with an uneasiness about the applicant. Nothing came of his search. By spring he decided to venture to Eastern and Southern Europe to collect material for a series of free-lance news stories and "perhaps a book."

He described what this time was like for him in a letter he wrote the following summer to Anna: "I hated being alive. I had no incentive to make anything of myself. I couldn't work. The wonderful stories I obtained in Europe wouldn't come out of my mind or my typewriter. I knew I had ability, but there are times when incentive is killed, and no driving or forcing can bring it back." He took to reading about a variety of religions, holding several exploratory conversations with a Catholic priest. What comfort these investigations promised seemed not to hold enduring appeal.

What Anna picked up, in bits and pieces, of John's state of mind she occasionally transmitted to her mother.

"*. . . right or wrong I'd stick to you . . .*"

29 Washington Square West
New York 11, N.Y.
Feb. 13th [1948]

Anna darling,

I was a little sad when I got your letter. . . . F jr. telephoned me today. He had talked to you & said you felt the paper situation was steadier & the personal gossip worse. That was what I thought would happen but I think you must do all you can to succeed with the paper & hope that John may be clearer thinking someday. I'm sorry he felt we were not interested but I can't talk to him. I can't know so many things & it will be better in the long run if we haven't said things we might regret. I'm very fond of John but right or wrong I'd stick to you in whatever you did as you know. John is coming up for Sunday & I hope he'll be there when I get back Sunday afternoon. Elliott is trying to get him off to Russia & he should sell to outside magazines. George Bye just phoned that he'd sold John's story on the Governor of Arizona which ought to please John. You are right on having to be careful in Arizona about articles & it will be better for John to sell outside.

I feel I've been little help to you in this but I don't know the business nor people to help you so I've felt both helpless & useless. On personal things I'll do all I can & with Sis' wedding I hope I can carry some expense for you. . . .

238 | MOTHER AND DAUGHTER

Four more chapters are done on the book, do you want to see them?
. . . Keep up your courage & I feel all will be well.

A world of love always,
Mother

"... *News looks worse & war looks nearer* . . ."

Val-Kill Cottage
Hyde Park
March 9th, 1948

Anna darling,

I've sent [John] a little note to Warsaw. He certainly should see much. He wrote me a line from the steamer thanking for some print I sent. Elliott says he has had no luck on Russia & fears he won't get the visa because things are deteriorating so fast that he doubts now in spite of the invitation to him whether they would let him in.

Before I forget, I must tell you that the paper looks very good to me. I always go thro' it critically. . . . It is swell that both circulation & advertising are improving. I long for the day to come when you can have a little leisure but I know with good nights of sleep you are still young enough to do a lot of work. I wish John would understand that you couldn't quit. Curtis [Dall] quit & you despised him but you couldn't carry on his business & pay his debts. This time it must have seemed like a nightmarish repetition but you could carry it. If John is himself again he may understand, but it will be hard to take if you succeed because it means that he, never having carried the full financial responsibility (he didn't carry it in Seattle) [,] was not in a state of mind to carry it. Perhaps it was lack of experience, perhaps it was the war. I hope you can both accept it & go on for the sake of your own happy companionship which means much as one grows older & for Johnny's security. Even the other two will be better off if they don't feel more instability in their home emotions.

I am interested that Buzz has decided on the University of Arizona. That means he'll live at home & perhaps help you? . . .

The research on the 2d vol. of letters should be nearly complete this month & ready for me to go over on my return. I won't finish my book but the rough draft will be done & I'll do final revising. . . .

Of course I'll give Sis & Van their flat silver, probably 6 of each & a full set & add year by year till they have 12 of each. If they don't get married in the Summer would you like me if I go abroad to the Assembly in Sept. to invite Sis to go? I wouldn't know till late August. . . .

Tommy & I were in Washington two days last week & I found my State Dept. contacts depressing. Everyone is so fearful! News looks worse & war looks nearer & I can't see anyone capable of clearing the atmosphere. Sec. Marshall did not want me to go to Russia. I don't believe I could now. We have no courage in action & talk too belligerently. . . .

We sail on the Queen Elizabeth March 27th at noon & Claridge's Hotel, London will be our abode till April 15. Then 15th–17th Zurich to see Dr. Gurewitsch, 17th–19th Brussels to speak night of 17th, 19th–21st Holland with Juliana & 21st back to London. Sail 22d & should land here 27th. Human Rights drafting com. begins May 3d which is also your birthday, bless you. . . .

Devotedly
Mother

". . . What friends Father made everywhere . . ."

[Holland]
April 20th [1948]

Anna darling,

My thoughts turn to you very constantly as these days go by & I wonder too about John. Have you news of him? Here there is interest in the Italian situation but work goes on from day to day & there seems less nervousness than at home.

Prince Bernard [Bernhard of the Netherlands] flew us over the tulip fields yesterday afternoon then over the Islands which were submerged & over Rotterdam & other bombed cities. All repaired & cleaned up. The docks almost entirely back into operation & the land in cultivation. Last night we saw films of destruction & the Welfare Minister sitting by me said "We do not think of the war. There is work to do day by day & we do it." Not such a bad motto for life is it?

Restrictions are severe for city people on food but better than in England. The rich can drive across the border into Belgium & buy Dutch eggs for .50 cts a doz.! No cheese here but plenty in U.S.A.! Germany was a source of supply & bought from them & that is gone. The East Indies, till political peace returns produce no revenues so they are badly off. They will make good use of the Marshall plan however & I feel buoyancy in the people.

This has been a strenuous trip, the only relaxed time was in Zurich & I was glad to find David Gurewitsch practically well. My first & probably only European degree has a most beautiful red & white silk hood & I am the first woman to receive an Honorary doctor of laws from Atrecht & it seemed to give the Dutch women great pleasure to have a woman so recognized! Apparently the Dutch women are moving forward, even after the war with considerably difficulty!

Here it has not been stiff & the welcome is warm everywhere. What friends Father made everywhere for the U.S. It ought to bring tangible results to us in the future if we are wise. . . .

Devotedly
Mother

". . . I love . . . you darling but get a job . . ."

Val-Kill Cottage
Hyde Park
July 15th [1948]

Anna darling,

I await anxiously some word from you & hope the delay means you are making arrangments to sell. I also want to hear about you, & John & Johnny. Do write when you can but don't push yourself.

I fear Buzz can have no job, but I can take him. I am a delegate & we sail Sept. 13th. He should fly East several days before & I'll arrange for his ticket. He can work for us in Paris & tell him to brush up on his french as Tommy knows none. I'll send him off on trips & try to make it profitable for him. They tell me they don't expect we'll sail for home till Nov. 24th & we might be later. . . .

Tommy & I loved being with you & the wedding was lovely & Sis will always have a wonderful day to look back on. How you went through all the strain I do not know. . . . I love & admire you darling but get a job & a salary & have less responsibility. I hate to suggest it but I wish you'd come East where in little ways we might make life easier now & then. Elliott would love it as much as I would.

. . . Tell Buzz we look forward to having him with us.

Devotedly
Mother

Anna decided at last to abandon the newspaper, assuming its huge accumulated debt, and, at the urging of her brothers, James, Elliott and John, to move to Los Angeles with Buzz and little Johnny. Elliott had gone into the radio broadcasting business and had concocted an idea for a daily mother-daughter conversation program starring the two Roosevelt women. It was to be produced by John Masterson and John Reddy, who became known in later letters as "the two Johns." The American Broadcasting Company agreed to take the "Eleanor and Anna" program, considering it highly salable to a sponsor, and it was scheduled five days a week on two hundred stations. Gleeful over this new involvement of Anna, Eleanor wrote to Maude Gray, "I'll record my part twice a week from wherever I may be! She'll get *all* the pay & it will help her pay her debts."

Also, Anna had taken a writing-editing assignment with a magazine called *The Woman,* her chief involvement to write a six-part article about her life with Father.

". . . what a let down you would go through . . ."

> Val-Kill Cottage
> Hyde Park
> August 16th [1948]

Dearest Anna,

I saw Mr. Masterson yesterday & liked him. I agreed that any decision made by you I would abide by but pointed out certain things I had to consider. Type of sponsor, trips, etc. He thinks I can record here which after I return fr. Paris will make it easy. I think I know what he wants & it won't be difficult. I'm finding out if anything would conflict with L.H.J. *[Ladies' Home Journal]* or U.F. [United Features] contracts. I hope he puts it over & that the magazine thing works out for you also.

George Bye told us today "Look" was interested in John's article (the first) Sat. Ev. Post turned it down.

Johnny [Roosevelt] told me his scouts were looking for an apartment for you. . . .

A Mr. Welsh a lawyer in Poughkeepsie has been asking me to find out if you & John ever had the paper destroyed making Pa legal guardian for the children? If not he feels you should.

. . . I knew what a let down you would go through as the tension eased. Giving up great hopes & going thro' great emotional upheavals take it out of one too. . . .

I'll write Curtis [Buzz] next week & send him the money for the trip & if you let me know what his tuxedo costs I'll pay for it. . . .

> Devotedly
> Mother

". . . we are being given a lesson in values. . . ."

> Val-Kill Cottage
> Hyde Park
> Aug. 28th [1948]

Anna darling,

Wire me when you hear just how far things extend with Buzz [who at eighteen has contracted a mild case of polio]. What I hope is that with a light case[,] involvement of any muscles may be temporary. You remember how badly Father's hands & arms were affected & they were normal very quickly. A prayer is in my heart for you & for him all the time. When you know if & when he can come let me know as I want to have all arrangments made for him. If by some marvellous chance he can still go with me I will see he gets a rest & good food & not too much work.

I am glad you found a house. What are you living on? Did the radio people give you an advance? I can spare you little out of income till November but should be able to pay your rent from then on & if you need cash there are always "things" I can sell & get a few thousand.

It will probably not be possible for you to fly on now before I leave but I will go over everything with Mr. Reddy if he comes. As long as you get paid I don't mind if we don't start till Nov. 1st though I was amused at the Republican director not wanting us on the air during the campaign. I wish I thought we could have that much influence.

Perhaps when things like this happen which seem just too much to bear, we are being given a lesson in values. There is no use trying to teach the weak but the strong are worth training. When a child is ill you know that the other losses were of little importance, his life & happiness is all that counts. You work to repay money losses to others because you have a sense of integrity & responsibility. You work for some future security so as not to be a burden on the young but you learn that the satisfactions that come are in doing the work well & in making those you love happy. You are one of the strong people of the world & I love you dearly & grieve that you have this added burden. . . .

. . . Let me know where to phone you these next weeks & what Johnnie is doing. He can come here & stay with Elliott & go to public school with Scoop if it would relieve you at all.

Devotedly
Mother

". . . Tommy had an attack of pain . . ."

Hotel Crillon
Paris
3d October 1948

Anna darling,

Buzz is taking a french lesson daily from one of the "girls" (she is now at least 74) where I stayed as a student. . . . He's heard most of the important speakers once but done little sightseeing as he gets tired so easily. I think the illness slowed him mentally & physically & only rest will bring him back. Dr. Gurewitsch is giving him some concentrated vitamins & I've written for more. He needs that as the food is good but there is no milk or cream. He is such a dear & I love having him & Tommy would be lost without him. . . . I fear Tommy had an attack of pain which was not just indigestion but may have been a slight heart attack so I make her stay here & not go to the office as she can't stand rushing off in the morning. I leave at nine & get home at 6.30 & usually lunch with people to discuss problems between the morning & afternoon sessions. . . .

The Sorbonne speech is done & went well. Buzz went tho' he could understand nothing. . . .

Devotedly
Mother

". . . Talk of . . . war with Russia is everywhere . . ."

236 So. Orange Drive
Los Angeles 36, Calif.
October 7, 1948

Darling Mummy:
Two letters from you and two letters from Buzz (plus the fact that I've been writing sample radio scripts and therefore having to read reams of copy off the wire service machines) have made me feel not too far away from you both. . . .
In the meantime, or rather between times, I've managed to get pretty well settled. Everything is unpacked. Most of the pictures are not hung, and some of the books are mixed up. But all in all, the place has a homey feel to it. . . .
Talk of imminent war with Russia is everywhere here—in restaurants, taxis and with people you talk to casually. But, somehow, the people here still don't seem to realize the horror of another war or what it would mean to those in Europe who experienced it so closely and drastically.
The Presidential and Vice Presidential candidates have got to the mud-slinging stages—with such things as [Republican vice presidential candidate Earl] Warren laying the blame for present foreign relations difficulties at the door of FDR and Truman for secret agreements at Yalta, and Potsdam—ending up with breast-beating to the effect that it is the people who must know all that goes on at all meetings and make all decisions! I imagine there are a good many American and European delegates and diplomats who wish they could put all the responsibilities on the broad shoulders of what we call "the people"!
I'm distressed about Tommy's not feeling well, and know it must be tough on you to have this worry. I do hope she didn't really have a heart attack, even a slight one. Buzz' tiredness doesn't really worry me. The doctors as much as admitted that he shouldn't have left the hospital so soon and that he would be quite a while in recuperating. But, they all said that after talking to him repeatedly they realized they would have a bad psychological case on their hands if he didn't take this trip with you. . . .
Big John is still having a tough time. I wrote Buzz he was here with us for a day and a night last week. I still wish he had written his articles in the east and contacted the publishers himself, mapping out articles in rough and then getting their suggestions for the finished product, after they showed an interest. He has nothing but rejections, thru Geo. Bye, and now his articles are getting so old he has much less chance if any, of selling them. He is not interested in writing a book. I've been keeping in close touch with him and trying to give him constructive suggestions and encouragement. But, I fear he is still not being too realistic. For instance, he told me at breakfast here, after Johnny had gone to school, that he would like to settle in a really small town so that Johnny could have a normal life, close to the earth, rather than the cityfied, Hollywoodish-radio life that I was giving him. He said that he gathered from listening to Buzz talk here, that the people I was associated with are brilliant but unstable, and he doesn't feel I can therefore give Johnny the right environement while working with them in this field. I answered

only by telling him of the normalities of Johnny's life—with baseball, Cub Scouting, etc. He just doesn't like Los Angeles as a place to work or live, and says he can't understand my feeling that it doesn't make much difference where you live as long as you're doing what you think you ought to do. He went to New Mexico from here to investigate a newspaper situation (on a part ownership basis) which he felt sounded good. . . . If that doesn't work out he goes to Chicago—but says he doesn't want to live or work there either. I wish to goodness I knew what to suggest or how to help! I've told him I hoped he'd get settled soon enough so that he could plan to be here for Xmas.

Did Buzz tell you that Sis has a job as secretary to one of the execs of Gilman's dept. store in Portland. . . . She and Van sound well and very happy.

That's all my dull news! But this takes you so very much love, darling, and the biggest of hugs—and my everlasting thanks for doing so many wonderful things for Buzz, as well as bringing him back to good health.

Anna

". . . I have a letter from big John . . ."

Hotel Crillon
Paris
October 14th 1948

Anna dearest,

Buzz seems much better & with improvement he wants to do more so Tommy suggested he go with Henry Morgenthau to Palestine & Henry cabled he would be glad to have him. . . . I go to Germany the following Sat. the 23d for a night & he wanted to go but I've promised if he isn't back to try to arrange for him to go with someone else later on. . . . He'll go to Oxford with me & to Westminster Friday afternoon for the unveiling of the tablet to Pa. Tommy will go along to London but I'm not sure about taking her to Germany. I think what was bad for her here at first was trying to go to the office when I went every morning & having once or twice to climb three flights of stairs. . . . Buzz has stopped his French till he returns from Palestine. It bores him because his progress is so slow. Johnny is at a better age to study a language! . . .

I like to think of you as settled again & tho' I fear Jimmy can be of little use to you but I am delighted that you & Johnny & Anne & little Johnny & Haven all make some family for you. I am thrilled that Sis has a job. . . .

I have a letter from big John for my birthday. I feel sorry for him & for you darling. He may not be able to help what has happened to him.

All my love darling & Buzz said to send you his. . . .

Mother

". . . My conscience just kills me when I think that I'm responsible . . ."

[Letterhead of Masterson, Reddy & Nelson,
Radio and Television Productions]
Hollywood, California
October 17, 1948

Mummy darling:

The night the 2 Johns [Reddy and Masterson, radio producers] sailed for Europe they called me on the phone with a request they asked me to transmit to you. They said the request came as a suggestion from the N.Y.C. American Broadcasting people, and that they thought it an excellent one. I told them I could see many difficult angles to it, but would give it thought and then write you.

The request is that you invite a "big name" to be with you on the first broadcast. The Johns pointed out that we will not have a commercial sponsor, which might make it easier for you to invite someone.

My first thought was that it would be too embarrassing for you to do this. Then the thought occurred to me that one of the foreign "big shots" might think it advantages [sic], from the standpoint of relations between the peoples of his or her country and ours, to get a message across by talking on the program with you. Despite the commercial angle, I still think of this program as a chance to get things across to the average person, in a simple and understandable way,—things of importance, but which are hard to understand as they are generally written up in snatches by the press.

There is no doubt, of course, but that a "big name", to start off with, would focus the right kind of attention on the program, and help it off to a good start. This from the eventual commercial and successful angles!

But, as I explained to both Johns, the decision on this would have to come from you, as you are on the spot and will know what is possible for you to do and what is not. So, for my part, I'm only presenting both sides, as I see them from afar.

Oct. 19

As usual I got interrupted! Your grand letter of the 14th arrived this afternoon. I'm so relieved and happy that Buzz is feeling so much stronger, and think Tommy's suggestion that he go to Palestine with Henry M. is excellent. Also, I'm tickled with the rest of your plans for him. It seems to me he is going to get a wonderful bird's eye view of much of interest. And, he's old enough to remember it and really benefit from it.

Your letter for John also arrived, and he called me on the phone this evening and asked me to read it to him.

His whole attitude is better, it seems to me. He set his heart on acquiring an interest in a paper in Roswell, N.M. It is, however, a $300,000 proposition, and I've tried to warn him it may be difficult to arrange the financing, (on a basis which would be satisfactory to him while he is personally insolvent) so he should not be too disappointed if it doesn't go thru. So, last night I was pleased to have him say what I've been hoping for so long that he would say, which is that he is well aware the deal may not go thru, and so he is also looking for almost any type of newspaper job he can get, and in almost any spot. He added he'd come to the conclusion that the most important thing for him to do is to get something definite to do, and that he's finally started making himself stop worrying about the future and is just doing the best he can from day to day—until his plans have jelled.

He is now in the middle west so has no permanent address.

In your letter to John you mentioned that you hoped the radio program does well quickly, in the hope that as soon as possible someone can be found to take your place. My conscience just kills me when I think that I'm responsible of adding one more burden onto the many responsibilities you already have. But, in this case it kills me even worse because only today I was reading over the informal letter—contract already signed, and the firm contract to be signed before we go on the air—because this contract signs us *both* up for a period of 2 years, if and when we get a sponsor. John M. and J. G. Moser tell me that most contracts read five years, and that the two years is a big concession. They point out, of course, that if the program is a big success, and if I can build enough of a personal following, that then we can break the contract and probably make a new one, with either me alone or with me and someone else. But, John M. was very firm in telling me that it's terribly hard to build yourself firmly with the radio listening audience, and that if you were not going on with me it would take me a long time, even if I should manage to be very good. Also, alone, I would have to start out on a local basis, and at a very small salary.

. . . Quite honestly, if it were not for the damn debts, I'd so much rather keep the program on a sustaining basis—and just be grateful beyond words to you for giving me a wonderful (but as short as you wanted) start.

Of course, the 3 Johns are in this for the dough, too.

They have been big enough to say that they will take no cut out of the amount paid to us on a sustaining basis. So all that will be deducted from the $1250. a week, which will be paid us on this basis, will be writer's expense, announcer's expense, secretarial, recording, air express for shipping your recording out here and office expenses. But, of course, they are counting on getting the program on a commercial basis as fast as possible because then they will get one third of the net proceeds.

They have given me a rough estimate of what the expenses will be on a sustaining basis, and if they are correct, we should net, per week, approximately $650. while you are in Europe, and $750. when you get back to N.Y. This sounds like a heck of a lot of dough to me! But, I realize I haven't lived here long enough yet to figure out what my monthly expenses will actually run, and therefore, how much I can set aside to pay off debts—on a sustaining basis for the program.

My only reason for writing the Johns is that I would have a fit if I signed something you were not in complete agreement with, and I do want to be sure it won't be too much of a burden on you, as the agreement is now drawn up. . . .

All my love, darling, and a big hug.

Anna

". . . Churchill might do something awful . . ."

> Hotel Crillon
> Paris
> October 25th, '48

Anna darling,

I cabled you today that of course I don't mind signing for 2 yrs. I'm sure once we get into the swing it won't seem any more trouble than the column. The two Johns are here & we've seen a good deal of them tho' we've done no work yet. I suggested tonight that we do one or two samples & John Reddy said ok day after tomorrow. The big name business I'm uncertain about as Churchill might do something awful so I'm going to suggest Mrs. Pandit for the first or Nehru her brother, who will be here any day, then Marshall & Dulles. . . . I don't know if I can get them but they might like the idea, anyway I can ask! As I make out from your estimates you should net about $2600 a month while I'm here & $3000 when I'm home. If you can live & pay your 2 boys expenses on $1300 & later $1500, you should have the equivalent each month toward debts. Someday will you send me a list of what you feel you should repay so I'll have a faint idea of the progress you can make? Will the magazine be extra or is that included in your estimate? Also income tax has to come out & it can't come out of your living expenses.

I don't think I can send you $200 a month unless you need it badly but tell me if you do because I can manage it. Expenses run high here & I don't know how much I'm making while I'm here. . . .

I'm glad big John is in a better frame of mind & doing better. . . .

I spent Sat. & Sunday in Stuttgart, Germany. Human misery is widespread over here. If you see my columns they'll tell you about it so I won't repeat. All my love darling.

> Mother

". . . at the last minute the 2 Johns came . . ."

> Hotel Crillon
> [Paris]
> Nov 14th, 1948

Anna darling,

Just a line to tell you that I'm so glad to hear from the Johns that all has been going well & they are pleased. I hope the programme sells soon.

We all went to London last Thursday night. . . . Buzz seems to love London & being with Lady Reading. He says it "reminds him of Granny." The most secure part of his life perhaps? . . .

Tommy & I flew back today & at the last minute the 2 Johns came because food in London wasn't good! No more recordings for a time as they feel we are too far ahead. I'm so busy anyway that it is a good thing. . . .

Do write me what your first weeks check was & the ensuing weeks. I'll be very interested in what expenses run. . . .

> Devotedly,
> Mother

". . . The Palestine question has kept me jumping . . ."

> Crillon
> Paris
> Nov. 22d [1948]

Anna darling,

. . . Our working hours are getting bad as they do at the end of the Assembly but yesterday, Sunday, was a fairly quiet day. Next Sat. & Sunday if all goes well Tommy, Buzz & I will go & see the landing beaches in Normandy. . . .

People are beginning to leave by air since boats are still unavailable. Sen. Austin [Warren R., of Vermont, head of U.S. mission to the United Nations] went home for an operation. The Secretary & Mrs. Marshall are gone. . . . I get restless to finish & go too. Well, one two or three weeks should do the trick. In the meantime I hope boats are available. . . .

The Palestine question has kept me jumping but I think we are in the clear at last.

I had a nice letter from Sis which I answered yesterday. Her working week sounds long & her pay she says is rock bottom but she likes it. I was interested that she is working with the League of Women Voters. Now that she is away from home some of the home influences will take effect!

The two Johns went to Rome & will be back in a day or two. We mailed you 2 records last week. . . . I haven't heard them but I hear that on short wave my voice sounded far away. I'm sorry.

What did your first two weeks checks amount to? Is there any prospect of a sponsor? . . .

> Devotedly
> Mother

". . . the name Roosevelt . . . worries the possible advertisers. . . ."

> 29 Washington Square West
> New York 11, N.Y.
> February 11, 1949

Anna darling,

By this time you must have the schedule of my trip and my very belated letter making suggestions for the one evening I am free.

I do not want to make any other engagements. I might meet the Democratic women if they want to see me, for an hour one afternoon. I told the man for whom I am lecturing . . . that I would not go to a luncheon for him. . . .

I want to go to see Jimmy and Rommie's children and Johnny and Anne's children—go to one on one afternoon and the other the next day. Will you arrange for that at whatever time is convenient? Don't let the Democratic ladies interfere. I want to spend at least an hour with the children.

It is wiser for me to stay at the hotel, I think, because of the ever lasting telephone and because there are other people whom I will have to see. I am scheduled to stay at the Biltmore. . . .

I was in St. Louis this week and I find that every where people talk about the program so I am sure we have a good audience. I am afraid it is fear of the name Roosevelt which worries the possible advertisers. Five times a week I think is right. I do believe people get into the habit of listening at the same hour every day and they do not like to have to remember that the program is on only three times a week.

. . . Do not get too tired because if you get sick or even get a cold which bothers your voice you will not be able to do the job. . . .

Personally I would not do anything for Look. I thought that last article was outrageous. As far as I am concerned I do not intend to do anything for them because we have been rather nice to them though they paid for anything they used. . . .

I have done altogether too much speaking since I came back from Paris and this lecture trip is really a foolish performance. If I find it too tiring I will decide never to do it again.

Ever since I heard Buzz on the March of Dimes I have been meaning to write to him. He sounded so natural and his voice was so good. Is he getting to like his life as an undergraduate? I hope so because I think on the whole he was too old for his years and was with older people too much.

Couldn't the radio cocktail party be *after* I see Jimmy's children?

The book is done, tho' of course there will be revising to do. . . .

> Devotedly
> Mother

". . . Sad, but nothing can be done. . . ."

> 29 Washington Square West
> New York 11, N.Y.
> March 19th [1949]

Anna darling,

. . . F jr. & Ethel are getting a divorce & she goes to Reno in April. Sad, but nothing can be done. F jr. is running for Congress if he gets the nomination. . . .

How come *we* gave Marion Davies an award? She isn't exactly my ideal!

I'm trying to get Talulah [Tallulah] Bankhead for an interview & I did 7 recordings yesterday as I can't again till the 25th at Hyde Park. If I can think of anyone to interview there I will. . . .
A world of love to you,

Mother

"*. . . we have to think up new ideas for the program, . . .*"

May 4, 1949

Mummy dear:
This is a business letter!
John Masterson says he explained to you in New York that we have to think up new ideas for the program, so that salesmen going back to accounts they have contacted before would have an excuse in making another presentation. John has come up with an idea which I think is really good, and which should, therefore, accomplish this purpose.
The suggestion is that when you do your five recordings (once a week) you should interview five club women from clubs such as the Federated Women's Club, League of Women Voters, PTA's, etc. Polly [Anna's assistant] would line these women up in advance; ask each one to think up a couple questions they want to ask you about, and tell her in advance so that she may tell you what these questions may be; and ask these women to publicize through their membership the day the program will be on the air, so that they will all listen in. The idea is that these women would be asking you questions of special interest to their own memberships. But, at the same time, Polly could talk with you and steer the questions into channels which you and she think would be of widest interest.
John thinks this has merit, because it will give the program a very specific audience as so many of these clubs have nationwide affiliations, and Polly would ask these New York members to publicize the broadcast through their national publications, as well as locally.
I am sending a copy of this letter to Polly.
Let me know as soon as you can what you think of the idea, and of any additional suggestions you may have.
All goes well. Lots and lots of love.

[Anna]

". . . nor do I have the responsibilities you have towards the people of this world. . . ."

May 25, 1949

Mummy, dear:

This is a beezness letter! And, as you may be hearing on this subject from John Masterson, who is now in New York, I thought I should write you about it and give you my own views.

The day before John Masterson left for New York, he called me to his office and told me that he had been thinking of new ideas for a show for you and me, as this one seemed to have almost no chances of being sold.

The new idea is a once-a-week show in the evening for 15 minutes. You would have three guests and I would have three guests. Yours would be leaders in all fields of endeavor, including government. Mine would be mostly Hollywood people. The show would go something like this:

The announcer would introduce you first. You would then say that (for instance) Jimmy Fidler [a gossip columnist and radio personality] had, during the past week, made the following allegation against—and then you would name one of your prominent guests. At this point the announcer would come in and read the allegation—whether it was from a newspaper column or a radio broadcast. Following this reading, you would then come back on the air and say that the prominent gentleman would now answer the allegation just heard.

The same theme would run throughout the entire show. Actually you and I would serve purely and simply as moderators.

Masterson says that the idea comes from a man out here, Mike Shore, whose business, I gather, is to dream up new radio and television ideas for shows. Masterson dropped the information that this is not a new idea, and that, in fact, he (Masterson) had once before turned it down. But that he now thought that with you and me it could work into a program very acceptable to a sponsor.

Masterson said he would approach ABC on the idea, and, if they went for it, he would then talk it over with you.

Now for my own views. I think for the sake of maintaining friendly relations with Masterson, Reddy and Nelson, which, of course, I want to do, that if you agree with me you should tell John that you and I have talked over the idea and agree in our thinking—not that I have sold you off the idea away ahead of time.

Quite frankly I do not like the show idea for a good many reasons:

1. I do not feel that people in prominent places, except perhaps for movie, radio and television stars or near stars, would want to dignify the often irresponsible allegations directed against them by the large majority of columnists and commentators today. I honestly think it would be wrong for such prominent people to do this.
2. I think it would be most inconsistent with your own policy over many,

many years of ignoring slanderous allegations against you and your family. And that it would look very strange for you to now be turning around and asking other people to adopt a policy you have apparently never agreed with.

3. I do not think it is a dignified type of thing for you to do.
4. I do not feel that, in actuality, you could get people of the caliber that they would want to go on this type of program with you—anymore than I feel you would want to ask them.

What I do, entirely on my own, from a standpoint of earning a living, is another story. I do not have the position you have, nor do I have the responsibilities you have towards the people of this world.

I feel that the truth is that our present program was never properly sold. In the first place, it seems to me that as Masterson is the only salesman in his organization, and as he stayed in Europe until Christmas, he must have felt that the program would sell itself and would not need his help. In fact, Buzz says he made this statement in Paris on several occasions.

In the second place, from the very beginning Masterson, Reddy and Nelson and ABC have been afraid of the political angle, and have approached it entirely negatively. It has always seemed obvious to me that either you or I talking on general topics would have political implications because everything of interest to people as a whole today has political connotations of one sort or another. And, as I have written you before, I have now proved my suspicions that the ABC selling force has never wholeheartedly sold this program of ours as being something they considered a top-notch program for them, and one that they believed in 100%. They and Masterson, Reddy and Nelson undoubtedly also believed that because of the results of the November election that a sponsor would come to them without any urging.

The result of all this is that I find Masterson, Reddy and Nelson now thinking in terms of shows for you and me which have what is known here in Hollywood as "gimmicks". Gimmicks are devices for attracting attention by hook or crook.

The result of all of the above is that I plan to ask to be released from our present 13 week contract (which is due to end on August 5th) on July 29th. This, I hope, will mean that I will be able to reach Sistie before her baby arrives. I will motor up there, and then when her ordeal is over, I will go up to Seattle and have J. G. Moser meet me there so that I can have a meeting with Mr. Sick and Mr. Green, the men to whom John and I owe the large sum of money. I must meet with them as soon as possible in order to work out some sort of a deal with them.

In the meantime, I am certainly not sitting still from the standpoint of future plans for myself. In other words, I am working on program ideas. And, if all goes as I hope it does, I will have something for me to start working on by the first of September.

Regarding the magazine, I think I told you that my contract reads to the effect that if we stay on the air for a certain number of weeks and then go off, Masterson, Reddy and Nelson will receive a cash sum of $10,000. My understanding with them is that I will receive $6,000.00 of this. I don't have the contract before me, but my recollection is that the magazine is then allowed to go on using me as editor (at no further pay) for several months—3 or 4. But, if we should stay on the air with our present program for 52 weeks, then Masterson, Reddy and Nelson acquire a fairly good sized amount of the stock of the magazine, and whatever dividends there are will be divided between Masterson, Reddy and Nelson and me. Frankly, I am not sold on this stock deal for the simple reason that even if we should stay on the air for 52 weeks, we would be very minor stockholders, and, as you know in cases of this kind, it is very easy to do some trick bookkeeping so that dividends are very small. I, personally, do not like this particular magazine outfit too well, nor would I feel like trusting them too far. They are definitely a penny ante outfit. Therefore, I would be quite satisfied to get out of the whole business with the cash settlement mentioned above, rather than carrying on with the stock deal proposition. As you know, I have never had any cash to date from this organization.

What would be your reaction to a labor sponsorship of our program? By that, of course, I mean a good solid labor organization such as Mr. [David] Dubinsky's [International Ladies Garment Workers Union]. Or a sponsorship by a group of such similar unions. I ask you this question because I could, if you think it's all right, ask John Masterson to go in to see Lew Novick who is in charge of all radio for the AFL. Or, if John Masterson doesn't seem the right person to do it, I could ask some person from here to do the initial spadework, and then pull John Masterson in if there seems to be any interest on the part of Lew Novick.

Do let me know what you think about this last by wire, if possible, as I haven't the slightest idea how long John M. plans to be in New York. But, come to think of it, I don't think it makes any difference whether he is there or not as I can make my contacts from here, and, if Novick is interested, he can be contacted by someone on the ABC selling force. I guess an airmail letter will fill the bill, and be far cheaper.

. . . Should you see John Masterson I would prefer that you don't talk about any future plans I have mentioned for myself, as they are still in such a nebulous state. Actually, the three Johns, but particularly Masterson and Reddy, have been awfully nice to me and all three of my kids, and I'm very grateful to them, and I would never want to do anything now or in the future to hurt them. But, after watching their operations for some time now, I know that they are head over heels with television ideas, and actually do not have the time to devote to launching a new type program for me, either nationally or here on the West Coast—in case that is the line of work which seems most advisable for me to follow this coming fall.

Please forgive the length of this. I did feel, however, that I should give you as full a picture as possible.

Much, much love,
[Anna]

". . . people feel the program lacks appeal . . ."

[29 Washington Square West]
New York, N.Y.
June 17, 1949

Dearest Sis:

This is a purely business letter to let you know what happened. John Masterson came to see me and told me of his idea which he sold to ABC for a program, once a week in the evening on which I would interview two people who had been attacked either by the government or by a columnist, and you would interview a Hollywood or west coast personality who had been attacked. He thought it could be extremely interesting and you would get the same as you are getting now.

I thought it over very carefully and for you I think it might be a valuable program, but in view of the fact that I am still on the UN and do have a certain responsibility to them and that I do not intend to give up working with the UN as yet, I decided it was unwise for me. I might get involved in all kinds of difficulties.

Perhaps I am too fearful and I hate not doing anything which might eventually be helpful to you. Perhaps the inability to sell our program shows that something is fundamentally wrong. I have inquired around and find that some of the advertising people feel the program lacks appeal and if that is the case, then something should be done about it. I will have more time to work on it after this next week when the Human Rights Commission ends, and I will be in Hyde Park and more free. However, I do not really feel I am capable of thinking up new ideas without direction.

I told John Masterson how worried I was for you and yesterday I had a little talk with [brother] Johnny. He feels you should look for other things and seemed hopeful that in public relations you would get something that would pay you as well or perhaps better in the long run.

I realize your feeling about staying in the west and I would not urge you for a minute to come east because I know how hard it would be to be further away from Sis and that both Buzz and Johnny really like that part of the world.

The letters from you and John make me very sad. In a way as long as you have to get a divorce I wish it had been possible to get it over with and he could get away since he has taken this new job. . . .

I will do anything and everything to help you, my dear, and you can count on me. I asked Elliott if he would have a talk with John Masterson thinking that between them they could think up something new but I haven't heard whether they did meet or whether anything came of it.

Let me know as soon as you know what your plans are.

All my love to you,

[Mother]

". . . There's too much that I don't understand . . ."

June 22, 1949

Mummy, dearest:

. . . As you know, I didn't see how in blazes you could possibly do the program on the once-a-week basis as outlined to you by John Masterson.

But here's some additional news. It appears that for about three weeks now McCall's magazine's advertising agency has been discussing with the sales force of the American Broadcasting Company the possibility of McCall's using our program as a means of not only continuing interest in the fact that you are now connected with McCall's, but as a means of giving general promotion to McCall's. In telling you this both John Masterson and Tom Frye of ABC have asked that I stress it is important that no one at this point discuss or even mention this possibility to anyone on McCall's, as it seems there is a very set protocol about going through their advertising agency on a proposition of this kind. I gather that this is all still in a very formative stage. At least up to the moment, as far as I know, the advertising agency is interested in the general format of the show as it exists now, and not in any new crazy idea.

So please keep your fingers crossed and stay very mum until such time as I know something definite and can contact you directly. If this idea falls through, we are, of course, definitely off the air on August 5th. . . .

I, too, wish it were possible for me to help John by starting divorce proceedings sooner, in order to help him get started earlier on his new job. I wrote him this at the same time that I wrote him that it was impossible for me to move until Mr. Moser's return, because, unfortunately, I don't know of any other lawyer I can work through. Mr. Moser has an assistant in his office, but he is only a statistical man and does not handle actual cases. I found out what ship Mr. Moser is arriving on from Europe, and have written to him so that he will know that we should get going at the earliest possible moment. I also gave the name of the ship to John, so that he could contact Mr. Moser if he (John) is still in New York on the 28th of June when Moser is due to land.

I hope that you were able to understand a little, from the copy of my letter to John which I sent you, how deeply I feel about what has happened between him and me. There's too much that I don't understand about the situation, but, as time has passed, I feel I can understand some things more clearly. This, however, does not change the sadness of it all—particularly, to my mind, as it affects Johnny. . . .

There's no news outside of all this—except that we're all well and happy.

Lots and lots of love,
[Anna]

". . . I haven't spoke to a soul on it. . . ."

Val-Kill Cottage
Hyde Park
June 26th [1949]

Anna darling,

. . . I hope McCall's comes thro' & if they do I imagine they will want you to come on. I haven't spoke to a soul on it but Elliott mentioned casually to me that he hoped they were interested but if you didn't want to work in the East it might not work out. I told him definitely you liked the West.

. . . I gathered how you felt dear, from your letter to John. He telephoned & may phone again before going west. I wish things could have worked out for both of you as I don't think he'll be happy & I know you are not.

F. jr. has decided to announce his engagement to Sue Perrin around Aug. 1st & get married the latter part of Aug. if Congress is over & go to Campo for 2 or 3 weeks. . . .

A world of love to you

Mother

Via Western Union
POUGHKEEPSIE NY 22 11:08 AM
JULY 22, 1949

MRS ANNA BOETTIGER
236 SOUTH ORANGE DRIVE LOSA-
JUST RECEIVED LETTER FROM ROBERT KINTNER INFORMING ME
OUR PROGRAM IS CANCELLED IS THERE ANYTHING ELSE YOU
WANT ME TO DO PLEASE ADVISE MUCH LOVE-
MOTHER-

". . . I can't think of you as a grandmother . . ."

Val-Kill Cottage
Hyde Park
Aug. 11th [1949]

Anna darling,

. . . I'm so happy over Sisty & the baby & wait anxiously for a letter. Was Van happy & did they both want a boy? She did not keep you waiting, did she? Was she in labor long? Do tell me all the details. I can't think of you as a grandmother or Buzz as an uncle.

. . . The A.B.C. thing Elliott thinks means McCall's showed interest but on *their* terms. He says you can't get more than $2000 a week at present as no one is paying the old prices.

I am glad the divorce is over. I hated it all for you & what you tell me about

John saddens me. There is no use trying to figure out something like this & it does no good & only brings more bitterness which hurts you. . . .

The watch is the one Father gave me when we were married. The pin was stolen a year ago & with the insurance money I had the new one made as nearly like the old one (but it isn't the same) as I could. I'm glad you like it. I'd so much rather see you use things now than wait till I die!

A world of love to all & a hug to you

Mother

"*. . . if I should continue in radio it will be alone. . . .*"

August 18, 1949

Mummy, dear:

This goes to you post-haste as you should read the enclosed copy of the release I have prepared for ABC for the reason that you will undoubtedly get queries from the wire services on the termination of our program.

I should also tell you that for reasons of self protection ABC and Masterson, Reddy and Nelson wished permission to say that the program was being terminated either because you were too busy or that I was entering into other fields of endeavor. I have refused to allow us to be made "the goats". During the arguments I was asked if I had consulted with you about using the reason that you were too busy to carry on, and I answered "Yes", and that you and I were in complete agreement. . . .

If I'm queried by the wire services as to why ABC cancelled it, I'm merely going to tell them that I do not know, that they merely notified us that the program is terminated, and that, therefore, I suggest they contact ABC. I think that's a safe premise for both of us to stand on.

As I wrote you previously, I have several lines out for new jobs, and those who are interested here all know that if I should continue in radio it will be alone. So I suggest that if you are asked if you and I are going to try to go on another network together that you say neither of us have any plans along these lines at the present moment.

That's all for now. I'm swamped—but having fun!

All my love,
[Anna]

". . . the book will . . . show Father as the 'people's man' . . ."

236 South Orange Drive
Los Angeles 36, Calif.
September 2, 1949

Mummy, dear:

Enclosed is a copy of a letter to me from Donald Day [a free-lance writer] which I would like you to read very carefully and let me know as soon as you possibly can if you will be willing to go along with his suggestions concerning you.

The book will be written in chronological order, that is, starting with the early years and going through to the date of Father's death.

The reason the title of the book includes the word "Autobiography" instead of "Biography" is because the book will be an attempt to show Father as the "people's man" through his own words and not through personal recollections or the thoughts and recollections of people who knew Father. The only editorial matter in the book will be the facts concerning dates and places which will identify either Father's speeches or what he wrote.

Donald Day and his wife have become good friends of mine and he and I believe that this type of book which eliminates all emotion about Father can be of real value today.

We propose to get the book roughly finished by this coming January 1st, but it would not be published until the Fall of 1950.

Lots of love,
[Anna]

". . . I wish that you were closer . . . so I knew . . . what goes on . . ."

Hyde Park
Dutchess County
September 5, 1949

Dearest Sis:

I just talked to Elliott who called from Fort Worth where he just arrived after driving his children back, because I was worried for fear this book suggested by Donald Day would be valueless in view of the material that will be put into the third volume of the FDR letters. That will include many things which I think would have to go into the type of book which Mr. Day contemplates.

Joe Lash is working with Elliott and has been through hundreds of thousands of items and papers in the library. They have it pretty well in shape and Joe is going to work on it all winter. The book comes out in 1950 and Elliott thinks it may run to two or three volumes, sold in a box together.

It is the kind of a book that will not have any tremendous sale any more than the other volumes of letters have had. I do not think the type of book you contemplate would have a very big sale either.

Also the use of the word "autobiography" seems to me completely misleading. An autobiography is something that the person himself had written and taking father's own words to show a certain trend of mind is still not an autobiography because he did not write with that purpose in mind.

Elliott says if you would be interested he would love to have you as co-editor with him and give you all of the money that might come in, but that, of course, would mean you would have to be here to work on it and while Elliott hopes it is going to bring in some money, the sales of the previous volumes do not indicate any great increase.

I am very anxious to hear whether the job which [brother] Johnny wrote me you and he were talking about has materialized. In fact, I wish that you were closer, close enough so I knew day by day a little more of what goes on in your family. Let me know what news you have of Sistie and the baby. I hope all goes well.

I just finished your article in The Woman and I think it is exceptionally good. In fact, all of your articles have been good. I wonder why you don't try to publish them in book form. It would have a better sale I think than the type of book Mr. Day has suggested.

With much love from Tommy and a great deal from me, I am

> Devotedly yours,
> Eleanor Roosevelt

If Mr. Day still wants to go on with his book I think you or he should come & see what is going into this last period of "Letters."

[This letter, unlike almost all others to Anna, was dictated, typed and probably signed in a pile of many others, which presumably accounts for the mistaken formality of the signature.]

Anna was scarcely settled in Los Angeles with nineteen-year-old Buzz and ten-year-old Johnny, still deeply strained from the folding of both the Phoenix newspaper and her marriage, when she came down with an ominous cough and persistent fever. Brother John's wife Anne directed Anna to a physician she trusted—trained in, of all things, surgery.

Stepping outside the norms of his specialty, the doctor, exuding certainty, diagnosed Anna's condition as tuberculosis, commanding her to bed and to prepare for two or three years in a sanitorium. Johnny would have to be removed from exposure to her disease. Frantically, Anna and her brothers searched for a suitable place to harbor the child. The selection was peculiarly delicate because Johnny was clearly shaken by his father's recent departure. (Many years later he was to tell his mother that her illness, so soon after the marital breakup, made him feel abandoned by both parents.) Anna made a fortunate choice, a camp school run by a man named Harry James, a rare friend and mentor of boys, in the mountains south of Los Angeles.

Within a couple of weeks after the diagnosis, the symptoms receded significantly. That rapid change indicated the diagnosis of tuberculosis was wrong. Anna went to see a chest specialist near San Francisco. He and a colleague identified Anna's malady as coccidioidomycosis—valley fever, a less serious and noncontagious disease. Anna started planning a move to Berkeley so her new doctors could take over treatment.

". . . you've suffered more than you would admit . . ."

29 Washington Square West
New York 11, N.Y.
Sept. 18th [1949]

Anna darling,

I am sorry for you to have this horrid attack but glad Johnny [Roosevelt] was there to make you behave & go to the hospital. You've driven yourself & been under a great strain for several years & you've suffered more than you would admit even to yourself I'm sure & it takes a toll physically.

I wish you'd come East & stay at Hyde Park & rest. Johnny could go to a boarding school in Dutchess Co. & Buzz could transfer to a college here in the East. I can swing the expense I'm sure! I'll write you a business letter tomorrow but this is just to tell you that I love you dearly & wish you were here now.

Devotedly,
Mother

". . . briefing is over. . . . I cld hardly keep awake! . . ."

29 Washington Square West
New York 11, N.Y.
Sept. 19th [1949]

Anna darling,

I wrote you a line last night but Tommy addressed to your home address so I write again fearing the first may be lost.

I think of you & hope you won't worry. [Brother] Johnny told me he would be here Friday & I can give him out of some money for serial rights in papers which has just come in money enough to pay all yr. bills & I'll send Buzz a gift too to cover what you would give him so don't worry about money.

The first day of briefing is over. By afternoon I cld hardly keep awake! There are lots of new people & they are so slow at grasping what the advisers tell them! Tomorrow there will be the opening at Flushing. . . .

Tommy & I have just been saying how we wished you were all here where we could take care of you! She sends her love.

A nice letter from Sistie today. She says she couldn't have managed without you. She sounds happy & competent & very pleased with "Nick"!

All my love darling
Mother

Most of the Roosevelts (including Eleanor in her memoirs) have told, rather proudly, how argument among the youngsters had always been a feature of family life, indeed, was encouraged by FDR at dinner table and elsewhere. As revealed in previous letters and others to come, argument not always reflects intellectual disagreement, but often revolves around money matters, conflicting ambitions, distrust of one another's motivations. This could easily be misread as evidence of a splintered, feuding, unloving family. The first paragraph of the following letter more accurately portrays the family instinct when one of its members is in trouble.

As for the less affectionate second paragraph, brother Jimmy had written each member of the family on September 16 that he and Rommie had decided that the family Christmas would be "nicer" if everybody quit sending everybody else presents. Therefore, Jimmy and Rommie were requesting all relatives and close friends to exclude their names from gift lists—presumably a message not to expect any gifts either. He adds the note that for the Roosevelts, at least, the Christmas spirit can "better be fulfilled in other ways." He expresses the hope that the others will understand.

They don't.

". . . It was so pompous & selfrighteous, I couldn't stand it . . ."

29 Washington Square West
New York 11, N.Y.
Sept. 29th [1949]

Anna darling,
Johnny tells me the news was a bit encouraging from the specialist. He expects to go back Monday midnight so before long you will have your big, little brother close at hand again! Elliott, F jr., & Johnny all met here this afternoon late & I was back from U.N. & we are sure that one way & another we have worked out the plans so you will have no financial worries until you are quite well again. Johnny will have $3000 to pay all the present bills on his return. He will give you details.

I hear you & Anne got the same incredible letter from Jimmy on Xmas. It was so pompous & selfrighteous, I couldn't stand it & was both hurt & mad so wrote just what I felt & sent a copy to Rommie. I have had no word since.

I went to a dinner for Trygve Lie [UN Secretary General] tonight & the speeches were good but too many & too long.

After two days of discussion in the U.N. we passed a resolution without changing one word which seemed to me a bit wasteful of our time. . . .

Do you need bed jackets, wrappers, nighties, shawls? Would you like an electric blanket? Are there any books you want?

A world of love
Mother

By November 18, the returns from the precincts were in and Jimmy threw up a white flag. Declaring that his and Rommie's "intention was not understood," Jimmy implored his mother and siblings to "forget we ever mentioned the subject."

Meanwhile, almost immediately after the family meeting on September 29 at Mother's house regarding Anna's trials, Elliott writes this remarkable letter in behalf of the family to his sister in California.

". . . When I heard of your latest hardship. . . ."

Top Cottage
Hyde Park
[October 1, 1949]

Dearest Sis:

It is hard for me to realize that life could be so cruel as it has been to you. You have always been such a gay, gallant, courageous and loving person that I cannot understand why you should have had to bear so many blows. You have been so wonderful in facing each successive situation which would have crushed a lesser person, that when I heard of your latest hardship I just couldn't believe that God could have been so cruel. Whatever the outcome of the tests, I know you will come through to health and happiness, and that your life will have great joy in the future.

Mother and Johnny and I have discussed what we could do, and Johnny will be home soon to tell you. All, we all hope for is that you will banish all worries from your mind and let us all be of as much help as we can in our small ways.

Remember we love you dearly, even though our paths have been so divergent in the past. We will always feel that we have been enriched by our relationship to you. I just thought I'd write and let you know how we felt.

I'll arrange to get out very soon to see you.

Your ever loving brother

Elliott

The family concocted a plan, chiefly at Elliott's suggestion, to take care of Anna by creating a weekly radio program for Eleanor, and to write Anna into the contract as producer. The only hitch in this creative design was that an Eleanor Roosevelt show must include Eleanor Roosevelt, thus adding another burden to her overburdened schedule. But Eleanor insisted on her availability—her eagerness—to do it if it would help Anna.

In 1950, the program began on WNBC, New York, not weekly but daily for forty-five minutes starting at noon. Elliott cast himself as the announcer. His duties included delivery of commercials for some products, informing listeners that "Mother uses" this toilet article or that kitchen item. A trade paper, the *Billboard,* voiced a suppressed embarrassment widely felt: "The show proves that a boy's best friend is his mother." Eleanor appeared 99 and ⁴⁴/₁₀₀ percent free of embarrassment. She was doing it for Anna and Elliott. Besides, she did enjoy the unmatchable public forum of radio. If the price of access to it was a faint label of commercialism, so be it.

Earlier letters illustrated Anna's predilection, while not hesitating to accept money and favors from her mother, for expressing guilt and apologia and do-you-really-think-you-want-to-do-this-Mother? In a letter no longer to be found, Anna obeyed that inclination again, this time over Eleanor assuming the added burden of the radio program. The response and assurances came not from Mother, but from her emerging spokesman, Elliott.

". . . how irksome it must be to have . . . so-called standards . . ."

October 10, 1949

Mummy, dearest:

Brother Johnny told me that Elliott was about to sign up with [industrialist] Henry Kaiser to take over [columnist and radio news personality] Walter Winchell's spot. That sounds simply wonderful and Elliott deserves heaps of congratulations.

Brother Johnny also told me that you are about to sign up with U.S. Steel to do a weekly radio program for them and that Elliott had suggested that I be the packager for the show—in other words that I run the show and that the agreement to "produce ER" at specified times be written up in a contract between me and U.S. Steel, rather than between you and U.S. Steel.

This sounds like a wonderful idea, but I would feel very, very badly if you went on the air for U.S. Steel. And I have a hunch you'll find that a lot of other people would feel about this as I do. After all, we can't deny that you are doing a most important piece of work in the world today, and one which would, I feel sure, be severely jeopardized if you should go on the air for any such corporation as U.S. Steel. After all, all thinking people in this country know what U.S. Steel stands for—and they certainly stand for all things directly opposed to what you and Father have always stood for.

I think I know just how irksome it must be to have to live up to certain so-called standards—or the faith that people have in you! I guess all of us in the immediate family have to face a little of that, although only a fraction of it compared to what you have to face.

But it seems to me with the present world crisis, that any such big step as going to work for a corporation such as U.S. Steel has to be considered most carefully.

I told Johnny none of the above, but did tell him I'd have to think about it from the standpoint of whether I was capable of producing any kind of a radio show, as I have never done work of this type before and have had no training from a research standpoint. Johnny's answer was that he had understood that whether I ran the show or not, you were just about ready to sign up anyhow.

So, for whatever it is worth, I thought I'd better get this off to you—just based on my own personal feelings—as soon as possible.

I did so love talking to you on the phone last night. Everything is really going smoothly at home now, and I'm feeling lots better.

Jimmy called this morning—said he had been out of town lately—and said he just plain forgot about his breakfast date with Johnny and would call him after talking to me. All much too casual! He is now scheduled to come over to have lunch with me today.

[Anna]

". . . Mother would like to knit us all together. . . ."

29 Washington Square West
New York 11, N.Y.
Oct. 21st [1949]

Sis Dear—

Mother showed me your letter that arrived this morning, and I thought I would drop you a line to clear up certain points. (Please pardon the pencil but my pen is on the fritz!)

First of all what Mother is doing she loves to do. It gives her a pride and feeling of really doing something worth while. It makes her feel closer to her own family, and she yearns for the affection and appreciation which you give her. Secondly, this was temporary emergency. You will soon get well and be more vigorously active than ever, if you relax mentally and physically and take care of yourself now. Whatever is done for you now will come back a hundred fold when you are back on your feet. Furthermore, and most important, Mother would like to knit us all together as a family unit, united in good times as well as bad. If she helps you today, maybe you'll have to help her some other day. I only regret that my contribution is not larger, but I guess everything helps!

The truth of the matter is that if Mother didn't do this for you she'd probably do it for someone else like a Lash or Gourevitch [David Gurewitsch]. She's just made that way.

So, for God's sake, forget, for the moment, the thought that she is doing anything unusual for you. She's not, she's doing what any Mother would do in similar circumstances for her Daughter. Particularly, one she has such admiration and pride in!

You can repay her a thousand times over by concentrating *all* your energies on a complete recovery.

You asked Mother to have me keep my eyes open for permanent job openings. There are several, but mostly here in the East. Would you consider one here if it was lucrative enough? . . .

Your ever loving Brother,
Elliott

". . . life . . . can not very well be lived in sections. . . ."

29 Washington Square West
New York 11, N.Y.
October 13, 1949

Anna darling:

I am dictating this so you will get it more quickly.

Of course, Elliott and I will see Donald Day. I however, feel that a book of this kind is entirely impossible in view of the publication of the letters which hold so much of the personal material, and the impossibility of writing a good biography before a good deal of historical study, and some of the material still unavailable, is free to students.

Elliott is going through the last negotiations with the publishers on the theory that you have as much right as he has to an interest in this. He is trying to arrange for you to be paid the advance and whatever future royalties there are on this last publication. The boys, at least Franklin and John, have been consulted and agree and I will write to Jimmy and I am sure he will be quite willing to agree too.

Of course, if Elliott and Donald Day find that it is possible to do the kind of book Mr. Day has in mind, both Elliott and I will do anything we can do.

John [Roosevelt] did not understand very well what Elliott must have said to him. The people who are negotiating for the weekly program for me, are the same people who handle US Steel. I am not thinking of going on the air for the US Steel. I have made it plain that whoever I go on the air for has to have very careful scrutiny as to their labor situation. I will not sign up at all unless it can be arranged that you do the research work on the program and therefore get paid certain expenses such as a secretary and for anything you do in the way of writing the scripts, etc. All I will do is to deliver the script either by recording or in person. This probably will not come through until nearly Christmas time and I never count on anything until it is actually signed up. However, I think it would net you a certain amount and give you the kind of work which by that time you might be able to do without over-taxing yourself.

I will be anxious to hear more about Jimmy. The difficulty is that big and little things get very much mixed up in life, and life has to be lived as a whole and can not very well be lived in sections. . . .

Many thanks for my birthday telegram. . . .

Devotedly,
Mother

". . . I wrote [John] . . . to wish him and his bride happiness, . . ."

November 4, 1949

Mummy, darling:

I am starting this out dictating to Peggy . . . I owe you so many letters it's terrible! . . .

I hope my long letter about doctors made it clear that the one doctor who has given me the jim-jams is Dr. Urabec, because of his insistence a couple of weeks ago that I immediately enter a TB sanitarium and start pneumo-thorax treatments, to be followed up with further surgery if he thought it necessary.

Recent developments are that an upper right molar has begun to bother me and must definitely be filled before I go away—particularly as I did not have a dentist in Phoenix whom I had any great confidence in. I am not strong enough to have much work done at one sitting, so it takes longer than usual. I went down to the dentist yesterday to have this looked at however. Therefore, I have been checking into a doctor whose name is F. M. Pottenger. All my checks have been to the good. Strange to say he is a good friend of Helen Gahagan Douglas' family physician here. So even though Helen doesn't know it, as she is away on a speaking tour until this weekend, I will probably get my first introduction to Pottenger through Dr. Gabriel Segall.

This means that I will very frankly tell Pottenger why I did not have confidence in Urabec, and ask him to tell me very frankly if he feels I should stay here until there is a definite diagnosis, or until the [lung] cavity closes, or if he feels I would heal faster by going to a place like Phoenix.

This also means that I will have to call Eagan and tell what I tried to avoid telling him—namely, that I lost confidence in Urabec, even though I realize that this is purely personal on my part, and doesn't mean that he is not a very fine physician.

The wonderful bed jacket made from Granny's material arrived safely. I have been wearing three bed jackets which Katy made me when Johnny was born. They are still in fairly good condition, but the new one is a most welcome change. The funny part is that it has been so blooming hot here this past week that any bed jacket is too hot! Many, many thanks. . . .

I still have not heard anything further from John B. than the one letter I told you about which was dated Oct. 20, and which told me he had written to Johnny about his marriage plans. The letter to Johnny has still not arrived. Yes, on the 6th I wrote him that I was ill. And when I wrote him a couple days ago to wish him and his bride happiness, I told him that I had a cavity in my right lung.

I, too, felt very sad about Ed Stettinius' death. As you said in your column, it's sometimes very difficult to understand the reasons behind the work of the "Grim Reaper".

[from Anna's carbon copy of her secretary's typing; no signature]

". . . Just a place to sleep & see people . . ."

29 Washington Square West
New York 11, N.Y.
Nov. 10th [1949]

Anna darling,
Your letter of the 4th was enlightening but not conclusive!
. . . David Gurewitsch was very happy that his letter was helpful. He has a keen understanding of all you are going through & a great impatience with doctors etiquette! . . .
I have had no word from John Boettiger so I imagine he has decided that there will be less contact in the future. . . .
I am trying to rent this apartment furnished & take rooms with Elliott in a hotel. It is an experiment till next September but I think may be better & a little cheaper. I don't need a home & more to care for here. Just a place to sleep & see people & an office & no servant problems seems a wise arrangment, if we find we like it! If I don't I'll move back here in Sept. . . .
Would you like some books or have you all you want?

Much, much love darling
Mother

". . . I am so happy . . . it turns out to be desert fever . . ."

29 Washington Square West
New York 11, N.Y.
Sunday night Nov. 13th [1949]

Anna darling,
I am so happy for you that it turns out to be desert fever & therefore means a quicker recovery. What a relief to everyone but above all to you for I know how you hated to be tied down & uncertain of your health. . . .
Neither Tommy, Elliott or I were very favorably impressed by Mr. Donald Day. He seemed vague & I doubt if he realized what research on a book of any kind on Father would mean. I'll be interested to hear what he tells you. . . .

A world of love darling,
Mother

". . . I'll try to compete adequately with you! . . ."

December 14, 1949

Mummy darling:
I think of you so darn much despite my very bad habits as a letter writer!
All of your wonderful packages have arrived, and so far I have refrained

from opening them and sorting them only because in this apartment I have no place to hide them from one young Johnny Boettiger. . . . Mummy, as usual, (from the number of things that have arrived) you are spoiling the living daylights out of us. You know, of course, that we love it! It does appal me a little however to think of all the trouble you have gone to and the time it must have taken you.

We three will go to [brother] Johnny's and Anne's for Christmas dinner and the rest of the day will be a very quiet one around here. But the quietness seems to be what [ten-year-old son] Johnny particularly wants as gradually it has developed that last year he felt overwhelmed by our very numbers at our Hyde Park Christmas! By the way, Johnny has improved just loads since he's been going to this school. He's nowhere near as selfish, seems far more secure about his home and me, and is ever so much more affectionate.

I'm sorry that you and Elliott and Tommy didn't like Donald Day. But of course we're such a large family that it would be impossible for all of us to feel the same about the same people. It happens that Donald Day is not a close personal friend of mine even though I do like him very much. The thing is that our contracts and conversations have been purely on the basis of history, political philosophy and world human relations—and that is the basis on which we will do the book. So we are proceeding and hope to get the manuscript completed by next July 1. I do so hope that as it proceeds you will all like it and feel that it's a worthwhile contribution.

Of all the tests that I had taken in San Francisco the last time I was there, the only one that I have heard results on was the one which was to show whether or not my lesion was a tumor. The report, thank goodness, is negative. All of the doctors, including the TB specialists, continue to feel sure that it's a pretty sure bet that I have desert or valley fever. And therefore Dr. Charles Smith is going to continue following up on me. I had word from Leo Doyle yesterday that he had phoned and said that he would like another stomach washing. And as I am to have another X-ray this coming week, I will go back there again for a day, probably next Tuesday or Wednesday. Western Airlines has a subsidiary company called Western Airlines of California. It uses DC4's, is a coach-like arrangement and costs only $22.88 round trip.

We all felt that it was wiser if I didn't go to visit Sis until after the middle of January when I will have answers to these last guinea pig TB tests. This is of course purely an ultra-conservative preventative decision, and I'm doing it just because I don't like to take the personal responsibility of running a chance in so far as Sis and Van and Nicholas are concerned. . . .

Darling, I hated to have you bothered by that damn guy Pegler's nosiness. [Westbrook Pegler, in his column, is pressing a rumor that Lucy Mercer Rutherfurd was at Warm Springs on a romantic visit when the President died.] But it struck me that Madame Schoumatoff [Shoumatoff] did a very good job when interviewed. I can't imagine why Olive Clapper [widow of Washington columnist Raymond Clapper] felt it necessary to go into this subject at all in her book. I had always understood that she was a pretty nice person, but now I have changed my mind.

It's grand to hear from Tommy that you all like the apartment at the Park-Sheraton. It sounds like a wonderful idea if it saves all of you from any of the wear and tear of housekeeping and the expense that goes with that particular part of our lives. Have you let the Washington Square apartment on a furnished or unfurnished basis. I hope the latter unless you have rented to people you know will take care of things for you. Don't forget I still don't have your private phone numbers at the Park-Sheraton.

My present schedule is that I must be in bed in a reclined position for 12 hours a day, and must make every attempt to "lounge" during the greater part of the other 12 hours. As my lesion is closed and there are no bugs running around in my system, I do not have to take any kind of medication. I'm avoiding all large gatherings, meetings or parties, like the plague, as it is impossible for me to go to one such thing and not to many others. And of course I'm forbidden any late nights, etc.

Mummy, I hate to tell you but I'm still 100% sold on trying to work out a way of making my living out here, and therefore of not moving back East. Naturally I'm not going to be pigheaded, if, after I get entirely well and have made every effort out here, I cannot find any work. But I'm sure going to make the effort! And, of course, I'm going to try to get back on the air even if it's only on a Westcoastwise basis. Besides that I may do some other writing. But none of this can be decided definitely at the moment. When I go back on the air I'll *try* to compete adequately with you! . . .

[typed; no signature on carbon copy]

". . . I don't like being in competition . . ."

> Val-Kill Cottage
> Hyde Park
> Dec. 29th, 1949

Anna darling,
   The basket is lovely & the colors in the fire give me pleasure every evening. You should not have thought of this but I love it & many thanks.
   I wait as anxiously as you must the result of the last tests.
   As long as you want so much to stay West I hope that it will be possible for you to do so. I had hoped my radio programme could be owned by you & Elliott but if you are not here to work on it we must think of something else. I don't like being in competition & when you go on again I will try to get off as soon as possible though Elliott says I cannot run out on my contract. When Mr. Day wants to work at the library let me know as I can speak to them. It will be heavy work to get a book out so soon. . . .

> A world of love,
> Mother

". . . he doesn't realize what he is taking on. . . ."

Val-Kill Cottage
Hyde Park
April 7th [1950]

Anna darling,

I haven't quite recovered yet! Buzz [who has just made it known that he plans to marry] seems young & I fear he doesn't realize what he is taking on. Jobs aren't plentiful & he has no college degree or special training. The girl may have a baby & then they'll have to live on Buzz's earnings. I'm afraid there are worries ahead for you & just now I'd like you to be free from care for a while. You'll be lonely too for Johnny should stay in school & that leaves you alone. Oh! Well, I don't suppose one can make the young look on life with the eyes of experience!

Of course I'll come to the wedding & so will Tommy unless preparations to go abroad get her down. . . . What would they like as a wedding present? You were sweet to give them the ring you like. . . .

A world of love,

Mother

". . . just now I'd like to stay home. . . ."

Hyde Park
June 1st, 1950

Anna darling,

. . . The children arrived last Sunday. . . . They are to spend next Sunday on their own in the stone cottage as all my people are off. So far Robin [Buzz's fiancée] has been too dazed to say much but she is self possessed & sweet & they seem to be easy together.

I hope you get just what you want for the summer & that you improve steadily & don't overwork. I don't believe you should drive your car much.

This is my last night here & I hate to go especially as my little dogs go to the kennel for the week end & I feel sorry for them! I know the trip will be wonderful & once off I'll be interested but just now I'd like to stay home. . . .

I loved seeing you darling & being at the wedding & I wasn't at all tired, I thought I would be but I wasn't!

Take care of yourself, all my love

Mother

". . . all of Noway was bicycling to the beaches . . ."

[Norway]
June 5th [1950]

Anna darling,
    . . . You know how lovely this place is. The view is beautiful & reminds of Campobello. Our trip was smooth & comfortable. . . .
    Yesterday was quiet. We lunched with the King & all of Noway [sic] was bicycling to the beaches on what I gather was the first warm & sunny Sunday. It was a pleasant sight. Sightseeing begins today & a speech & press conference for me.
    Take care of yourself darling & all my love,

Mother

Tommy sends love & so would Elliott but he's out taking pictures with the children.

———————

In California James Roosevelt won the Democratic primary for the nomination for governor, to run against the Republican incumbent, Earl Warren. California law permits "crossover" filing: a registered Republican may choose to vote in the Democratic primary, or vice versa. Warren, of course, has taken the Republican nomination and will be James's opponent in the general election.

". . . How do you feel about Jimmy's victory? . . ."

June 10th [1950]

Anna darling,
    We've been gone a week today & I feel as though much more time had gone by.
    The time here has been interesting & busy but I think we are doing something to re-enforce the courage of these people. Small wonder they are fearful! I hope it is worth while!
    Elliott & the kids seem to be enjoying it & tomorrow we go to Finnish Lapland & see the midnight sun.
    How do you feel about Jimmy's victory? From the news bulletins it looks as though Warren must have polled a good many democratic votes, which makes the next campaign [the general election] pretty tough. . . . We've all been buying some Xmas presents as we go along & getting everything sent home by the embassy! . . .
    How are you? All my love

Mother

". . . I should stay home like a well behaved old lady . . ."

Copenhagen
June 17th [1950]

Anna darling,
. . . Tommy doesn't seem to me too well. She gets tired & last night was ill all night & could do very little today. I suppose I should stay home like a well behaved old lady or not take Tommy on these strenuous trips! . . .

Hamlet done in the courtyard of the old Castle of Elsinore was really an experience & the children seemed to enjoy it.

The midnight sun & Finland are the most impressive things I've seen. What a people & they can still smile & rejoice at the summer sun! . . .

I realize Jimmy will have a fight & hope he gets a rest at Hyde Park. . . .

Devotedly,
Mother

". . . all Europeans are afraid of Russia . . ."

Hotel De Crillon
Paris
June 23d, 1950

Anna darling,
. . . I do hope Buzz & Robin keep their feet on the ground but it isn't easy as you know when people try to use you & flatter you.

Primarily all Europeans are afraid of Russia then secondarily they are not sure of us. The two fears have "nuances"; Norway & Finland seem to me to have the best spirit; Sweden & Denmark less secure. All countries seem to be recovering very well & the contrast in the countries I saw two or three years ago & now is enormous. Some countries may not be quite ready to give up all aid in 1952 but some may & all will be far on their way to be again on a competitive basis.

Luxembourg, at least in the northern part is one of the loveliest corners of Europe. . . . I am not sure I entirely like Mrs. [Perle] Mesta [leading Washington hostess, appointed by President Truman as ambassador to Luxembourg] but I think she is doing a good job as is Mrs. [Eugenie] Anderson [ambassador to Denmark]. I liked the latter better than Elliott did tho' I don't see how she can put her husband through something which so obviously makes him uncomfortable & both her children quite unhappy! . . .

All my love darling, don't overdo & let me know how you get on. . . .

Devotedly,
Mother

". . . we will know the horrid facts about the house. . . ."

Campobello Island
August 21st [1950]

Anna darling,

. . . I was very busy before leaving trying to clear up all my commitments so Tommy could have a real rest here. . . . I am carrying out my plan of doing my own column every day and all my letters and I do improve a little and Tommy sits and reads and I think is a little bored. . . .

My trembling is only bad in writing, it does not bother me in typing at all. Might not be so harmfull as far as legibility goes if I had not written so carelessly for years so that I run all my words together. It is emotional in part at least for I notice if I am upset about something that is the way it shows up. Nevertheless I type so slowly that it is going to be hard to make it a habit as nothing seems important enough to put on paper this way, and I leave words out constantly because my thoughts outrun my fingers. . . .

Elliott got the best carpenter on the island and in a few weeks we will know the horrid facts about the house. Granny's house will be all torn down by next spring. If it isn't too expensive, and we do decide to put this house in order, I'd like to use her cellar excavation for a swimming pool and turn our old and very poor tennis court into a deck tennis and badminton court at one end and a croquet court at the other. The expense on the house will be great however and I may not feel it worth while unless all of you children think you will enjoy coming here when you come east in the summer. . . .

Electricity is here and in all cottages and tourists abound but the fishermen are unhappy and say their business is very bad!

The Korean reports sound a bit better, and I hope it may create a better atmosphere to listen to proposals of diplomatic settlement. The only way I get any news here is to turn the radio on in the car, as our papers are two days old.

I am not resigning from the U.N. but I wanted them to feel free to name a stronger person in view of the fact that the reason for having me on this time was the fact that the first covenant on human rights would be up for decision, now it will either go back to the commission from the economic and social council or just be discussed in committee three for guidance on general principles. I could listen to that without being a delegate.

Jimmy is discouraged I think. . . . It will be hard for any democrat to win this year, because of Korea. [Secretary of Defense] Louis Johnson, [General Douglas] MacArthur, and [Senator Joe] McCarthy have won this campaign I fear for the Republicans. He insists that I come out to speak for him and for Helen [Gahagan Douglas], which seems a mistake to me but I have agreed to go on Sunday evening Sept. 10th to Los Angeles. . . . I intend to see you and your little house and Johnny if he is home. . . .

Buzz and Robin and her Father were coming to Hyde Park the last week end before I left, but she phoned they could not come and I wonder if Buzz has learned yet how to keep well in New York. Competition is so great it is a constant strain. I am glad they got around to writing at last. They will get some things they want for their apartment out of Cousin Susie's house. [Susie Parish had recently died.] That business I hope to finish the week after I get back from here as far as taking out things goes, as the tax people from the government should be through. . . . On appraised value I can equal in things what James, Elliott, and Franklin want. John wants very little that is there, so you and he should get the equivalent out of sale money if it goes well. At most it will mean some seven hundred dollars for you and you were left a cameo pin surrounded by pearls, not very valuable but quaint and old fashioned.

A world of love darling and take care of yourself, you are very much needed so don't be careless and don't get reckless.

Devotedly
Mother

". . . I work night and day . . . I thrive on it, . . ."

The Park Sheraton Hotel
New York 19, N.Y.
October 21st, 1950

Anna darling,

I've been very bad about writing because I work night and day while the U.N. is on. I thrive on it, and get fun out of working with Elliott on the radio show. We do the whole thing now on recordings at night, but I will do some live once the U.N. is over. We have our twelve sponsors and they are gradually getting set so in about three weeks you should get the show on the coast. The television show should in a few weeks also begin out there on film. I've done all shows live so far, but next week I'll try one on film. . . .

I've written the three boys that you want a clock and that I've bought it and they can pay me, so I hope you like my choice. . . . We get it cheap as Emerson is one of our sponsors. . . . Robin is improving[,] Tommy and I think, and she is learning what things cost. . . .

John Golden [the theatrical producer] gave me the smallest and lightest typewriter for my birthday and I am just learning to use it and I think I am going to like it very much.

Elliott and I went to see Connie [the Roosevelt children's governess] this afternoon after the television show was finished. She has a very nice apartment and a nice young doctor has a room with her. I should have gone years ago because she lives on her memories of you as children. She looks well and is not much changed. . . .

Buzz is doing well I think with his work, and I thought he looked better last Sunday. They are coming to supper, and Henry Morgenthau who is just back from Palestine & will tell us about his trip. He's bringing a Mrs. Hirsch and he brought her to Hyde Park just before he left so Elliott thinks there is a romance. . . .

ſ

We lost our battle for a good permanent plan on the children's fund, but I still hope we may improve it in the plenary. Now we are on the covenant of Human Rights.

I must dress so love to Johnny and a heartfull to you darling,

Mother

Living in New York, just a few blocks from where it happened, Mrs. Roosevelt heard the shocking word before Anna did. At 6:20 A.M., October 31, 1950, John Boettiger rose from his bed in a seventh-floor room of the Weylin Hotel, 40 East Fifty-fourth Street. At first, the rising did not stir the apprehensions of a young male nurse who had been engaged by a physician to spend the night keeping an eye on him. But then the motion assumed a deliberacy as Boettiger headed toward an open window. The nurse, Joseph Payne, lunged to seize Boettiger's arms.

"Joe, let go of me," Boettiger huskily commanded. "Good-bye and be a good kid."

Payne was later to recall: "He pulled me right along to the window. He thrust aside the chair [a heavy armchair that Payne had earlier placed as an obstacle to the window, just in case]. I was still grabbing his arms and I was half out of the window with him. I had to let go or go along too. I watched him go down. He landed on the curb on the Fifty-fourth Street side. It was horrible."

After failure to find a suitable newspaper job, John had become a partner with Theodor Swanson in a public relations business which, like the other recent enterprises of John's, was failing.

Two days before, on Sunday afternoon, October 29, Swanson was called at home by the excited manager of the Weylin Hotel, reporting that Boettiger was unconscious in his room, beside an empty bottle of sleeping pills. That's when the male nurse was hired to stand guard.

By Monday night, John's mind appeared to have recovered its clarity and he had "practically agreed," according to Swanson's personal physician, to enter a psychiatric hospital the morning of October 31. Off and on through the night he talked to Joseph Payne. He expressed love for his wife of scarcely a year, Virginia, regretting the difficult days and nights he had caused her. At one point, he picked up a picture of Virginia, talked to it and kissed it. Then he talked of Anna. He spoke of her with endearment and speculated that she might still love him. He fascinated the young listener with daubs at a word portrait of the First Lady of the World, his former mother-in-law, "a wonderful person," and of the larger-than-life dimensions of her husband. At one point John broke a long silence to utter, in puzzlement and frustration, "Why didn't it work? Next time I'll take a whole drugstore full."

The police found several letters. Thoughtful letters, composed not in hasty scribble, but with a sure hand that bespoke intention.

Among them was one to Anna:

Dear Anna

This is to say goodbye and to say thanks for all our wonderful years together.

I'm sorry to have failed in so many ways, but my memories are so filled with happiness and a sense of having accomplished a great deal. You know I always believed in fate. I still do and today, after years of having fought against the decision with all I could produce, I have added it all up and it seems to me that the fairest thing is for me to take off while I can still leave something for Johnny and Virginia.

I know you will make Johnny into a wonderful man. May he give you the happiness I couldn't.

Please send my love to LL and Tommy, and to Sis and Buzz.

And my love and a world of good luck to you and our Johnny.

John

Into the envelope for Anna he tucked another letter—to his eleven-year-old son whom he had not seen for a year. Anna decided to conceal that letter from Johnny until some indefinite future date. Almost a year later Anna explained this decision in a letter to a friend: "Johnny still hasn't reached the stage where he talks naturally and normally about his father. . . . Johnny has been almost completely 'bottled up' about his father since he died." Sometime in 1952, in a driven search for some glimpse of his father, he secretly searched through a file drawer he knew contained his mother's most private papers. Johnny came upon the letter, but would stay silent about it until his mother showed it to him many years later.

My dear Johnny,

Goodbye my son. I love you dearly. I have faith and pride in you. You will make a great and useful man.

I wish I could watch you grow.

I love you.

Pops

For his recent bride, Virginia, he reserved what he omitted from all the others: an explanation of his stunning action, and some view of the bleak road that led him to it. The extraordinary effort and achievement of this letter have several possible explanations: a desire to clear Virginia and any other individual in his life from responsibility for his action; perhaps an expectation that all or parts of it would be published; a caring, at a time when there was nothing left to care about, for how he and his life would be remembered and judged. "It was a most difficult letter to write," he says in still another farewell note, to his partner, Ted Swanson, "and I am not happy with it, but it is the best I could do."

Virginia, my Darling, I have reached the end of the road. I can see no path ahead that offers any promise of a useful life.

I am filled with sadness that the manner of my leavetaking is such as to bring an unwonted grief to you and others who love me. How comforting it would be if one could slip away quietly and unnoticed!

I would hope to leave with you and my other loved ones the sense that here departs an uncomplaining man who has tasted far greater joys of life than are given to most men.

In thinking about others who have taken their own lives, I have always felt that when a man in good reasoning arrives at the supreme decision that his usefulness in life falls short, his self imposed death should not invoke condemnation or dismay.

I do not challenge the thought that the man who dies to escape his responsibilities is less than admirable. But if he weighs the assets and the liabilities of his life, and the scales fall on the debt side, then his decision might be accepted, at least by those who care for him, as right.

It has seemed to me that the fates have held my life to have been lived. My Darling, I have struggled against such a decision, even up to yesterday when I talked with more people in my efforts to find a right way to carry on. But today I have a full sense of finality. I have searched myself most earnestly, and I have concluded that my course has been run.

The crushing irony in this scheme of fate is that in my personal life I am supremely happy. You have given me deep, inward happiness born of your boundless capacity for devotion and loyalty, companionship and love. Your beauty is of the mind as well as of the body. From you and Victoria I have received great gifts of human relationships. Bless you both, and my equally staunch and devoted Johnny, and may the fates deal more gently with you all, the rest of your days.

The insurance which I leave will help you three in your material needs. This, and the memory of our happy days together, are all that I can bequeath.

I am anxious that you and some others know the thoughts which are in my mind and contributed to my decision.

Some men achieve high purposes and accomplishments in life, and later slip gracefully into an acceptance of lesser aims. I could do this, and would do it gladly, so long as I could feel that I could provide a reasonably good life for my family, and so long as I had a feeling that my tasks were useful ones.

I could never take refuge in a life of intellectual asceticism, nor could I submit to a life of mediocrity. It would be frustrating beyond my power to bear to submit my family to a meager life, even though I know that your love and faith would endure. My Darling, you are made for much better things.

I am a newspaper man. Twice in 29 years I left my profession and entered other work. Both times I was privileged to work with able, successful and sympathetic colleagues. But in my present association, as in the other, I have felt ill adjusted and unable to exert what abilities I possess to real advantage. Quite frankly I feel I am more of a hindrance than a help to my present working companions.

You know how earnestly I have tried to find a place in my own profession. I have sought out publishers and editors of newspapers, and newspaper brokers, all over the country, and in every honorable way I have endeavored to discover a suitable newspaper pursuit. I have uncovered situations in which I knew in my heart I could render highly useful services, to those with whom I proposed connections as well as in society itself. But the proposals failed for one reason or another, and in some instances because people, while conceding my fitness, found it difficult to overlook my past associations.

They could not reconcile the strangely conflicting relationships I had with Franklin Roosevelt, Colonel McCormick and William Randolph Hearst. I must confess that were I on the other side of the table, I myself might hesitate to join efforts with an amorphous character such as I might seem to be!

But the people where my writings were observed, in Chicago and Seattle and Phoenix particularly, know that I searched for the truth and was not afraid to print it.

Life for me has never been dull, and for all the interesting and exciting and worthwhile things I have been permitted to do I have high gratitude toward all those who helped me in the doing. It's been a wonderful world filled with wonderful people!

My spirit rises now in happy memory of all the years I have lived, from the days of my earliest recollections, when my mother gave me her full devotion, through the years gay and full with joys and loves and good jobs to be done, down to the present in which I have cherished your glowing devotion.

Good night, Darling.

I love you.

John

P.S. Please, Darling, don't come to New York now. I want you and Victoria to think of me in our happy times. I am leaving a note that there's to be no funereal folderol.

The sun had scarcely risen when police at the Weylin Hotel, finding the letter to Anna and recognizing the name in the hotel register, telephoned Elliott. As the only Roosevelt brother currently in New York, he drew the grim duty of identifying the mutilated body. From the morgue, Elliott proceeded to the Park Sheraton Hotel to break the news to his mother. Her silence was long, brooding, heavy, as though suffused with her responsibility for the self-destructive violence. When she finally brought herself to say something, her voice, directed at no one, reached out to claim that responsibility. "Is there nothing I might have done to help poor John? What dreadful things can happen when people *fail* each other. I did try to offer him friendship, but what *good* did it do?"

There was another responsibility to face: calling Anna. Mrs. Roosevelt did it herself.

Scarcely minutes later, a newspaper reporter reached Anna by phone for a comment. How does a former wife shake free of the confused thicket of memories, emotions, regrets, guilts, to make an appropriate comment? Anna's years in the public eye and, indeed, on newspapers served her in composing the kind of foamy sentimentality that satisfies a news reporter at such moments: "It's one of those terrible and sad things. Even though there's a divorce, I feel very deeply."

Mrs. Roosevelt remained shaken. Later in the week at a musicale she met a well-known psychiatrist, Dr. Lawrence S. Kubie. Uncharacteristically for her at a social event, she questioned him, pumped him, about psychiatry, the family troubles of her children, testing for her degree of responsibility—and to what degree that responsibility might be laid to her husband. She invited him to spend the coming weekend at Hyde Park.

"That Sunday," Dr. Kubie was to record, "we drove alone around the country after church and she brought up very frankly her sense of guilt over John Boettiger's suicide, that he had written to her out of his depression and she had brushed it aside with hearty impatience and now felt that this had been insensitive and ruthless etc. She then turned to her concern over Elliott who was just then moving towards his divorce from Faye Emerson. This led Mrs. FDR to talk of all the children, of her role as the disciplinarian, and of the President's role as the comforter, and of what it had done to each of them to have him disappear into illness, into the governorship, into the presidency, into the war; until they had to make appointments in order to see him. She talked of how this had hit each in turn, and especially of how it had destroyed Elliott, which was why she felt such concern for him and did so much more for him than for the others. . . . She would catch glimpses of what I meant [about the ways of the mind and of psychiatry], understand it, and then lose it again. She never completely freed herself from the feeling that if one had courage enough, guts enough, and worked hard enough, one could hoist oneself up by one's own emotional bootstraps. . . . I do not think the arguments left a trace of anything except perplexity, and on my part at least, a warm and affectionate admiration."

". . . What dark days we are living through! . . ."

The Park Sheraton Hotel
New York 19, N.Y.
Dec. 6th [1950]

Anna darling,

The days go by & we are nearly through our work in Com. 3 & I hope to begin to have more time. You've found me very silent these last months because I really had little to tell you & no time in which to tell it.

What dark days we are living through! We are really struggling for survival & yet the daily round & plans go on as usual & of course they must. Elliott has been touring the country & now has 42 cities signed up for the radio & is busy about other business so I've hardly seen him for 2 weeks. . . .

I had a very nice letter from Rommie after election. Perhaps the defeat [of James by Governor Earl Warren in the general election] drew them closer together. . . .

Tommy is fine & seems very well & Hick has moved in at H.P. for her winter writing effort! . . .

A world of love dear,
Mother

". . . I thought of you on Father's birthday . . ."

727 Creston Road
Berkeley [California]
Feb. 13, 1951

Mummy darling:

I thought of you on Father's birthday and wondered if you wouldn't be going over to the grave, so it was good to know from what you actually did that day and some of your thoughts.

All goes well here, and Johnny and I flourish. . . . So far, I'm lucky when I want to go out in the evening, for Johnny has 3 young friends who live close by and who take turns coming to spend the night with him. This means Johnny is not alone during the evening, and, believe it or not, the kids are well behaved and go to bed at a decent hour. Most parents around here who have boys of Johnny's age prefer this sort of arrangement to hiring a "baby sitter" because these boys delight in making a sitter's life miserable! . . .

Mummy, you're wonderful to offer to pay my trip east and back this summer, if such a trip works out. I'm not making any plans until I decide what's best for Johnny this summer and get the results of my medical exam in April.

Financially, my "estimated" income (what I have and what I can count on coming in) will take care of me until Sept. 1, 1951, on my present scale of living. So, the most I would have to ask you for during 1951 would be $3000.00. I checked with a well known lawyer, who is also a friend, and he said an individual may make a gift up to $3000.00 to another individual, in a given year, without having to pay a gift tax on it. So, I'm wondering why your situation is different, as you write you "have to pay a tax on gift money."

And, of course, you know, darling, that I'd rather bust than to have you work harder than you do now—particularly in moneymaking fields. Also, I'm sure you know that I want to get back to financial independence just as soon as I can—without being an idiot and running a chance of landing myself once more on the sick list, thereby costing you a helluva lot of dough! . . .

Johnny just came in from school & sends his love to you, too. And so much of it to you from me.

Anna

". . . The President did the only thing he could do I think . . ."

Hotel des Bergues
Geneva
April 15th, 1951

Darling Anna,

Here we are safely settled in lovely rooms that face the lake & the snow capped mountains. Flowers bloom here but just a little way up in the hills the snow still lies on the ground. It is cold at night but the sun shone today & it felt warm.

Last night in London was cold! We dined with Lady Reading & I did two & half hours of radio interviews in the afternoon. . . .

I think Tommy will be happy here, nearly everyone speaks English. We will take her to our office tomorrow & install her with girls who can translate so the work shouldn't be too hard. . . .

We are three weeks ahead on all the radio programmes & Elliott will be here about the 26th to do more which added to those I do alone will keep us going. He is doing the next two T.V. shows & then those done over here should be on & then I'll be home! . . .

I wonder if you will see McArthur's reception? [On April 10 President Truman fired General Douglas MacArthur from his Pacific command.] The President did the only thing he could do I think but it is going to be stormy for a while. I don't know how long the other republican presidential aspirants will like McArthur however!

All my love to you & Johnnie
Mother

". . . a strange little complacent country, . . . a U.S.A. in miniature . . ."

Hotel des Bergues
Geneva
May 2d [1951]

Anna darling,

It was wonderful news . . . to know the cavity was smaller. Let me know how all the tests come out. . . .

Tomorrow will be your birthday & I shall think of you & send you many wireless messages to wish you a happy day & so many happy returns. What will you do to celebrate?

I hope people wake up soon to McArthur's policies & their meaning. Trude [Lash] wrote me his first 3 calls in N.Y. were on the D.A.R., Herbert Hoover & Cardinal Spellman! Here feeling, as in England & France[,] is strong against widening the area of the [Korean] war. This is a strange little complacent country, in many ways a U.S.A. in miniature but of course nearer the center of disturbance! . . .

Our work does not progress too fast but we may finish. Spring is lovely here & if I can't be home this is the next most beautiful stop I've seen! . . .

All my love to you darling,
Mother

". . . only 7 children for lunch. . . ."

Val-Kill Cottage
Hyde Park
August 20th [1951]

Anna darling,

Two letters from you & one from Sisty yesterday. What exciting news. [Sisty's husband, Van Seagraves, has landed a job with the Mutual Security Administration in Paris.] I'm glad for them as it will give them a chance to travel a good deal in Europe. They'll have to find a place to live in Paris & that will be hard. I'll write to people to keep an eye out. I know some people near their ages & living on about the same salary so I can help them to get started. . . .

We are having a quiet day only 7 children for lunch. . . .

Robin is very much the pregnant woman & Buzz dances attendance on her. It annoys me but why should I be annoyed? I'm only afraid Sisty may show her disapproval? . . .

Devotedly
Mother

". . . Johnny . . . doing a good job this year with his paper route, . . ."

Berkeley [California]
Oct. 16 [1951]

Mummy darling:

Your letter of the 10th was so very welcome. . . . Of course, I'll give the most serious consideration to [motion-picture producer Stanley] Kramer's offer. Mary Baker of the Jaffe Agency phoned me after she'd seen you in the east and I have told her I will plan a visit with her and Kramer, in L.A., within the next month or six weeks. It makes me very happy to know you have so much confidence in me in this regard. How did you like Kramer? The trade paper, VARIETY, says that the final financial arrangements will not be completed for a year, but that you plan to take a lump sum from Kramer and put it into a family foundation, deducting this from future profits. This sounds interesting. Mary Baker said legal papers would be ready for you to go over when you are home for Xmas. VARIETY also said you do not or will not have final say on the script or picture as it is being shot. I guess this would have been an impossible clause to get, and that all we can do is HOPE that both Kramer and Columbia will agree with whatever ideas we all have. The trip to L.A. will also give me a chance to look into two other job opportunities which sound interesting. . . .

I keep forgetting to tell you that your Rolex watch is perfect for me. It keeps such perfect time and the face is big enough so even my far-sighted eyes can read it at all times. Also, the linen from Campo arrived and is most welcome. The small bathtowels are perfect for Johnny's swimming and as hand towels as he and his pals are too rough on good towels. And the double bed sheets were much needed. The single sheets are mostly marked "nursery" and are a little small to use on Johnny's bed for bottom sheets, but are fine for top sheets. Thanks ever so much.

I've had wonderful letters from both Sis and Van in Paris. All goes so well with Johnny that I'm holding my fingers crossed! He's doing a good job this year with his paper route, and is doing well in school where he has a considerable amount of home work for the time. . . .

So very much love, & the biggest of hugs.

Anna

P.S. Anything new on your trip to India?

". . . I can swing a trip for you & Johnny to Paris . . ."

[On board S.S. America]
Oct 25th [1951]

Anna darling,

Franklin jr. & Sue came to lunch the day I sailed & said Sis & Van were wonderful. They told him it would be grand to have you & Johnny over there & you could work in E.C.A. [Economic Cooperation Administration]! F jr. is all set to ask Averill [Averell Harriman, director of newly formed Mutual Security Agency] to get you a job & wants me to speak to him. I don't think we should[,] as if you want one I think you should write him yourself & ask about possible openings. I think I can swing a trip for you & Johnny to Paris next summer so start planning now! You'll have to go on this ship for I can get you better accomodations cheaper!

. . . I'm really resting & reading Donald Day's book carefully. Tell him there is one error shld be corrected in other editions. In '32 he [FDR] went to Chicago from *Albany not* Hyde Park. I like it very much & will write again in the column about it. . . .

Mother

". . . with time and a half for contemplation, . . ."

Berkeley [California]
Nov. 6, 1951

Mummy darling:

. . . Your last letter, written after your first night in Paris, arrived with a grand one from Van and Sis. There is a Down-to-earthness and honesty about those two which is very refreshing these days. They have some good, realistic synacism *[sic]* about the many jobs the US is trying to do in Europe, and they're very realistic about their own "brushes" with people and events of historic importance, and, at the same time, they're determined to enjoy every second of their stay in foreign countries. On the personal side, you can imagine what a warm feeling it gives me to know that those two would like to have me over in Paris. And, naturally, to be near them would be such fun. But, I don't want to write Averill or do anything definite in that field for the moment. Suddenly, job opportunities are popping all over the place and two of them are in the international propaganda field which interests me so much. Yet, somehow, experience has made me very wary of making sudden jumps or decisions—and this time, I'm taking my own "time"! After all, I am 45½ years old, and still have a 12½ year old child to consider from all angles. These two years, with time and a half for contemplation, have made me realize how easy it is for all of us FDR "kids" to "spread ourselves very thin", allowing people to use us in an inordinate number of so-called "worthwhile" projects and programs, where, almost invariably we do "spotty" jobs. We have not the time or energy to do anything else.

Naturally, too, I'm terribly interested in the FDR picture—with the big hope it will be well done. It worries me to hear from several sources that you do not have final approval of the script, and to learn that Stanley Kramer is far more under the thumb of Columbia Pictures, Inc. than I had thought, and therefore not independent when it comes to the final say as to what he wants in the picture. Have you already signed anything in the way of an agreement or is all agreement still in obeyance *[sic]* until the legal papers reach you on your return to this country?

Jimmy was up here last week, on his way east. . . . He disturbed me a bit by saying that he'd never even received a word from Buzz—even an acknowledgement of the check he sent him. He was going to call Buzz and have a talk with him, and I'm curious to know what happened. I wrote Judy Edwards I'd be in LA at Xmas and got a nice letter back—but she said she'd had to call Robin on the phone because she hadn't a letter from her "in months". Same here!

Nov. 8

As usual I got interrupted, and this evening has been a riot because Johnny has recovered (tho he still itches) and had a pal over for dinner. The two of them had so much pent up energy, after dinner, that the whole place was upside-down—and right after I had a cleaning woman for the first time in 3 weeks! A phone call came in for me. Johnny [now twelve] answered and told the person who called that Mrs. B. didn't live here, that this was Kelly's Pool Hall. His pal, John Warner, then got on the phone and continued the clowning. Needless to say, by the time I got to the phone, there was no one at the other end! Next they tied an apple to the tin chandelier and tried to bite it as it swung—the point being to apparently see which of them could konk his teeth and face the hardest. Finally, they took to a chasing game around the circle, which means they run thru the living room, study, kitchen, my room and little hall. The dog joined in—and I finally put a halt when Johnny bounced off one door and into the stove. At that point I booted one John home and the other is getting ready for bed!

Back to more serious things. I don't even dare tell Johnny of your offer to give both of us a trip to Paris next summer because he would die of joy! It does sound too good to be true, Mummy, and my one big hope is that I don't get tied up in some job which will keep me from doing it. There are two job possibilities which might work out that way—so I'll just keep my fingers crossed, and HOPE!

I'm so happy you and Tommy got a chance to really rest on the trip over, for from news reports, there's going to be plenty a-popping at the Assembly. I thought the President did a good job with his speech last evening. The only two people I've talked to today were Democrats, but not the pro-Truman kind. Their opinions were, however, that they felt for the first time that our foreign policy was on a positive rather than a negative basis, and were pleased. . . .

Loads and loads of love to Sis, Van, Nick, Tommy, and a world of it to you, darling, with a big hug to boot.

Anna

". . . This picture is a 'sure seller' abroad . . ."

727 Creston Road
Berkeley, California
November 11, 1951

Dear Frankie:

I was delighted to get your letter because I've been wondering what you felt about the FDR picture project. . . .

To the best of my knowledge, and judging by two interviews I had with him, one on the air and one in his office, and by the pictures he has produced so far, I would say that Stanley Kramer has the ability and right ideals to turn out at least an interesting picture. . . .

Thru a friend in Hollywood, I got the story that under Kramer's deal with

Columbia, the latter have the final say on any arguments over script and final screening, and that the Columbia people have never been FDR fans. I was also reminded that the movie industry has been suffering because its foreign market has fallen off so badly in the last years, and that this picture is a "sure seller" abroad because of FDR's popularity there. The clipping says this is to be "a very personal picturization". . . . "The international conferences, the war, the speeches will enter in, but they will be only a back-drop." The rest of that paragraph makes me wonder how a Kramer would cover the "silver spoon" angle, our family way of living (which was certainly not average), and still get across to the people here and abroad what Father stood for and why he became known to all as "the friend of the people". . . .

When Jimmy was here, I pointed out to him that I felt the family should have NO share or financial interest in the project unless they had final say as to script and final screening (this last because in screening so many inuendoes can be put in which do not actually appear in the script), and unless the financial arrangements were such that the picture was not designed to make a killing for a lot of people connected with Columbia. . . .

Of paramount importance to me is that the family would be putting a stamp of approval on the picture if they are legally and financially tied up with it; that I feel that in this day of world turmoil and radically new evolvements, the leaders of history who mean as much as Father does to the people's of the world, must be depicted in such mediums as movies, on the basis of the "total man"—the man whose personal values and actions were such that he was able to do what he did as a leader. I feel that a vast majority of people today are groping for the inner security which comes from the growing buildup of respect and idealism with which people surround those who have passed into history but whose accomplishments still stand for all to see. Historically, Father's death is so recent, and still may well be five years from now, that many people (particularly in this country) hate him with the same intensity as if he were alive. Perspective won't come for many years.

I know, too, that any movie company would be asses to give the family a final approval of both script and screening. We are not dramatically trained; we are very personal about all this; we are individualists and might differ strongly among ourselves.

Practically speaking: anyone can make a picture of FDR without our consent. Our only recourse, if we as individuals are in the picture, and don't like the depiction, is to sue for damages we think we can prove have accrued to us thru the picture. Nevertheless, with a Stanley Kramer doing the picture, I don't think the family can ignore it. (I feel that the publicity to date was most premature, however, as the whole family was never given a chance to think thru all these details and come up with at least a family agreement.) I feel that *all* of us have something to contribute to the making of any serious picture about Father. Therefore, my present suggestion is (for our own long run protection, and completely aside from financial gain which seems to me more than secondary considering Father's importance in history) that we do not enter into any financial agreement concerning the picture; that we agree to help in ways we, individually, feel able to with an agreement between ourselves that we will only accept remuneration where actual expenses are incurred by us as individuals in the course of giving the help; that there be an agreement between Kramer-Columbia and the family that any member of the family can see any part of the script and/or screening at any time, but that unsolicited perusals of this sort by any of us must be done at our own expense. And, I believe, there should be a signed agreement whereby any publicity concerning any family affiliation with the picture must be okayed by Mother and either you, Jimmy or me,—the latter 3 of us can be in addition to Elliott and Johnny, but one of these latter 3 should always be included in a release okay.

All of the above can be termed "just thinking out loud", but I do feel strongly about it all. Please think it all over very carefully, and irrespectively of any family (individual) needs for financial gains of the moment or the future. My present thought is that I should write Mother, shortly, incorporating the thoughts in this letter—expressed as tactfully as I possibly can, realizing that she may have already gone much further than we know in her thinking regarding the financial help this could be to some members of the family. So write me your further thoughts as soon as you can.

I've just re-read the notes I made while I was talking to Elliott on the phone when he was in L.A., and according to them Mother is to receive $25,000 on signing the contract. This is to be in addition to her ⅓ interest, and will be made a "family pool" (Elliott's words) to be disposed of as ER wishes. Also, my notes say that Mother is to receive a $50,000 advance on her ⅓ interest, when the contract is signed. My notes say that the Jaffe agency will receive 10% on all phases of the contract, including whatever salary I would get if I worked for Kramer. Jaffe is to handle all legal representation.

Enough of that lengthy subject! On the possibility of the job in Paris, I want to hold off entirely for the present. Of course, it would be great fun being near my family of three over there. There are 3 possible jobs "on the pan" which I am cautiously proceeding towards. I've got enough dough to live on here, as I do now, until next June 1. And, I feel it would be a mistake for me to jump headlong into something, just because it seemed like a good idea at the time. . . .

Johnny has turned his heavy old bike in as part payment on a light English bike. This is his only Xmas wish this year, so he asked me if, instead of sending him a Xmas wish, you would send him a little cash toward the new bike. I told him you *might* be able to send him 2 or 3 bucks, but that was all, and that at least I'd ask you. He's saving his own dough, too, from his paper route, towards it. Forget it, if you want—but I did promise to ask!

How is Sue? And is the baby due just before or just after Xmas? . . .

Lots of love to you and Sue.

[Anna]

". . . I hope to . . . have Xmas at home . . ."

Claridge's
[London]
Sunday Dec 16th [1951]

Anna darling,
    . . . We [Van, Sis, Eleanor and Tommy] went to the Tower of London yesterday morning & drove all around the "City" & I showed them where the King has to be met by the Lord Mayor before he can enter & also took them to see the Blitz' damage. We saw St Paul's & Westminster in the p.m. All of us went to "South Pacific" in the evening & back stage to meet Mary Martin.
    This a.m. they saw the changing of the guard & went back to Westminster to hear the organ while Tommy & I stayed here & worked till Lady Reading came to see us. We all lunched with her & she has invited Sis & Van . . . on a motor trip to spend a couple of days at the "Manor House" she . . . [has] just bought. King Alfred is supposed to have signed his will in it & much of it dates back to the 11th century & one corner of the 9th! . . .
    I'll be horribly busy tomorrow but these days have been fun & Friday or Sat. I hope to get off for home . . . & have Xmas at home & talk to you & Jimmy that day. . . .

Mother

". . . I'll be walking on eggs in the Arab countries . . ."

Hotel de Crillon
Paris
Feb 7th 1952

Anna darling,
    I get off with Miss Corr [Maureen Corr, filling in for Tommy as Mrs. Roosevelt's secretary] for Beirut at 1.45 on Saturday the 9th, & I'll send you P.C.'s [postcards?] even if I can't write for a little while. They seem to be arranging a very tight schedule! . . .
    We all went to the Greene's (my advisor) for cocktails & then what remains of those who worked with me gave me a party at a nice little restaurant with wonderful food.
    My work is really done but I still have to go to the office tomorrow morning & sign mail. My reports are written but I have 2 columns to write & I still want to rewrite the 1st chapter I wrote of the book & write the 2d! I'm loaded with information & all kinds of people are prepared to show me things so if I don't learn something on this trip I just can't learn! I'll be walking on eggs in the Arab countries because they know I believe in Israel but so far with the Arab press I've got by!
    David arrived Tuesday & is busy as can be & enjoying Paris to the full. He'll go to Israel Sunday night & we will meet in Jerusalem on the 15th.
    I am sure you were sad over Mr. Ickes' [Harold Ickes, FDR's secretary of the interior] death. Do tell me what you hear from Jane [Ickes' widow, who

was much younger than he, and a close friend of Anna's]? The King of England's death was a shock. All my love darling & love to Johnnie.

Devotedly
Mother

". . . Arab states were hostile as I expected . . ."

Governor's House
Lahore [Pakistan]
Feb. 25th 1952

Anna darling,
    You must wonder what has happened to me but I have lived on such a close schedule that I've had a hard time to write the column & letters have been few & far between.
    . . . The Arab states were hostile as I expected tho' their officials tried to be friendly & I hope I left them more friendly. Isreal was a great experience & if only there could be better feeling & those pitiful refugees could be resettled, Israel could enormously help the Arab countries & get some much needed food stuffs & other commercial advantages in return. Their collective communities are most interesting but it is the quality & ideals of all government people that is so impressive. If it can be preserved I think it must be a great nation some day.
    Here problems are staggering but top people are able & fine but such a mass of ignorance to carry! Everyone has been very kind but I feel there is so much to be done & will I have time & strength just to set the ball rolling. Who knows? No one may listen after I get home!
    We go to one of their big development projects tomorrow, all except David who has bad sinus & hopes to stay home & flirt with some lovely ladies! The next day we leave for India & I hope from there on for a somewhat lighter schedule on lunches & dinners at least!
    I hope all is well with you & I long to hear. My love to Johnny & much, much to you darling.

Mummy

". . . I feel rather lonely & far away. . . ."

Lalitha Mahal
Mysore [India]
March 6th 1952

Anna darling,
    . . . We've seen a good bit of village life & the level in the village & the city slum is far below anything we know. The spirit, religious life & dignity of these people is also something astounding however. . . .

We've seen a princely State, we've of course been a government guest so there have been endless schedules & every meal official & speeches without end. So far I've had a good press & I don't think I've made any bad mistakes. I've cut . . . my programme & that may mean hard feeling but I didn't think it wise to take 2 long flights they had planned. The State Dept. & [U.S. ambassador] Chester Bowles I hope will feel that on the whole I've done my job & been helpful.

No letters from home so I feel rather lonely & far away.

All my love
Mother

CHAPTER VIII
May 15, 1952–December 12, 1962

Last New Year's Eve Anna attended a party in Los Angeles at the home of Frank and Doris Hursley, whom she didn't know intimately although they had mutual friends. More than four years had passed since Anna's separation from John Boettiger, and more than a year since his death. She had learned to handle the loneliness—yet one never learns. Through the special receptors of the formerly married, she sensed in the crowd an uncoupled other, a tall, restrained, cultivated Easterner whose bespectacled eyes offered inviting, personal contact. She learned he was a doctor, recently transplanted to California to engage in research, and currently enduring the one-year "waiting period" for a divorce as required by California law. At seconds before midnight, the convivial throng was in a circle holding hands to sing "Auld Lang Syne" and, as though by accident, Jim Halsted was next to Anna, his hand holding hers. They exchanged good wishes and small talk, none of it memorable except for its undercurrent of potential. As the party broke up, and Anna was departing in the company of a former Truman adviser, David K. Noyes, and his wife—Jim still recalls it vividly: "The front door was up some steps from the living room, and as she went out I remember her looking at me very interestingly and, well, fondly."

Several weeks later, again as though by accident, Doris Hursley made known to Jim that Anna was returning to Los Angeles for a few days for job interviews. More than a little intimidated by Anna's illustrious origins, Jim asked Doris how Anna would take to being asked out to dinner. She'd love it, assured Doris. He took her to downtown L.A., to a place called the Captain's Table "where you sit next to each other at small tables against a wall down along a line of tables." Next evening they dined together again, and that evening he said something to Anna that touched a special place in her heart. Perhaps he had no suspicion it would, or perhaps some instinct stirred his tongue. The only thing standing in the way of what he was learning to feel for her, Jim said shyly, was that he kept wishing that, instead of being a Roosevelt, her name was just Anna Smith. Years later she was repeatedly to tell Jim of her appreciation of that remark. For the remaining days of her visit they lunched together every day, dined every evening. By week's end she had decided to move to Los Angeles.

The romance between Anna and Jim bloomed swiftly. By April, they were fully sharing a residence and committed to marrying in the fall. In addition to their rented apartment in Los Angeles, they had bought a modest piece of land and cabin in the hills, which they chose to call their "ranchito."

Mrs. Roosevelt was quite aware of Anna's and Jim's informal arrangement and apparently accepted it without a quiver, although such premarital housekeeping remained far beyond the conventional in the early fifties. On several occasions, Mrs. Roosevelt turned over her Val-Kill cottage to young couples among her friends for weekends and vacations in advance of their marriages.

"(. . . if they decide to break a precedent and hire a woman). . . ."

> 664 Kelton Avenue
> Los Angeles 24, Calif.
> May 15, 1952

Mummy darling:

It now seems such ages since I left you—and all because there has been lots going on. First of all, I had to go and get a cold as soon as I got home, and had to really take it easy for 3 days. Then, I've been pursuing job possibilities like mad—the Ford Foundation (another appointment coming up tomorrow), 2 job possibilities in the University's Industrial Relation's Institute (at too small a salary), a possible job as organizer for a World Affairs Council here in L.A. (an appointment on this on Saturday), and a possible job as a saleswoman for the American Broadcasting Co. (I've had 2 appointments on this but still have to hear if they decide to break a precedent and hire a woman). In addition, the 3 boys [Johnny Boettiger and Jim's two sons] and Jim and I have spent as much time as possible at our little ranch starting to get it cleaned up—at least enough so we can spend week-ends there. So far we only go up during the daytime, and occasionally (once so far) Jim and I have gone up for 4 or 5 hours after he finishes work. The boys are all thrilled about the place and are really doing a job of "pitching in".

Once again I walked off with your apartment key! And, here, also, are the sales slips for all the wonderful clothes you gave me. They have arrived (and so has the box of stuff I left and which Tommy had mailed to me), and as Jim approves of them as much as you I'm very happy! I feel I really bought too much and that I should contribute something out of my first pay checks—I mean those I HOPE to get. But, until I can do that, I can only say thanks and thanks again for so very, very much, Mummy.

Your letter to Jim arrived today, and we both loved it. I'm glad you liked the picture of me.

Somehow, I got so much satisfaction from being with you on this last visit. Perhaps it's because my own life seems to be finally taking a positive and happy course. But, whatever the reasons, the all too short times with you were very happy ones.

F. Jr. phoned and asked if I would do the Harriman [for the Democratic presidential nomination] organizing job for the west coast from now until the convention. This would of course mean a lot of traveling and night work, and I explained to him I couldn't do this. Also, I'm not looking for a temporary political job! But, it was nice of him to think of me.

What do you hear from Elliott? I'm writing him tonight about Johnny's going up to their ranch this summer. Johnny wants to earn $30 per month because that is what Charley Halsted will earn at the ranch where he will work this summer. Charley, however is 15 years old, though not much bigger than Johnny.

All my love, darling, and do write soon.

Anna

". . . And now for a very important matter! . . ."

P.P.S.: *Read FIRST!:* As I finished this letter, a letter arrived from Minnewa [Elliott's wife] saying they can not hire Johnny to work but would be happy to have him visit them for a couple of weeks in June or July. Johnny prefers to visit his other friends, so I'll write them immediately, & also write his regrets & thanks to Minnewa.

Lots of love, again, darling,
A

664 Kelton Avenue—L.A. 24
[California]
June 9, 1952

Mummy darling:

Do you have any way of finding out, pronto, from Elliott as to whether he and Minnewa want Johnny to visit them in Colorado? I wrote him weeks ago and have had no answer. Then I wrote him again about 2 weeks ago, to Cuba, and sent a copy of the letter to Tommy asking her if she knew a better way to get it to him. And still not a peep! Elliott suggested Johnny work on the

Colorado ranch. . . . Anyway, you can see that just to have definite word from Elliott is just about imperative!

And now for a very important matter! Jim and I plan to be married next November 11th. It's Armistice Day and a Tuesday. We would so much like to have you here *if* you can make the trip without too much inconvenience. Tell Tommy that of course we'd give our eye teeth to have her too! We want to be married at our ranchito. Counting family and friends (and hoping that will include you and Tommy!) there will not be more than a dozen people. Jim's Unitarian minister friend will marry us. You are the only person we have mentioned this "big" date to—knowing how many months ahead your plans are made.

UCLA and the Fund for Adult Education (Ford Foundation) are still working on a position for me—one where I would be appointed by UCLA and paid by the Fund. But it all remains very hush-hush and slow because there are people at the top of both groups who are afraid, still, of the political implications. So, as usual, I wait. . . .

> All my love and a big hug.
> Anna

P.S. . . . Jim says please to give you his best & to tell you he so much appreciated your letter to him. Also, he wants me to thank you for inviting Nell [Jim's twenty-year-old daughter] to spend a weekend at Hyde Park. Nell wrote him how sorry she was that she could not go.

> A.

". . . all too few . . . know anything about Nixon. . . ."

> L.A., Aug. 17 [1952]

Mummy darling:

This time I'm the real wretch about writing! I know I haven't written since shortly after your Convention speech, and when I told you about moving out of my apartment . . .

Since August 2nd Jim and I have been minus children and have thoroughly enjoyed it! Jim has had a 2½ weeks holiday and we have come up to the ranch almost every day or had friends to stay up here with us.

I sold my Plymouth, so from now on we're a one car family—plus busses. The apartment *should* be sublet between now and Sept. 1. And all my furniture (plus what I still had in Phoenix) is now either being used at the ranch or at Jim's house in L.A. or stored in Jim's cellar.

I have a room and bath at the Frank Hursleys, and can stay there, rent free, until Nov. 11. The phone number there is Arizona 9-6758 but as I'm at Jim's most of the time, his number is the best to try if you want me in a hurry. It is Arizona 7-4385. My mail is still going to 664 Kelton Avenue, but later this week I will take a box at the P.O. nearest to Jim's house, and will send you the number pronto.

Cha [Jim's son] Halsted gets home this coming week-end and Tom turns up the following week. Johnny won't be home until the day after Labor Day. He writes he is having a wonderful time. . . .

Mummy, is there any chance that you could give Jim and me a very special wedding present in the shape of coach plane fares to N.Y. and back next December?! We would plan to leave here either the night of December 26th or the morning of the 27th. We could not be away more than 10 to 12 days, and would spend part of the time with you and part of the time in Boston so that we can see those of Jim's kids who will be there, and so that he can introduce me to some of the other members of his family (a sister, brother-in-law and their children to be exact) and to some of his old friends. This we would like more than anything else. It's something we could not swing on our own financially. Both tickets, round trip, and including tax, come to $460. We know this is a walloping big present, so if it's too much you know we will understand.

I'm sorry F., Jr. feels bitter about Stevenson [Franklin, Jr., avidly worked for Averell Harriman's presidential nomination], and hope he gets over it and finds he can sincerely work for Stevenson. It seems to me that Stevenson was honest all the way thru the pre-convention and convention times, and that he would have much preferred it if Harriman could have been nominated. I mean I think Stevenson was sincere in his pre-convention praise of Harriman and sincere in saying that he personally did not want the nomination. Also, I believe him when [he] says he feels the office of the Presidency is too big from a responsibility standpoint to be turned down with a flat refusal *before* it has been offered to you. In fact, I'm (and so is Jim) very pleased with the ticket! And, I thought before the convention and still believe that Stevenson is the only one who can defeat Eisenhower. By the way, I hope the Demos are going to do a good job of "exposing" Nixon [Senator Richard M. Nixon had been selected by General Eisenhower as his running mate], on his record. I find that all too few people, outside of this state, know anything about Nixon.

No job—as Johnny R. will tell you. So, I've decided to quit breaking my neck trying to get into something "worthwhile" and am, this week, going to ask Jimmy if he still has open the part time job he offered me before (as lately as 2 weeks ago) which would entail public relations work in his insurance office. In the long run this would probably be better for me—what with a husband and kids!

Jim sends his love—and lots and lots of it with a great big hug from me.

Anna

". . . I am . . . trying to do a little for Stevenson around here . . ."

29 Washington Square West
New York 11, N.Y.
Oct. 5th [1952]

Anna darling,

. . . 2 of Johnny & Anne's kids have had polio. I think Sally had it first but it was not recognized. She was ill with 104 temp. the day Anne brought 8 day old Joanie home from the hospital. Luckily thro' it all Anne has been a brick & gained her strength & seems well & the baby flourishes. Two weeks after Sally fell ill, Haven [John's son] was ill, quarantined in Tommy's spare room, & no mistake in diagnosis as his whole right side was weak & David who was with us knew at once. He is fine & goes back to school tomorrow. Two weeks after he came down Nina [John's daughter] took his place in Tommy's room & she did lose the use of her right leg. They all moved to town however, finally & today David allowed Nina to walk to the bathroom without crutches & she can do it so in a month or so she will be o.k.

Tommy & I won't get to L.A. till very late the night of 8th or around noon the 9th as I lecture in Tucson the evening of the 8th. . . . I'll surely be on hand for dinner on the 10th. I'd like to get a plane back on the 11th which would get me in around 2 a.m. so I cld have an hour or two in bed before the 9 a.m. morning meeting. I'm getting *all* my expenses & Tommy's pd by Colston Leigh, the lecture manager in lieu of any other payment & he will make arrangments for rooms at the Beverly Hills Hotel. . . .

Tommy doesn't seem very well to me but it is nothing I can put my finger on.

I am on the delegation to the G.A. [UN General Assembly] & trying to do a little for Stevenson around here & so busy I hardly have time to breathe. The finishing touches on the book seem impossible to do!

My love to Jim & Johnny & a world of love to you darling,

Mummy

". . . the last person I have known as long as I can remember. . . ."

The Park Sheraton Hotel
New York 19, N.Y.
Oct. 23d [1952]

Anna darling,

. . . Tell Jimmy I am annoyed with him! He was here to speak & never even phoned me. I heard about him from Dorothy Schiff [owner of the *New York Post*], who asked affectionately for you. Incidentally, she said both Jimmy & she were booed which at that Forum was no surprise to me. . . .

David is here & quite wonderful. It seems impossible that Maude is gone. We met so little of late & I'm so busy that I can't mean much to anyone, but she is the last person I have known as long as I can remember. I love the young about me, but I remember all about them & they can't know anything of my past so with Maude that particular tie is gone forever.

I don't look forward to the Chile trip but if I live thro' this coming week end, I should live through anything! . . .

I wonder what you think Stevenson's chances are? I never saw a campaign in which the regular organization seems to have done so little & the amateurs & volunteers seem to have run the show. . . .

Devotedly
Mother

On November 11 Anna and Jim were married. Mrs. Roosevelt attended, and returned immediately to New York.

A new life was about to begin for Mrs. Roosevelt as well as for Mrs. James A. Halsted. With the election the previous week of Dwight D. Eisenhower to the presidency, Mrs. Roosevelt assumed—quite correctly—that her pro forma resignation from her UN post would be accepted by the new President. Ike was the first Republican to occupy the White House since the day almost twenty years earlier when her husband took possession of it from Herbert Hoover.

". . . the advertisers think I'm too controversial! . . ."

Park Sheraton Hotel
[New York 19, N.Y.]
Friday night Dec. 19th [1952]

Anna darling,

I have been a wretch about writing but today we had our last Com. meeting & tomorrow our work will go thro' the plenary so I feel care free, with plenty of time on my hands! In one way it is sad to leave the U.N. officially but working with U.N. Ass. will be a challenge & seems to me very necessary. I may fail but it is worth a try.

It was wonderful to see Jimmy & hear that you had taken the job with him & I'm sure you'll enjoy it once you learn the business. . . .

How does your housekeeping go? Don't get too tired.

Sis writes she has a good baby & can't wait for you to arrive! . . . It looks as tho' I'd go to Japan June 1st for 6 weeks so I can't decide whether to go to Europe for May or come back via Europe but it is nicer there in May & I do want to get home by the end of July.

I haven't got any radio or T.V. yet, the advertisers think I'm too controversial! . . .

My love & a Merry Xmas darling to you & Jim. I feel so much happier about you & Johnny this year than I have for many years. Give Jim my love &

thanks & Johnny & the other boys too. The best of New Years to all & a big hug to you,

Mother

Late in the afternoon of April 12, 1953—to the hour, eight years after the death of FDR—just as Mrs. Roosevelt was arriving to visit her, Malvina "Tommy" Thompson, for years her ever-present secretary and friend, died in a New York hospital.

Mrs. Roosevelt was undergoing the ordeal which some say is the heaviest price of longevity: watching the departure of friend after friend, each death feeling like an abandonment, each a foreshadowing of the inevitable. In 1949, it was Elinor Morgenthau, her dearest Hudson River neighbor. In 1950, cousin Susie Parish, in whose town house President Theodore Roosevelt came to attend Eleanor's and Franklin's wedding, and whose inventions of dire illness were to amuse Eleanor for the rest of Susie's life. In 1952, Aunt Maude, the last remaining soul Eleanor had known all her life. And now Tommy, faithful for almost thirty years and who, Eleanor was soon to say, "gave me a reason for living."

"The people who worked with them," Anna was one day to explain to me concerning her parents' relationship with their closest employees, "had to be just as if they had no lives of their own. . . . I used to just cringe sometimes when I'd hear Mother at eleven thirty at night say to Tommy, 'I've still got a column to do.' And this weary, weary woman who didn't have Mother's stamina would sit down at a typewriter and Mother would dictate to her. And both of them so tired. I remember one time when Tommy with asperity said, 'You'll have to speak louder. I can't hear you.' And Mother's response was, 'If you will listen, you can hear *perfectly* well.' At twelve o'clock at night this was going on between these two women—and on went the column.

"During most of the years that Tommy was with Mother—Tommy had been divorced—there was a man [Henry Osthagen] who wanted desperately to marry her. She kept him as a boyfriend. She never married him. After all, working for Mother, she saw him so little. Tommy died before he did, and Mother helped support him."

But why would anyone devote her life to serving another the way Tommy did for Eleanor, the way Missy, then Grace Tully did for FDR?

"It's a queer combination of devotion to a person and the excitement that person provides in your life, a status you never dreamed you'd have, a kind of excitement and challenge and importance. Mother first met Tommy, I think, through the Women's Division of the Democratic State Committee. Tommy and, I'm sure, Tully didn't have college educations. What would Tommy have been if Mother hadn't come along? She'd have been there all the rest of her life, keeping somebody's calendar straight, fending off people someone didn't want to see. And here came this woman who propelled her into things she never dreamed of."

". . . She . . . died just as I reached the hospital . . ."

The Park Sheraton Hotel
New York 19, N.Y.
April 12th [1953]

Anna darling,

I wired Jimmy to tell you & Elliott that Tommy died this afternoon. She had a hemorrhage in her abdomen last night but at one o'clock Dr. Ingerman said she rallied but I came down as soon as the people who came to H.P. to lay wreaths in memory of Father had had lunch at the cottage. She had another brain hemorrhage & died just as I reached the hospital about 5.30. She was unconscious & had just a slight convulsion & Dr. Ingerman was with her. I doubt & so does Dr. Ingerman whether she could ever have fully recovered & I think being unable to live normally would have been very hard for her. We are all going to miss her sadly, young & old.

I have thought all during the past twelve days of all the many adjustments that we might have to make so it has not come as a shock but there are many things that have to be done. So far I've found no will. . . . Henry [Osthagen] will have to come & get his things. I think Miss Corr, & Miss Muller can manage till I go away & then in the autumn I may have to take an extra girl, but I hope not.

I'll see you on the 20th I hope & meantime a world of love,

Mother

". . . not having her around is going to be hellishly hard . . ."

In the office
Apr. 13, 1953

Mummy darling—

My heart is heavy today—thinking of you & of Tommy. I know it was best to have her go, after all that had happened to her; but that's no comfort when your mind & feelings are inundated (as they have been since you first wrote of her illness) with thoughts & memories of what she meant to each one of us. She was a very great person—with her unfailing interest in & understanding of others, her intuitively sound advice, & a sense of humor, & proportion & perspective very rarely found in such a great degree.

I know there is no use dwelling on how much you (& we 5, & Sis & Buzz & some of the other older grandchildren) will miss her—but still, not having her around is going to be hellishly hard to take.

I'd like to be with you Wednesday, but as that can't be I've sent a small spray of spring flowers.

Minnewa as the press phoned & said you'd still get here next Sunday, so we will see you then & that will be wonderful.

All my love, darling, & the biggest of big hugs.

Anna

". . . I was briefed . . . on Japan's 'Life & Culture' . . ."

Imperial Hotel
Tokyo
May 26th evening [1953]

Anna darling,

Tomorrow you will all be in Paris & how I wish I could be there with you! This is a fascinating experience & in a way I am meeting more Japanese from every walk of life than I met Indians in India. I begin to understand many things! Minnewa goes everywhere valiantly & seems to be enjoying it & I'm sure she is learning much but she'll have to tell you her impressions. They will be in L.A. on their way home early in July & again later I think. Elliott will meet her in Honolulu & they will have a few days holiday there.

The trip was comfortable but I was tired the first days here but I am recovered now & as I am interested I'm sure I shan't get weary again.

Saturday we drove deep & high into the mountains in the rain. I was briefed all evening & morning on Japan's "Life & Culture" & have had 2 more long evening sessions here on labor & agriculture & youth. . . .

We did get a glimpse of Fugi [Fuji] on Sunday, snow capped with clouds floating about the base. The Japanese houses are delightful but they must be cold in winter. Tokyo was so badly destroyed that much of it looks like flimsy slums. . . .

Sunday we go to Kyoto, the old capital, untouched in the war, very beautiful they tell me & I will see some typical homes. I've made 2 speeches & had one question period with university students & all seemed to go well. How I hate translated speeches! The night of our arrival we heard Marian Anderson in a concert & she has had real success here. . .

Devotedly
Mother

". . . I cannot flop on my knees gracefully, . . ."

Osaka
June 5th [1954]

Anna darling,

. . . Two things I find difficult here. I cannot flop on my knees gracefully, sit back on my heels for an hour or two without moving & rise without effort! Next, I did not bring shoes that I can walk in thro' mud, slip off when I go indoors or thro' a temple & put on again easily without sitting down! I'm really not sold on Japanese food either, tho' I never miss trying a new thing. It is a little like having a whole meal of hors d'oeuvres, an endless variety of bites is put before you, rice is all you get in any quantity! I do like the idea of doing your guest honor by the flower arrangment & the particular art objects you bring out on display for the occassion. The houses with their matting or even wood floors are spotless because no dirt comes in on shoes!

This place is the Chicago of Japan & I spent 2 hours yesterday p.m. listening to the business men's woes. I've been thro' factories with the most modern Du Pont machinery & others where all the work is done by hand. The economic situation is basic to establishing a democracy & making them feel free & not *driven* by us is basic to good will between us. Sometimes I wonder if we wouldn't be safer with Germany & Japan unarmed. It would at least show what we hoped for in the world & if we do arm them, we or the U.N. will have to really defend them, they can't be trusted to do it alone. Many of these people just don't want war again, period, & if Russia invades[,] well, it may not be worse than present conditions is their feeling. Freedom & democracy are so new & so hard for the masses to understand & the communist ideal is easier to grasp & they know nothing of the reality!

This Committee does a wonderful job of having you meet small groups of various kinds of people & hear & discuss their views.

I'm not really tired as yet & I do find it interesting. Minnewa has been a good soldier, gone to nearly every meeting, been nice to everyone & very helpful. She & Miss Corr are out shopping right now. I must go to meet with a group of women & students for an hour & a half. We're free tonight but I have a column to do & an article to start so I'll stop. Welcome home, love to Jim & Johnny & a world of love to you.

Devotedly
Mother

"*. . . Hiroshima was painful. . . .*"

Imperial Hotel
Tokyo
June 17th [1953]

Dear Jim,

. . . This trip of mine has been most interesting & I have learned a great deal. We've had fun & seen lovely scenery & beautiful art, but some days have been a strain. Hiroshima was painful. Yesterday for example was a long tough day, 2 hrs. in the morning answering questions from some 30 men, members of the Civil Liberties Union, 2 hrs & a half standing, speaking & answering questions & going to a reception . . . & 2 hrs in the evening on a panel discussing the status of women in Japan! Today however is easier.

Life is hard for the people here & the economic problems are basic to the solution of many others. The changes have come so fast that assimilation is difficult & the west & the east meet in the life of every household. There will be a dining room table & chairs but the grandmother may insist on a cushion on the floor & a low table, there will be 2 beds & the others prefer mats. I don't like Japanese food tho' it is better in the home than in the restaurants. . . . The morals of the East have been a bit too much for our boys. If we are going to have bases all over the world we need a change in our education & it should begin with parents.

Anna darling, my reports will go back from Greece . . . to you & some others so you should begin to get them about July 20th. . . . My love to Jim & the boys & ever so much to you.

Devotedly
Mother

". . . I want to learn about the British point of view . . ."

Peninsula Hotel
Kowloon
Hong Kong
June 25th evening [1953]

Darling Sis,
. . . This place [although] a crown colony is much more oriental in feel than Japan & the population teems. . . . I want to learn about the British point of view *out here* on China (communist) I mean. We sat on the [illegible] after dinner looking across the harbor with its myriad lights & the moon shining & it was unbelievably beautiful. This is a gorgeous harbor & the sampans are something fantastic. The sails are patched till you can't see *any* original sail! Must go to bed. All my love to you & much to Jim & the family,

Mother

". . . A weary Consul had met us but he perked up . . ."

[Athens]
Monday June 29th [1953]

Anna darling,
. . . I've been adamant about engagements here but on the 1st I must lunch with the King & Queen & all of us dine at the Embassy. David [Gurewitsch] arrives tonight & we got in this morning because I expected to reach Istanbul yesterday noon but instead we were held 12 hrs in Delhi & only arrived at 5 a.m. this morning. . . . We saw 3 mosques [in Istanbul] & drove thro' the narrow streets of the old town at 6.30 a.m. A weary Consul [Robert Macatee] had met us but he perked up & took us home to breakfast at 7:30 with his wife

& daughter. We had it on an enchanting 2d story porch with a view of the Golden Horn & all its shipping! I loved it & so apparently did Maureen & in the end the Macatee's!

We unpacked, bathed, had lunch, then we did the column & I dictated the first draft on an article about my interview with the Emperor & Empress of Japan. Maureen is tired but Adlai Stevenson is coming in for tea & I think her curiosity will keep her awake to meet him.

Hong Kong was a fascinating place. I'll dictate my round robin diary tomorrow. I'm so glad that it is full moon so we can see the Acropolis by moonlight. It's warm so I shall try to get my companions to sightsee early & be home the midday hours & perhaps go to the beach in the late afternoon & find a place we can dine. Adlai Stevenson has been & gone, a most interesting man, with vision & common sense. . . .

Devotedly
Mother

At the end of 1954, Jim Halsted, whose job is in medical research at the Veterans Administration in Los Angeles, unexpectedly receives a call from a VA hospital director in Syracuse, New York—Jim's hometown, where his father was once a prominent physician—asking if he'd like to come to Syracuse and take over as chief of staff. Feeling remote from their roots, Jim and Anna give in to the temptation without much investigation or thought. Before long, Anna is also to land a job in Syracuse as public relations representative of the State University of New York College of Medicine, Syracuse.

". . . It will be good to have you near again! . . ."

Hotel Adolphus
Dallas
Jan 9th [1955]

Darling Anna,

. . . I haven't written because I've been so uncomfortable I didn't want to do anything I didn't have to do! Tuesday a.m. after Xmas I sat minus clothes on a *very* hot radiator in my bed room in H.P. thinking no heat was on & burned my behind painfully. Thought it was nothing & found I was wrong & have suffered discomfort ever since & probably will for ten days more I'm told. This trip has been successful but not comfortable!

Of course I'm overjoyed that you will be so near & Buzz too will be happy. I'm sorry for you about leaving the "Ranchito" but you may find something not too far from Syracuse you will like almost as much! I'm very happy that Johnny is not upset. . . .

Buzz telephoned me from N.Y. & I have a letter from him. . . . Will write soon but sitting is uncomfortable. . . .

It will be good to have you near again!

Devotedly
Mother

". . . I don't care if a movie is ever made . . ."

211 East 62nd Street
New York 21, N.Y.
February 23d [1955]

Anna darling,

Your letter of the 20th is here. I would send your whole wedding dress, *on loan* to the library. Someday you may want that lace. It is the old family lace. The same should be done with my wedding handkerchief, but only *on loan*. Sis or Buzz may want them or even Johnny for their daughters wedding!

I'm having the part of your letter on a movie copied & sent to each of the boys. Personally I don't care if a movie is ever made but if it is to be done I still think a better script might be written while some people who knew Father are alive. . . .

Buzz & Ruth will be married on the 6th at 4 p.m. I leave the next day at 4 p.m. for Europe.

All my love
Mother

". . . Just a few more holes in this life . . ."

211 East 62nd Street
New York 21, N.Y.
June 20th [1955]

Anna darling,

. . . This last week end was hard for me. I spent Friday in Fall River [Massachusetts] for Mrs. Louis Howe's funeral. She had 2 strokes & death was merciful. Sunday I came down for John Golden's funeral. I shall miss him very much for he was a dear & thoughtful friend always, but he had suffered of late & so death was probably merciful in his case too. After 40 we all live on borrowed time & there should really be no cause for grief in the passing of one's contemporaries. Just a few more holes in this life to warn us to be prepared! I've tidied up much in the house this year but this summer I must see that all the papers I can get rid of are destroyed & the rest properly filed! . . .

My love to all & a big hug to you dearest. I do look forward to your visit.

Mother

". . . a good contract. . . . plenty of social conditions to study. . . ."

> Peninsula Hotel
> Kowloon, Hong Kong
> August 24th [1955]

Anna darling,

Maureen said you . . . were glad at my losing weight. My clothes & girdles hang on me so I think when I get home & get them all fitted I really will look a bit better!

We left Japan last Sunday night after a really nice visit & I felt I learned more about how the people lived & how they felt than ever before.

This is a good contract. No temples to visit but plenty of social conditions to study. There is just the ordinary crowding of Chinese poor & then the refugees from Communist China & I cannot tell you what conditions are. Harlem is luxury! We drove to the border this a.m. saw the fishing village of Aberdeen yesterday which is just hundreds of junks moored together on which the whole population lives & dies. . . .

Friday we leave early for Jakarta in Indonesia.

I can hardly realize I've been gone 3½ weeks & in 3½ more . . . I will be home. . . .

Perhaps Oct 8th you could come down to H.P. for the night but I have to leave at one on Sunday as I have to be in Boston for a U.J.A. [United Jewish Appeal] speech that night. That means taking a 4 p.m. plane to Boston and an 11 p.m. back! . . .

Have you found work?

All my love to you & give Jim his share. David wants to be remembered to you both.

> Devotedly
> Mother

". . . how easily one could slip out of life & not have it even noticed. . . ."

> Bali
> Sept. 1st, 1955

Dearest Sis,

Your letter . . . reached me here today & is the first word I've had from any member of the family since I left. Maureen, of course cabled me about Sisty in Japan & I cabled at once. I'm glad for her the baby came early & 8 lbs 5 oz. is a good weight. . . .

This is a strange island, seems worlds away, no outside news since Sunday last! In town, I suppose someone might get an Indonesian newspaper. Bali seems to have none! The climate is soft & out of the sun cool. It is very tropical, many women are naked to the waist & they carry enormous loads on their heads. This is the part of the world where you have a dipper bath. You get soaped first & your bathroom has a stone floor & a water outlet, through which lizards & mice etc. can come in! Then with a basin or pitcher you pour water over yourself. There just is no hot water! Here I've been swimming about 6 a.m. because it is high enough tide to swim inside the reef. Sharks are outside. At low tide you can walk out to the reef in a bathing suit & walk along it. Indonesians & Ballinese [Balinese] like very "hot" spicy food but served cold! rice is the basic food but they have fish & chicken & the Dutch influence brings cheese & the smallest eggs you ever saw. They have an enormous orange bigger than a grapefruit but good, many varieties of bananas & papaya.

Dances are woven into the life of the people & there are only a few professionals. All the people dance, but only little girls. When you are married (at thirteen) you are too old & no longer a virgin so you can't dance! There is an infinite variety of dances for all occasions.

I've written a diary in my column so as you see it you know all I've done & seen. David has taken hundreds of pictures & someday I hope he will have a chance to show them to you. I know of no better travelling companion, he knows so much & is so interested. I love being with him. . . .

My love to Jim & all the family. A special hug to you & thanks for writing. Being away makes one realize how easily one could slip out of life & not have it even noticed.

A world of love
Mother

". . . This year I'm not going to celebrate my birthday . . ."

On way to Geneva
Sept. 12th [1955]

Dearest Anna,

. . . The Thais were wonderful & most hospitable & especially kind to me. . . . I think these areas of the world we've been in are hard on people who have had T.B. Our colored boys who are prone to T.B. came down with bad cases very often in the war. It really hasn't been very hot but it is humid (my hair [illegible], my shoes get muddy) so I'll be glad to have David in a more invigorating climate after tomorrow. I have not been ill a minute & have found I could manage the column easily & never give up doing anything. I really do get tougher with age!

This year I'm not going to celebrate my birthday, last year shld last till I'm 75 & we can forget it till then. No gifts for I need nothing & now I should give & not receive! If you can come the week end of Oct. 8th I'll try to get David to come & bring his pictures. . . . He took a great many & is working out an interesting talk to go with them, tho' that he'll probably refuse to do for us & reserve it for his hospitals.

I think I've learned a lot on this trip, & I've enjoyed it & now I'll be glad to be home & at work for a while. I'll be doing quite a bit of travelling this autumn for lectures & for A.A.U.N. [American Association for the United Nations] but no long trips.

. . . I got a Cambodian knife for Johnny & one for Haven. They are used by the country boys but nicely engraved & rather swank I think. . . .

Devotedly
Mother

". . . [Harriman] isn't happy that I am for Stevenson openly . . ."

211 East 62nd Street
New York 21, N.Y.
Oct 31st [1955]

Darling Anna,
    I sent you last week a black coat partly lined with lamb which I thought you could have made to fit you & which would be good as a rough coat for the cold Syracuse winter. I also sent some furs I thought might come in handy. You certainly cld have the Shaker cape made into a good coat. I have at H.P. a very old fur *jacket* which could be worn over a sweater with a heavy skirt for everyday. It is shabby but still warm & doesn't look too badly for weather when you would spoil your mink. Shall I send? I won't be at H.P. to get it till Nov 17th.
    I hope you enjoyed your dinner with the Harriman's. I fear he isn't happy that I am for Stevenson openly & tho' F jr. I suppose will say nothing I think he is also for Stevenson.
    On the 16th of Nov I get in to Syracuse at 10.22 a.m. by Am. Airlines. Pray for good weather. The Jewish ladies drive me to Cornell & I return here by the night train. . . .
    All my love dear to all & a hug for you,

Mother

". . . spontaneously a thrilled 'yes, how wonderful' . . ."

511 Van Buren Street
Syracuse 10, N.Y.
March 13, 1956

Mummy darling,
    As usual I am way behindhand in writing. First and foremost, Jim, Johnny and I think it would be wonderful to celebrate my birthday here, with you, Franklin and Sue, and Ruth and Buzz (if they can afford the trip, which they have always said they could not), on Saturday, May 5. Franklin wrote me a very nice letter right after seeing you, and he asked me to make a hotel reservation here for him and Sue that night. So, I'll make two reservations

(one for he and Sue, and one for you), all in F.'s name in order to try to avoid publicity. It will be such fun, too, to be able to show Franklin and Sue (I *do* hope she really comes, too) the farm on Sunday morning, as Franklin suggests in his letter. Franklin also suggests that we go with him to Ithaca for the day on the 5th to a special pure-bred cattle auction (where he has 4 entries), but I'm afraid we can't do that because of work obligations. I really feel quite overwhelmed at the idea of a *real* birthday party—at your giving up a previous engagement, etc.—but it would be great, great fun to all be together, especially if Buzz and Ruth can make it in addition.

We wish so much we could go to you at H.P. for Easter Sunday. Darn it all, our contractor starts work on the farm house the very next day and wants to take time that week-end to go over the earliest renovation details before starting the work, so we'll have to be here.

. . . I tried "sounding out" Johnny about your tentative plan to take him and Haven to Europe from Aug. 17 to Sept. 9, but his immediate reaction was so spontaneously a thrilled "yes, how wonderful" that I had to tell him all you'd written, emphasizing, of course, that it was all still indefinite. Johnny will be 17 on March 30, so he only has a junior driver's license, with which he is entitled to drive, alone, until one hour after sunset, and at any time, day or night, if a licensed driver is in the car with him. In Europe he would have to get a special license anyway, so maybe Maureen could find out from the N.Y. passport division, or a travel agency, what the rules are over there under the circumstances. He was told today that he can have the summer job with the building contractor to whom he applied some time ago. And tonight we figured out that if he starts work the day after graduation he could work for 7 or 8 weeks and make enough money to pay his clothes and personal expenses at college at least through the first term, and then he can get a job at college for the 2nd term.

. . . No more now—but *thanks* for being the amazingly thoughtful person you are, in so darn many ways!

Tons of love from the three of us, and a big hug from me.

Anna

". . . No one here has the slightest doubt about your energy-ability . . ."

511 Van Buren Street
Syracuse 10, N.Y.
March 24, 1956

Mummy dearest,

Johnny is thrilled you're giving his commencement address. Many, many thanks from the three of us. Also, we're tickled because it means another glimpse of you!

. . . No one here has the slightest doubt about your energy-ability to take Johnny and Haven to Europe next summer! But, we do think that, in Johnny's case, there is a possibility that after a year in college he may have developed some sort of special interest which may take him elsewhere next summer ('57). In other words he may have reached an age when he wants to do something entirely on his own. But this year he's very very anxious to go with you. He thinks, too, that rather than take a long motor trip it would be easier to plan to fly to different spots and depend on renting a car and driver at each spot.

The snow has really been so beautiful. We love it—despite the big amount we've had here since last Nov. But these last 2 big storms (the last one last night) made the roads more slippery than any other snowfalls all winter long—and skidding I don't like!

Much love from the 3 of us, and a special lot from me.

Anna

"... *Today we've visited the Queen,* ..."

Hotel Des Indes
[Holland]
Monday eve. Aug 20th [1956]

Anna darling,

... Your Johnny is a joy to travel with. So interested & the year between Haven & himself seems to mean much more maturity. It is hard to tell what the impact of all the new experiences are but he will tell you & in any case I think both boys are having a good time. Grania [young daughter of Dr. Gurewitsch] has not joined us yet as she was ill in London but I hope David will come to his meeting in Copenhagen & bring her. . . . The 2 hrs in museums in the p.m. may have seemed long but they apparently saw a great deal in spite of crowds. It is a wonderful collection of Rembrandts. . . . Today we've visited the Queen, . . . seen a publishing house & a small Dutch home & now to bed & tomorrow to Copenhagen. . . .

Devotedly
Mother

"... *Here we are in Paris* ... *though Johnny begins to be tired!* ..."

Hotel de Crillon
Paris
26th August 1956

Anna darling,

Here we are in Paris after an interesting 3 days in Copenhagen which I think the boys enjoyed though Johnny begins to be tired! He is more interested than Haven so gets more out of it but he's been tired the last 2 days in Paris. . . . Yesterday p.m. we went back to see . . . Marie Antoinette's farm village & walked up thro' the Versailles gardens just as the fountains came on which was lovely. The flowers are brilliant in color due to the rain I think. One other piece of luck. We heard the liberation day commemoration service in Notre Dame, just a little of it but the music was lovely & one so rarely hears music in that cathedral. Today the 3 are going sightseeing alone & meeting me at the Embassy for lunch & then they go off again. They seem to get on well & say this a.m. they are rested. Tomorrow we start on 4 days motor trip which I hope they enjoy. The weather will make a difference & it seems very changeable. David has a friend & patient who is very ill here so I doubt if he goes with us. I can hardly realize I have only been gone ten days, the past seems another world!

. . . My dear love to you & Jim & thanks for letting me have Johnny. I love him.

Devotedly
Mother

"... you are the number I practical politician . . ."

At the office
September 7 [1956]

Mummy darling,

You have been so wonderful about writing and sending us interesting clippings on this trip with the boys that I feel particularly guilty at my writing delinquency. It's just that we've been snowed under household-wise, and when we took our one weeks fishing trip we were 105 miles north of Quebec city, out in the wilds where there is only a once a week mail delivery. When we left for our fishing trip we left 3 kids to close up the house, and when we got home on Labor Day we cleaned up the joint for our next influx which started arriving the next day. Sue and F., Jr. have been with us since Tues. and left this morning. Chris stayed with the cattle on the Fair grounds. We were particularly happy that Sue could come because we so rarely have a chance to see her that we felt we didn't know her too well. F., Jr. did a wonderful job of giving us a blow-by-blow description of his "inside" experiences at the convention—including Finnegan's remark to him that you are the number I *practical* politician in the country!

We have shared your letters, clippings and columns with all visiting family, and are saving your columns written on the trip for Johnny so that he may have a special record. Now, of course, we can hardly wait to see you and get the inside dope of some of the funny experiences and happenings that *must* have occurred while traveling with young people! And, of course, we look forward to Johnny's versions too!

Beginning tonight we will only have 2 kids with us, until Johnny arrives home. They are Chuck and Bella [Jim Halsted's son Charles and daughter Isabella]. They and we can hardly wait to see Johnny and have a chance to "catch up" with him before he takes off for college early the morning of Sept. 14. That is the day, too, that Jim and I start our real vacation of two weeks. (We're going to stay home!) Chuck goes back west on the 10th and Bella will go to Boston on the 14th to stay with her mother until after Oct. 1 when she returns here, we think.

Van motored over in a borrowed truck on Labor Day to pick up our dining room table chairs, an old over-stuffed chair we're not using, an old children's desk, and a couple of scatter rugs. . . . They picked up an old Frigidaire for $33! . . .

We have no more news—but I did want to have this awaiting you when you land on the 9th. . . .

Much, much love to you from both Jim and me. We're so grateful to you for giving Johnny not only such a wonderful trip and chance to see so many things but also a chance to see them with you, as what you personally added to it all is immeasurably valuable to him. He's a very lucky guy—as I'm sure he knows.

Anna

". . . we could have prevented the USSR's move on Hungary . . ."

211 East 62nd Street
New York 21, N.Y.
Wed. Dec. 5th [1956]

Anna darling,

I've been so constantly on the road that I only just got a letter off to Jim about his Father. He will miss him tho' I realize he must have expected it & accepted that it was a release.

The U.N. is proving more effective than I thought it could be without force in spite of Hungary. If we had moved faster, I think we could have prevented the USSR's move on Hungary but we delayed & the Nagy Gov. fell. We may learn but our leadership is very weak.

I saw Mr. Stevenson & he still seems tense & tired to me.

Have you got an Encyclopaedia Britannica? I might get one to give you in the winter if you want it.

Much, much love
Mother

". . . a frontier gone when someone goes from the older generation . . ."

211 East 62nd Street
New York 21, N.Y.
Dec 6th [1956]

Dearest Jim,

I've been meaning to write ever since your Father died. For him it must have been a blessed release but even though you knew it must come, just because you did so much for him, you must miss him. It is always a frontier gone when someone goes from the older generation even tho' they may have long ceased to be a protection. The funeral & the large family must have been a strain too & I hope now you & Anna can rest a bit.

I am still travelling much too much but it seems inevitable! Much love to you

E.R.

"... re-adjustments are hard for men ..."

211 East 62nd Street
New York 21, N.Y.
Feb. 6th [1957]

Sis darling,

... I guess I was more tired than I knew & that was probably why I was so hard hit by whatever bug I had on my last trip. David says I had pneumonia & a near pleurisy but I'm back & more rested than I have been in a long time. I'm still being quiet because I leave Sunday on a pd. lecture trip & don't get back till the 19th & have to write 2 articles by March 1st so Maureen & I must get some work done in odd moments.

... I won't hurry with my $350, but I'll send it later in the spring. ... Just the next few months expenses are high as I bought a new station wagon & must turn in my car & pay more than usual on a new one. Of course if you are getting John's insurance policy money & you really feel it will cover all expenses I won't pay but you let me know & I might be able to give you a bit more. ...

I had quite a talk with Adlai the other day & re-adjusments are hard for men but I think he's going back to law & trying to do largely international work which should be good.

Much love to Jim & a world of love to you

Mother

"... I haven't Father's gift of making interviews valuable! ..."

Morocco
March 26th, 1957

Darling Anna,

... Could you come to H.P. sometime for a week end or for Memorial Day? I think Harry Truman *may* come this year. ...

Morocco is a place of contrasts but fascinating. ... It turned out a bit as I feared, too big a party but Elliott has been interested. I have enjoyed it, but

I'm very tired & I'll be glad to get home on the 1st. This is a beautiful spot & I have Churchill's suite! The Sultan is charming but I haven't Father's gift of making interviews valuable! . . .

Devotedly
Mother

Clearly Anna wrote many more letters to her mother than appear in the Hyde Park library or in Anna's private files at the time of her death. Since Roosevelts are compulsive savers, it has seemed unlikely to the compiler of this volume that Eleanor would have disposed of these letters. The following probably explains where they went.

". . . You can decide if they have any historical interest . . ."

Val-Kill Cottage
Hyde Park
June 30th, 1957

Anna darling,
 . . . I am reading letters before giving any personal ones to the library. I have many from you. Would you like them back & then you can decide if they have any historical interest or you want to destroy?
 . . . I forgot to say that I probably have to take a private plane from here to Syracuse & back as I have the [United Automobile Workers president Walter] Reuther's here & don't want to be away long. . . .
 All my love to you darling

Mother

". . . 'Tivoli' that incomparable spot in which to be frivolous. . . ."

Hotel Codan
Copenhagen
[early September 1957]

Anna darling,
 We've had wonderful flights & 2 nights in Berlin. The days were full of interest in Frankfurt & Berlin. I can't write of the refugee work which I saw till I get home & even then I will have to be careful for much must be secret.

Tonight we spent in "Tivoli" that incomparable spot in which to be frivolous. I really like Denmark & it was fun to come in & be greeted by . . . our very Republican new Ambassador, Mr. Peterson. I hope he'll do well here for his parents came from here. . . .

Well, day after tomorrow I'll know what I'll be able to do in the Soviets. We leave at 10.15 & get there at 6.35, so there isn't much we can do but see a ballet or something tomorrow night. All my love

Mother

". . . A strange 'Alice in Wonderland' world. . . ."

[Moscow]
Sept. 16th, 1957

Dearest Anna,

Back here just for part of a day yesterday as we were half a day late in leaving Tashkent because of fog here in Moscow. Went with the Indian Ambassador . . . to see a touching Russian war film just finished & some scenes from a film about a Russian traveller in India in the 15th Century which is being done in collaboration with Russia.

The days in Central Asia were fascinating[,] not the least interesting is the contrasts of 50 yrs ago & now. The life of the people is enormously improved & most of them don't worry about politics. On every hand "peace" is preached & we are depicted as the one danger to peace. They have no news that is truthful about the outside world so they believe & are grateful for all the improvements at home. A strange "Alice in Wonderland" world. . . .

A world of love
Mother

". . . and to continuing payments on my newspaper debts . . ."

Sentinel Heights Road
Lafayette, New York
New Year's Day 1958

Mummy darling,

As usual we have so many wonderful Christmas presents for which to thank you—and so much thoughtfulness. They are all perfect—from the electric blanket, to the stockings check, to that really lovely ring from India (which I wear with joy in the evenings), to the recordings (which we all enjoyed while the gang was here), to the "personalized" cocktail napkins and matches, to the Tugwell book, and the Hyde Park honey! And yesterday we received your records, etc. of Berlitz Spanish, and hope to start putting them to good use very soon. Oh, and I forgot the stockings—which are always most particularly needed. You couldn't have spoiled us more, and we loved it. Many more thanks than can possibly be put into a letter.

Then your letter which also touched me very deeply arrived yesterday. I guess you know that your yearly, by the month present goes into our holiday, travel for me in between, and much needed extra household help from time to time. The extra $200 was practically "heaven-sent" this month! You are wonderful to think of making it $1200 this coming year "if next year is as good as last", but don't forget that I know well all the demands on you—both personal and for those things which carry on and build toward the fulfillment of your beliefs and principles, with which we both so heartily agree. All I mean is that I want you to know always that whatever you decide on this will be "swell by me" while at the same time I am terribly appreciative of what it means to us to have this extra.

Now for a tough part—which has to do with Jan. 30th. As I think I told you, we have a new president of the Medical Center and dean of the College of Medicine. He started here on Dec. 1 but as he has been very active for 15 or 20 years in medical education at the national level he has been away most of the time since Dec. 1. In addition he feels that in the long run it will benefit this school if he keeps his national positions in the field. Therefore more responsibility at a local administrative level is being delegated to people like me. Because of the opening of the play [*Sunrise at Campobello,* Dore Schary's play about the Roosevelt family] on the 30th I consulted with his [the dean's] secretary on his schedule and found that he expects to be here all of that week and has scheduled administrative meetings for Wed., Thurs. and early Friday afternoon. My job in the public relations field is tough because I have to keep au courant through many types of faculty and administrative meetings. And, of course, into this picture comes the old problem of financial security because a new dean can (and often does) change administrative personnel according to his own desires. And at the age of 51½ I don't particularly relish job hunting—and know that the money I make is a necessity to our family economy and to continuing payments on my newspaper debts (Messrs Sick and Greene in Seattle). All of which boils down to the fact that I don't dare take off the afternoon of the 30th and the morning of the 31st. BUT: two weeks ago Jim was notified of a symposium in his specialty being held in N.Y.C. on the 31st and 1st of Feb. which is most important to him because of his research. So, my suggested compromise is that I fly to N.Y.C. on a 3 or 4 p.m. plane on Fri., the 31st (Jim having taken a midnight train the night before), and that Jim and I go to see the play that evening. We'd hate to miss it, and we hate not to be with you at the opening, but this seems the only solution. . . .

No, we have not met Johnny's girl. A month or so before Xmas he invited her to come up here during the holidays but her parents said no. Since then he has apparently "cooled off" on the relationship, at least for the time being. She is the daughter of a surgeon and Johnny, who has been there once for a meal, says they are very "stuffy"! . . .

Anna

". . . The articles are definitely well written . . ."

Sentinel Heights Road
Lafayette, New York
March 5, 1958

Mummy darling,

. . . Many thanks for the offer of the table linen. I really don't need any because it's impossible for me to take care of the washing and ironing—so I almost always use paper napkins and plastic stuff. And I do have lots of old and beautiful family table linen for special occasions. . . .

Yes, Jim and I have loved the Sat. Eve. Post articles. We have heard many favorable comments, and feel that they are of interest to a very broad audience. Your memory is fabulous, and it's been such fun to renew mine through yours! The articles are definitely well written, and they hold one's interest. There is so much variety, and a good mixture of the serious and the human interest. The book should be EXCELLENT! . . .

A Mr. Hyman Rosenblum, a lawyer in Albany, whom I met at a State University gathering in Albany last spring, and who says he was a legislative page boy in Al Smith's days, is "in your hair and mine"! He said he was phoning you to ask you to a dinner (he gives them yearly) on April 12 for high school students to whom he gives Consideration Prizes. I enclose one of the pieces of literature he sent me so you'll know what it's all about. He invited Jim and me 3 months ago, and not having any excuse for saying "no" at the time I figured I'd dream up a reason for getting out of it as the time approached. I'm told he's a very sincere guy, but I learned, personally in Albany, that he's very publicity minded, and "names" mean much. I'm sure that if he got you on the phone, or if he had to write you, that you gave him a bonefide excuse for not being able to be there. Please tell me what it was, so that I don't cross wires with you. It would be nice to be able to do all these "nice" things, but even if I start doing one or two I'm swamped with a million more!

We're busier than ever here—and thoroughly enjoying it. Our new medical school dean is a dinamo—and, incidentally, a good liberal! As soon as our snow drifts disappear we've got lots of little repair jobs to do around the place.

Loads and loads of love from us both, and a big hug from me,

Anna

P.S. I almost forgot to thank you for the $50 Bond presented to you by the N.Y. Newspaper Women for your articles on Russia. That was a most thoughtful gift, Mummy darling, and is so much appreciated.

". . . I want to live alone and be entirely independent. . . ."

211 East 62nd Street
New York 21, N.Y.
August 12, 1958

Dearest Anna:
     You will get at sometime in the fairly near future a request from the Estate to agree that they should invest in a mortgage for me which will be guaranteed by my Estate at my death, in order that I may buy a house. I will tell you the details over the weekend but I assure you that you will get your five percent interest on the mortgage no matter when I die and this would be about as good as you would get from any other type of investment. Until all other bequests would be paid out you would get only one-half of the income but afterwards you will get the full income from my small estate until your death when this will be divided among all the grandchildren living except of course Sarah and Kate [daughters of Franklin, Jr., and the former Ethel Du Pont] who certainly don't need it.
     I hope you will be willing to agree to this arrangement because I would like, as I grow older, to be in a house with someone I know, though I want to live alone and be entirely independent. The house we are hopefully planning on will give me more room and will mean I will have a permanent home in New York City. I am going to give up my present apartment on the day I leave for Brussels because they want to raise the rent by $150 a month which seems to me ridiculous.

Much love,
Mother

     In the late summer of 1958, Mrs. Roosevelt departed for a second visit to the Soviet Union, stopping en route at the Brussels World's Fair.
     It was a moment of importance in her daughter's life. Jim Halsted had applied for and been granted a Fulbright Fellowship as an exchange scholar to visit Iran for a year where he would teach medicine and conduct research. The award excited him—and one aspect of it surprised him. "For years Anna and I had talked," he would one day recall for me, "of how interesting it would be to live in an underdeveloped country for a year, where you would really get to understand it, rather than just travel through it treated as VIPs. When this opportunity came up, I jumped at it. What surprised me was that she didn't really jump the way I did. She groaned a bit that we were enjoying the little farmhouse we'd resurrected outside of Syracuse, and that she hated to pull up stakes."

". . . one advantage of being footloose & fancy free! . . ."

Hotel Metropole
Bruxelles
Aug 31st, 1958

Anna darling,

I shall be thinking of you both as you start off soon after this reaches you. I hate to have you so far away but after you get there let me know your telephone number & I'll try to reach you at Xmas. No place in the world is really far away nowadays so remember if you need me any day I can come! That is one advantage of being footloose & fancy free!

The [Brussels World's] fair is interesting, not as gay as some others I have seen, crowded all day but empty after the early evening. Our buildings & ground layout are delightful, much the best I've seen so far, but we have a theatre & the audiences are poor because at night people don't go out there. It is far out & they are tired. Our primitive & modern art Exhibits are fine & I like not showing big automobiles & machines. We have plenty in the science exhibit but our building shows the comforts of American life & its simplicity & I like it & so do all the foreigners. The Russians show vast areas of machines, sputniks, automobiles & it is jammed but I don't think people enjoy it & they do enjoy ours. The Czech building & exhibition is lovely & that is about all I've seen so far because I wanted to see ours thoroughly & report in the column as there had been so much controversy.

Mr. [William] Warfield, the very good Negro singer whom I like is here & we have seen him often & will go to his concert Monday night. We saw the new Menotti opera, & the Russian ballet last night so we've been busy!

A world of love & good luck to you & Jim & a special hug darling.

Devotedly
Mother

P.S. Johnny should appear today. . . .

". . . We need some realistic re-thinking in high places . . ."

[Leningrad]
Sept. 12th, 1958

Dearest Anna,

We reached Leningrad yesterday morning & were lucky to find a beautiful day so we went out to show Edna [Mrs. Gurewitsch] this really beautiful city. Very many beautiful buildings, parks & monuments, more sophisticated in every way than Moscow but not as interesting for there one feels the pulse of change & a dynamic drive. None of the beautiful buildings seem much damaged by the 900 day siege in World War II tho' there was much destruction in the outskirts. We had a delegation meeting with the local USSR

UN organization from 4–7. Today Edna spent the morning in the Hermitage & came home starry-eyed & David & I went to the Pediatric Institute which I visited last year but he missed seeing. I was glad to have a second look & I learned more. This afternoon we all three visited the Central Youth Palace & I was much impressed. They have used the palaces well! Every district has a pioneer Youth House where children go for certain activities a number of times a week after school. One child said twice a week for ¾ of an hour of gym, twice a week for 1½ hrs of dancing & to the Central Palace twice a week for some activity.

It is difficult to assess the value of contact unless you accept the need for our recognition of realities. If we accept Mr. Dulles theory that men want to be free so communism can't last, then there is no value in what we did as a delegation or are now doing as individuals. If, however, we believe that communism is here to stay awhile & that we must live together & very slowly changes may be coming in both our systems which will make co-existence possible, then I think intercourse has value. Now, we talk, but we don't mean the same things & we dare not try to clarify unless we manage to talk alone with one individual. We need some realistic re-thinking in high places I think about the USSR & China.

Take care of yourself dear. My love to Jim & a world of love to you.

Mother

". . . my time is limited & I should see new things . . ."

Moscow
Sept 18th, 1958

Dearest Anna,

I'm sending this to Shiraz hoping it will welcome you on arrival.

Our trip is going successfully. I've pretty much seen all I hoped to see & I've learned much more I think. David does not feel he's been as well treated but on the whole he too feels a gain. Edna will I think take back a good exhibition, so we are all happy. They will probably be back many times but I imagine this is my last trip for I feel my time is limited & I should see new things or stay at home!

If you find you want papers or magazines mailed to you let me know & I'll see to it. One can feel very cut off from world news I find.

I wonder if you'll get through by telephone, if you haven't called by the 24th, I'll try to reach you at the Embassy.

We go to Paris the morning of the 26th as we feel we will be all thro' & would like 4 days there. I'll go the Ste. Chapelle & the Louvre, eat a dinner at my favourite restaurant, & buy some Xmas presents! . . .

I met with 71 American Educators tonight who have been touring the Soviet Union for a month & I was pleased to find they knew no more than I did.

I spent the morning in a school. The usual pattern is to have all 10 yrs of school in one building but when it is overcrowded they go on 2 shifts & certain grades come at 2.30 instead of in the morning.

You'll be busy till you are settled but then do write me in detail so I can picture your life.

Blessings on you. . . .

Mother

". . . I believe that discontent exists aplenty . . ."

Shiraz, Iran
10/4/58

Mummy darling—

Your cable from Moscow reached me here 4 days ago and your so very welcome letter from there came a couple of days ago. From a communications standpoint we really are in the stix—Teheran being the only place in Iran where foreign mail comes thru fast. We came down here on Sept. 23rd after 5 days in Teheran. . . . I could find no way to phone you from Teheran. There had been a little stupid trouble with the USSR Embassy and the only way I could have tried to get you would have been through that Embassy. Our Embassy was alerted for a call from you but as you know we missed you. It was a big disappointment because there is no way that overseas calls can be put thru from here. The phone service is so lousy that you can hardly hear someone calling you from across the street. Also, no one has a phone in a private home. This is really a most primitive country—but a most interesting one because industries are gradually creeping in and bringing with them [a] growing middle class. At the same time radio and movies are reaching even a good many of the *very* poor masses. I believe that discontent exists aplenty (I *know* it from talking to professional people) but initiative is slow in coming to the fore because of the strength here of the caste system. From the coolie to the Shah are hundreds and hundreds of caste gradations. The system is so ingrained in all of them that those with leadership qualities, education and abilities, see few opportunities here, and too many of them talk only of ways and means to go elsewhere. I don't see how this can be changed except by leadership from the top or revolt from the middle classes. The poor people in the towns and villages are too malnourished to have initiative. Discontent does exist among some of the tribes people, however, and there have been some uprisings which have to date been squelched by the army. The tribes are better fed. But I have met no tribesmen yet—but we are planning on a 3 day trip to the winter camp of one of them (not too far from here) around Oct. 26th—camping out. . . . The Univ. found a nice house for us . . . and [it] is being renovated—with Western toilets, kerosene cooking stove (all natives cook with charcoal, hence there is the usual terrible need for a conservation program), refrig., etc. We hope to move in in two weeks, but work here is very slow. All I have seen of Iran so far is very similar to parts of Arizona and N.M. Stark, bare, brown mountains rise on all sides of Teheran, Isfahan and

Shiraz. Dust is a constant curse, but this is the worse time of year for it as there has been no rain since last March—and we're due for some some time next month or anyway by Dec. 1. The food is pretty tough because it's cooked in tons of grease, most of it rancid; but we're *very* lucky because we found that we have Embassy Commissary privileges and can, once a month, get an order of canned goods, Danish butter, powdered milk, toilet paper and the like, which comes down here by truck which takes 4–5 days. Bruscillosis (sp?) abounds here [so] one eats no local dairy products. The foreign colony is small but interesting (mostly) consisting of Danes, French, English, Swiss[,] Belgians and Swedes as well as Americans—really only a handful of each. . . . The Saadi Hosp. is a horror to behold—but it is "the people's" hospital. There are 250 beds and 4 trained nurses, who are helped out by very ignorant maids. Jim is finding his work most interesting and challenging, and really loves it. Without a doubt there is one H of a lot to be done—and it's a satisfying feeling to know that you are really contributing. I have had some interesting visits to local schools—not the really poor ones, unfortunately, as the Irani school officials won't let Americans see them—not even the USOM [United States Overseas Mission] people attached to the Iran Ministry of Education as advisors. And I've volunteered to write English letters for the Univ. Chancellor—who rattles off what he wants said in broken English before I've read the letters—then I tap my meager knowledge of Univ. affairs here, and try to write an English letter with a Persian flavor! . . . Yes, I do feel you did the right thing in not paying Johnny's way to Moscow for the meeting there. I'd so love to have had him with you, but agree wholeheartedly that it was far better for him not to do what another boy in his position would not have been able to do. Good letters (one from each) have come from Sis and Johnny, but not a word from Buzz. *Please* send me all you can of any reports you make on your trip! The fastest mail to us is c/o Faculty of Medicine, University of Shiraz, Shiraz, Iran but it takes either a 25¢ air mail stamp or one of these letters which have a 10¢ stamp printed on them. Heavier mail should come: Point Four, Shiraz; American Embassy, APO 205, New York, N.Y. This takes longer to get here because the pouch from Teheran only comes down here 3 times a week—*if* the *old* Iranian Airway D.C.3's fly, which they don't always do! We would love it if you can come here next spring. Our house is going to be at least comfortable, and by that time we'll know more about the country and interesting things to see and do. Jim just came in and sends you lots of love. A world of it from me to you, dear—and I'll write again soon.

Anna

P.S. Jim thinks my letter only gives you pessimistic viewpoints, but it's not meant to be so! Perhaps I've had my "adventuresome" ears knocked flat too often in the past; and perhaps not having a specific task to perform here makes me unconsciously try to look at everything I hear and see on a too realistic basis—leaving out the romance, which I honestly haven't felt much of as yet. Anyway, I'll try to be objective!

A.

". . . don't go camping where you might get kidnapped! . . ."

Hotel Park Sheraton
[New York, N.Y.]
Oct 19th, 1958

Darling Anna,

I was so glad to get your letter of Oct. 4th. It doesn't sound too comfortable but I'm glad Jim finds the work interesting & I think you'll find something to do. Just be careful, both of you & stay well & don't go camping where you might get kidnapped! . . .

I'm settled comfortably here [Mrs. Roosevelt has moved back to the hotel while house hunting] but the cooking facilities are *very* poor. We will survive but I hope we find a house soon! I've been very busy ever since I got home, speeches, people & much mail & some writing but after the next two weeks I ought to be freer. . . .

It sounds like a good democratic year but many feel Averell [Harriman] is not too sure of winning here & if he loses [New York Democratic leader Carmine] deSapio will be responsible.

. . . Do write if you want a check. Mailing things seems senseless & you can probably buy what you want better than I can unless you tell me what you need. Would you like books? or subscriptions to some magazines? . . .

I go out tomorrow for AAUN & will be all over the lot till Friday. . . .

Much love to Jim & more than I can say to you dear,

Devotedly
Mother

". . . because the owner was told that I have famous parents! . . ."

[covering note]

Mummy—Because the attached kind of mail can be so easily opened, & because some of what I wrote might not be appreciated by the Iranian government, we decided to send this via APO pouch!

A

How is your house hunting (& Edna's & David's) going?

[Shiraz, Iran]
October 21, 1958

Mummy darling—

Your letter from Moscow dated Sept. 18 just arrived today! I have a hunch it was well inspected along the way, but was so glad to get it I didn't give a hoot. You are right that one feels very out of touch—both with family, and with news—in a place where communications are so poor. So letters are looked for avidly, and we buy the Tehran News, which is written in English but which carries some excellent editorials translated from Iranian papers as well as fairly good coverage of news from abroad. And we listen once a day to BBC news—which is jammed far less than Voice of America news. (We get the Tehran News here about 5 days late!) Also we have started getting the Saturday Review but the Reporter, which we also ordered mailed to us by APO has never come. We'll write them again, and that plus the S.R. and the Tehran News should keep us sufficiently up-to-date—considering our remoteness. It's strange how little interest there is among Iranians we've met here in Iranian news, Middle East news or world news. We're told that this is so because even those few who hold government key positions here are completely controlled by Tehran and just obey orders from there without having the slightest idea of the "why" of an order. This is a habit they do not seem to question. We've started horseback riding 3 times a week and as you can imagine I'm loving it! Mr. Glines (USOM director & our host here for the past 3 weeks) arranged it through the commanding general in the area who has a cavalry battalion under him. Jim loves it too, and as Glines is a horseman and polo player from way back we all have a good time. Two days a week we go out at 8 a.m. and one day at 7 a.m. One of these days is a Friday, the Moslem Sunday, and Jim's one day off a week, so on that day we can ride for 2 or 3 hours. Mrs. Glines and Mr. G.'s Iranian assistant (a member of one of the wealthy, prominent families here) took me this afternoon to what is known as the most beautiful garden in Shiras [Shiraz]. It's the worst time of year for gardens here (no rain for 8 mos. so leaves are all dusty) but it was lovely, with many varieties of flowers, shrubs and trees, from the U.S., Europe and here. The owner is a screwball and apparently typical of a certain group of rich Iranians who are poets, philosophers, dabble in such things as photography and painting. Someday I'll write more of this gentleman's philosophy—it was very shallow, and the Iranian who took us told us ahead of time that our host would either decide he likes us—and then entertain us lavishly—or that he did not like us and then he would fast disappear. He liked us and we found ourselves drinking the usual tea and eating kabob—after a big luncheon! All the old family houses, with the big, walled in gardens have the same type of architecture with slender fluted columns. They all have a delapidated appearance (at least the half dozen or so that I've seen) and remind me a great deal (in atmosphere) of old, run-down Southern mansions; mostly depressing, with dirt and dust inside and out. Our newly hired cook and bodje (maid) will start work tomorrow scrubbing our new house—which has been renovated—the biggest work being two of the flossiest western bathrooms existing in Shiraz, I'm sure. Also, I'm sure that this last special treatment comes because the owner was told that I have famous parents! It is going to be wonderful to be able to unpack, after almost 2 months, and to be able to be alone once in a while! Privacy doesn't exist as it does at home, however, because lack of phones means that people drop in on one at any and all times of day and evening without any notice. Social invitations are delivered by messenger, and we've learned that when you sign a receipt for one this means you have accepted—and we haven't learned yet how one refuses, particularly as most invitations arrive only a few hours before the event! We're learning a few words of Farsi but not enough to get along satisfactorily as yet in ordinary daily living. Our cook has worked for an Englishman so speaks some English. All servants need constant supervision, and none of them know what it is to clean or wash according to our standards. And their personal cleanliness is most questionable—but we've had chest X-rays (TB is rampant), stool and blood tests done with the cook, as he will handle food, and an X-ray for the bodje, and both of them are okay. Eventually we will have pretty, walled-in gardens both back and front of our house. I think I told you that this house will be used only for visiting University professors. We hope to move in on the 27th or 28th. I asked David Lillienthal to get in touch with you when he gets home and tell you of our evening with him and his wife. (And I wrote Sis, in the letter she will send you, something about his project.) And I asked a Mrs. Mahon of the Committee of Correspondents to call you when she gets back to N.Y.C. I saw her at a meeting she had here. I have been feeling so badly because I let your birthday go by without planning ahead so that I would at least get a note to you on time. I just plain forgot it until October 12th suddenly was here, and then could only send you "thought-waves" of love and "many happy returns"! . . .

Anna

P.S. We've found out: 1. That Jim's teaching here doesn't end until July 1, '59. #2. That he gets a 2 week vacation in March (we don't know the dates yet), and we think we'll take advantage of this to blow ourselves to a trip to India. Sometime, let me know what you think would be most worthwhile for us to see and do in India. There is an Indian couple here (both M.D.'s, with 3 small children) whom we like very much, and we will get ideas from them too. But they haven't been home in 6 years as they were in the U.S. until a year ago, and are now leaving for a month's vacation with their families. They say that the people in India, when poor, are just as poor and miserable as here; but here they have found it as hard as I am finding it, to adjust to both a tangible and intangible lack of "spirit" here among people of all classes. Sometimes Jim and I wonder if we are revolutionaries at heart! We are sure, however, that there is hidden unrest here about which we know nothing as yet. I believe the Shah does want his country to catch up with this century, but [I] also believe that more drastic measures are needed to bridge the gap of approximately 1000 years. Five years from now it will be interesting to see what has transpired! A world of love, again.

A.

". . . We asked and asked . . . and got no answers. . . ."

Shiraz, Iran
Nov. 2, '58

Mummy darling,

. . . We moved into our house last Wednesday after 4 weeks of inflicting ourselves on the Glines as house guests—and while they were wonderful to us, I'm sure they are as happy as we for a little privacy! Our trunks arrived 2 days ago and we're pretty well settled. Curtains are up because Mrs. Glines was good enough to let a seamstress who works for her make them at her house. I chose the material (which is poor but adequate and attractive, I think) and the University paid for it. But, we both are going to try to persuade the USIS office in Tehran to get up a list of things which people like us should bring from the States with them—in the way of household goods. We asked and asked for information and got no answers. We guessed pretty well, but could have done better. Of course, the other side of the picture is that things do get lifted from trunks en route. For instance, we lost 3 cheap washable bedspreads, a cheap wood salad bowl, and a very good, large white linen table cloth, and some Japanese stainless steel knives, forks & spoons from Woolworth's. Right now we're in the throws of trying to get our little garden fixed up. The lawn part has been sewn, and this afternoon we bought 10 rose bushes. Shopping here is a scream. Nothing is bought without heated bargaining—and we can't shop without an interpreter because our few words of Farse are utterly insufficient for "trading"! Bargaining is *expected!* (JAH) Jim loves to bargain and I get a kick out of listening for a while but finally my feet wear out as bargaining means that it takes 2 and 3 times as long to buy what you want—and I'm not too fond of shopping anyway! Also, of course, we pay more as Americans whenever we go into a shop. There being nothing in the way of a dept. store or dime store, one also spends lots of time going from shop to shop to find what one wants. Tomorrow we give our first dinner party—invited guests: an Austrian couple (he is professor of anatomy at the Univ. & she is an artist), and an Indian couple who have 3 young children. . . . Our young Iranian friends in Syracuse (not anywhere near as brilliant as these Indians) are coming back here—but only because they *have* to, and they go to Tehran and not where they are needed because of the living conditions elsewhere (their 3 year old son was born in the US and they dread the disease adjustment for him). Anyway, it would seem that there are many gaps in our thinking and planning, at a practical level, of professionals from backward countries such as this. Added to the dreads of living conditions are those human dreads of the difficulties of living in countries such as this. The Syracuse Iranians admitted that they hated to face losing super markets and department stores; that they hated the old bargaining routine and the time consumed, with the added knowledge that many of the things they had become accustomed to, even on a small salary in the US, would not be available to them unless they lived in Tehran.

We spent the morning going through the Public Health Center here. It has excellent programs—though they only scratch the surface from a needs standpoint because funds are lacking for expansion. There is a Jewish Center here which in many ways duplicates the regular PH [Public Health] service— but as there are 20,000 Jews here (in Shiraz) it is much needed. No one has asked us to visit there yet so we don't have the story, but we'll get there before long.

We got good letters from Buzz and Ruth; nothing from Johnny since I last wrote, nor from Sis and Van whom I know have been busy with the Seagraves Sr. and with getting settled. Chuck writes good letters from Rochester Med. School, and apparently all goes well with Jim's other kids.

And, speaking of dates: We have a letter from a Mr. Moshe Kol, inviting us (on behalf of himself and Youth Aliyah) to visit Israel on our way home from here. He says that you will be with him in Israel from March 22nd to April 2nd to participate in their World Conference. The No Ruz holiday in Iran is from March 21 to April 5—the only holiday we'll get as far as we know. Could you possibly plan to come here before you go to Israel? We could then go with you to Tehran from here on the 20th or 21st of March—and from there we would take off for 2 weeks in India. On our return from India, the present plan is for us to go to Meshed and Tabriz—for Jim to lecture and to confer on Med. School problems in both places. His way is paid because such trips are a part of USIS curriculum. We could have gone in Dec. to both places, but first of all Jim is swamped with work, and secondly both places are really cold, with lots of snow, until late March—and we have no winter coats! . . .

Has F. Jr. been active in this campaign? I started this letter 2 days ago and today is election day, so tomorrow evening we will do our best to get the Voice of America on the short wave radio which Sis and Van gave us, in the hope of getting some returns.

We can hardly wait to hear that Edna has found a house which all of you like! And we can imagine how tired you must be of Park Sheraton cooking facilities.

Ever and ever so many thanks for giving Jim the summer suit as a present. . . . For a while he had a tough time with only one summer suit— which I washed every Friday (the Muslim Sunday and therefore our "day off") and drip dried!

As usual this has turned into a book. But it takes you a heartful of love, and much love from Jim, too.

Anna

P.S. On the 16th of this month we fly to Isfahan for 36 hours of sightseeing by ourselves, and from there we fly to Tehran on the 18th. We will be in Tehran until the 22nd when we're due to fly back here. There is a conference in Tehran for all of this year's Fulbright professors, and Jim has some Med. Education work to do. We will stay again with the Wailes' at the Embassy.

I am doing more and more work for the University here—such things as helping them with the English part of their catalogue, making a statistical study of the different "Faculties" as they call them of the Univ., and I still write their English letters. So I'm busier and enjoying it. Also my tummy is better behaved and my nose has quit sneezing and running like a pump most of the time!

P.P.S.—We use A.P.O., which has to go by truck from here to Tehran, in writing you, because after all this *is* a police state & mail addressed to you could very well be opened. [added by Jim:] Dear Mrs. R—We love your letters and it is a joy to hear from you. We do hope that you can arrange to visit us and the weather and countryside should be at its best in the Spring. Our house is quite comfortable and our garden ought to be blooming then. Our bodje (maid) is about to give us several goldfish for the garden pool! Much love—Jim

"... *the Shah is 'allergic' to American ... interviews, ...*"

I've fired so many questions at you in the following that I'm sure it will be simpler for you to dictate the answers to Maureen!

Tehran
Dec. 27 [1958]

Mummy darling,

Despite our lousy connection it was perfect to be able to talk to you, Johnny, Buzz and Ruth on the phone Christmas day. The U.S. Embassy has just one phone with the type of "booster" needed for international calls, so we sat in an Embassy office for almost 2 hours HOPING that the call actually would go through!

I think I understood you to say that you and Nina [John Roosevelt's daughter] would arrive in Tehran on Wednesday, March 11. Is this correct; and if so, on what airline and what time of day are you due? (Any day you arrive is fine with us because with so much time we can lay our plans ahead.) . . .

We are taking for granted that you want your stay here to be unofficial— simply on the basis of your coming to see us. But, [U.S. ambassador] Tom Wailes will have to tell the Minister of the Court that you are coming and he believes that this will mean you, Nina, the Wailes and Jim and I will be invited to a "family" lunch with the Shah. We won't know until later, however, if the Shah will be here at that time or on an official visit to Paris and London. If he's not here we'll probably all have to go to some sort of shindig at Mr. Ala's (Minister of the Court). Be sure to confirm to me the unoffficialness of your visit here, as it will make planning far easier. It appears also that the Shah is "allergic" to American newspaper and news magazine interviews, so it appears he has to be assured that you will not be interviewing him, though you will be saying (in all probability) in your column that you lunched with him or had an audience with him. (Time mag. recently interviewed him, at Tom Wailes request, and their subsequent article contained spurious remarks about his mother and his sister—so that all Time mags coming into Iran that week had two pages torn out of them before they hit the stands or were delivered to subscribers!)

Tom Wailes wants to know if you would like the services of a secretary (for your column or any letters) while you are in Tehran. The Embassy could supply you with one. (Columns *cannot* be cabled out of Shiraz or any place in Iran except Tehran.) (And in Tehran I'd probably have to make arrangements with the one paper using wire services. Are there any special things or types of things you would like to see, or people you would like to talk to, while you are here?

We will have 13 days in India. Is Delhi (and environs) a good spot to concentrate on for such a short visit? Any suggestions will be gratefully received!

Unless the weather is bad, we fly to Isfahan tomorrow and drive from there to Shiraz the following day.

So very, very much *love* from us both, & an extra lot from me.

Anna

". . . I have to live to be 84 . . . to pay off the mortgages! . . ."

Val-Kill Cottage
Hyde Park
Sunday, Dec. 28th, '58

Darling Anna,

. . . I had a bad time with my left knee & it bothered my whole leg but David finally has it under control & I think a day or two more & I won't have to think about it anymore. The financing of the house was difficult too because we have, since Mr. [Dutchess County attorney Henry J.] Hackett died, a bank as our trustee & finally I gave up borrowing from them & David & I have a 1st & 2d mortgage & each put in an equal amount of cash. Luckily I had invested a little income each year so I had a little capital of my own & so had David. I am surprised I ever was wise enough to do it for I never expected that I would want to buy anything! Now, I have to live to be 84 at least to pay off the mortgages! For 2 yrs. I may have to live on one floor unless a present tenant whose lease runs to '61 in Sept. moves out voluntarily but I'll be at least as comfortably established as in 62d St. & it will be everything I want when I get the 2 floors. The address is 55 East 74th St. & I hope the sale goes through tomorrow or next day. I can't move in till next Sept. however. David & Edna can get their floors very soon, so I can profit by watching any changes they make! I called Sisty Xmas day. . . . I tried to get her tied in to talk to you but couldn't arrange it. I'd like to pay you for the call so please let me know whether to send you a check or add it to your check here. By the way, I gave you $100 a month last year because I feel you will miss your own earnings.

I look forward to March & my trip to you. . . .

Devotedly
Mother

". . . The President wouldn't send me anywhere . . ."

202 Fifty-sixth Street West
New York 19, N.Y.
Jan 4th [1959]

Sis darling,

Your letter . . . can't be answered till the travel bureau gives me definite flight numbers but I'll get it to you soon. Of course I am coming unofficially dear, the State Dept & the President [Eisenhower] wouldn't send me anywhere & I have no official position! I have to mention what I do in my column but I can easily interview people [illegible] with work in Iran & not say anything beyond mentioning his[,] the Shah's[,] interest in development. We would like to see Isfahan. I would like a stenographer as I plan to do my own column & notes on trip & . . . to have someone take dictation at the start & finish of my visit would be wonderful. . . .

I know a young Iranian woman working with her husband in a village. I'll write her as I'd like to see her if she isn't too far away.

New Delhi is a good place to see as a starter. You should see Benares & Bombay & walk in the villages & of course you must . . . see the Taj & to the 2 places for monks carvings & frescoes. I'll ask David what in a medical way would be important for Jim to do.

Much, much love
Mother

Mrs. Roosevelt had clearly come to enjoy certain aspects of her celebrity, which she once considered onerous, to be borne as a duty. Especially she liked going on television, rationalizing that it enlarged her ability to influence. In fact, at age seventy-four, she had turned loose the secret ham in her. A few weeks earlier she had been offered an impressive sum to go on TV, not to arouse concern for the world's starving—but to sell a brand of margarine. Her agent warned she'd get a lot of criticism. But, on the other hand, he pointed out, if her reputation survived it—and if she moved lots of margarine—she would have demonstrated that even as a "controversial" figure she could be an asset to a sponsor. Translating the offered fee of $35,000 into CARE packages, she announced to her agent, "I'll do it. For that amount of money I can save six thousand lives." She soon reported to a friend, "The mail was evenly divided. One half was sad because I had damaged my reputation. The other half was happy because I had damaged my reputation." An aftermath is noted in the letter that follows.

". . . I'll write Ben Gurion & Goldie Mayer you are coming . . ."

New York City
Feb. 19th, 1959

Anna darling,

. . . I'll write Ben Gurion & Goldie Mayer [Golda Meir] you are coming &
I've written Gideon Tadmor in the Embassy here to do all they can for you.
I'll write Mr. Baratz . . . & if you want to see a Kibbutz he'll give you lunch.
It is near the Syrian border on the Sea of Galilee so you may not be allowed to
go there. . . .

I went on Frank Sinatra's show in Hollywood (the pay for 5 minutes was
fantastic & my part rather nice) but I'm not very good at "entertainment." I
have never had so many compliments however & I found watching the
mechanics amusing! . . .

I started to fly to Pittsburgh last Sunday a.m. for 2 speeches & we couldn't
land so had to go to Columbus, Ohio. They sent us back in a greyhound bus
that got in a ten mile tie up on the West Va. road & we took 12 hrs to reach
our destination & I just got a night train at midnight for N.Y.! I'm so glad
you are coming home & do get here for Johnny's wedding. All my love

Mother

". . . the subject of 'women's rights' is 'hot stuff' ! . . ."

Tehran
Feb. 25 [1959]

Darling Mummy,

Many thanks for replying so promptly to my cable asking for date of your
arrival, etc. (It must have sounded very terse—but cabling from here is very
costly!) As was to be expected, more darn people and organizations have been
after the Wailes and me in an effort to set up something for and with you that
we decided it would help to know when you get here! . . .

Enclosed is a copy of a tentative schedule made up for your time here. . . .
Under March 19, on the schedule, the *"Lunch 'out'"* is the time reserved for
the possible family lunch with the Shah. This would probably start at 1 P.M.
and last until 4 P.M. Apparently it can't be confirmed until a few days before
your arrival. . . .

Unfortunately for you, we will have to have large teas for you in Shiraz on
March 15th and 16th! These will be for both Iranians and Americans, and we
have to use the "official" lists. But, we do want to take you to Persepolis, and
if possible to the village of a progressive landowner who is a friend of ours.
Both trips take the better part of a day, each.

One more thing about the schedule: The suggested dinner for the
diplomatic corp is tentative. It happens that March 21st is the Iranian New
Year—a big national celebration when Iranians do everything together and
not with foreigners, and on the 20th they're all busy with preparations.

The only political tip I've picked up here this week, which might be helpful to you, is that the Shah has been having trouble with the religious Mullahs (as there is no division between church and state, the church is all-powerful in some areas). Some of his trouble stems from his efforts to emancipate women in Iran who are pitifully restricted, and the Mullahs are dead set against any emancipation and have apparently been devising ways to make life difficult for the government. So, for the time being, the subject of "women's rights" is "hot stuff"! And, of course, we're not supposed to know that any such trouble exists! . . .

All my love to you, and much from Jim.

[Anna]

". . .so the lid is off! . . ."

Hamadan, Iran
March 26, '59

Mummy darling,

We so loved having you and Nina with us, and saying good-bye would have been infinitely tougher without the knowledge that we'll be seeing you again in 3 months. And, we're still tickled at the chance to know Nina better and to find that we felt so close to her.

Our flight here was as rough and uncomfortable as usual around here. Hamadan has no airport and no control tower—you just land in a big prairie, and as this is the north country the weather is still very cold and cloudy, with flying uncertain. So, as we must get back to Shiraz by a certain date, we now plan to go to Tehran by bus next Wednesday. It will be our first bus trip in this country and foreigners we've talked to say it's quite an experience!

We've written all our flock of seven off-spring about the plans to return here for 10 months—so the lid is off! We'll mail everything from Tehran, however, as mail from here is *most* uncertain. . . . I also wrote my three that we are due to arrive in N.Y.C. from London, on BOAC, the morning of June 25th, that we will stay with Buzz and Ruth (if they can have us), and that we plan to go to H.P. the afternoon of the 26th (I need to do some shopping at Arnold Constables!). . . .

Do you have the name of the little Dutch girl who did your secretarial work in Shiraz? If not I'll send it to you as I'm sure a little note from you would mean more than a gift.

We particularly thought of you and your stay in Israel this afternoon. We hiked into town to find the Jewish shrine where Esther and Mordecai are supposed to be buried. After being conducted by an ancient rabbi through the shrine we sat down to put on our shoes and a woman (with a very beautiful face) spoke up in French and asked us if we were Jewish. After our polite denial she and a man and we had a long talk about Jews in Iran, the differences between the various Jewish communities, and Israel. She confirmed, by the way, that the Jewish community in Shiraz is a particularly difficult one because some of the Jews continue to live in filthy surroundings even though they have some money and that the wealthy ones do not take the responsibility for the many really poor ones to the degree they should. Then they asked us if we would join them this coming Sunday morning for some sort of special celebration at their church. We accepted and are to meet them at a little pharmacy in the middle of town. Afterwards I'll know more about the celebration—my ignorance of their celebrations and other observances is great and their French lapsed into Hebrew terms. We will also be celebrating Easter by going to a Presbyterian service conducted in Farsi, to which we have been invited by the Americans at the mission here. After that service we have "Easter dinner" at the home of one of the two doctors at the mission hospital. The other doctor is a negro. Their hospital is really pretty sad and we don't think either doctor is very well trained. The minister is pretty ancient but that's all we know about him. And that's all there is to the mission except for the 3 wives, umpteen children (of the doctors) and a nurse (American). There is only one other American in town, a queer looking man who represents an American road construction company. The only other foreigners are 2 Swedish road engineers, and their families.

If all our plans go well we'll be back in Shiraz on April 3rd. . . . So many, many thanks for taking all the trouble to come and see us way out here.

Anna

". . . I should be sylph like when you arrive! . . ."

202 Fifty-sixth Street West
New York 19, N.Y.
April 19th, 1959

Dearest Anna,

I am home & it is good to be here tho' I have been very busy. . . .

Sis & Van are coming down Thursday p.m. this week & I've lined up all the plays I can & by luck I got three tickets for the Bolshoi Sat. night so they can go. . . .

You'll be interested to hear that I have some T.V. & radio offers & I hope something will be settled to start in the fall.

I'm dieting hard so I should be sylph like when you arrive! I'm also working on my neck & on my feet so my body is taking up much time & thought. I'm as busy as I can well be.

David & Edna moved into the house last Tuesday but have only one floor so far. My lady hasn't moved yet but all the preliminaries are getting done so work can get under way on my floor as soon as she goes. . . .

Devotedly
Mother

". . .would give you a more interesting job . . ."

> 202 Fifty-sixth Street West
> New York 19, N.Y.
> June 17, 1959

Dearest Anna:

Ever since I left Iran I have been thinking of the problem of the women in the villages and wondering if it would not be possible for some UN agency or US agency to set up a project whereby some young home economics people could go to Iran for three months briefing and then live in the villages for a time as demonstrators. It might be started on a small basis—10 to 15 people at first, and they would work under the supervision of that remarkable lady we met, but under your direction. This would give you a more interesting job, difficult as it would be to travel about occasionally, but it might make your time there more interesting.

Mr. Paul Hoffman [former administrator of the Marshall Plan, now a UN official] wants to talk this over with you and I have made a tentative engagement for you to lunch with him on June 25th at 12:30 or 1:00 o'clock. He is going away and this seems to be the only time you could be sure of seeing him. He is at the UN★ and his phone number is Plaza 4-1234, ext. 683.

This is rather an awful thing to greet you with on the day of your arrival but nevertheless I thought it important.

I will be calling you this morning! Welcome home and,

> Much love,
> Mother

". . . The childish sensitivity to criticism of these people . . ."

> Nemazee Hospital
> Shiraz, Iran
> October 11, 1959

Mummy darling,

First I have to ask your help and advice, then I'll tell you about our trip over here and how things are going.

Upon our arrival at the Wailes in Tehran, Tom said he would get the disagreeable news over with first: During the time we have been gone from Iran, the Shah has called Tom in twice, and Mr. Ala, the Minister of Court has called him in twice to complain that you wrote and said some things about Iran after your visit here last March which they deeply resented and were sure you could not have thought of yourself as you were not here long enough, therefore I must have instigated your remarks. Tom said that both gentlemen said they had been sent copies of newspaper clippings by their Ambassador in Washington. Tom says they resented most remarks to the effect that until the wealthy people of Iran came out from behind their high, protective walls and

★Notation in margin by Anna: "11 a.m.—U.N.—Rm. 2997."

took responsibility for the people of Iran at a social level that you did not feel much progress would be made here; that you therefore felt sad upon leaving Iran, but happy upon leaving Israel as there you felt that the people were working together in coordinated teams, with well-worked-out goals. These are of course not your actual words. Then last evening, at the dedication ceremonies for the new headquarters of the Shiraz Iran-American Society, the new Governor General of this Province came over to me, and before a good sized audience, told me in French that he wished to have Jim and me to dinner within the next week or so because he has been sent a portfolio from Tehran enclosing statements from the Iranian Ambassador in Washington purported to have been said by you. Among these statements he says is one in which you said that Shiraz is the dirtiest city in the world! He wishes to go over the memorandum with me as he has been requested to answer it after talking with me, taking me on a personally conducted tour of the city, and telling me where I erred in information I gave you! Then comes the final pay-off: After this brainwashing I am to write articles (for both Iranian and U.S. consumption) refuting your statements. In addition, I of course realize that the tour of the city, in his mind, means that he and I would be accompanied by a corp of photographers. Naturally I denied that you ever made any such statement as that Shiraz was the dirtiest city in the world, but I was quite well aware that my denial made no dent. In addition, I told him that we would be delighted to discuss anything he wished at dinner—and that while I have already made several tours of the city I will be happy to make another (though naturally I won't do so until he has agreed to no photogs). Furthermore I told him that he and his Ambassador and the government should know by now that you are a trained observer and that whatever comments you make are always your own.

I have here a set of your columns written after your visit to Iran and Israel. (I re-read them carefully last evening, and so did Jim, and neither of us can find anything in them that is not strictly true and fair (except where you make a few historical mistakes concerning Persepolis!). . . . I would guess that the Iranian Ambassador to the U.S. has some sort of grudge, but what, I can't imagine. I do know, however, from what has been going on here at the educational level that while the Shah and the Minister of Court are publicly on record as wanting Jim's and my help in setting up the plans for an American-type university here, that practically everyone else in the government is "agin" such a university—preferring to keep the present set-up where Provincial universities are run by Tehran and the university there. So, it may be that the Iranian Ambassador is taking this means to attempt to poison the Shah's and the Minister of Court's minds about me, in an effort to make us both personna non grata in this country. This is, of course, only a guess, but it happens that all I.C.A. [E.C.A., for Economic Cooperation Administration, or Marshall Plan, subsequently the Agency for International Development] grants for this medical school (and therefore the Nemazee Hospital, also) are being held up because the Cabinet Ministers are agin' the projects here. And, there is no doubt in both Jim's and my mind that there is a growing anti-American feeling in this country.

As soon as you have the time could you dictate a letter to me telling of any recollections you may have of things you said in interviews or speeches, on your return from here and Israel last spring to the U.S., concerning Iran? Ruth Appleby told me this summer you made an excellent speech about your trip which she heard in Washington—either to the Women's Democratic Club or to the Women's Press Club, I can't remember which. Any information will give me ammunition in talking to these jokers. And, I certainly am not going to be caught apologizing, or be trapped into public statements or publicity stunts!

The childish sensitivity to criticism of these people was brought out this morning by an American doctor's wife (from Portland, Ore.) who said that last summer they showed some slides taken in Iran of such things as the donkeys laden down, the camels, and village scenes. Present was an Iranian M.D. who promptly blew his top and complained bitterly that all Americans take pictures such as that and never show pictures of "the good things such as our paved streets and our motor cars"!

Since starting the above I've talked with the Point Four Director and he believes that I can be protected from misquotations in the newspapers (Iranian), when talking to the Gov. Gen'l (whose invitation I have to accept he says) by saying from the outset that as an American citizen living in this country I come under the jurisdiction of the State Department and may make no public statements without the Dept.'s permission. At the same time, from the standpoint of going on living here I should point out that Jim and I would not have come back here for a 2nd year if we had not liked Iran and Iranians. So, we'll just wait and see what happens next—and I'm sure now there is no use in your sending me any recollections on what you said.

Now that I've finished the disagreeable part of this letter, first and foremost comes the happiest of birthday wishes to you from us both along with some extra hugs. When you write tell us what you did to celebrate the occasion. We would have loved so much to be "in on it". . . .

Since our arrival here on Sept. 30 we've been living temporarily in a house next door to the one we are to settle in. So we remain half packed, though the living room is quite comfortably fixed up. We HOPE to move next door in another couple of weeks.

Our two 7 months old Collie pups are quite a handful as they had no training during the summer—and they are huge, particularly the male. But they're fun for me and I love having them. We've had no time yet to even think of horseback riding.

Jim found things pretty well snafued at the hospital and has been working like a dog, but loves it. Now things are getting into shape for him. . . .

One last line on my present unpopularity with the Iran government: It appears that I am also frowned upon because I accepted Faroc Bi Bi Quash Quai's invitation to take you there last March. She is, as you will remember, the head of the tribe because after that tribe's uprising in 1952 all senior male members of the family were outlawed from the country—with two of them, only, allowed to occasionally come into Tehran for a visit. The government's philosophy on handling this tribe remains beyond me—it just does not make sense. No over-all plan exists for settling them and teaching them how to live when settled. Therefore, the poorer members of the tribe become poorer and poorer. As one settled member of the tribe (an educated man according to Iran standards, and a very intelligent one) said to us the other day: if a sufficient number of the people of this tribe get poor enough, and become desperate through lack of any hope, they are apt to take to the wild mountains and plains which begin only 30 miles east of Shiraz, and become bandits. For the time being the military have control, but fighting in the wilds would be different—and military rules and strict government regulations don't answer the economic, health and educational problems of these people.

Once again, a belated Happy Birthday, which we hope was a really happy one. And loads and loads of love from us both,

Anna

". . . in this country this is tantamount to an order! . . ."

Nemazee Hospital
Shiraz, Iran
October 26 [1959]

Mummy darling,

Five weeks ago today we left home—and I'm really getting worried because I haven't had one line from you. I'm surmising that there's nothing drastically wrong because I did receive from Maureen a few days ago the book you so thoughtfully remembered to send along to Jim after you'd read it. He sends you many thanks for this.

Are all four boys, plus wives and children, okay? Has Sue had her baby? Have you seen Buzz (and Ruth?)? I've heard nothing from Buzz, but have had wonderful letters from Sis and Van, and two good letters from Johnny. And, are you well and happy? And how is your apartment coming? And have your TV shows sold?

We are fine, and even busier than last year. Jim really has a tremendous load of work, and I help wherever I can. Tomorrow we start moving to the house we will have for the rest of the year, because the hospital needs the house we've been in for the Aga Khan who is coming "just for a visit". The Gov. Gen'l of the Province requested that he be housed on this compound—and in this country this is tantamount to an order! We've had a doctor from Boston as house guest for the past 5 days but he left today. The Ambassador and Mrs. Wailes arrive on Friday to spend 3 days with us, for medical check-ups, and, he, to visit Persepolis for the first time. . . .

There's nothing new to report on the Iran government's irritation with me over you! Mr. Glines, the Pt. 4 Director, told his Iranian counterpart who evidently told the Gov. Gen'l, that wives of ICA appointees in foreign countries are forbidden by the State Dept. to make public statements (oral or written) which have political implications, and that I was annoyed by the Gov. Gen'l's way of approaching me on the matter. So I'm hoping it can be forgotten.

Much, much love from both of us, and a great big hug from me—and do write soon, even a few lines.

Anna

". . . hope I'll stay awake at the meetings . . ."

On plane near San Francisco
Nov. 6th [1959]

Anna darling,
Your letter has just come & I hope by now my second letter has reached you. I wrote you one right after you left but that must have been lost.
Buzz is back with a Mexican divorce. He found Juliana [his daughter] well & seems quite happy about her. I saw him on his return. . . .
The elections are over & both sides claim gains! In N.Y. City, the Mayor's strength has waned. The bond issue for city schools was voted down. The Adirondack Northway was voted, so a road will go thro' 75 miles of the Forest Preserve. . . . I would have liked the route along Lake Champlain.
I've done a lot of travelling & am now on my way to San Francisco for a *one* day regional meeting [of AAUN]. I slept well last night & so hope I'll stay awake at the meetings & speak well at the lunch! Tomorrow I'll fly home[,] catch up on mail & go to Boston Sunday for T.V., a class Monday & then 4 days of lectures in Ill. Mich. & Ohio. Home Friday.
The apt. is coming on. The 24th of Nov. I move the furniture from storage in & the 27th I'll return from H.P. & sleep there for night. Mrs. Levy [Adele, head of women's division, United Jewish Appeal] has given me a beautiful rug for my front room (living room). It is big 24 x 17 & the rug will make it lovely.
On return flight Saturday Nov 7th
All went very well in S.F. . . . I met a doctor the other night who said he'd been consulted when you were ill there & that his advice had been followed so he was happy over your recovery.
Jimmy's book [*Affectionately, F.D.R.*] seems to be going well & is much enjoyed. . . .
I went to the opening of Dore Shary's [Schary's] play "The Highest Tree." He dramatized the results of "fallout" & it is a courageous play but not really good & I doubt if it has much of a run. . . .
Tell me, do you have any work to do? . . .
Much love & a big hug to you

Mother

". . . Mr. Truman & I had a 'little difference' again. . . ."

55 East 74th Street
New York City
Thursday, Dec. 17th, 1959

Anna darling,

What long silences I put you through! I can only say that I never seem to have any free time anymore, even now it is 1 a.m. & I've just finished the mail! I'm awake enough to write however! . . .

Buzz seems busy & happy & asked me to give him a new Tuxedo for Xmas so he can't be a hermit.

The mail has increased to appalling proportions & being 75 was no help!

I love my apartment. . . . In a year & a half "he" [the unwanted tenant] will have to move & then it will be perfect. Now, I sleep on a couch in the dining room & dress in the one bathroom & the kitchen is fine, very modern, but our office is tiny! Someday it will just house the maid! . . . I had my Xmas party for the AAUN office force today (35 of them) & it went well & they loved it. I go to Hyde Park Sat. p.m. & Sunday will have the party for the people on the place. I've been to 4 AAUN regional meetings & done much lecturing for Leigh because everything you do costs so much that I've wanted to earn more. I'll need to do very little downstairs, only add a guest bathroom.

I spoke in Hollywood Florida last Sunday night & on Monday went to Sarasota to see Uncle David. He seems well & working & happy & gets thro' the English mediums long letters from Maude.

At the dinner the Dem. Advisory Com. gave for me, Mr. Truman & I had a "little difference" again. I thought I was gentle but the papers played it up. Adlai's speech seemed much more mature than any of the candidates. . . .

Devotedly
Mother

". . . The Western Jew in Israel has no patience with these people . . ."

Nemazee Hospital
Shiraz, Iran
Feb. 8, 1960

Mummy darling,

. . . I'm delighted that we'll have a full week in Israel with some concentration that should give us time to get some of the "flavor".

Our Dutch doctor friend, Jay Groen, is spending ten days here as a visiting lecturer and teacher. He tells us that he and his friends feel it is just a matter of time before Nasser invades Israel; that Nasser's present manoevers have shown his present military forces to be well trained for the first time. (He says they are trained in Czechoslovakia and operate with USSR equipment.) He says it is their (Israel's) hope that the hostilities will not go beyond a Korean war-type. I keep wondering how the U.S.A. is planning to handle this situation; what policy they intend to pursue.

I took Jay, at his request, on a tour of the Jewish ghetto here (led of course by the American Joint people) and he was most upset by what he saw. The places which have been "cleaned up" were, he felt, no better than the worst Arab quarters he's seen. But what jolted him most were the number of people he met who told him definitely they did not want to go to Israel. He even met quite a few who had been to Israel and returned. The answers are tough but understandable: These Jewish people have lived here for some 2600 years. Historically they have had two previous chances to return to Jerusalem but have always refused. Over the years they have become more Muslim than Jewish and have no religious leadership. Their rabbis are not bonefide—just "sons" of rabbis, who have adopted the roles of the Mullahs—that of being judges in family and other disputes and advisors in financial matters. Those who went to Israel expected the proverbial land of milk and honey, but without having to work any harder than they do here. And hard, sustained work here is unheard of. Jay says that Israel has had a very tough time with the Jewish refugees from Iraq who have the same Muslim background as the Jews here. The Western Jew in Israel has no patience with these people and can't understand them.

Many many thanks for writing to Ben Gurion, Goldie Mayer [Golda Meir], Gideon Tadmor and Mr. Baratz. Jay says that Ben Gurion sees very few people and that his American wife is a pain in the neck to most Israelis because she's very "loud" and self-assertive!

Johnny B. wrote that he and Debbie had such a wonderful five days at H.P., and I was happy they had this time for some peace and quiet together. Gosh I'm happy we'll be home in time for the wedding on Aug. 20th. AND, gosh how we hope they are both mature enough to make a go of married life!

How we wish we were seeing your once a month TV programs at Brandeis. Does Brandeis sponsor them or do they have a commercial sponsor?

. . . Do take care of yourself—despite the constant temptations to stay over-active. I've been happy that so far this winter you don't seem to have written about having a bad cold and respiratory infection; but now I read that N.Y.C. has had 13½ inches of snow, and HOPE this hasn't undone your good record to date.

Love from Jim—and all my love,

Anna

". . . I don't think Nixon unbeatable . . ."

55 East 74th Street
New York City
Feb 19th, '60

Dear Jim,
. . . I don't think Nixon unbeatable but I haven't found the candidate yet among those running I think can surely do it!

I am very well but I have been much too active, but somehow one finds it so easy to be on the go! . . .

Much love
E.R.

". . . Mrs. B.G. . . . complains a bit but she is good really. . . ."

55 East 74th Street
New York City, 21, N.Y.
Sunday March 20th, 1960

Anna darling,

Tomorrow is the first day of spring & it feels like midwinter! I hope Sisty is landing in Tel Aviv tonight & is met & has a place to sleep. . . .

I saw Ben Gurion alone for 15 minutes & he & Mrs. G. are looking forward to seeing you three. . . . He looks a little frailer, but full of life & vitality & seemed happy about his talks here. Don't think harshly of Mrs. B.G. She takes good care of him & complains a bit but she is good really. . . .

Brandeis & Boston Educational T.V. sponsor my once a month "Prospects of Mankind" show & they are talking of having another series next year. . . .

I only had one cold all winter & David found the right pills & I wasn't even in bed. A big hug to Sis & to you a world of love

Mother

". . . I feel David & Edna need a rest! . . ."

55 East 74th Street
New York City, 21, N.Y.
Sunday, April 10th [1960]
really Sat. night

Darling Anna,

. . . Now, I must tell you that I stood back of an automobile on 8th St. last Sunday & got myself backed into & knocked down! I was up at once & no crowd gathered & I walked away but I found my right foot functioned less & less well. I opened the cancer benefit I was going to, & luckily Joe and Trude [Lash] were picking me up to bring me home & I greeted & fed a group of some 24 kids 8–10 with their chaperones on arrival here, & then I called David because I had to speak at a cloak & suit Industry dinner for Brandeis & I was finding my foot less & less use! David did all he could & I got thro' the evening but Monday a.m. David insisted on an x-ray at the medical center & their best surgeon to see me. Nothing was broken just torn ligaments but under the instep so the foot would bear no weight. They told me if I didn't be still & keep it up *all* the time it would bother me for weeks whereas a week might cure it with complete rest. So I've been here a week, but far from alone & not too restful. Whenever it was possible my activities were just brought here! Yesterday at least 40 reform N.Y. City candidates were photographed here with Sen. Lehman & me! I've done 3 recordings, tons of mail each day & seen *all* the people who intended to see me here or elsewhere!

To-night for the first time I went out to the loveliest Philharmonic concert with David & Edna & tomorrow p.m. I'll go to a radio station for 2 hrs to tape the show. I'm going to use the foot as an excuse to cut out a number of things because David found some signs that my heart was overstrained a bit. He's making me go for a check up . . . next Thursday. (We, Maureen, David & Edna & I) are going to H.P. Wednesday night to stay till Monday morning after Easter because I feel David & Edna need a rest! I have felt for sometime that this might be so therefore I'm going to cut out a number of things & say the foot has to be rested! . . .

I hope you get a holiday on the way home & remember you can stay in H.P. as long as you like & use this apt. when I'm not here or I can get you a hotel room 1 block away. . . .

My love to Jim, a heartful to you, & I hope you can read this, I'm writing in bed. A big hug darling from,

Mother

Habitually resistant to medical examination and treatment, Mrs. Roosevelt had to give in to a light going-over as a result of her seemingly minor accident—at the age of seventy-five. Dr. Gurewitsch did not like some signs he discovered—and the implications were soon to become worse.

". . . astonishing . . . how stirring he was. . . ."

Val-Kill Cottage
Hyde Park
Saturday, April 16th [1960]

Anna darling,

. . . My ankle progresses steadily but slowly. I can use it, but then I have to lie up & rest it. I had a partial check up. Found I was aneamic (how do you spell it?) which might account for the heart skip. In itself the heart is nothing, just a warning & I am slowing up in earnest! So, nothing to worry about where I'm concerned!

The Gurewitsch's & I came up Wed. eve. & have been very quiet. I went to the library yesterday because a Mr. Bialek is doing a complete collection of records of all of Father's recorded speeches & wanted me to write a foreword. It was astonishing how good they would be now & how stirring he was. We have had nothing like it since. I will give each of you the collection next Xmas for I feel sure you & Jim will like it.

. . . Joe [Lash] will be here this morning & Grania & her present beau will arrive too & tomorrow Hick and Laura will come to lunch so we will be a big party.

We've had two lovely spring days but it is gently raining off & on today. The daffodils & tulips just begin to bloom. . . .

Devotedly
Mother

". . . I decided I had to come out for Stevenson . . ."

55 East 74th Street
New York City 21, N.Y.
June 19th eve. [1960]

Darling Anna,

I wish you & Jim could have seen Johnny graduate "cum laude" last Sunday. He led the class & looked fine & had a rousing hand clapping. Buzz went up, Debby was there. She graduated "Phi Beta Kappa" & has her job for next winter. Everyone young & old said good things about Johnny. . . . I like Debby better every time I see her. . . . I have been bad about writing but I've never been busier & there are some worisome things about the boys & wives again.

Politics are very active because I decided I had to come out for Stevenson & now I have to go out to the convention.

. . . I love you very much

Devotedly
Mother

The following was written on a Wednesday after a devastating half-week. The previous Saturday John Roosevelt's teenage daughter Sally fell from a horse near Mrs. Roosevelt's Hyde Park cottage and died. The Democratic candidate for President, Senator John F. Kennedy, offered to cancel his obligatory pilgrimage to see Mrs. Roosevelt at Hyde Park, scheduled for the next day. As always in her moments of crisis, duty took command. She told him to come.

Seemingly lowest on her list of concerns were Dr. Gurewitsch's findings about her health.

". . . I assure you both I feel quite well! . . ."

55 East 74th Street
New York City 21, N.Y.
Aug 17th [1960]

Dearest Anna & Jim,

. . . You'll never know how glad I am you were home & with us this week end. It meant so much to Johnny & Anne. I find it hard to realize even now that I'll never see that child running thro' my house again.

David has just been in to tell me today's results & I suggest he stop worrying & we forget about it. I'll take my pills & pay a fortune for these tests from time to time to satisfy him but I assure you both I *feel* quite *well!*

My love to you both,

Mother

Near the end of Jim's fellowship period in Iran, which was extended into a second year, Jim accepted a post as assistant dean of a new medical school in Lexington, Kentucky.

". . . no screens . . . no washing machine . . ."

3498 Tates Creek Road
Lexington, Kentucky
[margin note] Telephone number:
Lexington 6-6194
September 5, 1960

Mummy darling,

. . . Leaving the farm was hectic because we had a housefull until the night before the movers (packers, I mean) arrived. Then the moving van did not arrive on the scheduled day and we finally left, in our V.W. and Sis' and Van's Ford station wagon which we've bought, in the early afternoon, leaving everything for the movers to do alone the next day. At 8 that evening we arrived at the Lindleys [Ernest K. Lindley was a newspaper columnist and FDR biographer] in Bucks Co., Pa. and spent a delightful evening and early morning with Betty and Mark. It's a lovely and interesting old house and place, but apparently Ernest doesn't like it there any more according to Betty, so he's rarely there. The second night we were lucky to find a motel, immediately, which would accept our dogs. And the following evening we hove into Lexington about 7 P.M., having driven 950 miles—and without having lost each other once! We went 100 miles out of our way, first to go to Betty's and secondly because of getting lost several times.

We left the dogs in a kennel for 4 days. The day after our arrival was busy with trying to get the builders to fix up obvious deficiencies such as no screens on the windows, and no washing machine—which we picked out when we were here before, and which is a real necessity now because having visiting kids to the last moment means that I brought along one heck of a lot of soiled linen.

It's now the 6th and the washer-dryer machines are being worked on and *should* be ready today, and the screens are promised for this evening. I sincerely hope for the screens because misquitoes have eaten me up during the last 2 nights! We spent the first 2 nights at Dean and Mrs. Willards. The weather is in the 90's and the humidity very high so we've done plenty of just plain sweating!

Jim started work today. As it's a new medical school there's more than enough work for everyone, but it should all prove very interesting, particularly as the medical education policies and thinking are all progressive and forward-looking. There is a nepotism problem concerning putting me on the payroll, and the Dean and the President of the University want to avoid any possible interpretation that Jim and I were hired in a "package deal". Therefore, it will be a couple of months before anything starts to be worked out for me. This is undoubtedly just as well because I have quite a few problems relative to getting settled: the house here won't hold all the stuff we had at the farm (the rooms are smaller and there is no storage space except in the garage), and it's going to be quite a job to go through all the stuff we accumulated in Iran as well as all the stuff I packed away at the farm before going there. And in the meantime I'll have a chance to "sort out" the faculty and some of the other dozens of new people to be met and remembered!

We are fine—and hoping that you and David and Edna all had fun and a good rest in Switzerland. . . .

So very much love from us both & a great big hug from me.

Anna

Although not acknowledged in the letters of this period, Anna and Jim received a disturbing phone call soon after settling into their new home in Lexington. It was from Dr. Gurewitsch. As one doctor to another, David confided to Jim about his fears for Mrs. Roosevelt's condition. Jim, a gastroenterologist, was mindful that David had been trained in rehabilitative medicine. Neither had a high degree of authority in the ailments Mrs. Roosevelt was said to have. David reported, as Jim was to recall, "that Anna's mother had aplastic anemia, and that it might really be leukemia, and he thought she was going to die. He was awfully upset about it. Actually, the diagnosis was made at the Rip Van Winkle Clinic in Hudson, New York. She made herself a patient there because she felt that, from a social point of view, this new idea of having a clinic with lots of doctors together was a good development in medical practice. Anna and I suggested to David that he ought to get a good internist to take charge. He handled this by going to Mrs. Roosevelt and saying, 'Well, Jim and Anna don't think I can take care of you properly. They want me to turn you over to Dr. So-and-so.' She said, 'Well, David, if you don't want to take care of me, I won't have *any* doctor.'

"In the long run, it probably wouldn't have made too much difference—probably didn't make any difference. Nevertheless, it was the proper thing to do. He shouldn't have taken care of her. Doctors don't like to take care of their own families or of people very close. David's relationship to Mrs. Roosevelt was of a greatly emotional character; among other things, emotionally beneficial to his own ego. E.R. always needed people around who were devoted to her. That was true ever since she discovered the affair between Lucy Mercer and her husband way back in 1918. She needed devotion from people, and she gave it as part of getting it. Whenever she went to Europe, she used to take David. I don't think David was ever her lover.

I'm reasonably certain of that. In any case, he was too close to her to have taken care of her as her doctor."

". . . either be dancing a jig . . . or . . . licking my wounds! . . ."

3498 Tates Creek Road
Lexington, Kentucky
ELECTION DAY 1960!!

Mummy darling,

I find this a difficult day to live through with calmness, particularly as the university involvement keeps me from even working at the polls or driving people to them! Other university wives are working at the polls because there will be no publicity about them. It's a good thing that Iran taught me to control frustrations—and now I'm hoping so hard that I may soon find really interesting work in the Community Services division of the Medical Center. Next Monday we spend two days in rural Kentucky (Hazard and Hiden) and the Community Services' director (a really fine and capable person) goes with us. Dec. 1 is the present target date for my starting work—let's hope it doesn't get delayed! . . .

Please don't worry about the extra $100 a month for me. This is something I do not spend and therefore do not need—and Elliott obviously does.

I'm so hoping that after today you will cut down drastically on your schedule. You have done yeoman's work for the ticket. People in Miami told me they'd seen you on the Jack Parr [Paar] *and* the Dave Garraway [Garroway] shows—not the most desirable hours for you to be working—but they said you were wonderful! Has your virus bug disappeared completely?

Even the staunchest of Democrats here feel that there's little chance that Kentucky will be in our column, and this county is due to go overwhelmingly for Nixon and the ticket. I have to admit to being nervous about even the key states. So darn many people seem to have felt Eisenhower to have been highly effective. While foreign policy does seem to be the major issue in most peoples' minds, it is terribly over-simplified by them so that they remain impressed with the statement that Ike kept us out of war, and that Ike says Nixon has the experience and will do the same. Oh well, I'll either be dancing a jig by tomorrow morning or sticking my chin out and licking my wounds! (We voted by absentee ballot from Lafayette.)

A world of love to you, Mummy,

Anna

P.O.—Jim would send his love, too, but is at work.

". . . So relieved [it's] Kennedy and not Nixon . . ."

3498 Tates Creek Road
Lexington, Kentucky
Nov. 25 [1960]

Mummy darling,
    . . . From a weather standpoint I'm told that January and February are the worst months here—wet and cold, sometimes down to zero and below but with lovely and snappy, sunny days occasionally. March has more sunny days but is still cold. In other words I gather that the climate here is very similar to Washington, D.C. Whenever you can get away to come here will be wonderful with us—even if you don't combine your visit with a speech—and even if you do!!
    Do you think that because of you we might be invited to the inauguration in Washington? If you think there is a chance we will be[,] we will put it on the calendar so that Jim will be sure not to be away on one of his faculty-hunting trips. Jim has never been to an inauguration, and we're so relieved that Kennedy and *not* Nixon will be sworn in, that, if invited, we thought we'd go.
    Jim has been out of town more than here, and I haven't been going along because of the expense, but we hope that after Dec. 6th he'll be through with traveling until after Christmas. We both go, overnight, to Harlan, Ky. on Dec. 5th—so I will have been able to see a good deal of the southeastern part of this state. And, it's now definite that I start to work on Dec. 7th. . . .
    Very much love from us both, & a special lot from me,

Anna

". . . I'm quite a bit older than my boss . . ."

3498 Tates Creek Road
Lexington, Kentucky
Jan. 2, '61

Mummy darling,
    We loved talking to you on Xmas Day. After 3 years this *really* made it Christmas—even though we couldn't be with you! It was wonderful having Buzz here. . . . He really needed a rest and slept long hours. We admire his courage and perseverance and hope to goodness he can afford to see his study program through, emerge with his M.A., and get a job which will really interest him. Buzz will be able to tell you about our house and surroundings.
    We had snow for Xmas and zero weather, and this week-end more snow came but with less severe cold so we've enjoyed walks with the dogs. The kids found our house cold—it "leaks" like all the new and not too well-built houses! But our "portable" fireplace makes things very snug and cozy in our study. Buzz, with his flare for interior decorating, moved around the furniture in the study so that the whole room is better now.
    My job is slow getting underway but I'm sure it will grow in interest and

satisfaction. Once again (like in Syracuse) I'm quite a bit older than my boss (a nice guy, with an M.S. in public health) and this unconsciously makes him a bit leery of me, particularly as he didn't choose me but was needled into "needing" me by the Dean! The hours are long, with a 5½ day week and I must observe them scrupulously while I'm "new"—which makes it tough to get marketing done or any shopping as I'm in the office by 8.30 and don't leave until 5.15. But I take 1½ hours for lunch and that helps. There's still some question about my appointment—nepotism being the alleged excuse, though I'm not on the State payroll (as is Jim) but supposed to be paid from a grant—however no pay has been forthcoming. The Dean seems convinced he can straighten it out with the president of the Univ. Everyone's afraid of publicity about me, so I'm on a temporary status! It is, of course, a State Univ.

Buzz got us invited to the reception for you and Gov. Lehman on the 19th, so we'll fly to Washington that afternoon. Where will you stay, and for how long, and what plans do you have while there? We'd love to see you quietly even for a few moments. . . .

Elliott phoned us the day after Xmas and said he and [his new wife] Patty will be in Wash. for Inauguration and also in N.Y.; that he now works for an aviation company who have put a plane at his disposal so that he'll fly himself East if the weather is okay. They sent us a huge box of S.S. Pierce cocktail goodies, too. So, I guess the financial pinch is off—thank goodness—though I wish he'd save. . . .

By the way, our invitation to the Inauguration hasn't arrived—but it's bound to turn up soon. . . .

We send you worlds of love, and so many thanks for everything, and a big hug from me. What fun that we'll at least get a glimpse of you soon!

Anna

". . . he seems relaxed & affluent! . . ."

55 East 74th Street
New York City 21, N.Y.
Sunday Jan 15th, 1961

Dearest Sis,

I have seats for the inaugural ball & parade for you & I hope you have your own invitation by now to the ceremonies. The concert I'm not sure about, but I'll see. I'll be going to Frankie's house to dress. . . .

Elliott & his wife came in this afternoon & all went smoothly. We were not alone but she was at ease & pleasant, he seems relaxed & affluent! . . .

I dined last night with Johnny & Debbie. They seem happy & manage their lives well. A world of love

Mother

". . . Two thousand bucks is an awful lot . . ."

3498 Tates Creek Road
Lexington, Kentucky
February 22, '61

Mummy darling,

For a week I've been laid low, first with an intestinal virus and now with diverticulitis. This is a nuisance because the Univ. Board of Trustees finally passed my appointment last Friday and I was supposed to go to work "formally" this past Monday. Now, Jim says it will be next Monday before I can put in a full day's work. But anyhow I'm lucky, (and feeling lots better than yesterday) because the pain on the left side of my tummy is subsiding. It was swollen and very painful.

We're very hopeful that your "bug" left you, and that you took enough time from your regular schedule to really get rid of it.

What are your thoughts about the enclosed? I don't ever remember seeing or hearing about the Sara Delano Roosevelt Community House at Warm Springs, but then I haven't been there for so many years that I've never seen the place as it is now. Two thousand bucks is an awful lot of money. We might be able to scrape $25 together. $425 is our monthly living allowance (including travel and donations), and that includes your check for $100. (This will of course be improved when I start getting paid.) And the rest goes into overhead—mortgage, alimony, newspaper debts, putting Chuck through medical school, etc. The 2 years in Iran took most of the Sunrise at Campobello money, plus an odd loan or so to kids and occasional small travel or other gifts to them—and what is left is in a not too large savings account for "old age" or emergencies. But I don't want to seem like a tight wad, and so wonder if all five of us (I should say four of us because I know that Elliott is not even solvent) couldn't send you whatever we can give and have you send it to Mrs. Barnes as an inclusion with your gift. This is admittedly a face-saving device (for me and Elliott) because I know that the others can afford more than 25 bucks—so that Mrs. Barnes won't think that two of us just ain't as interested as the rest!! It still amazes me how often it is "thrown" at me that everyone of us are "rolling in dough". As I'm sure you don't want to put up most of the $2000 (and I see no earthly reason why you should), do you suppose that the Historical Society of Georgia would help out through some money raising gimmick down there? Or, are any of Granny's old and wealthy friends in N.Y. still alive who might be interested? . . .

We're delighted as can be to hear that you get the second floor of your apartment so soon—and accept with the greatest of pleasure to stay with you when we're there next!! This really is the best news in a long time—I've hated to have you so cramped, and feel that now you will really enjoy the apartment, and have more freedom of feeling than you do anywhere else.

A world of love—& from Jim, too.

Anna

In March, Jim was offered a job as chief of the Department of Medicine at the Metropolitan Hospital and Clinics in Detroit. Dissatisfied with his purely administrative position at the University of Kentucky, he accepted the offer, and he and Anna moved to Birmingham, Michigan, in early June.

". . . 'Praise be, she has . . . humor.'. . ."

> 3498 Tates Creek Road
> Lexington, Kentucky
> May 15, 1961

Mummy darling,
. . . We'll be at our new house in Birmingham [Michigan]—32766 Bingham Lane—(no phone until we get there) until June 8 when we will start driving to N.Y.C. so as to get there in time for lunch with Buzz and his new bride—going afterwards to the church ceremony—and from there to H.P. Johnny B. writes that he is to be Buzz' best man at the church ceremony and that he and Debby will go with us to H.P. afterwards. How does all of this fit in with your plans? As you know we *had* planned to reach you at H.P. in time for lunch on the 10th. Now, I don't even know what time the church service is to be, and therefore, what time we will arrive at H.P. Are you planning to be at the church ceremony?

According to Johnny B., and to a pupil of Jeanette's whom we met at the Ethridges in Louisville on Derby Day, Jeannette is a really fine person. Johnny and Debby say they like her very much and (as Johnny puts it) "praise be, she has a good sense of humor." We were in Detroit when the civil marriage took place and found Buzz' letter telling about it on our return 3 days after the event! We phoned him right away. Our only hope is that both have found *real* happiness. Buzz sounded blissful!

When I've talked to you on the phone I've forgotten to thank you for the wonderful Vermont maple syrup and sugar. We've missed that so much during our years in Iran, and it does seem so good to have it again.

We can hardly wait to see you. There are so darn many things we want to talk to you about and ask you about and, as usual, the time seems so very short.

The Tuskegee Institute (Dr. Dibble) sent both my plane fare and a $200 honorarium. The latter was most welcome—what with moving; a leak under our present house which must be fixed and which is caused by the excessive rains; and the fact that we still haven't been able to sell this house. Our actual moving expenses will be paid by the Detroit Hospital, but there are always so many incidental expenses to a move. But our financial picture is fine. I started working part-time at the Med. Center today (until we move) but will be paid full time because of the fiasco when I first went to work.

Ever & ever so much love from us both,

> Anna

". . . I decided the taste was too rich . . ."

Val-Kill Cottage
Hyde Park
July 23d, 1961

Dearest Anna & Jim,

You are right, it is fun watching Edna & David's baby grow! They come next Saturday for a week & I look forward to it. . . .

I tried Metrocal 3 weeks & didn't lose a lb. I guess it has to be 3 times a day & no other food but I decided the taste was too rich & I'd try to just eat less for a time & see if I could lose without starving! We'll see! . . .

At last I am doing some reading but not all I want as yet. . . .

Mother

". . . I shall take your letter up . . ."

55 East 74th Street
New York City 21, N.Y.
November 24, 1961

Dear Jim:

. . . I thought you might both like to have your Christmas checks ahead of time, so here is yours with all my love and best wishes.

I enjoyed your letter very much. I saw Mr. [H.E.W. Secretary Abraham] Ribicoff at breakfast last week and he told me all his troubles, but I think you give him credit for being better informed than he really is! I shall take your letter up with Mrs. [Mary] Lasker when I see her, which will be when I can get Mr. Ribicoff to come to lunch with her and Anna Rosenberg [a former FDR adviser, now in public relations].

With much love,

Affectionately,
E.R.

". . . lectured me roundly on the inferiority of women . . ."

Feb. 18, 1962

Mummy darling,

I hope this meets you in Israel. We've already received your first column from Paris—and can imagine how busy you were both there and in London. We envy you in Israel and hope we, too, may go back some day.

We didn't get back to Detroit until midnight the day we left you because of weather problems, and have been as hectically busy as ever at the hospital since then.

Now it's the 19th and I'm in the hospital (my office!). The phone rings and rings and I dictate madly, in between on a dictaphone—almost entirely on patients' problems! We had a young Negro patient in here complaining last Saturday because he had been taken care of by a woman doctor in the Emergency Room. He lectured me roundly on the inferiority of women versus men—even quoting the Bible to the effect that women's function was limited to waiting on men. His only real complaint was that he had demanded a penicillin shot for a slight head cold and had been told he didn't need it!

We really had a wonderful time in New York last week. Our luncheon with you was perfect, and we only wished we had longer to just chat with you. Debby and Johnny were very dear—but obviously they are still working on their troubles, and heaven only knows how things will work out in the end. Jeanette and Buzz were wonderful—so happy and relaxed. Their old house has real possibilities, and by next September they will be moving into their floor and one-half apartment. I think they are the kind of people who don't mind taking a long time to get things in shape—unlike Jim who likes to have things *settled* almost as soon as one has moved in! I practically bought out Arnold Constable—on my once a year buying spree. As I loathe shopping, it's perfect, however, to be able to get it all done at once, and under the same roof.

We drove Dorothy Roosevelt and a friend of hers to the ADA [Americans for Democratic Action] Roosevelt Dinner this last Saturday evening and she asked if she could drive you to the airport from our house the morning of March 30. She pointedly said this was the only way she'd get a chance to talk to you. With this last I agree because I'm going to be selfish enough not to invite her over the afternoon before nor for breakfast the next morning—unless you insist! . . .

Jim sends you lots of love—and a great, great lot from me with a big hug,

Anna

"*. . . I have endless begging letters in German . . .*"

Kulm Hotel
St. Moritz
Tuesday March 6th, '62

Anna darling,
The past two days have been snowy & tho' it is not cold out & quite lovely for walking, there is no sun to lie out in on steamer chairs. This is no longer considered "the season" & many are leaving but I find it very pleasant & have never had such a good rest. I believe the same could be had in places at home & probably no more expensive! The air does give you lift & no one has colds tho' they are wet every day. The sun is trying to come through today but it doesn't look very hopeful.

Needless to say I have endless begging letters in German which Maureen can't read & when I'm stumped we have to get David to decipher but I am being hard hearted for the number of rich, arrogant Germans I've seen in this place makes me feel they are simply able to care for their own.

There is much speculation about the meeting in Russia these 2 days &

whether Krushev's [Khrushchev's] milder policy will be approved or whether China's position will be upheld in which case I suppose we can expect more & more difficulties. . . .

All my love & I'll call you when I get home on the evening of Sunday, the 11th. A big hug to you,

Devotedly
Mother

". . . feeling stronger all the time . . ."

Campobello Island
August 13, 1962

Dearest Sis:

I am sure you are anxious to know how the trip went. Everything went smoothly and while I am feeling stronger all the time I imagine it will be quite a while before I feel entirely normal.

I hope the improvement in your arm is continuing and I look forward more than I can say to seeing you and Jim on the 23rd [at Hyde Park]. Come as early as you can. . . .

Much love,
Mother

". . . the most frustrating job I've ever had. . . ."

32766 Bingham Lane
Birmingham, Michigan
Wednesday evening Sept. 5, 1962

Mummy darling,

You sounded so wonderfully chipper on the phone last Monday evening that you made us both feel happy—happy in the knowledge that you really are getting stronger all the time.

My news of the moment is that I got called in by the hospital director, Dr. Rosenfeld, this afternoon, and fired! Actually it was not put that way. I was merely told that the Board of Directors and he had decided that my position (as director of community relations) is to be abolished as of Dec. 31 because the hospital deficit is so great that retrenchments must be made. He added that the final decision (about my position) had not been made because it has to be ratified by a joint meeting of CHA (the prepayment, comprehensive medical care program) and Metropolitan Hospital heads next Thursday, September 13, but that the projected hospital deficit for the current fiscal year is based on $400,000 so that there didn't seem to be much chance that there would be a reversal in decision. Never once in our talk did the bum have the courtesy to say he would be sorry to see me go, or that he thanked me for working full time (most of the time) when I was hired and paid on a part-time basis. This was typical of what I've observed with this guy in the little more than a year that I've worked there. People in just every type of responsible position, from doctors to supervisors, have remarked to both Jim and me during this time that no feeling of approval of their work or of them as human beings has ever come through to them—and some of them have been there from 4 to 5 years. Actually, this has been the most frustrating job I've ever had. It's never been defined and I've never known whether what I made of the job was what was wanted—though I did know that it was needed. It's an unhappy place to work, as too many employees have dropped during lunch periods—and it shouldn't be this way because of the purpose of CHA, and the hospital as the instrument for implementing the plan, is so damn worthwhile.

Anyway, regardless of what happens on Sept. 13, I've decided to resign—giving them 2 weeks notice from that date—for the simple reason that I am holding the only responsible position being abolished, and it is therefore obvious that, to them, what I have done or have to offer, is not what they want. In the meantime I'm telling no one of this decision—until I hear the result of the Sept. 13 meeting.

The whole business has a rather ludicrous side to it: for the first time I was with an organization which had purposes of particular interest to me personally and what I've done has not worked out—and yet the two Deans of the two Medical Schools where I worked previously wrote embarrasingly (to me) warm recommendations to the Metro Hosp. Board (when this Board asked me to get these), each one saying that they would be happy to re-hire me at any time! In fact, the State University, Syracuse, Dean never would formally acknowledge my resignation (when we returned for a second year in Iran)—and never has.

We mailed to you today the copy we borrowed of "Conversations with Stalin", and feel we learned much by reading it. I'm not returning "The Liberal Papers" for a little while because it has a few things in it which will come in handy when I moderate a symposium of Wayne Univ. foreign students being sponsored by the Detroit Congress of Jewish Women in about ten days.

Be sure you stick to that new schedule you've been working on! We both send you much, much love—and a big hug from me.

Anna

". . . as you could not read if I wrote . . ."

55 East 74th Street
New York City 21, N.Y.
September 12, 1962

Darling Anna,
I will be calling you some time soon. But as you could not read if I wrote I am just dictating this to say that your letter reached me with all its changes. I am not sure that in the long run these will not be beneficial. I am sure there is more interesting work to do.

I am looking forward to seeing you both on October 7 and you will let me know later the flight Tubby is to meet.

Much love,
Mother

During 1962, as though moved by a premonition that her time was ending, Mrs. Roosevelt occasionally wrote checks to fulfill promises and obligations far in advance of their due dates. To godchildren whose school tuition she had taken on, to organizations whose fund drives she always remembered, she sent out checks as much as six months early. She prepared a memorandum on how she wanted to be buried: in plain wooden coffin, covered with pine branches from the woods of Val-Kill, no embalming. And there was a further instruction that her veins were to be cut. She explained the latter oddity to a friend: A fear had always haunted her that after her burial she might wake up in her coffin, finding herself trapped by the pile of earth atop her. When David Gurewitsch left for a short trip to Peru, she wrote him: "To me all goodbyes are poignant now. I like less & less to be long separated from those few whom I deeply love."

Just before David returned, Mrs. Roosevelt grew suddenly weak, was given a blood transfusion and ran a fever of 105.5 degrees. She improved, was released from the hospital, and, over David's protests, insisted on a trip to Campobello for the dedication of an FDR memorial bridge linking the Canadian island to the United States. On a short morning walk in front of the Campo house—her first steps outside since her illness—she told a friend that she learned on the night of her fever how easy it is to die. She was just slipping away without regret or pain, pleading with David to just let her go.

On September 26, she was taken to the hospital again. Anna and Jim arrived from Detroit, taking charge of Mrs. Roosevelt's household. Mrs. Roosevelt instructed David that she did not wish to linger as an invalid and that she expected him to save her from an artificially dragged out, pain-wracked death. David made it clear he could not cooperate. She clenched her teeth in resistance to pills proffered by her nurse, spitting them out if the nurse succeeded in inserting them. One day, an intravenous tube in her arm and sustained by an oxygen tank, Mrs. Roosevelt stated simply to her nurse that she wished to die. The nurse responded that the Lord would take her in His own good time, when she was finished with the work she was put here to do. Mrs. Roosevelt replied, "Utter nonsense."

On November 7, 1962, her wish for surcease was fulfilled.

Anna was fifty-six when her mother died. Roosevelts do not make a display of mourning and grieving. Perhaps Anna had worked through her sense of loss during the ups and downs of her mother's illness. In any case, her husband Jim told me that Anna exhibited "less grief than one might expect." When Anna did talk to Jim of her mother in the weeks and months that followed the death, it was often of how "depressed" a person Mother always was. Trained as a diagnostic observer, Jim adds today that he did not see in his mother-in-law the clinical signs of depression, but would not dispute the sensitive, subtle reading that a keen daughter might make of her mother. He adds that, as many daughters do of their mothers, Anna felt more enlightened than—in a sense, "superior" to—her mother, not in a sense of ability for worldly accomplishment, but in awareness of her emotions and feelings and her right to have them; in permitting her life to be a fulfillment of her own needs. That sense of difference, implies Jim, may have been an ever-present barrier between daughter and mother, for all their appearance of affinity and communication.

In 1970, Jim retired from his job in Michigan—he was sixty-five, Anna, sixty-four—and they moved to a simple, woodsy home designed for them off a winding, unpaved road in Hillsdale, New York, about thirty miles up the Hudson Valley from Hyde Park. Jim began a medical practice in the nearby city of Hudson. Now returned to the geographical center of her mother's life, and to the vacuum left by her mother's death, Anna, as the oldest Roosevelt child, was drawn into a prominence that all her life she had avoided. The Roosevelt Library, headquarters for what amounts to a Roosevelt-remembering industry, came to her frequently for counsel. The Wiltwyck School for infractious boys, which increasingly occupied the interest of Eleanor, now possessed Anna as the school's chief fund raiser. Continuing contact with the vast network of old Roosevelt lieutenants and friends and allies and retainers and supplicants, a demanding load of correspondence and special-date remembrances, of requests for opinions and all varieties of succor—all these now took up a major part of Anna's attention and life, as they once did her mother's.

And, while appearing burdened by it all, clearly Anna liked it. Jim offered the observation that after a long, exciting, but never quite secure and satisfied life of observing her mother's conspicuous position—a life of never quite feeling her mother was reachable and touchable—Anna now sensed herself as occupying her mother's space, at last being in touch with her, in a sense *becoming* her.

Unlike her mother's, Anna's final illness—in 1975, thirteen years after Eleanor's death—was unheralded, and took her relatively quickly.

INDEX

357

Other Fromm Paperbacks:

FLAUBERT & TURGENEV
A Friendship in Letters
edited and translated
by Barbara Beaumont

SECRETS OF MARIE ANTOINETTE
A Collection of Letters
edited by Olivier Bernier

KALLOCAIN
A Novel
by Karin Boye

TALLEYRAND
A Biography
by Duff Cooper

VIRTUE UNDER FIRE
*How World War II Changed Our
Social and Sexual Attitudes*
by John Costello

PIAF
by Margaret Crosland

CHOURA
The Memoirs of Alexandra Danilova

BEFORE THE DELUGE
A Portrait of Berlin in the 1920's
by Otto Friedrich

THE END OF THE WORLD
A History
by Otto Friedrich

J. ROBERT OPPENHEIMER
Shatterer of Worlds
by Peter Goodchild

THE ENTHUSIAST
A Life of Thornton Wilder
by Gilbert A. Harrison

INDIAN SUMMER
A Novel
by William Dean Howells

A CRACK IN THE WALL
Growing Up Under Hitler
by Horst Krüger

EDITH WHARTON
A Biography
by R.W.B. Lewis

THE CONQUEST OF MOROCCO
by Douglas Porch

THE CONQUEST OF THE
SAHARA
by Douglas Porch

HENRY VIII
The Politics of Tyranny
by Jasper Ridley

INTIMATE STRANGERS
The Culture of Celebrity
by Richard Schickel

BONE GAMES
*One Man's Search for the
Ultimate Athletic High*
by Rob Schultheis

KENNETH CLARK
A Biography
by Meryle Secrest

THE HERMIT OF PEKING
*The Hidden Life of Sir Edmund
Backhouse*
by Hugh Trevor-Roper

ALEXANDER OF RUSSIA
Napoleon's Conqueror
by Henri Troyat